총신·장신 신학대학원 입시를 위한
마스터 영어

조영태 교수 지음

The Master English

by

Jo Young-Tae

2004

Agape Culture Publishing Company,

Seoul, Korea

□ 머 리 말 □

　영어에는 "왕도가 없다"라는 말이 있다. 영어를 읽고 듣고 말하고 쓰려면 오랜 시간이 걸려야 되는 것이 누구도 부인할 수 없는 사실이다. 그러나 수험영어에는 방법이 있다고 말할 수 있다. 그 이유는 어떤 시험이든지 그 시험이 가지고 있는 특성 때문이다. 수험생이 자신이 준비하고 있는 시험의 출제경향을 잘 파악하고 적절한 대책을 세우고 준비하면 목표에 도달할 수 있는 것이다. 필자는 1984년부터 외대, 성대, 숙명여대, 숭실대와 코리아 헤럴드 어학연수원 및 학원 등에서 영어 강의를 했다. 짧지 않은 경험을 바탕으로 수험생들에게 유익한 책을 제공하려는 일념으로 집필에 임했다.

　본서는 특별히 신학대학원 준비생들을 위해 쓰여졌다. 총신대 신학대학원이 올해부터 영어입학시험으로 TEPS를 치루기로 결정되었다. 그보다 먼저 장신대 신학대학원이 영어입학시험으로 TEPS를 이미 치르고 있다. 때문에, 본서에서는 TEPS에 들어가기 전에 본 시험의 실력 향상을 위해, 1부에서 Pre-Test로 틀린부분 찾기, 어휘력, 문장완성형, 어법, 장문독해 등의 문제를 다루면서 자세한 설명을 하였다. 이 부분은 객관식 문제에 대한 전체적인 대비를 위해, TEPS를 준비하는 예비 과정으로 매우 중요한 것이다. 왜냐하면 어떤 시험이라도 공통적으로 중요한 부분이 출제되고 있기 때문이다. 또한 이 부분은 다른 신학대학원이나 일반대 대학원 및 각종 객관식 시험을 준비하는데도 유익할 것이다. 2부에서는 실전 TEPS를 집중적으로 다루고 있다. 그리고 3부에서는 누구나 혼자서 공부할 수 있도록 1·2부의 모든 것을 쉽게 해설해 놓았으며, 마지막 4부에서는 어떤 시험에서나 자주 출제되는 빈출 어휘를 명쾌하게 정리해 놓았다. 본서는 시종일관 독자의 입장에서 상세하게 해설을 하려고 노력하였다. 수험생 여러분들이 본서로 성실하게 준비하면 목적달성은 물론, 전반적인 영어실력의 향상을 경험하게 될 것이다.

　이 책이 나오기까지 세심하게 배려해 주신 김영무 사장님에게 감사를 드린다. 또한 인생의 동반자인 아내와 항상 나의 기쁨이 되어 주는 성근이와 현주에게도 감사한 마음을 전하고 싶다.

　모든 영광을 하나님께!(*Soli Deo Gloria*)

주후 2004년 8월

방배동에서 저자 조 영태

□ 이 책의 특징 □

1. **다양한 문제를 수록했다.**
   - 1부에서는 TOEIC, TOEFL, 대학원 및 각종 시험에서 출제되는 부분을 다루었다.
   - 2부에서는 TEPS문제를 수록하였다.

2. **책 속에 책이 있다.**
   - 문제집과 해설집이 한 권 안에 들어있다.
   - 시종일관 독자의 입장에서 상세하게 설명하려고 노력했다.

3. **TEPS 빈출어휘를 수록했다.**

4. **시험에 자주 등장하는 영어표현을 정리했다.**

5. **중요한 이디엄을 수록했다.**

6. **꼭 알아야 되는 영어 속담을 소개했다.**

7. **기독교인에게 힘을 주는 은혜로운 신앙명언을 실었다.**

8. **본서를 통해 모든 영어에 자신감을 갖도록 집필했다.**

차 례

- 머리말 · 3

제 1 부 Pre - Test · 9

Ⅰ. 신대원 입시 출제경향 · 9

Ⅱ. 틀린 부분 찾기 · 11
    1. 실력문제 1회·11 / 2. 실력문제 2회·14
    3. 실력문제 3회·17 / 4. 실력문제 4회·20

Ⅲ. 어휘력 · 23
    1. 실력문제 1회·23 / 2. 실력문제 2회·26
    3. 실력문제 3회·29 / 4. 실력문제 4회·32

Ⅳ. 문장 완성형 · 35
    1. 실력문제 1회·35 / 2. 실력문제 2회·38
    3. 실력문제 3회·41 / 4. 실력문제 4회·44

Ⅴ. 어법 · 47
    1. 실력문제 1회·47 / 2. 실력문제 2회·50
    3. 실력문제 3회·53 / 4. 실력문제 4회·56

Ⅵ. 장문독해 · 59
    1. 실력문제 1회·59 / 2. 실력문제 2회·66
    3. 실력문제 3회·72 / 4. 실력문제 4회·78

Ⅶ. 종합 문제 · 84
    1. 최종 점검문제·84 / 2. 최종 독해·90

제 2 부 TEPS - 총신 · 장신 신학대학원 준비 · 93

Ⅰ. TEPS 시험안내 · 94
    1. TEPS란 무엇인가? · 94
    2. TEPS의 구성 · 94
    3. TEPS의 특징 · 95

Ⅱ. 유형별 문제-영역별 문제 유형 · 96

1. 듣기 / PartⅠ·96 / PartⅡ·97 / PartⅢ·98 / PartⅣ·99
2. 문법 / PartⅠ·100 / PartⅡ·100 / PartⅢ·101 / PartⅣ·101
3. 어휘 / PartⅠ·102 / PartⅡ·102
4. 독해 / PartⅠ·103 / PartⅡ·104 / PartⅢ·105

Ⅲ. 실력 문제 · 106

1. 문법·106
    * [Part Ⅰ]
      ·실력문제 1회·106 / ·실력문제 2회·108
      ·실력문제 3회·110 / ·실력문제 4회·112
    * [Part Ⅱ]
      ·실력문제 1회·114 / ·실력문제 2회·116
      ·실력문제 3회·118 / ·실력문제 4회·120
    * [Part Ⅲ]
      ·실력문제 1회·122 / ·실력문제 2회·123
      ·실력문제 3회·124 / ·실력문제 4회·125
    * [Part Ⅳ]
      ·실력문제 1회·126 / ·실력문제 2회·127
      ·실력문제 3회·129 / ·실력문제 4회·130

2. 어휘·132
    * [Part Ⅰ]
      ·실력문제 1회·132 / ·실력문제 2회·134
      ·실력문제 3회·136 / ·실력문제 4회·138
    * [Part Ⅱ]
      ·실력문제 1회·140 / ·실력문제 2회·142
      ·실력문제 3회·144 / ·실력문제 4회·146

3. 독해·148
  * [Part Ⅰ]
    ·실력문제 1회·148 / ·실력문제 2회·153
    ·실력문제 3회·157 / ·실력문제 4회·161
  * [Part Ⅱ]
    ·실력문제 1회·165 / ·실력문제 2회·171
    ·실력문제 3회·177 / ·실력문제 4회·182
  * [Part Ⅲ]
    ·실력문제 1회·188 / ·실력문제 2회·190
    ·실력문제 3회·192 / ·실력문제 4회·194

Ⅳ. 최종점검 문제 · 196
  1. 문법 / Part Ⅰ·196 / Part Ⅱ·199 / Part Ⅲ·202 / Part Ⅳ·203
  2. 어휘 / Part Ⅰ·204 / Part Ⅱ·208
  3. 독해 / Part Ⅰ·212 / Part Ⅱ·218 / Part Ⅲ·229

제3부 TEPS 문제에 대한 해설 및 해답 · 231
  Ⅰ. 제1부 PRE-TEST · 232
  Ⅱ. 제2부 총신·장신 신대원 TEPS 문제분석 · 315

제4부 빈출 어휘 정리 · 431

제1부

Pre-Test

I. 신대원 입시 출제경향

어떤 시험이던지 가장 좋은 대비는 기출문제를 많이 풀어보고, 기출문제와 비슷한 유형의 문제, 난이도가 비슷한 문제 등을 많이 다루는 것이다.
　요즈음 신학대학원 입시가 TEPS로 치러지는 추세이다.
　TEPS는 서울대학교 영어 능력 검정시험이다. 이 시험은 청해, 문법, 어휘, 독해 4개영역에 걸쳐 총 200 문답으로 구성되어 있다. 신대원 입시에서는 청해(L·C)부분을 제외한 나머지 3개영역만 테스트 한다.
　TEPS의 효과적인 수험대책은 다음과 같다.

　첫째, 청해 부분은 같은 테이프를 반복해서 3번 정도 듣고, 대본을 보고 확인하는 식으로 공부를 하는 것이 좋다. Native Speaker의 보통 속도의 발음 규칙을 체계적으로 알아두는 것이 도움이 된다. 속도나 전달력의 변화에도 유의하고, 발음 현상을 기억하는 것이 도움이 된다. 어려운 문장이나 많이 등장하는 상황은 통째로 암기해 두는 것이 유리하다.

　둘째, 문법 부분은 많이 출제되는 분야를 집중적으로 공부하는 것이 좋다. 우선순위는 다음과 같다. ① 동사와 관련된 분야, 즉 동사의 유형, 시제,

태, 가정법, 부정사, 분사, 동명사, 조동사 등이다. ② 연결 장치인 전치사, 접속사, 관계사 등이다. ③ 수식어인 형용사, 부사, 비교 등이다. ④ 명사, 대명사, 관사 등이다. ⑤ 특수 구문(도치, 강조, 생략), 병행구조(Parallelism) 등 이다. 문제를 풀면서 나름대로 위의 5가지 영역으로 나누어 세부적으로 어떤 문제가 많이 출제되는가를 연구하는 것이 도움이 될 것이다. 구어체 표현이 많이 출제되므로, 문법 지식을 구어체에 활용하고 암기해 두는 것도 유용하리라 생각한다.

셋째, 구어 표현이 많이 출제되므로 구어에 자주 등장하는 숙어나 회화 표현 등의 감각을 기르고 암기하는 것이 좋다. 시사 영어(신문, 방송)에 익숙해지는 것도 유리하다고 생각된다. 이디엄도 외워 두자.

단어를 암기할 때 연어(Collocation) 상태로 기억해 두는 것이 매우 도움이 된다. 어원에 의한 단어 공부도 추천할만한 방법이다.

넷째, 독해 부분에서 일반적으로 출제되는 질문 유형은 다음과 같다. ① 글 전체의 흐름 파악 문제 ② 세부 내용 파악 문제 ③ 주제 파악 문제 ④ 추론 문제 ⑤ 글의 응집력을 파악하는 문제 등이다. Part Ⅰ은 빈칸 채우기 문제이다. 이런 문제는 첫째 문장을 읽고 주제를 먼저 파악해야 한다. 만약에 첫째 문장에서 주제가 파악이 안 되면, 둘째 문장이나 마지막 문장을 읽고 주제를 파악하여야 한다. 다음에는 빈칸 앞뒤의 문장을 정독하면 답을 구할 수 있다. Part Ⅱ는 주제 파악 문제, 세부 내용 파악 문제, 추론 문제, 글이 응집력을 파악하는 문제 순서로 풀어 나가면 좋을 것이다. 세부 내용 파악 문제를 푸는 요령은 먼저 주제를 파악한 후에 질문지를 보면서 본문의 내용을 확인하는 것이다. 추론 문제는 첫째 문장과 마지막 문장에 유의하면 정답을 구할 수 있다. Part Ⅰ과 Part Ⅱ를 읽을 때 접속사, 전치사, 부사에 주의해야 한다. 예를 들어, 'Despite'가 나올 경우는 콤마 뒤가 중요하다. 'However'가 나오면 그 문장이 중요하다. Part Ⅲ에서는 첫째 문장(주제문)과 나머지 네 문장과의 관계를 따져, 관련이 없거나 적은 것을 고르면 된다. 독해 부분을 푸는 요령은 Part Ⅰ, Part Ⅲ, Part Ⅱ의 순서로 하는 것이 좋다.

유형별 문제 분석

II. 틀린 부분 찾기

실력문제 1회

* 아래 주어진 문장에서 문법적으로 옳지 못한 부분을 고르시오.

1. <u>Neither</u> the God he served nor the learning he <u>preserved</u> count for
     ①   ②
   much in the world from <u>whom</u> he had retired.
   ③   ④

2. As I <u>had</u> finished <u>to read</u> the newspaper, I began <u>to think</u> about
         ①   ②   ③
   the terrible accident <u>reported</u> in the paper.
                         ④

3. Upon <u>both</u> agreement, the price may be <u>converted</u> to other
        ①   ②
   currencies <u>according</u> to the <u>published</u> exchange rate on the invoice date.
              ③   ④

4. <u>In light of</u> economic cutbacks, many airlines <u>are planning to</u>
      ①   ②
   <u>improved</u> comfort <u>and</u> service <u>at lower fare levels</u>.
      ③   ④

5. The financial consultant you <u>select</u> should <u>have knowledge</u> of your
                                  ①   ②
   industry and <u>an interest</u> in <u>to learn</u> more about your company.
                   ③   ④

6. <u>Some of</u> the <u>finest examples</u> of <u>cave draw</u> and <u>paintings</u> are found in France.
      ①   ②   ③   ④

7. Jenny Lind, <u>the most famous</u> soprano <u>of the</u> nineteenth century,
                  ①   ②
   <u>was called as</u> "<u>the Swedish nightingale.</u>"
      ③   ④

8. There were <u>no survivors</u> in the <u>crash</u> and officials <u>say</u> there is still
             ①   ②   ③
   no indication of <u>that</u> caused the crash.
                  ④

9. Even <u>at the elementary school level</u>, especially <u>in rural areas</u>,
                 ①   ②
   <u>the number</u> of boy students greatly exceeds <u>girl students</u>.
      ③   ④

10. Group therapy <u>refers to</u> the <u>simultaneous treatment</u> of several clients
                    ①   ②
    under the guidance of therapist who <u>try to</u> facilitate <u>helpful interactions</u>
                                  ③   ④
    among group members.

11. <u>For</u> now the official objective is <u>to smash</u> Milosovic's war
      ①   ②
    machine so <u>bad</u> that it will be unable to continue <u>its</u> genocidal
            ③   ④
    onslaught against Kosovo Liberation Army and Kosovar villages.

12. In North America <u>the name</u> chameleon is <u>popularly</u> given <u>to</u> several
                      ①   ②   ③
    lizards capable of <u>change</u> color.
                    ④

13. Wind and <u>oceans</u> currents <u>may move</u> icebergs thousands of <u>kilometers</u>
            ①   ②   ③
    from <u>their</u> source.
        ④

14. The concept <u>of folk</u> music, <u>though</u> generally understood by <u>most</u>
               ①   ②   ③
    people, has <u>not</u> simple, widely accepted definition.
            ④

15. Light from the Sun can penetrate only a few hundred meters below
        ①   ②   ③
    surface of the ocean.
       ④

16. A drought is a period of dry weather that lasts too long enough to cause
                    ①   ②   ③
    a serious imbalance in the water cycle.
         ④

17. The area of the United States was doubled as a result of the
                                    ①   ②   ③
    Louisiana Purchase, which made in 1803.
                            ④

18. Clouds perform a very important function in modifying the distribute
      ①   ②   ③
    of solar heat over Earth's surface and within the atmosphere.
                                              ④

19. Although months or even years may pass without rainfall in parts of
       ①   ②
    deserts, they are never complete dry.
                ③   ④

20. As the centrally control orange of the body, the brain governs the
     ①   ②
    functioning of the body's other organ.
         ③   ④

◉ 표현연구

네 말이 맞아.

You can say that again.
I couldn't agree with you more.
You said it.
I'll say.

실력문제 2회

* 아래 주어진 문장에서 문법적으로 옳지 못한 부분을 고르시오.

1. At a time when most people <u>would argue</u> that oil or water are the world's
                                    ①
   most <u>precious</u> natural resources, Marc Furrer believes that it is <u>actually</u>
        ②   ③
   knowledge that is the most vital <u>resourceful</u> for a sustainable future.
                                   ④

2. The summit will <u>took place</u> in a new century that has already <u>witnessed</u>
                    ①   ②
   the <u>rapid</u> development <u>of an information society</u>, which has made
       ③   ④
   knowledge and information valuable commodities.

3. Dr. John expressed <u>doubts that</u> he and his assistants would be able
                      ①
   to <u>deal the</u> casualties resulting <u>from</u> the earthquake without any <u>aid</u>
      ②   ③   ④
   from the authorities.

4. All aspects of the <u>case</u> that <u>needs</u> further discussion will <u>be taken</u> up
            ①   ②   ③
   in the next <u>regularly</u> scheduled meeting.
          ④

5. We <u>enjoyed</u> the concert <u>held in</u> Townsend Hall very much, but personal
      ①   ②
   matters prevented us <u>from</u> staying for the full duration of the <u>performers</u>.
                ③   ④

6. If you let the <u>publishing</u> department <u>to know</u> in advance how
             ①   ②
   <u>many</u> copies are needed, they can have them available <u>in a matter of</u> days.
    ③   ④

7. This <u>cleaning</u> <u>agent</u> will work best <u>if</u> applied to materials as <u>recommendation</u>
        ①   ②   ③   ④

by the manufacturer.

8. The speed of data transfer has doubled by the end of next month if current
      ①   ②   ③
   trends are any indication.
   ④

9. Improve customer service is central to making the company work better
   ①   ②   ③
   and cost less to operate.
           ④

10. An independent poll showers that Thomas is currently the most popular
                         ①   ②   ③
    politician in the state.
              ④

11. New computer technology makes possible for anyone to calculate payroll
    ①   ②   ③
    taxes with relative ease.
              ④

12. Executives responsible for Korean markets find themselves run hard to
                ①   ②   ③
    keep pace with opportunities and government policies.
                    ④

13. Final revisions were being made to the report just hours before he
          ①   ②   ③
    presenting it to the board.
    ④

14. That is probably a good point to emphasis, since marketing and
               ①   ②   ③
    distribution are where most self-publishers fail.
                        ④

15. After working for fourteen hours without rest, Tom felt very tiring.
    ①   ②   ③   ④

16. Service will be withhold until the client satisfactorily responds to our
    ①   ②   ③
    notices regarding the delinquent payment.
                         ④

17. The committee suggested that the new policy incorporates throughout
    ①   ②   ③   ④
    the company.

18. As discussing, committee leaders will give a five minute report
    ①   ②
    concerning what is happening in their area.
    ③   ④

19. Each country has an assessor who fixes the value of all real property
    ①   ②
    subject to taxable.
    ③   ④

20. This warranty does not cover normal wear of parts or damage resulting
         ①   ②   ③
    from misusing of the product.
         ④

◎ 표현연구

절대 안 돼!
No way!
Not in a million years!
Not on your life!
Nothing doing!
Over my dead body!

◎ 표현연구

참고 견뎌!
Hang in there!
Stick it out!
Tough it out!

실력문제 3회

* 아래 주어진 문장에서 문법적으로 옳지 못한 부분을 고르시오.

1. There <u>remains</u> many reasons for the <u>animosity</u> that <u>exists</u> <u>between</u> the Arab
       ①   ②   ③   ④
   countries and Israel.

2. The <u>best of De La</u> Vega's <u>pictures is created</u> with <u>masking</u> tape, which
          ①   ②   ③
   he uses <u>to making</u> line drawings.
              ④

3. <u>Travel uptown</u> on any <u>Sunday morning</u> and <u>you'll amazed</u> by the <u>scene</u> on
        ①   ②   ③   ④
   125th Street at 9:00 A.M.

4. <u>Within</u> the company's <u>policy of</u> matching <u>funds</u>, retirement contribution
      ①   ②   ③
   could soon amount to a <u>considerable</u> sum.
                                ④

5. Many companies are imposing <u>stern</u> disciplinary measures on <u>employees</u>
                                 ①   ②
   <u>who</u> use e-mail <u>and the Internet</u> for personal use <u>beside</u> office hours.
     ③   ③   ④

6. The Cancer Research Institute <u>applied</u> <u>to grant money</u> <u>that was</u> offered
                                    ①   ②   ③
   <u>by</u> several pharmaceutical companies.
     ④

7. Ski <u>clothing</u> is <u>not suitable</u> <u>in climbing</u> because it is often too tight or
           ①   ②   ③
   restrictive and <u>prevents ventilation.</u>
                         ④

8. If you <u>enroll</u> four people <u>from your</u> organization <u>to our seminar</u>, you may
              ①   ②   ③
   send a <u>fifth</u> person free.
             ④

9. This training seminar will <u>teach you</u> <u>how to make</u> great <u>presentations</u>
① ② ③
<u>even so</u> you are not an expert public speaker.
④

10. Mr. White was so <u>nervous</u> <u>while</u> he <u>put</u> the wrong file <u>in his</u> briefcase.
① ② ③ ④

11. Notebook computers are <u>small enough</u> to <u>transport</u> easily, <u>although</u> powerful
① ② ③
enough to handle <u>the same chores as</u> a desktop machine.
④

12. Another <u>ambitious</u> proposal to <u>improve</u> semiconductor design <u>were</u> <u>offered</u>
① ② ③ ④
by the research and development.

13. Consultants are increasingly <u>involved in</u> recruitment and selection
①
<u>though</u> <u>he rarely</u> make <u>the final</u> decision.
② ③ ④

14. <u>Although</u> I took a <u>four-month leave</u> of absence, I have worked <u>for</u> the
① ② ③
General Electrics <u>in</u> 1995.
④

15. <u>Plugging</u> phone lines or <u>other</u> peripherals <u>into your</u> computer
① ② ③
increases your <u>vulnerable</u> to power problems.
④

16. Once a public relations agency <u>took</u> over contact <u>with</u> the media, the
① ②
company's advertising <u>dramatic</u> <u>improved</u>.
③ ④

17. Regular aerobic activity <u>can make</u> the heart pump <u>much efficiently</u> and
① ②
it <u>increases</u> a person's <u>energy level.</u>
③ ④

18. Environmentalists <u>discourage</u> the <u>use</u> of household <u>disposal</u>, such <u>as</u>
① ② ③ ④

plates and napkins.

19. He was <u>complemented</u> <u>on</u> <u>having done</u> <u>a fine job</u>.
    　　　　　①　　　　②　　　③　　　　④

20. The chairman <u>specifically</u> mentioned that each department <u>should do</u>
    　　　　　　　　①　　　　　　　　　　　　　　　　　　　②
    its <u>respectful</u> work to the best of <u>its ability</u>.
    　　③　　　　　　　　　　　　　　④

◎ 표현연구

상대방의 말에 동의하는 표현들

Alright.
No problem.
I'd be glad to.
Yes, of course.
OK. Why not.

◎ 표현연구

나는 녹초가 됐어.
I'm dead put.
I'm worn out.
I'm exhausted.
I'm wiped out.
I'm beat.
I'm bushed.

◎ 속 담

혼자 힘으로 대세를 막을 수 없다.
A fog cannot be dispelled with a fan.

실력 문제 4회

* 아래 주어진 문장에서 문법적으로 옳지 못한 부분을 고르시오.

1. One thing <u>which</u> I'd like to <u>mention to</u> my boss <u>is that</u> he forgets
   　　　　①　　　　　　　②　　　　　　③
   <u>that</u> he promises too often.
   ④

2. The workshop <u>explores</u> the importance of learning styles <u>besides</u>
   　　　　　　①　　　　　　　　　　　　　　　　　　　　②
   they <u>apply</u> to personal and <u>organizational</u> learning.
   　　　③　　　　　　　　　　④

3. Construction of <u>new homes</u> has <u>steadily</u> decreased <u>over the last</u> six
   　　　　　　　①　　　　　②　　　　　　③
   months, <u>what</u> is a bad sign for the economy.
   　　　　④

4. A representative <u>of the timber</u> industry acknowledged <u>which</u> the price
   　　　　　　　　①　　　　　　　　　　　　　　　　②
   of hardwood would <u>continue</u> to go up as demand <u>increased</u>.
   　　　　　　　　　③　　　　　　　　　　　　　　④

5. In a business listing, <u>companies</u> should include <u>any</u> whatever <u>awards</u>
   　　　　　　　　　　　①　　　　　　　　②　　　　　　③
   they <u>have</u> won.
   　　　④

6. The more <u>unsettled things</u> are and <u>fast</u> they change, the more valuable
   　　　　　①　　　　　　　　②
   it <u>is to</u> keep multiple options <u>alive.</u>
   　　③　　　　　　　　　　　　④

7. The lawyer <u>used</u> a successful <u>combination</u> of <u>flattery</u> and <u>intimidate</u>
   　　　　　①　　　　　　　　②　　　　　③　　　　④
   to cross-examine the witness.

8. The <u>strength</u> of the German mark is having <u>its</u> greatest impact <u>at</u>
   　　　①　　　　　　　　　　　　　　　②　　　　　　③
   import growth and <u>inflation</u>.
   　　　　　　　　④

9. Marine biology, the study of oceanic plant and animals and their
            ①   ②
   ecological relationships, has furthered the efficient development of
                                  ③   ④
   fisheries.

10. The way of reasoning whereby people do conclusions by logical
                    ①   ②   ③
    inference from given premises is called the deductive method.
                   ④

11. Our toys are created with children's safety in mind, and we are
              ①   ②
    aware that babies sometimes put them in danger when small parts of
    ③   ④
    the boy are detachable.

12. Scientists and economists believe that human beings can never
                              ①   ②
    use away all the mineral resources on earth.
    ③   ④

13. Negotiable instruments such as personal checks may ordinarily be
    ①   ②
    transferred to another people by endorsement.
                           ③   ④

14. Baffin Bay played an important role in the explorer of North America
              ①   ②   ③
    by Europeans seeking a trade route to India.
                         ④

15. It is estimated that a scientific principle has a life expectancy of
         ①   ②
    approximately a decade before it drastically revised or replaced by
                    ③   ④
    newer information.

16. Radio waves, the same light waves, travel at a constant speed of
                 ①   ②   ③   ④
    186,282 miles per second.

17. Air law is <u>defined as</u> the body <u>of law</u> directly or indirectly
    　　　　　　　　①　　　　　　　②
   <u>is concerned</u> with <u>civil</u> aviation.
   　　③　　　　　　　④
18. <u>As</u> a glacier <u>melts</u>, rocks, boulders, trees, and tons of <u>dirt</u> <u>deposit</u>.
    ①　　　　　②　　　　　　　　　　　　　　　　　　　　③　　　④
19. The body <u>does</u> not <u>stay at</u> the <u>alike</u> temperature from morning till <u>night</u>.
    　　　　　①　　　②　　　　③　　　　　　　　　　　　　　　　④
20. Various <u>option</u> have been outlined <u>for</u> restructuring our manufacturing
    　　　　　①　　　　　　　　　　　　②
   <u>division</u>, but nothing will be finalized until after the end of the <u>next</u>
   　③　　　　　　　　　　　　　　　　　　　　　　　　　　　　　　　　④
   fiscal year.

◉ 표현연구

잘 했어.
You did a good job.
You've got a great job.
You made it.

◉ 속 담

천리 길도 한 걸음부터
A journey of a thousand miles begin with a single step.

◉ 속 담

분수에 맞는 생활을 해라.
Cut your coat according to your cloth.

◉ 속 담

은혜를 원수로 갚지 마라.
Don't bite hand that feeds you.

III. 어휘력

실력문제 1회

* 밑줄 친 단어와 가장 가까운 의미를 가진 단어를 선택하시오.

1. The <u>inadequate</u> supply of necessary military machinery eventually led to the downfall of Hitlers troops.
   ① substantial   ② inconsequential   ③ insufficient   ④ proper

2. We must not <u>relinquish</u> our rights as the citizens of Korea.
   ① change   ② surrender   ③ increase   ④ protect

3. The representative was asked to <u>verify</u> his earlier statement.
   ① confirm   ② withdraw   ③ repeat   ④ modify

4. The farmer <u>extricated</u> the dog from the barbed-wire fence.
   ① rankled   ② removed   ③ vaunted   ④ scrutinized

5. Everyday, millions of children "pledge <u>allegiance</u> to the flag of America and to the republic for which it stands."
   ① disloyalty   ② judgment   ③ sedition   ④ fidelity

6. The author's reasons for changing his novel are highly <u>pertinent</u>.
   ① imaginative   ② unrealistic   ③ relevant   ④ controversial

7. She would <u>portray</u> the city as a blend of Manhattan and Hollywood on the Arabian Sea.
   ① rehabilitate   ② impeach   ③ vitiate   ④ depicture

8. The priest <u>absolved</u> the boy when he confessed he had stolen some money from his father's desk drawer.
   ① exonerated   ② consoled   ③ blamed   ④ reproved

9. I try to be broad-minded but do feel <u>antipathy</u> toward people who

are dirty and unkempt.
① sympathy   ② empathy   ③ aversion   ④ antipode

10. If the unions were to <u>abrogate</u> their traditional role, they would be blamed.
    ① establish   ② revoke   ③ abscond   ④ assimilate

11. Your <u>belligerent</u> attitude is often the cause for your lack of popularity.
    ① courageous   ② cowardly   ③ hostile   ④ stupid

12. A <u>benevolent</u> employer has a sincere interest in the welfare of his employee.
    ① considerable   ② charitable   ③ miserable   ④ inventive

13. It is hard to <u>conciliate</u> the views of labor and management on this point.
    ① mediate   ② meditate   ③ commence   ④ consecrate

14. Ashamed to oppose the censor's morality, and afraid to <u>contravene</u> his authority, the writer's first reaction is evade the censorship.
    ① approve   ② concede   ③ manifest   ④ gainsay

15. Whoever did this must have been <u>demented</u>; no sane person would have acted in such a way.
    ① incessant   ② irrelevant   ③ insoluble   ④ insane

16. It wasn't <u>discreet</u> of you to call him around midnight.
    ① intelligent   ② violent   ③ copious   ④ prudent

17. The scars of battle were <u>effaced</u> during the incident.
    ① wiped off   ② effective   ③ groped   ④ stashed

18. Fathers, do not <u>exasperate</u> your children; instead bring them up in the instruction of Lord.

① coax　　　② deceive　　　③ frighten　　　④ infuriate

19. John F. Kennedy's <u>forebears</u> migrated to America from Ireland.
    ① ancestors　　② descendants　　③ dictator　　④ forecast

20. Many different racial and cultural groups are to be found in the <u>heterogeneous</u> population of a large city.
    ① homogeneous　② varied　　　③ congested　　④ intractable

◉ 표현연구

내가 살께.
It's on me.
It's on the house.
I'll treat.
Let me get the check.
I'll take the tab.
I'll foot the bill.

◉ 표현연구

비밀을 누설하지 마.
Don't let the cat out of the bag.
Don't spill the beans.
Keep it to yourself.

◉ 표현연구

너 무슨 일이 있니?
What's eating you?
What's bothering you?
What's bugging you?

실력문제 2회

* 밑줄 친 단어와 가장 가까운 의미를 가진 단어를 선택하시오.

1. It took several days for the wrecking crew to <u>demolish</u> the old building.
   ① abandon   ② raze   ③ ostracize   ④ rant

2. The most surprising feature is that she was such a <u>prolific</u> writer even at an early age.
   ① traumatic   ② saturated   ③ native   ④ productive

3. The <u>bedrock</u> on which psychoanalysis rests is a belief in the unconscious.
   ① impasse   ② perspective   ③ prejudice   ④ foundation

4. Many of his colleagues eventually agreed that Einstein's theory was <u>tenable</u>.
   ① tenuous   ② warrantable   ③ redundant   ④ tolerable

5. Only two of the girls protested when they were ordered off the field. The rest were too <u>meek</u> to complain.
   ① practical   ② aggressive   ③ submissive   ④ patient

6. Rubber is one of the most <u>elastic</u> materials in our daily life.
   ① indispensable   ② flexible   ③ invariable   ④ portable

7. The officer is <u>gallant</u> in his behavior toward the woman.
   ① obedient   ② brave   ③ pertinent   ④ courtly

8. Even today, when discussing the sinking of the Titantic, survivors tend to speak <u>solemnly</u> of their ordeal.
   ① slowly   ② cautiously   ③ somberly   ④ weakly

9. William's <u>pert and saucy</u> remarks always distress his wife.
   ① recessive   ② oblivious   ③ bold   ④ nimble

10. The vote approving the amendment was far from unanimous; six members are <u>dissented</u>.
    ① concurred   ② resented   ③ consented   ④ opposite

11. The handle is <u>fragile</u>; it will easily break if you use too much pressure.
    ① light   ② breakable   ③ temporary   ④ priceless

12. Eighty students came to the dance but only seventy-four tickets were collected at the door. Can you account for this <u>discrepancy</u>?
    ① discretion   ② discredit   ③ difference   ④ discomfort

13. What <u>enchants</u> him in this case was the nicety of procedure, which began by deceiving and ended by murdering.
    ① attracts   ② embarrasses   ③ imprison   ④ impute

14. Unethical behaviors by the political officials have become more <u>prevalent</u> these days.
    ① widespread   ② justified   ③ acceptable   ④ proper

15. The new global community faces many <u>pressing</u> issues.
    ① pressure   ② urgent   ③ perverse   ④ consequential

16. Judy wore an imitation fur coat that everyone thought was made of <u>genuine</u> leopard skin.
    ① perfect   ② imitated   ③ real   ④ valuable

17. Steam railways had their <u>heyday</u> in the 19th century.
    ① the hardest time   ② the most prosperous time
    ③ initiation   ④ decline

18. His listeners were amazed that such a thorough presentation could be made in an impromptu speech.
    ① interesting ② informative ③ expressive ④ extemporaneous

19. If some of the requirements for graduation seem complicated, see your guidance counselor.
    ① coarse ② lengthy ③ obsolete ④ intricate

20. Dad has no misgivings when Mother takes the wheel, because she is an excellent driver.
    ① confidence ② misconduct ③ doubt ④ coolness

◎ 표현연구

나는 바빠.
I'm busy as a bee.
I'm tied up.
I'm all booked up.
I'm behind in my work.
My hands are full.

◎ 속 담

빈 수레가 요란하다.
Big talk means little knowledge.

◎ 속 담

말 한마디에 천 냥 빚도 갚는다.
Kind words are worth much and they cost little.

◎ 속 담

누워서 침 뱉기.
He who spits against the wind fouls his beard.

실력문제 3회

* 밑줄 친 단어와 가장 가까운 의미를 가진 단어를 선택하시오.

1. A masquerade is always interesting because people come in such <u>outlandish</u> costumes.
   ① jolly   ② liable   ③ rustic   ④ queer

2. The president has been accused of serious <u>infractions</u> during the last few months.
   ① discrepancy   ② violation   ③ urgent   ④ revolt

3. The beach was not as <u>shallow</u> as we thought.
   ① beautiful   ② deep   ③ not deep   ④ windy

4. Once a commercial <u>impetus</u> is given to their development, the products should improve rapidly.
   ① impiety   ② timidity   ③ incentive   ④ distortion

5. Some <u>enterprising</u> couples slave for a combined 100-hour-plus workweek, a pace relieved by exotic vacations and expensive health clubs.
   ① vigorous   ② reluctant   ③ suspicious   ④ entertaining

6. They said they had been <u>interrogated</u> for 20 hours about political demonstrations.
   ① chased   ② praised   ③ examined   ④ intermingled

7. Hemp, a harsh, <u>stiff</u> fiber, comes from a plant that grows in both hot and mild climates.
   ① sticky   ② rigid   ③ dense   ④ woven

8. A neutron is so <u>tiny</u> it would take ten trillion of them to cover a square inch.
   ① indefinite   ② variable   ③ minuscule   ④ intangible

9. The doctor told me to cut down my consumption of carbohydrates.
   ① reduce   ② appease   ③ increase   ④ appreciate

10. The right of his opponent's attack enervate the young politician.
    ① avenge   ② avert   ③ weaken   ④ cripple

11. I was in a totally torpid state once after a grueling wrestling match.
    ① lethargic   ② energetic   ③ delightful   ④ harmonious

12. The newly employed clerk in the bank is known to be meticulous person.
    ① kind   ② ambitious   ③ tedious   ④ scrupulous

13. Cowboy films traditionally open with a view of an immense spread of rugged terrain.
    ① a beautiful   ② an unsettled   ③ a vast   ④ an immediate

14. The tendency of the human body to reject foreign matter is the main obstacle to successful tissue transplantation.
    ① factor in   ② impediment in   ③ occurrence in   ④ phenomenon of

15. Opera should have flourished in France during the decade of the Revolution.
    ① perished   ② discouraged   ③ prospered   ④ increased

16. The excuse he gave for his lateness was so preposterous that everyone laughed.
    ① primordial   ② prosperous   ③ absurd   ④ outstanding

17. The beaver uses its engineering proficiency to create intricate lodges and dams.
    ① excavation   ② labor   ③ skill   ④ experiment

18. You must not override other's happiness in pursuit of your own.

① reside　　② annul　　③ drench　　④ establish

19. Because the grapes of North America grow so <u>profusely</u> and appear in many varieties, the continent has been called a natural vineyard.

　　① robustly　　② persistently　　③ abundantly　　④ gratuitously

20. A sensation of <u>stupor</u> oppressed me as my eyes followed her retreating steps.

　　① responsibility　② anger　　③ resentment　　④ aspiration

◉ 표현연구

너 기분이 안 좋아 보여.
You look down.
You look blue.
You look under the weather.
You don't look very well.
Why the long face?

◉ 표현연구

오늘은 여기까지 하자.
Let's call it a day.
Let's call it quits.
So much for today.

◉ 속 담

말하기는 쉬워도 행하기는 어렵다.
From word to deed is a great space.
From saying to doing is a long step.

실력문제 4회

* 밑줄 친 단어와 가장 가까운 의미를 가진 단어를 선택하시오.

1. His <u>recurrent</u> absence at the conference was a big news item to everyone.
   ① periodic   ② perennial   ③ prolonged   ④ unacceptable

2. Human beings have an uncanny ability to <u>adapt</u> to the environment.
   ① refrain   ② adopt   ③ flee   ④ adjust

3. Once the water was <u>depleted</u>, the explorers had to give up hope.
   ① disproved   ② exhausted   ③ malingered   ④ appeased

4. His <u>parsimony</u> was legendary throughout the film world.
   ① charisma   ② affection   ③ stinginess   ④ retribution

5. Many of the audience walked out through <u>sheer</u> boredom.
   ① latent   ② absolute   ③ potential   ④ ambiguous

6. Frank felt it <u>incumbent</u> on him to pay for the damage, which was caused by his negligence.
   ① obligatory   ② reasonable   ③ submissive   ④ superfluous

7. Students who click their ball point pens in class <u>drive me up a wall</u>.
   ① enrage me   ② enervate me   ③ make me laugh   ④ make me diffident

8. During the rest of the week the man continued his <u>vehement</u> protests.
   ① forceful   ② weird   ③ absurd   ④ onerous

9. If wool is submerged in hot water, it tends to <u>shrink</u>.
   ① smell   ② fade   ③ unravel   ④ contract

10. Perhaps a year ago a <u>prescient</u> West could have stationed forces

to prevent the current war.

① pliable   ② intractable   ③ prophetic   ④ keen

11. The National Science Foundation <u>disseminates</u> information relating to scientific resources.

    ① records   ② discounts   ③ obtains   ④ disperses

12. Using extremely different decorating schemes in adjoining rooms may result in <u>discord</u> and a lack of unity in style.

    ① compromise   ② disharmony   ③ disillusion   ④ anxiety

13. While some bacteria are beneficial, others are <u>harmful</u> in that they cause disease.

    ① detrimental   ② prodigious   ③ intrusive   ④ mordant

14. At this point we are brought to those fundamental and <u>ubiquitously</u> held assumptions in our culture which lie unexpressed at the heart of this anomalous decision.

    ① contradictorily   ② omnipresently   ③ arbitrarily   ④ essentially

15. The Ford Foundation is one of the world's wealthiest <u>philanthropic</u> organizations.

    ① profligate   ② governmental   ③ humanitarian   ④ multinational

16. Many pure metals have little use because they are too soft, rust too easily, or have some other <u>drawback</u>.

    ① property   ② additive   ③ disadvantage   ④ disparity

17. The speaker explained the <u>nuts and bolts of</u> his plan to establish a new telephone system for the country.

    ① various arguments for   ② widespread passions for
    ③ expected advantages of   ④ basic practical details of

18. George knew all <u>the ins and outs</u> of the case.

① strengths ② weaknesses ③ details ④ answers

19. We excluded the problems with nuclear-generated fuels as they were not <u>germane</u> to our debate.

    ① relevant ② immaterial ③ essential ④ vague

20. He is all muscle and sinew and the most <u>indefatigable</u> hunter and trapper in the world.

    ① courageous ② excellent ③ defiant ④ untiring

◎ 속 담

어떤 나쁜 일이라도 좋은 면이 있다.
Every cloud has a silver lining.

◎ 표현연구

상대방의 제안을 받아들이는 표현들
All right.
You're on!
That would be great!
That's very kind of you.

◎ 표현연구

상대방의 제안을 정중히 거절하는 표현들
Thanks, but it's OK.
No, that's fine. I can manage.
Don't worry. I can do it myself.
Don't bother. It's OK.

◎ 표현연구

내 말을 믿어.
You have my word.
Take my word for it.

IV. 문장 완성형

실력 문제 1회

* 괄호 안에 들어갈 가장 적당한 단어를 고르시오.

1. United Airlines posted _____ financial losses in 2001 after the Sept. 11 attacks and again this year as revenues remained weak.
   ① real   ② massive   ③ mass   ④ realistic

2. There was a new report of the _____ between the terrorist groups and bombings in the Middle East.
   ① connection   ② agreement   ③ debate   ④ understanding

3. Union and management hope they can _____ a contract before the workers strike.
   ① negotiate   ② stipulate   ③ reciprocate   ④ correlate

4. Bob prefers classical music to modern music, which he says is noisy and _____.
   ① rapturous   ② raucous   ③ ravenous   ④ rigorous

5. The lines of communication between the conscious and the unconscious zones of the human psyche have all been _____, and we have been split in two.
   ① cut   ② connected   ③ diverged   ④ activated

6. Man requires the opportunity to do challenging work. I do not include in this category the many tasks which are merely repetitive routine. I am not interested in _____ work.
   ① creative   ② laborious   ③ monotonous   ④ necessary

7. His _____ and experience made him an excellent person for this job.
   ① competence   ② complacency   ③ compensation   ④ compunction

8. Because there was so little food, each family was _____ only one pound of rice a week.
   ① entreated ② alloted ③ resolved ④ detached

9. Thanks to the natural resources of the country, every American, until quite recently, could reasonably look forward to making more money than his father, so that, if he made less, the _____ must be his; he was either or inefficient.
   ① wealth ② fault ③ expense ④ possession

10. The speaker tried to arouse the emotions of the silent crowd by delivering a(an) _____ speech.
    ① erratic ② frustrated ③ irregular ④ passionate

11. John and Bob tried to move the large rock, but they could not _____ it.
    ① provoke ② dodge ③ arouse ④ budge

12. We can't make out what he says because he always _____.
    ① masters ② mumbles ③ molests ④ ridicules

13. Marketers have always exploited pretty faces and perfect bodies to sell everything from lipstick to lingerie, but worldwide _____ and tough times in the advertising business have made the supermodels one of the few reliable sales tools.
    ① prosperity ② plateau ③ boom ④ recession

14. Columbus' journey was the first step in a long process that eventually produced the United States of America, a daring experiment in democracy that in turn became a symbol and a _____ of individual liberty for people throughout the world.
    ① anomaly ② haven ③ shambles ④ inferno

15. To finance the program they had to turn to _____.

① the public in the bay of raising money
② the public for the funds they needed
③ appealing money from the public
④ fund raising for money of the public

16. The ultimate goal of their reform movement cannot be uniform, but must be composed of numerous diverse elements that will _____ the wholesome old ways.
    ① reinforce   ② continue   ③ replace   ④ reinstate

17. Judy is a nice girl but she has one great _____; she talks too much.
    ① crime   ② deviation   ③ mistake   ④ failing

18. Bush said only that economic sanctions against Baghdad would remain in _____ and that history has a way of taking care of tyrants.
    ① affect   ② force   ③ void   ④ effective

19. Don't let grass grow _____. You must learn to do things a little faster.
    ① on the ground   ② in the garden
    ③ under your feet   ④ under the trees

20. It would be difficult for one so _____ to be led to believe that all men are equal and that we must disregard race, color, and creed.
    ① emotional   ② broadminded   ③ tolerant   ④ intolerant

◎ 속 담

늦어도 안 하는 것보다 낫다.
Better late than never.

◎ 속 담

남이 당신에게 해주기 원하는 대로 남에게도 해 주어라.
Do as you would be done by.
Do to others as you would have them do to you.

실력문제 2회

※ 빈칸에 들어갈 가장 적당한 단어를 고르시오.

1. _____ drops of rain barely fell on our head as we walked down the street.
   ① Heavy   ② Intermittent   ③ Continuous   ④ Repeated

2. Since he had not worked very hard on his project, the student was quite _____ upon learning that he had won the contest.
   ① dismayed   ② apathetic   ③ composed   ④ enraptured

3. Tests showed that the driver was _____ when he had the accident.
   ① caring   ② undeniable   ③ intoxicated   ④ overexcited

4. He speaks so softly that his voice is not really _____.
   ① fragile   ② audible   ③ brittle   ④ decrepit

5. I don't think Johnson will succeed in his new job, for he is not _____ to do that type of work.
   ① compatible   ② consistent   ③ conspicuous   ④ competent

6. When the arsonist was questioned by the prosecutor, he denied his _____ in the crime.
   ① simulation   ② complicity   ③ exuberance   ④ contingency

7. Without Bob's testimony, evidence of bribery is lacking and _____ in the case will be impossible.
   ① verdict   ② sentence   ③ conviction   ④ acquittal

8. Massive amounts of data from mass media seems to overpower us and drive us to _____ accounts for an easily and readily digestible portion of news.

① investigative ② predominant ③ insular ④ synoptic

9. For a long time I fixed my eyes on the billboard. Its white attracted my eyes, and, as it were, _____ my brain. I tried to read it, but my efforts were in vain.
   ① affected ② tempted ③ washed ④ hypnotized

10. Many people, out of anxiety, became unable to contemplate their true situation and with it to plan accordingly. Anxiety, and the wish to _____ it by clinging to each other, and to reduce its sting by continuing as much as possible with their usual way of life incapacitated many.
    ① contradict ② counteract ③ frustrate ④ deprecate

11. An oppressive _____, and not the festive mood one might have expected, characterized the mood of the gathering.
    ① senility ② capriciousness ③ insanity ④ solemnity

12. His _____ remarks are often embarrassing because of their frankness.
    ① sarcastic ② sadistic ③ digressive ④ ingenuous

13. Jane would not talk to us, for she was shy and _____.
    ① recumbent ② redundant ③ resonant ④ reticent

14. After his long illness, the old man appeared so thin and _____ that a gust of wind might have blown him away.
    ① faint ② sinewy ③ flimsy ④ frail

15. Victims of glaucoma find that their _____ vision is impaired and that they can no longer see objects not directly in front of them.
    ① peripatetic ② peripheral ③ periphrastic ④ ocular

16. There appears to exist an inverse relationship between the birth rate and the degree of development of a nation. Thus, the greater the degree of industrial and scientific progress, urbanization, and elevation of the standard of living, the more the birth rate tends to be _____.

    ① sustained   ② higher   ③ depressed   ④ stabilized

17. The teacher gave the students extra work because she was _____ by all the noise and talking in the classroom.

    ① degenerated   ② exasperated   ③ consummated   ④ expended

18. Freedom of speech is an _____ right in a democracy.

    ① incoherent   ② inherent   ③ incessant   ④ incredible

19. Although nominal wages might fall, the removal of a tariff would result in a still larger reduction in price level so that the real wages must _____.

    ① rise   ② fall   ③ dwindle   ④ expand

20. Apparently the long drought has _____ this tree's growth.

    ① retarded   ② rebuked   ③ retreated   ④ retained

◎ 속 담

과한 욕심을 삼가라.
Don't bite off more than you can chew.

◎ 표현연구

흥분하지 마.
Keep your cool.
Don't lose your cool.

◎ 표현연구

그는 아직 위독한 상태이다.
He's still touch-and-go.

실력문제 3회

* 빈칸에 들어갈 가장 적당한 단어를 고르시오.

1. In the presence of God and of Christ Jesus, who will judge the living and the dead, and to _____ his appearing and his kingdom, I give you this charge.
   ① in view of   ② in spite of   ③ regardless of   ④ in terms of

2. Having written 57 books till his retired age, he may well be considered one of the most _____ theologians of the century.
   ① controversial   ② unheralded   ③ easygoing   ④ prolific

3. The novel Uncle Tom's Cabin, which effectively _____ the unfairness towards black people, was a major influence in _____ the anti-slavery movement.
   ① viewed – appraising   ② glamorized – launching
   ③ portrayed – strengthening   ④ exposed – condemning

4. The spies found that the secret code was impossible to _____.
   ① intercede   ② publish   ③ decipher   ④ unveil

5. Hospitals, prisons, and ____ asylums are places where people fear to go.
   ① public   ② psycho   ③ lunatic   ④ fantastic

6. He was though of as the most _____ man in our company since he accepted whatever his superiors suggested without reflexive thought.
   ① intractable   ② suspicious   ③ obsequious   ④ antagonistic

7. Many educators argued that a _____ grouping of students would improve instruction as the range of student abilities would be limited.

① intensive　② homogeneous　③ systematic　④ varied

8. The charm of her voice _____ her rough appearance.
   ① fascinated　② redeemed　③ illuminated　④ ratified

9. No artifacts have been _____ from the wreck of the Titanic so far.
   ① retrieved　② recalled　③ reprieved　④ restricted

10. Not wanting to be seen by the man he was following, he moved _____.
    ① snugly　② stealthily　③ modestly　④ moodily

11. If you are to stress points of difference in answering an essay examination question, the key word in the question is to _____.
    ① compare　② define　③ evaluate　④ contrast

12. Smoking may _____ your health.
    ① danger　② ameliorate　③ impair　④ enhance

13. Your _____ remarks has confused the discussion.
    ① insightful　② incongruous　③ prosperous　④ appropriate

14. He would spend more time _____ before making public statements about the matter.
    ① at overcoming　② recuperating　③ on getting over　④ from getting well

15. When Benjamin Franklin invented the lightning rod, the clergy condemned it as an _____ attempt to defeat the will of God.
    ① adventurous　② arrogant　③ decent　④ impious

16. We do not learn to construct sentences instinctively, as we learn to breathe or to walk. We repeat sentences from memory and we vary them by _____.

① initiation   ② record   ③ analogy   ④ instinct

17. Taekwondo is one of the _____ sports which has been developed in Korea.
    ① crude   ② manual   ③ congenial   ④ indigenous

18. Don't hesitate to give us your ideas; we are always _____ any suggestions.
    ① up to   ② in for   ③ open to   ④ content with

19. The concept of timelessness is paradoxical from the start, for adult consciousness is _____ by the awareness of duration.
    ① repelled   ② permeated   ③ measured   ④ intrigued

20. Lukewarm acceptance is much more bewildering than _____ rejection.
    ① resentful   ② prudent   ③ outright   ④ insulting

◎ 속 담

교만한 자는 오래가지 못 한다.
Pride goes before a fall.

◎ 속 담

하룻강아지 범 무서운 줄 모른다.
Fools rush in where angels fear to tread.

◎ 표현연구

비용이 정말 많이 들었구나.
That really cost you an arm and a leg.

실력문제 4회

* 빈칸에 들어갈 가장 적당한 단어를 고르시오.

1. Although Jesus was _____ by his followers who found truth in his teachings, his teachings constituted _____ to the Jewish leaders.
   ① accepted – a benefit   ② revered – a threat
   ③ slighted – a challenge   ④ denied – an innovation

2. Mr. Lee was frequently intolerant; moreover, his strange behavior caused most of his acquaintances to _____ the professor whenever possible.
   ① revere   ② shun   ③ contradict   ④ tolerate

3. Many buildings with historical significance are now being _____ instead of being torn down.
   ① built   ② repaired   ③ destroyed   ④ praised

4. A bank teller can easily distinguish the genuine ten-dollar bills from the _____ ones.
   ① authentic   ② contraband   ③ counterpart   ④ counterfeit

5. In eastern North America, the oak, on account of the _____ quality of its wood, is everywhere regarded as a symbol of strength.
   ① brilliant   ② splendid   ③ staunch   ④ starveling

6. It didn't take long for him to come _____ a convincing example.
   ① up with   ② down on   ③ into force   ④ to terms with

7. A young person who is _____ has very little experience or knowledge of the way he should behave as an adult.
   ① callous   ② arduous   ③ callow   ④ ardent

8. There is an _____ among classmates that is often as strong as loyalty to one's family.
   ① animosity   ② animus   ③ affinity   ④ equanimity

9. No punishment is too severe for such a(n) _____ crime; it is almost impossible to understand its enormity.
   ① arbitrary   ② egregious   ③ exemplary   ④ aimless

10. The members of the group did very competent work as individuals, but it was their _____ effort that produced the best results.
    ① extraordinary   ② collaborative   ③ brilliant   ④ persistent

11. If one speaks constantly in _____ there is little danger that others will take literally any of what is said.
    ① hyperboles   ② detail   ③ mischances   ④ comparison

12. Given a certain number of uncompromisable convictions and a certain number of unfulfilled expectations and the fact that marriage evokes in people not only their best but also their beastliest features, any couple is bound to have their share of _____.
    ① common experience   ② credibility gap   ③ cooperation   ④ fighting

13. Specifically our proposal would be to establish sufficient journeyman-level positions so that when capability and performance is achieved by individuals they would _____ achieve journeyman status.
    ① automatically   ② probably   ③ judiciously   ④ patiently

14. The consequences of the establishment of the colonies were rapid and careless _____ of natural resources, and _____ human suffering.
    ① disappearance - planned   ② development - unfailing
    ③ depletion - appalling   ④ disintegration - compelled

15. Some philosophers think that one's lifetime is _____ when considered from the viewpoint of _____ making humans appear

much less important than they think in the grand scheme of things.
① complimentary - prestige ② jaded - youth
③ ephemeral - eternity ④ gauche - theology

16. Assessments of the family are changing remarkably, from general approval of it as a worthwhile, stable institution to widespread _____ it as an oppressive and bankrupt one whose _____ was both imminent and welcome.
① flight from - restoration ② fascination with - deterioration
③ rejection of - vogue ④ censure of - dissolution

17. He is the victim of firmly fixed and deep-rooted habits. With him telling untruths is as frequent and customary an activity as brushing his teeth in the morning or ordering toast and coffee for breakfast. Then he is an _____ liar.
① notorious ② inveterate ③ incorrigible ④ consummate

18. If they can only forget their differences and _____, they may have a chance to win the election.
① pull up ② pull through ③ pull together ④ pull out

19. His Bohemian attitude toward sex should be told as open-minded. He is not a champion of _____, but he maintains a _____ attitude toward other people's behavior.
① decadence - strict ② promiscuity - tolerant
③ sexism - theoretical ④ licentiousness - personal

20. The young cricket is a carefree itinerant songster. It seeks no permanent home. A stone or a leaf is enough for its shelter. It finds its food along the waysides. In the insect world, it is a _____.
① worthless rascal ② nomadic herdsman
③ traveling salesman ④ wandering minstrel

V. 어법

실력문제 1회

* 빈칸에 들어갈 가장 적절한 것을 고르시오.

1. Social reformer Jane Addams _____ a prominent role in the formation of the National Progressive party in 1912.
   ① playing   ② who played   ③ played   ④ to play

2. Dams can be very beneficial to the areas _____.
   ① in which they are built   ② building them where
   ③ which they are built   ④ where are they built

3. _____ either by cooling or by depriving the fire of oxygen, and most do both.
   ① Working fire extinguishers   ② Fire extinguishers that work
   ③ Fire extinguishers work   ④ The work of fire extinguishers

4. From birth, nightjar chicks solicit food by walking to the front of an adult bird, reaching up, and _____.
   ① they peck at its bill   ② peck at its bill
   ③ pecking at its bill   ④ at its bill they peck

5. _____ wild dogs have very keen senses of sight, hearing, and smell.
   ① Like the cats,   ② Cats are like
   ③ Although   ④ They are like the cats,

6. A social system is _____ of social relations that draws the behavior of its members toward the core values of the group.
   ① a complex network   ② how a complex network
   ③ a complex network and   ④ a network that is complex

7. About 75 percent of all cadmium is used for cadmium plating of _____ such as iron and steel.
   ① easily corroded metals   ② metals are easily corroded
   ③ corroded metals that easily ④ how easily metals corroded

8. _____ astrology and alchemy may be regarded as fundamental aspects of thought is indicated by their apparent universality.
   ① Both are   ② What both   ③ Both   ④ That both

9. _____ in the southern and midwestern United States, ragtimes music reached its classic form in the 1890's.
   ① To have originated   ② Originating
   ③ To originate   ④ It originates

10. The harder the shrub is to grow, _____.
    ① the higher price it is   ② the higher price it would have
    ③ the higher the price is   ④ the higher is the price

11. _____ the alarming report of earth tremors nearby, the workers proceeded to lay the foundation of the building.
    ① On   ② Beside   ③ Despite   ④ Instead of

12. Jody looked _____ at the towering mountains-ridge after ridge until at last there was the ocean.
    ① to search   ② searching   ③ searchingly   ④ searching for

13. Good things long _____ cannot easily be given up.
    ① having enjoyed   ② enjoying   ③ enjoyed   ④ to have enjoyed

14. It is becoming more and more important for us to know _____ a computer.
    ① using   ② to use   ③ having used   ④ how to use

15. The frog escaped from its basket, and _____ caused all the

little girls to scream.
① these ② those ③ this ④ which

16. No matter how _____, it is not necessarily worthless.
① dry a desert may be ② a desert may be dry
③ a desert dry may be ④ may be a desert dry

17. Despite our _____ properly introduced prior to that evening, Dr. Benson and I had in fact been acquainted for some years, having taken to greeting one another in the street our of mutual recognition of our respective reputations.
① ever have been ② never been
③ having been ④ never having been

18. This statement means exactly what it says. Don't try to read anything else _____ it.
① through ② out ③ over ④ into

19. _____, the government was not doing enough to solve the pollution problem.
① As the public was concerned
② As far as the public was concerned
③ Much as it concerned the public
④ As long as the public was concerned

20. _____, I don't know him.
① Meeting not him before ② Not having met him before
③ Having not meet him before ④ As I having not met him before

실력문제 2회

* 빈칸에 들어갈 가장 적절한 것을 고르시오.

1. _____ to stand in a warm place, it sours because of the presence of bacteria that convert milk sugar into acid.
   ① When milk is allowed　② When is milk allowed
   ③ Milk, when allowed　④ When milk allowed

2. Pure naphtha is highly explosive if _____ to an open flame.
   ① it exposed　② exposed　③ expose it　④ is it exposed

3. Venus is perpetually covered by thick, opaque clouds _____ the planet's surface from view.
   ① that they shield　② the shield is　③ they shield　④ that shield

4. Ethanol tax subsidies were originally intended to be _____ that would allow alternative fuels to become economically viable.
   ① a measure which temporarily　② measured and temporary
   ③ temporarily measuring　④ temporary measures

5. _____ economic activity in terms of gross national product- a measure of the price of goods and services that sell on the free market.
   ① Economies that are gauging　② A gauge of economics and
   ③ Economists gauge　④ Gauged economy

6. Mr. Sam will have his assistant _____ the minutes of the meeting before passing them out to attendees.
   ① transcribe　② transcribed
   ③ be transcribing　④ to be transcribed

7. A lumberjack, or logger, is a worker who cuts down trees in a

forest, saws them into logs, and _____.
① the mill takes them   ② takes them to the mill
③ they are taken by the mill   ④ taken by their mill

8. Sunburn, _____, is caused not by heat but by rays of ultraviolet light.
① that a painful redness of the skin is
② is a painful redness of the skin
③ when is there a painful redness of the skin
④ a painful redness of the skin

9. _____ all cherry trees are very attractive when in bloom, some species with inferior fruit are cultivated especially for their flowers.
① Although   ② There are   ③ It is   ④ That

10. Through the ages, people have invented thousands of tools, machines, and techniques to make _____.
① easier than their work   ② their work easier
③ easier than work   ④ work is easier

11. To generate income, magazine publishers must decide whether to increase the subscription price or _____.
① to sell advertising   ② if they should sell advertising
③ selling advertising   ④ sold advertising

12. _____ Java Man, who lived before the first Ice Age, is the first manlike animal.
① It is generally believed   ② Generally believed it is
③ Believed generally is   ④ That is generally believed

13. Of all the cereals, rice is the one _____ food for more people than any of the other grain crops.
① it provides   ② that providing   ③ provides   ④ that provides

14. With advances in technology, the tremendous energy of the sun _____ within our reach.
    ① brings   ② to bring   ③ had brought   ④ is being brought

15. _____ withstands testing, we may not conclude that it is true, but we may retain it.
    ① If a hypothesis   ② That a hypothesis
    ③ A hypothesis   ④ Hypothesis

16. It is presumed that rules governing the sharing of food influenced _____ that the earliest cultures evolved.
    ① that the way   ② is the way   ③ which way   ④ the way

17. Canada does not require that U.S. citizens obtain passports to enter the country, and _____.
    ① Mexico does neither   ② Mexico doesn't either
    ③ neither Mexico does   ④ either does Mexico

18. To remain competitive, a company like Pearl Industries must be aware of _____ their competitors are planning for the near future.
    ① that   ② what   ③ which   ④ whether

19. Improvement in the overall financial situation is impossible unless there is a change in the way the company and its subsidiaries _____.
    ① manages   ② management   ③ managing   ④ are managed

20. _____ a few exceptions, most entrepreneurs will find the first few years of business to be difficult.
    ① On   ② With   ③ For   ④ In

실력문제 3회

* 빈칸에 들어갈 가장 적절한 것을 고르시오.

1. _____, Thomas Paine aroused both admiration and hatred.
   ① The most widely read author being of his day
   ② Of his day was the most widely read author
   ③ The most widely read author of his day
   ④ He was the most widely read author of his day

2. When people have a body temperature that is cooler than the surrounding air temperature, heat is _____.
   ① constantly flown into that   ② constantly a flow into these
   ③ constantly to flow into those ④ constantly flowing into them

3. Not only do sunglasses protect your eyes, _____ your skin from wrinking.
   ① and also are to prevent   ② as they are also prevented
   ③ but they also prevent   ④ also are prevented by

4. Wind and water _____ of energy, but they produce only small amounts of power.
   ① they are renewable sources   ② sources are that renewable
   ③ are renewable sources   ④ renewable source

5. _____ description occurs in ballads is brief and conventional.
   ① Some   ② Every   ③ How much   ④ Whatever

6. Before the commercial fertilizers became popular, farmers used marl, _____ for fertilizer.
   ① a kind of clay mixture,   ② it was a kind of clay mixture
   ③ a kind of clay mixture, which   ④ was a kind of clay mixture

7. The role _____ has played in shaping the local society cannot be denied.
   ① the valley was unique that
   ② that the unique topography of the valley
   ③ is the unique topography
   ④ although the unique topography is the valley

8. Newton's physics was _____ that the universe was fundamentally logical since it had been created by a powerful and rational creator.
   ① on belief based the   ② the based on belief
   ③ based on the belief   ④ belief on the based

9. Mold and mildew are fungi that van grow on _____ of most materials.
   ① that surfaces ② whose surfaces ③ its surfaces ④ the surfaces

10. The advantages of a large family are no longer evident _____.
    ① society is urban   ② and urban society
    ③ the society urbanized   ④ in an urbanized society

11. Send us the details of the item you are looking for and we will send you a list of companies that offer products most _____ matching your specifications.
    ① closely   ② closest   ③ closed   ④ closer

12. Mr. Williams _____ for 15 years as chairman of the faculty board by the time he retires.
    ① is served ② had served ③ has served ④ will have served

13. _____ the slight color adjustment that Harrison is currently making, the brochure is ready for printing.
    ① Except that ② Besides that ③ Aside from ④ Long since

14. Unlike most of _____ automobiles in its price range, the

Kamara comes with a sophisticated computer navigation system.
① other   ② another   ③ the other   ④ each other

15. The computer company readily agreed to the terms offered by the government, _____ its selection for the lucrative contract.
① ensures   ② ensuring   ③ assurance   ④ ensured

16. _____ coming out of the Chinese monk's hands that it was known to lift a grown-up man from his seat.
① So great was the force   ② The force was so great
③ The great force was   ④ So great force was

17. The teacher saw, out of the corner of his eye, someone _____ pass a note to someone else.
① trying to   ② tried to   ③ who try to   ④ to try to

18. In the end, Mrs. Thatcher lost her job because she _____ the new economic realities.
① didn't come to grip   ② could not come to grips with
③ would come to grips   ④ is able to come to grip with

19. A good many years of study and experiment will be necessary _____ anything very definite can be said on this subject.
① that   ② than   ③ since   ④ before

20. In spite of the deep-seated craving _____ love, almost everything else is considered to be more important than love; success, prestige, money, power- almost all our energy is used for the learning of how to achieve these aims, and almost none to learn the art of loving.
① towards   ② of   ③ in   ④ for

실력문제 4회

* 빈칸에 들어갈 가장 적절한 것을 고르시오.

1. If the binary signals of the brain were _____ for mental consciousness, then a computer could feasibly gain awareness and possess a mind of its own.
   ① requires all which has
   ② requirements all which
   ③ that all require
   ④ all that was required

2. _____ in a sand forest is partially due to the low level of nutrients available in the soil.
   ① The plants are spaced widely
   ② The wide spacing of planets
   ③ The spacing of plants is widening
   ④ The wide plants are spaced

3. Before Alexander Fleming discovered penicillin, many people died _____.
   ① infected with simple bacteria
   ② from simple bacteria infections
   ③ infections were simple bacteria
   ④ infecting of simple bacteria

4. Both liquids and gases flow freely from a container because they have _____.
   ① not definite shape
   ② none definite shape
   ③ nothing definite shape
   ④ no definite shape

5. All the cereal grains _____ grow on the prairies and plains of the United States.
   ① but rice
   ② except to
   ③ but for
   ④ excepting

6. _____ a teacher in New England, Webster wrote the Dictionary of the American Language.
   ① It was while
   ② When
   ③ When was
   ④ While

7. An equilateral triangle is a triangle _____ and three angles of equal size.
   ① that have three sides of equal length
   ② it has three sides equally long
   ③ that has three sides of equal length
   ④ having three equal sides in it

8. Unlike most Europeans, many Americans _____ a bowl of cereal for breakfast every day.
   ① used to eating   ② are used to eat
   ③ are used to eating   ④ use to eat

9. _____ discovery of insulin, it was not possible to treat diabetes.
   ① Prior to the   ② Prior   ③ The prior   ④ To prior

10. Not until a student has mastered algebra _____ the principles of geometry, trigonometry, and physics.
    ① he can begin to understand   ② can he begin to understand
    ③ he begins to understand   ④ begins to understand

11. Based on the premise that light was composed of color, the Impressionists came to the conclusion _____ not really black.
    ① which was that shadows   ② was shadows which
    ③ were shadows   ④ that shadows were

12. The people of Western Canada have been considering _____ themselves from the rest of the provinces.
    ① to separate   ② separated   ③ separate   ④ separating

13. Even today's sophisticated telescopes do not enable us to tell exactly how far _____.
    ① an object is distant   ② is a distant object
    ③ distant an object is   ④ a distant object is

14. Ball-point pen manufactures work with measurements _____ used in spacecraft.
    ① as precise as those   ② those precisely
    ③ as those are precisely   ④ they are precisely

15. Television now plays _____ in so many people's lives that it is essential for us to try to decide whether it is good or bad.
    ① such important part   ② such a part importantly
    ③ so important a part   ④ a part so important

16. We had the thrill of seeing three national records _____ by our own athletes.
    ① to break   ② be broken   ③ broken   ④ to be broken

17. The chief technician insists that the network _____ reinstalled, though there hasn't been a problem so far.
    ① be   ② are   ③ were   ④ has

18. Employes who are absent from work due to illness must hand in a doctor's note to their boss _____ make up the hours missed.
    ① without   ② or   ③ instead ④ until

19. The sudden burst of _____ that occurred because of the storm did not have any effect on our computer system.
    ① electrics ② electricity ③ electrical ④ electronic

20. Faced _____ a large budget deficit which had built up during nineties, the president decided to create more jobs and privatize big industry.
    ① in   ② towards   ③ with   ④ within

VI. 장문독해

실력문제 1회

* 다음 문장을 읽고 질문에 답하시오. [1 - 5]

To build a defense against terrorism's germ arsenal, we are (1) belatedly producing vaccines and awakening to public health needs.

Beyond that, government and private foundations are increasing support of basic research into ways to expand the capability of the body's (2) innate immune system without (3) triggering an autoimmune response.

A couple of years ago, I asked an official of the Centers for Disease Control when we might achieve the dream of a "universal vaccine" against all pathogens. He waved it off with "in 50 years, maybe." When he noticed I was a journalist, he cut it to 25 years. Now, under pressure, scientists are seeking "multivalent vaccines" against groups of diseases, which this generation may see.

Out of crisis comes unexpected bravery. And out of today's threat of biowar may come tomorrow's conquest of infectious disease.

1. Choose the main idea of the passage.
   (a) What should you do against the terrorism's biological weapons?
   (b) Great good can grow out of today's crisis.
   (c) There is a way to deal with the present jitters.
   (d) There is no way to overcome the present nervousness.

2. It is implied that officials or scientists feel _____ with journalists.
   (a) disillusioned   (b) frivolous   (c) absent-minded   (d) weighed down

3. Choose the closest meaning to the underlined word (1) belatedly.
   (a) predominantly   (b) overridingly   (c) too lately   (d) overduly

4. Choose the one that has the DIFFERENT meaning to the underlined word (2) innate.
   (a) inborn   (b) acquired   (c) congenital   (d) inbred

5. Choose the closest meaning to the underlined word (3) triggering.
   (a) capitulating   (b) activating   (c) alienating   (d) trapping

* 다음 문장을 읽고 질문에 답하시오. [6 - 8]

The temperance crusade was perhaps the most widespread of all the reform movements. The census of 1810 reported some 14,000 distilleries producing 25 million gallons of spirits each year. With a hard-drinking population of just over 7 million, the "alcoholic republic" was producing well over three gallons per year for every man, woman, and child, not counting beer, wine, and cider. And the census takers no doubt missed a few stills. William Cobbett, an English reformer who traveled in the United States, noted in 1819 that one could "go into hardly any man's house without being asked to drink wine or spirits, even in the morning."

The temperance movement rested on a number of arguments. First an foremost was the religious demand that "soldiers of the cross" lead blameless lives. Others stressed the economic implications of sottish workers. The dynamic new economy, with factories and railroads moving on strict schedules, made tippling by the labor force a far greater problem than it had been in a simple agrarian economy. Humanitarians emphasized the relations between drinking and poverty. Much of the movement's propaganda focused on the suffering of innocent mothers and children. "Drink," said a pamphlet from the Sons of Temperance, "is the prolific source (directly or in directly) of nearly all the ills that afflict the human family."

In 1833 a national convention was called in Philadelphia, where the American Temperance Union was formed. The convention, however, revealed internal tensions: Was the goal moderation or total abstinence, and if the latter, abstinence merely from ardent spirits or also from wine, cider, and beer? Should the movement work by persuasion or by legislation? Like nearly every movement of the day, temperance had a wing of perfectionists who rejected all compromises, and they passed a resolution that the liquor traffic was morally wrong and ought to be prohibited by law. The union, at its spring convention in 1836, called for abstinence from all alcoholic beverages—a costly victory that caused moderates to abstain from the movement instead. Still, between 1830 and 1860, the temperance agitation drastically reduced Americans' per-capita consumption of alcohol.

6. What is the main topic of this passage?
    (a) A brief history of the foundation of the American Temperance Union
    (b) American extremist fighting for abstinence from drinking
    (c) The reduction in America's consumption of alcohol
    (d) Summary of the American temperance movement of the 1800s

7. What is the main purpose of the second paragraph?
    (a) To illustrate the points of temperance supporters
    (b) To compare humanitarian and social views on drinking
    (c) To discuss the arguments against drinking
    (d) To support the temperance movement

8. Paragraph 3 is mainly concerned about the
    (a) performance of the American Temperance Union
    (b) comparison between moderation and total abstinence
    (c) process of making a resolution by the American Temperance Union
    (d) influence the American Temperance Union had on society

* 다음 글을 읽고 질문에 답하시오. [9 - 13]

When television entered the home in this country(i.e., the United

States of America), the air was filled with dismal prophecies. This meant the end of reading; the book was doomed. What has so far followed? A mounting dissatisfaction with the general content of TV; a steady rise in the sale of books. One must not underestimate the enormous latent power of the purely visual appearance. The movie and television, even the still photograph, have not yet been applied to all the uses which will finally be found for them. Nevertheless, it is questionable whether they will ever take in the place of the book and cause it to be thought of as merely a thing of the past. The simplest way to realize the importance of books as tools, which is one of their most valuable though not very noble functions, is to imagine how we would manage without dictionaries or encyclopedias. True, the usefulness of books as books is limited, and much of the practical work of the world is best learned by other means. All the same, within a limited range of usefulness, the books we use as tools have advantages lacking in the newer forms of communication. They can be studied over and over again, and what they have to offer can be taken in as slowly, with as many interruptions, as we wish or need. We can take them with us wherever we go, and use them without causing inconvenience or disturbance to anyone else.

9. The title below that best expresses the ideas of this passage is _____.

   (a) The importance of Books as Tools
   (b) Television and Books
   (c) The Usefulness of Books as Tools
   (d) The Movie and Television

10. If we were to break the second paragraph up into two, the additional paragraph would best start with _____.

   (a) "Nevertheless, it is questionable..."
   (b) "The simplest way to realize..."

(c) "True, the usefulness of books as tools..."
(d) "All the same, within a limited range of usefulness..."

11. According to the passage, TV in the U. S. _____.
    (a) brought about the end of reading
    (b) met the expectation of the general public
    (c) caused a steady rise in the sale of books
    (d) none of the above

12. The passage implies or states that _____.
    (a) the movie an television will replace the book in the end
    (b) the movie and television have great appeal
    (c) reading will no longer be enjoyable
    (d) the movie and television are yet to be maximally utilized

13. Which of the following statements about books is not true according to the passage?
    (a) Books are east to carry.
    (b) Books offer the best way to learn the practical work of the world.
    (c) Books have more advantages than the movie and television.
    (d) Books as tools are very important.

* 다음 글을 읽고 질문에 답하시오. [14 - 18]

We learned that Tom Brokaw's assistant at NBC had tested positive for anthrax after opening a threatening letter with powder inside. At that moment the New York Times was being (1) <u>evacuated</u> after another letter rained powder in the newsroom; this one was addressed to bioterrorism expert Judith Miller. Initial testing showed no sign of anthrax, but the threat still seemed real, and cunning. You didn't need to shoot the messengers; you just needed to scare them to death, (2) <u>because fear is bacterial as well</u>. It can spread in the air and over wires, infect the marketplace, (3) <u>lay waste to</u> whole industries and leave its victims at home in bed with the covers pulled up. And the worst part was that since there were so many scares, so many hoaxes, we were in some ways doing this to ourselves.

14. Choose the main idea of the passage.
   (a) Stopping evacuating mass-media buildings
   (b) Spreading fear about anthrax terrorism
   (c) Too many anthrax victims to count
   (d) Being careful about the envelope containing white powder

15. It can be concluded from the passage that _____
   (a) We needed not have worried about all the white powder mistaken for anthrax germs.
   (b) We are too fortunate to avoid the worst spreading of the germs.
   (c) Our fear can be another aim of the terrorists.
   (d) We are too sensitive to what's going on these days.

16. Choose the closest meaning to the underlined word (1) <u>evacuated.</u>
   (a) sanitized   (b) realized   (c) removed   (d) restricted

17. The underlined part (2) implies that _____
   (a) the terrorists are biological warfare experts.
   (b) the terrorists are psychologically sick.
   (c) the terrorists are waging biological war only.
   (d) the terrorists are waging both biological and psychological war.

18. Choose the closest meaning to the underlined expression (3) <u>lay waste to</u>.
   (a) destroy   (b) surround   (c) evacuate   (d) threaten

* 다음 글을 읽고 질문에 답하시오.[19-20]

Although the three currents which have been discussed so far in twentieth century painting may be found in sculpture as well, the parallelism should not be overstressed.

Whereas painting has been richer and more adventurous, its leadership as an art form has not remained unchallenged, and sculpture has often followed different paths.

19. The paragraph that preceded the passage most probably deal with _____.

   (a) movements in modern painting
   (b) nineteenth century art
   (c) the development of painting techniques
   (d) current approaches to art history

20. According to the passage, why are the similarities between painting and sculpture of limited importance?
   (a) The inspiration for painting rarely comes from sculpture.
   (b) Painters are frequently very critical of sculptors.
   (c) Sculptors' working methods are basically different from those of painters
   (d) Trends in sculpture often develop independently of trends in painting

---

◎ 속 담

침소봉대 하지 마라.
Don't make a mountain out of a molehill.

◎ 표현연구

힘을 내!
Keep your chin up.
Pull yourself together.
Don't let it get you down.

* 다음 글을 읽고 질문에 답하시오[1-3]

The explosive growth of world-population has not been caused by a sudden increase in human fertility and probably owes little in any part of the world to an increase in birth-rate. It has been caused almost entirely by advances in the medical sciences, and consequent decrease of death-rate in areas where the birth-rate remains high. This is some of biological interest. Nature takes as her motto that nothing succeeds like excess, and any living thing, including Man, if able to reproduce without restraint to the limit of its capacity, would soon occupy all parts of the world where it could exist.

1. Which of the following agrees with the contents of the passage?
   (a) The increase in birth-rate has been a result of advances in medical sciences.
   (b) In some areas the birth-rate remains high because of the decrease in the death-rate.
   (c) The sudden growth of world-population is chiefly due to advances in the medical sciences.
   (d) The population of the world has increased explosively owing to an increase in birth-rate.

2. "nothing succeeds like excess" means _____.
   (a) excess is the best means of success
   (b) nothing exceeds like success
   (c) nothing comes after success
   (d) no successful thing likes excess

3. What does "it"(last sentence) refer to?
   (a) Man   (b) Nature   (c) the world   (d) any living thing

* 다음 글을 읽고 질문에 답하시오[4-7].

All social animals need some method of communication. They use it to exchange information and to maintain an orderly community. Human beings communicate in many ways. One of these ways is the gesture. Men communicate approval by winking an eye, by clapping their hands, by whistling, by smiling or laughing. They communicate disapproval by pointing a thumb toward the ground, by putting the tongue out of mouth and blowing, by holding the nose with the fingers, or by frowning. They indicate direction by pointing, and they often communicate size by holding their hands a certain distant apart.

4. According to the passage, if a man whistles as a way of communication _____.
   (a) he may be angry
   (b) he may be surprised
   (c) he may be pleased
   (d) he must be unhappy

5. In order to exchange information, social animals use _____.
   (a) an orderly community
   (b) some method of communication
   (c) some particular parts of the body
   (d) he may indicate direction by pointing

6. The above passage says that if a person feels unsatisfied _____.
   (a) he must clap his hands
   (b) he should not use any gesture
   (c) he should disapprove the gesture
   (d) he may put the tongue out of the mouth

7. According to the passage, when a man wants to communicate how large a certain thing is _____.
   (a) he uses his hands
   (b) he keeps a certain distance apart
   (c) he winks an eye
   (d) he communicates in many gestures

※ 다음 글을 읽고 질문에 답하시오[8-12].

In these days of technological triumphs, it is well to remind ourselves from time to time that living mechanisms are often incomparably more efficient than their artificial imitations. There is no better illustration of this idea than the sonar system of bats. Ounce for ounce and watt for watt, it is billions of times more efficient and more sensitive than the radars and sonars contrived by man.

Of course, the bats gave had some 50 million years of evolution to refine their sonar. Their physiological mechanisms for echo location, based on all this accumulated experience, therefore merit our thorough study and analyses.

To appreciate the precision of the bats' echo location, we must first consider the degree of their reliance upon it. Thanks to sonar, an insect-eating bat can get long perfectly well without eyesight. This was brilliantly demonstrated by an experiment performed in the late eighteenth century by the Italian naturalist Lazzaro Spallanzali. He caught some bats in a bell tower, blinded them, and released them outdoors. Four of these blind bats were recaptured after they had found their way back to the bell tower, and on examining their stomachs' contents, Spllanzani found that they had been able to capture and gorge themselves with flying insects. We know from experiments that bats easily find insects in the dark of night, even when the insects emit no sound that can be heard by human ears. A bat will catch hundreds of soft-bodied, silent-flying moths or gnats in a single hour. It will even detect and chase pebbles or cotton spitballs tossed into the air.

8. The author suggests that the sonar system of bats _____.
   (a) was at the height of its perfection 50 million years ago
   (b) is better than man-made sonar because it has had 50 million years to be refined
   (c) should have been discovered by man many years ago
   (d) is the same as it was 50 million years ago

9. That bats had a well-developed system of echo location _____.
   (a) was discovered in the eighteenth century
   (b) is a very recent discovery
   (c) was discovered during World War II
   (d) was know to primitive man

10. Spallanzani's proof that bats could "see" in the dark was that _____.
    (a) the bats found their way back to the bell tower
    (b) they found their way to their feeding area
    (c) only one of the bats starved to death
    (d) their stomachs contained bodies of insects

11. The fact that "blind bats" will detect and chase cotton spitballs as well as insects is remarkable because _____.
    (a) bats do not eat spitballs
    (b) cotton is harder to track
    (c) spitballs make no sounds audible to human ears
    (d) there is purpose in the flight of insects

12. The following is the main point of the article _____.
    (a) A bat will catch hundreds of gnats in a single hour
    (b) There is a perfection in nature which sometimes cannot be matched by man's creative efforts
    (c) The phrase "blind as a bat" is valid
    (d) Sonar and radar systems of man are inefficient

* 다음 글을 읽고 질문에 답하시오[13-15]

With increasing development of computer technology, there is a new disease to worry about. Computer "virus" programs designed to sabotage computers are infecting computers in corporations, homes, and universities. These viruses spread rapidly, much like biological contagion, and then disrupt the affected systems. The virus secretly attaches itself to other programs and then can delete or alter files. The damage is generally activated by using the computer's clock. Then, any program that is executed may be exposed to the virus, including programs spread through telephone connections.

Because of the increasing incidents of virus infiltration, businesses and agencies are becoming wary of sharing software. Security policies need to be increased as immunity programs are being developed.

13. Which of the following is the best title of this passage?
   (a) Deleting Files   (b) Stop the Clock
   (c) Sharing Software   (d) Beware of Computer Virus

14. It is inferred that a company can best protect itself from the virus by _____.
   (a) keeping clean   (b) not using shared software
   (c) setting the clock correctly (d) spreading programs by telephone

15. If the virus infects a computer, the result would probably be _____.
   (a) sick personnel   (b) dead telephones
   (c) lost information   (d) a broken computer

* 다음 글을 읽고 질문에 답하시오[16-20]

Nevertheless, there is such a voluble hue and cry about the abysmal state of culture in the United States by well-meaning, sincere critics that I would like to present some evidence to the contrary. One is tempted to remind these critics that no country has ever achieved the complete integrations of haute culture into the warp and woof of its everyday life. In the wishful memories of those who moon over the passed glories of Shakespeare's England, it is seldom called to mind that bearbaiting was far more popular than any of Master Shakespeare's presentations. Who cares to remember that the same Rome that found a Juvenal proclaiming mens sana in corpore sano could also watch an Emperor Trajan celebrate his victory over Decebalus of Dacia in 106 A.D. with no fewer than 5,000 pairs of gladiators matched to the death? And this in the name of amusement!

16. The title that best expresses the ideas of this passage is _____.
   (a) The Hue and Cry of the Critics
   (b) Reflections on Culture
   (c) Dangers in Contemporary Criticism
   (d) The World's Amusement

17. The paragraph preceding this passage most probably discussed _____.
   (a) the increased interest of Americans in public affairs
   (b) the interest of Americans in the arts
   (c) the duties of a literary critic
   (d) Juvenal's contribution to poetry

18. According to the author, _____.
   (a) the lack of culture in America is amusing
   (b) those who criticize the lack of culture in America are outspoken
   (c) Emperor Trajan had a keen sense of humor
   (d) critics of our level of culture are insincere

19. The author's attitude toward culture is essentially _____.
   (a) despairing   (b) realistic   (c) distorted   (d) uncritical

20. One can conclude from the passage that _____.
   (a) the masses instinctively recognize artistic achievement
   (b) the popularity of culture depends upon economic factors
   (c) human nature has not changed too much over the years
   (d) Americans do not appreciate intelligence

실력문제 3회

* 다음 글을 읽고 질문에 답하시오[1-3]

The twentieth century has produced books of power not only in science and in politics but also in philosophy and literature. However, this being an age of specialization, we often find that the influential ideas contained in these books have first been propounded or mentioned in theses and papers for experts before reaching the layman. The popular magazine articles and the works of interpretation come last.

It is undeniable that science has influenced our world. But, without books to translate the language of science to the language of the layman, the strides would be minuscule instead of gigantic. The stage is now set for some of the most powerful books the world has ever seen. Books are needed to help man find the way to the one-world life that the sciences indicate must be developed if man is to continue on this earth.

1. The author of this passage seems to believe that _____.
   (a) books can influence man (b) science can save the world
   (c) our world is coming to an end (d) books and science go together

2. From this passage, we can infer or draw the conclusion that man has a choice between _____.
   (a) science and books (b) books and destruction
   (c) science and unification (d) science and destruction

3. Scientific papers for the experts _____.
   (a) follow popularized literature
   (b) precede popularized literature
   (c) are put into popularized literature
   (d) have no relationship to popularized literature

※ 다음 글을 읽고 질문에 답하시오[4-8]

Farther back in the brain, the hippocampus can lose about 20 percent of its volume between the ages of 50 and 90. This little sea-horse-shaped structure is crucial to forming as well as (1) <u>retrieving</u> memories. In normal aging, its levels of the neurotransmitter acetylcholine fall. Since acetylcholine is one of the molecules by which neurons communicate, its scarcity in the hippocampus provides "one of the most likely explanations of memory deficits in otherwise healthy old people," says Whalley. And in not-healthy older people? There is no definitive way to diagnose Alzheimer's (except through autopsy), but a test called the Mini-Mental State Exam comes close. It asks the date or year, for example, and has the person count backward from 100 by sevens, recall three objects named a few minutes before, read and obey the sentence "close your eyes," as well as do other simple tasks. A low score, combined with confusion about places, a loss of initiative and problems recognizing friends are more likely to (2) <u>presage</u> Alzheimer's than forgetting an appointment.

4. Which topic of the following can precede the above passage?
 (a) Another disease of the brain, cerebritis
 (b) Another part of the brain, the frontal lobes
 (c) The new recognition of cerebral diseases
 (d) The dissection skill of the brain

5. According to the passage, which of the following persons is most likely to be diagnosed as a patient of Alzheimer's?
 (a) a person who usually forgets to close or open his or her eyes.
 (b) a person who occasionally forgets an appointment.
 (c) a person who fails to recognize his or her close friends.
 (d) a person who has a deformed hippocampus.

6. According to the passage, what is the function of the hippocampus?
   (a) It prevents one's brain from aging.
   (b) It adds to or subtracts from one's whole memory.
   (c) It forms and retrieves memories.
   (d) It helps develop one's ability of communication.

7. Choose the closest meaning to the underlined word (1) <u>retrieving</u>.
   (a) repealing   (b) reprimanding   (c) rejecting   (d) recovering

8. Choose the closest meaning to the underlined word (2) <u>presage</u>.
   (a) ignore   (b) foretell   (c) prevent   (d) contract

* 다음 글을 읽고 질문에 답하시오.[9-13]

There are wars of choice, and there are wars of necessity. Wars of choice-Vietnam, Kosovo, even the Gulf War-are fought for reasons of principle, ideology, geopolitics or sometimes pure humanitarianism. Passivity might cost us in the long run. But we do not have to go to war.

A war of necessity is a life-or-death struggle in which the safety and security of the homeland are (1) <u>at stake</u>. The war on terrorism is such a war. So was World War II. Fifty years is a long interval, and it shows. The habits of waging such a war have (2) <u>atrophied</u>. The language we have mobilized to wage this war of necessity is the language of wars of choice, heavily (3) <u>freighted with</u> moral anguish, obsessively concerned with proving how delicate and discriminating, how tolerant and sensitive we Americans are.

9. Choose the best title of the above passage.
   (a) The war of choice on terrorism
   (b) Too much burden from the war of necessity
   (c) The war of necessity on terrorism
   (d) Too much burden from the war of choice

10. According to the passage, what is going wrong with the war on terrorism?
   (a) Nobody wants to show how tolerant and sensitive we Americans are.
   (b) While we were waging the war of necessity during the World War II, we had been accustomed to too much language of wars.
   (c) Since we waged the war of necessity during the World War II, we have used too much language of wars.
   (d) While we're waging the war of necessity on terrorism, we are using the language of wars of choice.

11. Choose the closest meaning to the underlined expression (1) at stake.
   (a) at peace   (b) at work   (c) at play   (d) at risk

12. Choose the closest meaning to the underlined expression (2) atrophied.
   (a) shortened   (b) lengthened   (c) strengthened   (d) degenerated

13. Choose the closest meaning to the underlined expression (3) freighted with.
   (a) cleared of   (b) burdened with   (c) discharged from   (d) relieved of

* 다음 글을 읽고 질문에 답하시오[14-16]

For centuries we have enjoyed certain blessings: a stable law, before which the poor man and the rich man were equal; freedom within that law to believe what we leased; a system of government which gave the ultimate power to the ordinary man. We have lived by toleration, rational compromise and freely expressed opinion, and we have lived very well. But we have come to take these blessings for granted, like the air we breathe. They have lost all glamour for us since they have become too familiar. Indeed , it is a mark of the intellectual to be rather critical and contemptuous of them. Young men have acquired a cheap reputation by sneering at the liberal spirit in politics, and questioning the value of free discussion, toleration, and compromise.

14. The title below that best expresses the ideas of this paragraph is _____.

   (a) Characteristics of Democracy
   (b) The Value of Free Discussion
   (c) The Weakness of the Democratic Way of Life
   (d) Unappreciated Advantages of Democratic Life

15. The writer resents the growing criticism of freedom as an attitude which results from _____.

   (a) too much freedom of speech
   (b) being too accustomed to freedom
   (c) questioning the rightness of democracy
   (d) the conservatism of young intellectuals

16. The writer's attitude toward young intellectuals is _____.

   (a) critical   (b) generous   (c) indifferent   (d) very contemptuous

*다음 글을 읽고 질문에 답하시오[17-20]

West Side Story, a famous musical tragedy, transforms the Montagues and Capulets of Shakespeare's play *Romeo and Juliet* into feuding street gangs, the Jets and the Sharks, on consisting of newly arrived Puerto Ricans and the other of native-born New Yorkers. It is set in the early 1950s, when gang warfare in big cities led to injuries and even death. The plot, tightly choreographed by Jerome Robbins, tells the story of the love of Maria, a Puerto Rican, for Tony, who, while attempting to stop a street fight, kills Maria's brother and is ultimately killed himself. Leonard Bernstein's musical score is brilliant, and Stephen Sondheim, making his Broadway debut, reveals a remarkable talent for writing lyrics. The play opened on September 26, 1957. It ran for 734 performances, toured for 10 months, and then returned to New York for an additional 246 performances. A film version was released in 1961, and a successful New York revival opened in 1980.

17. When does the action of the play *West Side Story* take place?
  (a) In Shakespeare's time
  (b) In the early 1950s
  (c) In 1961
  (d) In 1980

18. How many times was *West Side Story* performed during its initial appearance?
  (a) 26
  (b) 734
  (c) 10
  (d) 246

19. Who wrote the words to the songs of *West Side Story*?
  (a) Jerome Robbins
  (b) Leonard Bernstein
  (c) a Puerto Rican
  (d) Stephen Sondheim

20. It can be inferred from the passage that the Capulets and Montagues _____.
  (a) were rival families in Shakespeare's play
  (b) were two street gangs in 1950s
  (c) fought against the Jets and Sharks
  (d) were groups of actors, dancers, and singers

◎ 표현연구
이 상황을 어떻게 헤쳐 나갈래?
How are you cooking[managing/ handling] this situation?

◎ 표현연구
나는 곤경에 처해 있어.
I'm in a hot water. I'm in a jam[fix/blind].

◎ 표현연구
지긋지긋해.
I'm sick and tired of it. I'm disgusted with it.
I'm had enough of it. I've had it.

실력문제 4회

* 다음 글을 읽고 질문에 답하시오[1-4]

Philosophy presupposes such contemplation, a survey of phenomena; and in order to make his survey, the philosopher must remain a spectator, taking no part in the action; he must, like the spectator at the games, watch them outside the _____. But the objective judgment which the philosopher's contemplation of the scene calls for, though it is facilitated, is not to be induced by _____ distance alone; temporal distance is equally essential; time in which to retreat from and consider the events, so that he may, as a serene spectator, an _____ participant, appreciate the passions which possess men in life, and perceive the motives or ideas that stir those passions. From this withdrawn attitude, mentally detached from practical and individual interests, he can survey and sum up the phenomena.

1. Choose the one that is most appropriate for the blanks.
   (a) gymnasium, far, passionate   (b) gymnasium, near, passionate
   (c) arena, near, unimpassioned   (d) arena, spatial, unimpassioned

2. Which of the following descriptions does not characterize the philosopher?
   (a) Passionate contemplation   (b) An objective judgment
   (c) A serene spectator   (d) A mental detachment from practical interest

3. The title that best expresses the ideas of this passage is _____.
   (a) A survey of phenomena   (b) Philosopher's arena
   (c) Spatial and temporal distance   (d) Philosopher's attitude

4. Which is NOT true of the passage?
   (a) The philosopher has to make a survey of the phenomena
   (b) Spatial distance is essential in obtaining time in which to retreat

from and consider the events
(c) The philosopher is not moved in life by desire for action
(d) The philosopher has to secure detachment from practical and individual interests

* 다음 글을 읽고 질문에 답하시오[5-9].

A common pattern in many societies provides for a periodic relaxation of the rules of conventional behavior. In some societies this goes to the length of letting down all sex barriers, even to the relaxing of incest taboos. In other societies there may simply be feasting, drinking, or dancing along with some other forms of entertainment. We find a counterpart of such activities in our Halloween parties, masked balls, costume parties, and Mardi Gras. Some societies make provision for ritual teasing and joking, or occasions when buffoonery, ribald tricks or tales, and other such activities are permitted or even encouraged. The jester and the clown are stock characters in many societies.

By their uninhibited behavior they provide a vicarious outlet for socially restrained resentments and hostilities.

5. The best title for the above passage is _____.
   (a) Festivals in the World
   (b) Halloween and Mardi Gras
   (c) Relaxation of Conventional Rules
   (d) Why We Sometimes Relax Our Behavior

6. Who may have written the above passage?
   (a) historian (b) philosopher (c) anthropologist (d) political scientist

7. Which one of the following does not fit in with the above category of relaxed behavior ?
   (a) carnival   (b) mask play   (c) mask dance   (d) wedding ceremony

8. Which one of the following best summarizes the above passage?
   (a) People in many societies enjoy life by relaxing rules
   (b) Relaxation of morality is not dangerous in some cases
   (c) In some societies sex taboos are relaxed from time to time
   (d) People in many countries relax their rules of behavior at some intervals

9. The writer of this passage is likely to be _____.
   (a) a French (b) a German (c) an American (d) an Englishman

* 다음 글을 읽고 질문에 답하시오.[10-12]

Sometimes it is very difficult just to sit back and listen. There are three basic reasons why this is true. First, we are often so busy with our own thoughts and desires, related or nonrelated, that we are 90 percent sender and only 10 percent receiver. Second, some individuals are self-centered. Instead of hearing what is being said, they are merely waiting for the speaker to finish so that they can then talk. Getting their thoughts organized keeps them from being good listners. Third, some people allow themselves to analyze motives or personality traits of the person speaking and, again, fail to hear what is said.

10. Which of the following is the best title for the above passage?
    (a) How can we talk to others   (b) What makes us self-centered
    (c) Why is it difficult to listen   (d) When do we listen to others

11. Which of the following statements is implied in the above passage?
    (a) We aren't free to express our thoughts and desires
    (b) We must get our thoughts organized before we speak
    (c) We usually tend to talk much more than we listen
    (d) We should listen carefully to analyze other's speaking

12. Which of the following is the world that best characterizes the above passage?

(a) Explanatory   (b) Emotional   (c) Philosophic   (d) Metaphorical

* 다음 글을 읽고 질문에 답하시오.[13-17]

Misery may love company(depressed people are more likely to seek emotional support than people who are not depressed), but company clearly does not love misery. In 1976, psychologist James C. Coyne, while at Miami University, asked 45 female college students to talk on the phone for 20 minutes with other women, some of whom were depressed- although the students weren't told that. Later, the students indicated they had much less interest in spending time with the depressed women than with the others. Such reactions are part of a vicious circle that is all too common among unhappy people. Their behavior drives away the very people whose support and acceptance they need, thereby worsening their depression and intensifying their need for support. These findings are also important because they suggest that when depressed people say others view them negatively, they may well be right.

13. What is the main idea of the passage?
   (a) Misery loves company.   (b) Cry and you cry alone.
   (c) Birds of a feather flock together.   (d) Care killed the cat.

14. In the research mentioned here, 45 college students were students were asked to talk to _____.
   (a) depressed women
   (b) children in misery
   (c) both men and women who need support
   (d) women, depressed or otherwise

15. What was the students' reaction after the talks?
   (a) They were not interested in talking to the depressed women.
   (b) They became more sympathetic for the depressed women.

(c) They became more depressed.

(d) They found the problems of depressed people very interesting.

16. Before the talk, the students _____.
   (a) were told to be sympathetic
   (b) were asked to tell whether the people they talked to were depressed or not
   (c) were told about the emotional state of the people they talked to
   (d) didn't know the emotional state of the people they talked to

17. Which of the following statement is NOT true?
   (a) It is true that depressed people are usually viewed negatively.
   (b) Depressed people are very popular.
   (c) Depressed people usually need more support than others.
   (d) Depressed people tend to get more depressed.

∗ 다음 글을 읽고 질문에 답하시오.[18-20]

Although a jet engine and a rocket engine operate on the principle of Newton's Third Law, they differ in that a jet must take in oxygen from the air to burn its fuel, but a rocket must carry its own oxygen. Gases escaping under great pressure in one direction exert a push on the engine in the opposite direction. According to Newton's Third Law, to each action there is an equal and opposite reaction. You can illustrate the principle by blowing up a rubber balloon: it moves forward as the air escapes in the opposite direction.

18. What characteristic of rocket engines is not characteristic of jet engines?
   (a) Method of obtaining oxygen (b) Method of using oxygen
   (c) Reaction to the escaping gases   (d) Application of Newton's Third Law

19. Which of the following would be best explained by Newton's

Third Law?
(a) A balloon with a lower density than air rises.
(b) A bat strikes a ball and the bat breaks.
(c) A sled accelerates while sliding downhill.
(d) A rock, thrown horizontally, falls to the ground.

20. What propels jet planes?
    (a) Rocket motors   (b) Steam turbines
    (c) Propeller blades   (d) The thrust of hot gases

◉ 속 담

과거는 잊어버리자.
Let bygones be bygones.
Let's bury the hatchet.

◉ 속 담

두 마리 토끼를 쫓을 수 없다.
One cannot eat one's cake and have it.

◉ 속 담

똥 묻은 개가 재 묻은 개를 나무란다.
The pot calls the kettle black.

◉ 속 담

백지장도 맞들면 낫다.
Two heads are better than one.
Two hands make thing lighter.

◉ 표현연구

그녀는 아들을 찾을 때까지 온갖 수단을 다 할거야.
She'll leave no stone unturned until she finds her son.

VII. 종합 문제

1. 최종점검 문제

* 빈칸에 가장 적절한 단어를 고르시오.

1. For ancient people, myths were often attempts to explain _____ events such as volcanic eruptions.
   (a) optimistic   (b) comfortable   (c) joyous   (d) catastrophic

2. His _____ was so great that he became the _____ of all disputes about art and music.
   (a) erudition, arbiter   (b) pomposity, censor
   (c) speech, conspirator   (d) contribution, moralist

3. The new office is rationalized: machines are used, employees become machine attendants; the work, as in the factory, is collective, not individualized; it is standardized for interchangeable; quickly replaceable clerks; it is specialized to the point of _____.
   (a) automation   (b) dehumanization   (c) fascination   (d) frustration

4. A _____ liar lies constantly, continuously, without a break in time; a _____ invalid is always, or almost always, sick; a _____ smoker is a steady devotee of nicotine.
   (a) anachronistic   (b) synchronous   (c) chronic   (d) incongruous

5. In its search for means of inducing sleep in the grievously sick, modern researchers have analyzed many of the _____ compounds that primitive people have discarded.
   (a) biographic   (b) sadistic   (c) soporific   (d) bombastic

6. If a burglar breaks into my house and I knock him down, the law

will acquit me, and if I am physically assaulted it will permit me to _____ with reasonable violence.
(a) retaliate   (b) excuse   (c) sympathize   (d) behave

7. Soil samples showed that robbers had broken into the tomb about 2,000 years ago, _____ it of whatever gold and silver it contained, and then abandoned it.
(a) looted   (b) micturated   (c) cherished   (d) supplicated

8. Crime probably ranks as the number one problem in the minds of most Americans. Some say that _____ by juveniles is epidemic.
(a) aspiration   (b) reputation   (c) delinquency   (d) benevolence

9. It is the task of the International wildlife Preservation Commission to prevent endangered species from becoming _____ in order that future generations may _____ the great diversity of animal life.
(a) tamed-recollect   (b) evolved-value
(c) extinct-enjoy   (d) salient-appreciate

10. The awareness of health risks and the prospect of parental punishment rarely seem to _____ middle and high school students from experimenting with cigarettes.
(a) deter   (b) deepen   (c) deplore   (d) degrade

11. Our new copy machine will continue to deliver good service to the user _____ maintenance checks are performed as often as possible.
(a) in case that   (b) so that   (c) although   (d) as long as

12. The recent increase in accidents means that safety inspections _____ increased over the next two weeks.
(a) were   (b) are   (c) will have to be   (d) will have been

13. Marketing proposals should not be submitted to the planning department _____ accompanied by a fact sheet.
    (a) whatever   (b) withou   (c) unless   (d) and

14. Data of a sensitive nature should always _____ in the special filing cabinet.
    (a) locking   (b) be locked   (c) lock   (d) to lock

15. _____ last year's outdoor concert, when few people attended because of the heavy rain, this year's concert is expected to draw large crowds.
    (a) Dislike   (b) However   (c) Unlike   (d) Though

16. The headlines in today's newspaper about the early resolution of the ongoing labor strike were not as _____ as the board members had hoped.
    (a) encourage   (b) encouraging   (c) encouraged   (d) encouragement

17. Renewable energy sources are so called _____ regularly replenished by natural processes and are, therefore, in endless supply.
    (a) so are these   (b) because they are
    (c) that are since then (d) which follow them are

18. The capacity factor is the amount of energy actually produced by a power plant _____ with the amount that could be produced if the plant operated at full capacity.
    (a) compare   (b) compared   (c) to compare   (d) comparative

19. Rheumatism, bronchitis and digestive diseases are not _____ they once were.
    (a) too prevalent   (b) more prevalent   (c) so prevalent as   (d) all prevalent on

20. I would have arrived for the appointment on time _____ I not been detained at the last moment by an unexpected call.
   (a) because (b) if (c) since (d) had

* 밑줄 친 부분 중에 틀린 부분을 고르시오.

21. The expense (a)of renting a car for (b)the rest of the year (c)would be (d)comparable of purchasing a good used one.

22. I (a)know you will (b)never be (c)at peace until you (c)will have discovered where your (d)brother is.

23. (a)Drawing to Poland by high (b)growth and interest rates, investors are (c)fleeing now because growth is (d)faltering and debts are rising.

24. Inmates (a)return to the outside world contend (b)with the stigma of (c)being ex-convicts, an (d)obstacle to successful integration into the larger society.

25. (a)Economically, the dynamism of the East Asian region (b)is expected (c)to be remained although (d)the high growth rate of the 1960s and early 1970s may not be repeated.

26. All music (a)consists of two elements- expression and design. Expression is inexact and subjective and may be enjoyed in a (b)personal and instinctive way. Design, on the other hand, is exact and (c)must be analyzed objectively in order to be understood and (d)appreciation.

27. One might (a)object to that (b)since there were so few people in this research area, generalizations (c)such as the above are meaningless, but this (d)is not the case.

28. It is essential that the temperature (a)is not elevated (b)to a point where the substance formed (c)may become unstable and decompose into (d)its constituent elements.

29. Dissuading lawmaker Mr. Kim (a)to be seated, the chairman of the committee (b)on Foreign Affairs (c)asked him not (d)to foul up his plan.

30. Anthropologists, who make (a)it their business to discover just how human beings (b)perceive themselves as differing from one another and from other natural species, will tell you (c)what every community conceives of itself (d)as being uniquely human.

* 밑줄 친 단어와 의미가 가장 가까운 것을 고르시오.

31. Police cracked down on the selling of liquors to minors.
    (a) did a double take (b) did good (c) hit and run (d) enforced laws

32. Certain hostility to religious bigotry is not altogether surprising.
    (a) belief   (b) conflict   (c) ritual   (d) prejudice

33. After the ordeal he had a cadaverous look, but he was still alive.
    (a) discouraged   (b) dissatisfied   (c) ghastly   (d) empty

34. John was a skillful debater, and his calculated sarcasm went home. His opponent flushed under the attack.
    (a) folded up   (b) hit the target   (c) was misleading   (d) was ambiguous

35. Lack of employment outside the home tends to make women more vulnerable to depression.
    (a) futile   (b) feasible   (c) likable   (d) susceptible

36. In mammals embryo is more insulated from the external world but, of course, more directly dependent on its mother's physiological state.
    (a) indifferent   (b) sophisticated   (c) isolated   (d) saturated

37. The whole problem boils down to a power struggle between management and labor.
    (a) end up   (b) pile up   (c) pick up   (d) turn up

38. We tried to ignore her acrimonious comment, but that took considerable restraint.
    (a) crazed   (b) cunning   (c) confused   (d) bitter

39. Secure, however, in the inscrutability of my place of concealment, I felt no embarrassment whatever.
    (a) thoughtfulness   (b) untraceability   (c) intensity   (d) improbability

40. Dancing before Nadar's luminous eyes at century's end is the prospect of $ billion in annual revenue.
    (a) shining   (b) diminutive   (c) immense   (d) ravishing

◎ 표현연구

참 잘 되었다.
Good for you! I'm happy for you! I'm thrilled for you!

◎ 표현연구

그게 바로 이 문제의 요점이야.
That's the name of the game around here.

◎ 속 담

열 번 찍어 안 넘어가는 나무 없다.
Little strokes fell great oaks.
Small drops make a shower.

2. 최종 독해

*다음 글을 읽고 물음에 답하시오.[1-4]

I would like to express my concern at the growing number of lottery games in this country. _____㉠_____. First, the people who run the lotteries are taking substantial amounts of money away from people, many of whom are old and can least afford to _____㉡_____ it. The elderly couple down the street from me, for example, spent over $20 on lottery tickets last week, and they have only their ㉢ <u>meager</u> social security checks to support them. Second, while I do not object to gambling in principle, I feel that this particular kind, where no skill is required on the part of the player, is especially offensive to the intellect. Finally, the places where lottery tickets are sold often attract undesirable people to otherwise quiet neighborhoods. In conclusion, I wish to express my opinion that lottery games of all types should be _____㉣_____.

1. 빈칸 ㉠에 들어갈 가장 알맞은 것은?
   (a) I am addicted to lottery games myself
   (b) I want to suggest some ways to win a bet
   (c) There are many steps to play lottery games
   (d) There are several reasons why I object to this kind of gambling

2. 빈칸 ㉡에 들어갈 가장 알맞은 것은?
   (a) rob   (b) sell   (c) lose   (d) sprawl

3. 밑줄 친 ㉢ meager와 그 뜻이 가장 가까운 것은?
   (a) scanty   (b) spacious   (c) thorough   (d) notorious

4. 빈칸 ㉣에 들어갈 가장 알맞은 것은?
   (a) expanded   (b) classified   (c) abolished   (d) attempted

*다음 글을 읽고 물음에 답하시오.[5-7]

The press should not be expected to be what it is not. Literary critics chide journalism for not being literary enough, historians for lacking historical accuracy, lawyers for not marshaling facts by the rules of evidence. But journalism is not literature, not history, not law. Most of the time it cannot possibly offer anything but a fleeing record of events compiled in great haste. Many news storied are, at bottom, hypotheses, discarding them when errors are discovered, and ti does so, on the whole, without blame, even when a mistake costs lives.

The press, which lay no claim to scientific accuracy, is not easily forgiven its errors. Admittedly, the press often _____ⓐ_____ with insufficient information, responding to an occasionally mindless hunger for news. A utopian society might demand that the press print nothing until it had reached absolute certainty. But such a society, while waiting for some ultimate version of event, would be so ⓑrife with rumor, alarm and lies that the errors of our journalism would by comparison seem models of truth.

5. 밑줄 친 ⓐ에 들어갈 가장 알맞은 것은?
   (a) refuses to write   (b) rushed into print
   (c) calls into question   (d) denies the authorities

6. 밑줄 친 ⓑrife with와 그 뜻이 가장 가까운 것은?
   (a) full of   (b) happy about   (c) congenial to   (d) satisfied with

7. 윗 글의 내용과 일치하는 것은?
   (a) The press should adopt the scientific method.
   (b) The press can best thrive in a utopian society.
   (c) The press is not free from reproach when news stories are not true.
   (d) The criticism that the press is literary enough is all too natural.

*다음 글을 읽고 물음에 답하시오.[8-10]

The Frankenstein myth has a viability that transcends its original intentions and a relevance beyond its original time. The image of the frightened scientist, guilt-ridden over his own creations, ceased to be theoretical with the explosion of the first atomic bomb. The revulsion of some of the young, idealistic men who were involved in the actual making of the bomb or in the theoretical work that led to it, had a demonstrable influence in the scientists, who, now wary and forewarned, are trying to consider the ethical, social and political implications of their research. They are even starting to ask whether some research ought to be done _____. With the serious introduction of questions of "ought" ethics has been introduced-and is beginning to shake some of the traditional illusion of a "science above morality" or a "value-free science."

8. What occasioned scientists to think about their research in ethical terms?
  (a) the reading of the novel Frankenstein
  (b) the inevitability of doing team projects
  (c) the first serious accident in nuclear power plants
  (d) the explosion of the first atomic bomb

9. What is that most suitable phrase for the blank in the above passage?
  (a) at once   (b) at all   (c) at times   (d) at least

10. What is the best title for the passage?
  (a) The Meaning of the Frankenstein Myth
  (b) Scientists and Their Creations
  (c) The Generation Gap in the Field of Science
  (d) The Ethical Problem of Scientific Research

제2부 TEPS

총신·장신대학교 신학대학원 준비

총신대학교와 장로회 신학대학교 신학대학원 입시 영어는 최근에 TEPS로 치러지는데, 청해 부분은 빠져 있다. 2006년부터는 청해 부분도 첨가된다고 한다.

I. TEPS 시험 안내
1. TEPS란 무엇인가?
2. TEPS의 구성
3. TEPS의 특징

II. 유형별 문제 분석-영역별 문제 유형
1. 듣기(청해)
2. 문법
3. 어휘
4. 독해

III. 실력문제
1. 문법
2. 어휘
3. 독해

IV. 최종점검 문제

Ⅰ. TEPS 시험 연구

1. TEPS란 무엇인가?

TEPS는 Test of English Proficiency developed by Seoul National University의 약자로 서울대학교 영어능력 검정시험입니다. TEPS는 정부의 공인을 받아 32년 간 정부기관, 각급 단체 및 기업체를 대상으로 어학능력을 측정해 온 서울대학교 어학연구소가 국내외 영어 전문가 40여명을 출제위원 으로 하고 영어 교육계의 권위자로 구성된 자문위원회의 검토를 거친 후, 수차례의 다양한 집단을 대상으로 평가를 거쳐 시험의 신뢰도와 타당도가 입증된 한국인에 맞는 실용 영어 능력평가 시험입니다. TEPS는 다양하고 일반적인 영어능력을 평가하는 시험으로 대학교, 기업체, 각종 기관 및 단체, 개인의 다양한 목적을 위해 응시할 수 있는 시험입니다.

2. TEPS의 구성

TEPS는 청해, 문법, 어휘, 독해 4개 영역에 걸쳐 총 200문항으로 구성되어 있으며 시험시간은 약 2시간 20분입니다.

영역, 시간/배점, part별 내용, 문항 수는 다음과 같다.

◉ 청 해(Listening Comprehension) (55분/ 400점)
Part Ⅰ: 문장 하나를 듣고 이어질 대화 고르기 15
Part Ⅱ: 3개 문장의 대화를 듣고 이어질 대화 고르기 15
Part Ⅲ: 6-8 문장의 대화를 듣고 이어질 대화 고르기 15
Part Ⅳ: 단문의 내용을 듣고 질문에 해당하는 답 고르기 15

◉ 문 법(Grammar) (25분/ 100점)
Part Ⅰ: 짧은 대화(대화문의 빈칸에 적절한 표현을 고르기) 20
Part Ⅱ: 문어체(문장의 빈칸에 적절한 표현을 고르기) 20
Part Ⅲ: 대화문(대화에서 어법상 틀리거나 어색한 부분 고르기) 5
Part Ⅳ: 설명문(단문에서 문법상 틀리거나 어색한 부분 고르기) 5

● **어 휘***(Vocabulary) (15분/ 100점)*
Part Ⅰ: 구어체(대화문의 빈칸에 적절한 단어 고르기) 25
Part Ⅱ: 문어체(단문의 빈칸에 적절한 단어 고르기) 25

● **독 해***(Reading Comprehension) (45분 /400점)*
Part Ⅰ: 빈칸 넣기(지문을 읽고 질문의 빈칸에 들어갈 내용 고르기) 16
Part Ⅱ: 내용 이해(지문을 읽고 질문에 가장 적절한 내용 고르기) 21
Part Ⅲ: 흐름 찾기(지문을 읽고 문맥상 어색한 내용 고르기) 3
• *총 계 13개 Parts 200문항 140분/ 990점*

3. TEPS의 특징

TEPS는 실용영어의 능력을 평가하는 시험이다. 실용영어는 생활영어의 범주를 넘어서는 광범위한 분야에서 일상적으로 사용되는 영어이다. 따라서 문어체 영어보다는 구어체 영어에 더 강조점이 주어진다고 할 수 있다. TEPS는 듣기능력 위주의 시험이다. 선택지가 문제지에 주어지지 않고 모두 들려준다. TEPS는 속도 시험(speed test)이라고 할 수 있다. 짧은 시간에 많은 문제를 소화해야 하기 때문에, 습득된 언어를 자유롭게 구사할 수 있는 사람이 유리하다고 볼 수 있다. TEPS는 다른 시험에 비해 편법과 요령이 통하지 않는다. 다양한 테스트 방법이 동원되고 있는 시험이라는 특징도 가지고 있다.

TEPS는 문항 반응 이론(IRT: Item Response Theory)을 도입했다. 문항 반응 이론은 문항을 개발할 때, 문항별로 1차 난이도를 정의하고 시험 시행 후 전체 수험자들이 각각의 문항에 대해 맞고 틀린 것을 종합해서 그 문항의 난이도를 재조정한 다음, 이를 근거로 다시 한 번 채점해 최종성적을 내게 된다. 이 과정에서 최고점은 990점, 최하점은 10점으로 조정된다. 총 배점은 1,000점이 나오나, 실제로는 난이도가 높은 문제를 많이 맞춘 수험자가 더 좋은 점수를 취득하게 된다.

II. 영역별 문제 유형
1. 듣기

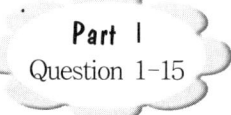

Part I
Question 1-15

* 다음 말을 듣고 연결될 수 있는 가장 적절한 응답을 고르시오.

You will now hear 15 items made up of a single spoken statement followed by four spoken responses. Choose the most appropriate response to the statement. For example, if you hear:

(speaker 1) Thank you for your help.
(speaker 2) _____.

  (a) You're welcome.
  (b) Nice to meet you.
  (c) Thanks.
  (d) What's that?

You should choose (a) because (a) is the most appropriate response among the choices given.

Now let's begin part one.

1-15. 답안지에 정답을 표시하시오.

◉ **표현연구**
무슨 생각을 하고 있니?
What's on your mind? What do you have in mind?

◉ **신앙 명언**
지속적인 영향을 끼치는 열쇠는 하나님께 순종하는 삶이다.
Obedience to God is the key to a lasting influence.

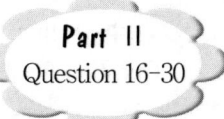

Part II
Question 16-30

* 다음 말을 듣고 연결될 수 있는 가장 적절한 응답을 고르시오.

You will now hear 15 dialogue fragments made up of three spoken statements followed by four spoken responses. Choose the most appropriate response to the last statement made. For example, if you hear:

(speaker 1) What time is it now?
(speaker 2) Let's see. It's 10:30.
(speaker 1) Really? It's 10:15 by my watch.
(speaker 2) _____.

(a) Your watch is fast.
(b) My watch is slow.
(c) My watch is dead.
(d) Your watch is slow.

You should choose (d) because (d) is the most appropriate response among the choices given.

Now, let's begin part two.

16-30. 답안지에 정답을 표시하시오.

◎ 표현연구

6시 정각에 여기 도착할 거야.
He'll be here at 6 o'clock sharp.
He'll be here at 6:00 on the dot[on the nose].

◎ 신앙 명언

그리스도의 십자가는 인간의 최악의 죄와 하나님의 최선의 사랑을 나타낸다.
The cross of Christ reveals man's sin at its worst and God's love at its best.

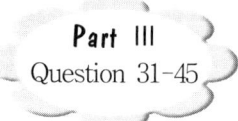

Part III
Question 31-45

* 다음 말을 듣고 질문에 가장 적절한 답을 고르시오.

You will now hear 15 complete dialogues. For each item, you will hear a dialogue and the corresponding question read twice followed by four spoken answer choices read once. Choose the correct answer among the four choices. For example, if you hear:

(speaker 1) Do you deliver?
(speaker 2) Yes. I do.
(speaker 1) Well, can you deliver it to my house?
(speaker 2) Sure. Do you have a specific date for delivery?
(speaker 1) Yes. I'd like to have it on Tuesday.
(speaker 2) That sounds fine. Thank you.

Question. When is a day for delivery?
 (a) Monday
 (b) Sunday
 (c) Tuesday
 (d) Saturday

You should choose (c) because (c) is the correct answer to the question.

Now let's begin part three.

31-45. 답안지에 정답을 표시하시오.

◉ 신앙 명언
 당신 속에 있는 그리스도의 능력이 당신 주위의 고난의 압력보다 더 크다.
 The power of Christ within you is greater than the pressure of troubles around you.

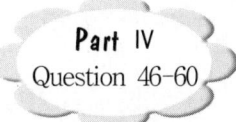

Part IV
Question 46-60

* 다음 말을 듣고 질문에 가장 적절한 답을 고르시오.

You will now hear 15 spoken monologues. For each item, you will hear a monologue and the corresponding question read twice, followed by four possible choices read once. Choose the correct answer among the four choices. For example, if you hear:

(speaker 1) May I have your attention please? Flight 208 to Boston will now begin boarding. Will all those passengers with children or special needs please proceed to gate F4 and board the plane as the seat numbers are called. As always, our Gold Club members may board at anytime. Once again, we are now beginning boarding of Flight 208 to Boston at gate F4. Thank you.

(speaker 2) Question. Which of the following is Not correct?

[The monologue and the question are repeated once again]

   (a) Flight 208 is about to land.
   (b) Boarding of flight 208 is beginning.
   (c) Gold Club members can board the plane.
   (d) The plane is at gate F4.

You should choose (a) because it is the correct answer to the question.

Now, let's begin part four.

46-60. 답안지에 정답을 표시하시오.

2. 문법

* 다음 대화문의 빈칸에 들어갈 가장 적절한 표현을 고르시오.

A: I was told your brother is an actor.
B: Yes, he _____ in several films so far.
 (a) is appearing   (b) has appeared
 (c) has been appearing   (d) appears

[해설] 빈칸에는 'so far'(지금까지)와 어울리는 현재완료가 와야 한다.
(해석) A: 네 형이 영화배우라고 들었어.
  B: 예, 그는 지금까지 몇 편의 영화에 출연했어. 정답 (b)

* 다음 글의 빈칸에 들어갈 가장 적절한 표현을 고르시오.
Non-profit corporations are established for purposes of public service and _____ special privileges by the government.
 (a) are giving   (b) has given   (c) give   (d) given

[해설] give는 수여동사이므로 목적어가 두 개가 필요한데, 본문에서는 special privileges라는 목적어만 왔으므로 빈칸에는 수동태가 와야 한다. 그런데 앞의 are가 있으므로 빈칸에는 given이 들어간다.
(해석) 비영리 기업체들은 공공 서비스를 목적으로 설립되며 정부에 의해 특전이 주어진다. 정답 (d)

◉ 신앙 명언
이 땅에서의 삶만을 위해 사는 사람은 영원히 그것을 후회하게 될 것이다.
The one who lives for this life only will have eternity to regret it.

Part III

* 다음 대화에서 어법상 틀리거나 어색한 부분을 고르시오.

(a) A: How do you like your new job?
(b) B: It's very good. It is different the one I had before.
(c) A: Why do you think so?
(d) B: First of all, I can have a lot of money.

[해설] 'be different from(-과 다르다)'을 묻는 문제이다.
(해석) (a) A: 새 직업이 어때요?
(b) B: 매우 좋아요. 전에 했던 것과는 달라요.
(c) A: 왜 그렇게 생각해요.
(d) B: 무엇보다도 돈을 많이 받을 수 있어요.
정답 (b) It is different→It is different from

Part IV

* 다음 글에서 문법상 틀리거나 어색한 부분을 고르시오.

(a) These days, in many families, both the mother and the father work. (b) The responsibilities of running a house and raising the children are now more equal shared between men and women than ever before. (c) Fathers have become more involved in raising the children and taking care of their everybody needs. (d) But mothers still spend more time caring for the children and doing the household chores.

[해설] 동사 shared를 수식하는 것은 부사이므로 (b) equal shared→ equally shared.
(해석) (a) 요즘에는 많은 가정에서 어머니와 아버지가 일을 한다. (b) 가정을 경영하고 아이들을 양육하는 책임은 전에 보다 지금 남녀 사이에 더 공평하게 분담된다. (c) 아버지들이 자녀를 양육하고 그들의 필요를 돌보는데 더 관여하게 되었다. (d) 그러나 아직은 어머니들이 아이들을 돌보고 잡다한 집안일을 하는데 더 많은 시간을 보낸다. 정답 (b)

3. 어휘

Part I

* 다음 대화문의 빈칸에 들어갈 가장 적절한 표현을 고르시오.

A: Are you free tonight?
B: No, I'm sorry I'm all _____.

 (a) full   (b) in time   (c) booked up   (d) behind schedule

📖[해설] 내용상 빈칸에는 '매우 바쁘다'의 뜻을 가진 (c) booked up이 와야 한다. (a) I'm full 배부르다. (b) in time 조만간 (d) behind schedule 예정보다 늦게

✎ (해석) A: 오늘밤에 시간 있나요?
   B: 아니오. 미안하지만 매우 바빠요.   정답 (c)

Part II

* 다음 글의 빈칸에 들어갈 가장 적절한 표현을 고르시오.

When students contracted the flu, they should study at home to prevent a _____ of the disease.

 (a) spread   (b) cause   (c) touch   (d) delivery

📖[해설] 내용상 빈칸에는 '전염'의 뜻을 가진 (a) spread가 와야 한다. (d) delivery 배달, 인도

✎ (해석) 학생들이 독감에 걸렸을 때, 병이 전염되는 것을 막기 위해 집에서 공부해야 한다.   정답 (a)

◉ **표현연구**

내 욕을 했으니까 당해도 싸.
It serves him[her] right for calling me names.

4. 독해

* 다음 글을 읽고 빈칸에 들어갈 가장 적절한 것을 고르시오.

Even in the safest home, accidents may happen. It takes only a second for a person to cut himself. He may burn himself for stumble and fall over something. Cuts, burns, and bruises are three accidents which may happen at any time in the home. Therefore, it would be helpful if you knew what to do in such an emergency to help a person who is hurt. This is known as _____.

　(a) operation　(b) first aid　(c) medical care　(d) immediate rescue

📖[해설] 빈칸에 적절한 것을 고르는 문제는 첫 문장과 빈칸 바로 앞에 있는 문장에 답을 고르는 키가 있다. 'Therefore'(그러므로)이하에도 힌트가 있는 경우가 많다. 본문에서는 'if you what to do in such an emergency to help a person who is hurt'에 정답을 찾는 단서(clue)가 있다. 따라서 빈칸에는 '응급조치'의 뜻을 가진 (b) first aid가 와야 한다.

✎(해석) 가장 안전한 집에서조차 사고가 생길 수 있다. 어떤 사람은 칼에 베이는데 몇 초밖에 안 걸린다. 그는 화상을 입기도 하고, 무언가에 걸려 넘어지기도 한다. 베이고, 불에 데고, 타박상을 입는 것은 언제라도 집에서 발생할 수 있는 세 가지 사고이다. 그러므로 그런 긴급 상황에서는 다친 사람을 돕는 법을 알고 있다면 도움이 된다. 이것이 응급조치로 알려져 있다. 정답 (b)

◎ **표현연구**
나에게 책임을 전가하지 마.
Don't pass the buck to me.

◎ **신앙 명언**
매 순간을 준비함으로써 마지막 순간을 준비하라.
Be ready for your last moment by being ready every moment.

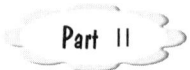

* 다음 글을 읽고 질문에 가장 적절한 답을 고르시오.

The word propaganda, as is generally used, is not a "bad" word. However, you can see that the propaganda in ads is made up of half-truths, and perhaps even lies. Propaganda comes close to being a "bad" word when the propaganda uses it to "stack the cards" against unsuspecting readers. Some advertisers want their readers to believe that they would like to give something for nothing.

Q. Which of the following is correct according to the passage?
(a) A piece of propaganda necessarily includes a lie.
(b) "Bad" readers do not believe in propaganda.
(c) Advertising is an essential part of modern business.
(d) Advertisements sometimes tell a lie.

[해설] However이하의 내용에 힌트가 있는 경우가 많다. 본문에서는 둘째 줄의 'half-truths'에 문제 해결의 키가 있으므로 정답은 (d)가 된다.
stack the cards 속임수를 쓰다(=arrange unfairly and dishonestly) for nothing 공짜로

(해석) 일반적으로 사용되는 것처럼 선전이라는 말은 "나쁜"말이 아니다. 그러나 광고문에 사용된 선전 문구는 반만 진실인 말, 그리고 어쩌면 거짓말 조차도 포함하고 있다는 것을 알 수 있다. 광고주가 선전을 의심하지 않는 독자에게 "속임수를 쓰기"위해 이용할 때 "나쁜" 말에 가까워진다. 어떤 광고 주들은 독자들로 하여금 그들이 무언가를 공짜로 주고 싶어한다고 믿기를 원한다. 정답 (d)

◉ 신앙 명언

하나님은 비극을 승리로 변화시키실 수 있다.
God can transform a tragedy into a triumph.

Part III

* 다음 글을 읽고 내용의 흐름상 어색한 부분을 고르시오.

For many years, men have been taught that hard work is noble. (a) They have been encouraged to work diligently for long hours. (b) Modern technology has removed the necessity for a life of constant hard work. (c) "Idleness is the devil's plaything," they have been told. (d) As a result, men have been busy for centuries.

📖[해설] 첫째 문장이 주제문인데 주제문과 다른 문장들의 관계를 따져 보면 된다. 주제문과 관련성이 적거나 없는 것이 답이 된다. 본문의 주제문은 '인간이 열심히 일하는 것이 귀한 것이다'이므로, 정답은 (b)가 된다.

✎ (해석) 여러 해 동안 인간은 열심히 일하는 것이 귀한 것이라고 배워 왔다. (a) 그들은 오랜 시간 동안 부지런히 일하도록 격려되어 왔다. (b) 현대 기술로 인해 끊임없이 열심히 일해야 하는 생활이 없어지게 되었다. (c) "게으름은 악마의 장난이다"라고 들어 왔다. (d) 결과적으로 인간은 수세기 동안 바빠 왔다. 정답 (b)

◎ **표현연구**
타협하지요.
Let's meet halfway.
Let's split the difference.

◎ **표현연구**
그녀는 해고되었어.
She got fired.
She got dismissed.

◎ **표현연구**
하나님은 일을 하도록 부르실 때 완성하도록 그의 능력도 함께 주신다.
God's call to a task includes His strength to complete it.

III. 실력 문제
1. 문법 · Part I

실력문제 1회

* 다음 대화문의 빈칸에 들어갈 가장 적절한 표현을 고르시오.

1. A : Are you waiting to see someone?
   B : Yes, I have some urgent business to _____ Mr. John.
   (a) discuss   (b) discuss on   (c) discuss about   (d) discuss over

2. A : Is Tom going to New York with you?
   B : I couldn't talk him _____ with me.
   (a) of going   (b) to going   (c) into going   (d) that he will go

3. A : Why are you so late this morning?
   B : I'm really sorry. I didn't hear my alarm clock _____.
   (a) go off   (b) to go off   (c) gone off   (d) went off

4. A : I can't make up my mind _____.
   B : Why don't you try the pizza? They make good cheese pizza here.
   (a) here what order to   (b) what to order here
   (c) what here to order   (d) what here to order

5. A : We are supposed to meet this coming Friday, aren't you?
   B : Yes, but it _____ if the president still has the flu.
   (a) was put off   (b) has put off
   (c) will be put off   (d) is put off

6. A : Jane, you look beautiful tonight.
   B : _____.
   (a) That's flattered   (b) They're flattering
   (c) I'm flattered   (d) Don't flatter to me

7. A : Must I phone home right away?
　　B : No, you _____.
　　(a) won't　　(b) may not　　(c) must not　　(d) don't have to

8. A : We're at stake recently.
　　B : If you _____ to me, we wouldn't be in danger now.
　　(a) has listened　　(b) listen　　(c) would listen　　(d) had listened

9. A : What's the weather report today?
　　B : Take your umbrella _____.
　　(a) in case it rains　　　　　　(b) in case that may be raining
　　(c) in a possible case it rains　(d) in any case it would rain

10. A : Anything wrong?
　　B : Yeah, Harris won't talk to me any more, and I don't know _____ to make of it.
　　(a) how　　(b) what　　(c) why　　(d) any

◎ 표현연구

누구나 때로는 감정을 발산해야 한다.
Everyone has to blow off steam sometimes.

◎ 표현연구

사과의 표현들
I'm so sorry.
It won't happen again.
Please accept my apologies.
How can I make it up to you?
I'd like to apologize for…

실력문제 2회

* 다음 대화문의 빈칸에 들어갈 가장 적절한 표현을 고르시오.

1. A : Did Mary attend the meeting last night?
   B : No, but I'd hoped _____.
   (a) her coming   (b) she comes
   (c) her to come   (d) that she would come

2. A : I heard you're moving into a new apartment before long.
   B : Yes. Once _____, I'll move in right away.
   (a) finishing to do the renovations
   (b) the renovations are finished
   (c) the renovations to be finished
   (d) the renovations being finished

3. A : How would you compare Tom with Jack in terms of their English fluency?
   B : Tom is just as fluent as Jack, if not _____.
   (a) the better   (b) more so   (c) no better   (d) more such

4. A : Do you know about the new rules?
   B : No, I don't recall ever _____ about them.
   (a) to inform (b) informing (c) to be informed (d) being informed

5. A : Jane has been sitting for 30 minutes _____.
   B : Probably she couldn't sleep a wink last night.
   (a) closing her eyes   (b) her eyes closing
   (c) with closed her eyes   (d) with her eyes closed

6. A : May I help you?
   B : I'm looking for a copy of the The Korea Herald. Can I

_____ here?
(a) pick up it (b) pick it up (c) pick up them (d) pick them up

7. A : How come you're so late this morning?
   B : I spent more than twenty minutes _____ a cab.
   (a) trying catching   (b) to try to catch
   (c) in order to try to catching (d) trying to catch

8. A : If only I _____ home a little earlier! Then I could have caught the train.
   B : It is of no use to say such a thing now.
   (a) had left   (b) left   (c) leave   (d) have left

9. A : I thought your team couldn't make the hike.
   B : _____ the weather wasn't cooperative, we went hiking anyway.
   (a) Despite (b) In spite of (c) Despite the fact that (d) Besides

10. A : Did you hear _____ there would be no year-end bonuses this year?
    B : I'm not surprised. It's the same in many companies.
    (a) of   (b) about   (c) that   (d) which

◉ 표현연구

옆 집 사람이 신경에 거슬려.
My neighbor gets on my nerves.

◉ 표현연구

한 번 시도해 봐.
Give it a try!
Give it a shot!

◉ 신앙 명언

남은 날들을 세지 말고 모든 날들이 의미 있도록 만들어라.
Better than counting your years is making all your years count.

실력문제 3회

* 다음 대화문의 빈칸에 들어갈 가장 적절한 표현을 고르시오.

1. A: I'm calling to ask if you carry floppy disks.
   B: Let me check and see if they're _____.
   (a) up   (b) down   (c) out   (d) in

2. A: I hear you got lost yesterday.
   B: Yes, I went to the museum and couldn't find _____ the hotel.
   (a) how to return to   (b) how I should go for
   (c) my way back to   (d) the way back for

3. A : Do you know why she quit the job?
   B : No, she did nothing but _____ the whole time she was here.
   (a) complaining   (b) complained   (c) to complain   (d) complain

4. A : I can't trust you any more. I guess you made up the whole story.
   B : Why are you talking to me _____ deceived you?
   (a) if I have   (b) as though   (c) as if I had   (d) as if I haven't

5. A : "Will you be able to carry it to the tennis court?"
   B : "I'll get there _____."
   (a) somehow   (b) by the way   (c) in a way   (d) by some way

6. A : I like the painting, although I never would have recognized it as a Pollack.
   B : This is _____. I had no idea he was so prolific.
   (a) a quite show   (b) quite a show
   (c) rather a show   (d) a rather show

7. A : How's your brother doing? I haven't seen him for a while.

B : He's fine but _____.
(a) busy to write his thesis (b) busy with writing his thesis
(c) busy for writing his thesis (d) busy writing his thesis

8. A : Can you lend me some money?
   B : I'm not _____ to lend you money again.
   (a) such a fool as   (b) so fool as
   (c) more foolish   (d) too foolish as

9. A : My car broke down so I walked all the way home.
   B : _____ you didn't take a bus?
   (a) How come   (b) What about   (c) Why not   (d) How often

10. A : Do you drink a lot?
    B : I can't drink much. Nor _____.
    (a) I wish to drink   (b) wish I to drink
    (c) do I wish to   (d) do I wish

◉ 표현연구
그는 업무에 필요한 능력을 갖고 있지 않았다.
He didn't have what it takes to do the job.

◉ 표현연구
내가 알기로는 아니야(없어).
Not that I know of.

◉ 신앙 명언
근심 걱정의 잡초를 제거하려면 무릎을 꿇어라.
To uproot the weeds of anxious care, get down to your knees.

실력문제 4회

* 다음 대화문의 빈칸에 들어갈 가장 적절한 표현을 고르시오.

1. A : Do you smoke very much?
   B : Yes, I should break _____.
   (a) the habit from me (b) the habit of myself
   (c) the habit myself   (d) myself of the habit

2. A : How's he doing in mathematics?
   B : He has no ability _____ in mathematics.
   (a) whatsoever (b) far from (c) nor (d) if ever

3. A : We've got to choose between Monday and Wednesday for the oral test. What do you think?
   B : Well, for me. Wednesday is _____ Monday.
   (a) more preferable to   (b) more preferable than
   (c) preferable than   (d) preferable to

4. A : What were you doing when Joe called.
   B : I _____.
   (a) was cooking in the middle of
   (b) was trying in the middle of cooking
   (c) was in the middle of trying the cook
   (d) was in the middle to cook

5. A : I guess she dislikes him.
   B : _____ you that idea?
   (a) Why does it make   (b) what gives
   (c) How is it that   (d) What is making

6. A : Who is Mr. Williams?
   B : The man _____ is Mr. Williams.

(a) having the brown suit   (b) in the brown suit
(c) on the brown suit   (d) wears a brown large suit

7. A : What do you say _____ out for a drink?
   B : That's a good idea.
   (a) going   (b) to going   (c) for going   (d) to go

8. A : What does he look like?
   B : He greatly _____ his father.
   (a) resembled   (b) is resembling   (c) has resembled   (d) resembles

9. A : I feel so sleepy this morning.
   B : You _____ to bed earlier last night.
   (a) should go   (b) had to   (c) should have gone   (d) went

10. A : It's pretty tough trying to coax him into joining the club.
    B : You can say that again. _____ I say, he always has something to disagree with.
    (a) However   (b) Whichever   (c) Wherever   (d) Whatever

---

◎ 표현연구

규칙을 어기지 마.
Don't hit below the belt.

◎ 표현연구

나는 배가 출발하는 시간에 아슬아슬하게 맞춰 도착했어.
I arrived just in the nick of time to catch the ferry.

◎ 신앙 명언

인생의 경주는 믿음으로 달리며 은혜로 승리한다.
The race of life is run by faith and won by grace.

문법 - Part II

실력문제 1회

* 다음 글의 빈칸에 들어갈 가장 적절한 표현을 고르시오.

1. Poets devote themselves to _____ their inspiration into words.
   (a) transform (b) transforming (c) be transformed (d) being transformed

2. _____ in a humorous tone, the story instantly catches the reader's attention.
   (a) Writing   (b) Written   (c) Having written   (d) To be written

3. _____ become blocked completely, the patient would have died.
   (a) If the cell   (b) The cell is   (c) The cell were to   (d) Had the cell

4. The golden rule is that "Do to others as you _____ "
   (a) wish to be done   (b) would be being done by
   (c) would have them do to you   (d) wish them to do for you by

5. I never saw him get mad _____ her like that before.
   (a) to   (b) in   (c) at   (d) about

6. I believe that our systems seem as odd to you as yours _____.
   (a) can   (b) will do   (c) does   (d) isn't

7. Agronomists _____ the quality of crops, maintain the quality of the soil, and increase the yield of fields.
   (a) work to have improved   (b) working in improving
   (c) work to improve   (d) working in having improved

8. _____ our school brochure and an application form.
   (a) Please enclose find   (b) Enclosed please find
   (c) Enclosed find please   (d) Please find enclose

9. Barbara agreed to conduct the meeting _____ the election of a permanent chairman.
   (a) to pend   (b) pended   (c) pending   (d) pend

10. Cancer occurs when body cells multiply in an uncontrolled way, producing abnormal _____ called tumors.
    (a) growing   (b) growings   (c) grown-up   (d) growths

◎ **Collocation(연어)**

1. abuse drugs 마약을 복용하다
2. administer first-aid 응급조치를 취하다
3. answer the phone 전화를 받다
4. balance the books 회계 장부를 결산하다
5. bear the expense 비용을 부담하다.
6. bounce[dishonor] a check 수표를 부도 처리하다
7. break one's word 약속을 어기다
8. catch one's eyes 시선을 끌다
9. claim a refund 환불을 요구하다
10. deliver[address/give/make] a speech 연설하다
11. draw a line 한계를 긋다
12. entertain questions 질문에 응하다
13. file[place] an order 주문을 하다
14. hold one's temper 화를 참다
15. identify the problem 문제를 찾아내다

실력문제 2회

* 다음 글의 빈칸에 들어갈 가장 적절한 표현을 고르시오.

1. Scientists hope to determine which genes are abnormal; then they want to develop treatments to fight illnesses, possibly _____.
   (a) use the known genes   (b) used such genes as these
   (c) using the genes themselves   (d) to use the gene pool

2. A black asphalt road _____ nothing shading it from the sun grows extremely hot in the summer.
   (a) has   (b) having had   (c) what has   (d) which has

3. All the advice _____ to him was ignored. He wouldn't listen.
   (a) was given   (b) were given   (c) given   (d) giving

4. In today's business world, it is crucial that you be able to _____ all types of communications when and where you need to.
   (a) access to   (b) be accessible   (c) have access   (d) access

5. The forest fire appears _____ when a domestic fire nearby spread across the dry ground aided by high winds.
   (a) to have started   (b) to be started   (c) to start   (d) started

6. Tom is very fit. He's just run six miles and he's _____.
   (a) even not out of breath   (b) not even out of breath
   (c) not out of breath even   (d) not out of even breath

7. According to the press release, the second annual awards ceremony _____ here next month.
   (a) holds   (b) is held   (c) is to hold   (d) is to be held

8. His financial situation was so desperate that he _____.
   (a) left no stone unturned   (b) left stone not turned

(c) unturned left no stone   (d) unturned no stone left

9. The judge assented to the suggestion that _____.
   (a) both of the criminals will soon be set freedom
   (b) some of the criminals there are of guilty only
   (c) that girl was to be paroled in the custody of a welfare society
   (d) the prisoner be sentenced to death

10. The impact of Thoreau's "On the Duty of Civil Disobedience" might not have been so far-reaching _____ for Elizabeth Peabody, who dared to publish the controversial essay.
    (a) it not having been   (b) it is not being
    (c) had it not been   (d) is it not being

◉ Collocation(연어)

16. issue a statement 성명을 발표하다
17. launch an attack 공격을 개시하다
18. lose heart 실망하다
19. meet a requirement 요구사항을 충족시키다
20. place an advertisement 광고하다
21. pull the trigger 방아쇠를 당기다
22. raise[make/voice] objections to
    …에 대한 이의를 제기하다, 반대하다
23. serve a three-year sentence 3년형을 살다
24. sue for[seek] damages 손해배상 소송을 제기하다
25. take chances 모험을 하다
26. take medicine 약을 먹다
27. take stock[inventory] 재고를 조사하다

실력문제 3회

* 다음 글의 빈칸에 들어갈 가장 적절한 표현을 고르시오.

1. The doctor _____ enter the room, for the patient was asleep.
   (a) said to us not to
   (b) told us not to
   (c) said us to refrain to
   (d) talked us not to

2. _____ the uncertainty over John's future I was left with little other choice.
   (a) It being given
   (b) Given
   (c) Given that
   (d) While giving

3. The special cabinet committee _____ Mr. Dick, Mr. Williams, and Tony Newton.
   (a) comprising
   (b) to comprise
   (c) comprised by
   (d) comprise

4. _____ in the physical universe, it is in man, in his love and hatred, his noble achievements and failures, that I am interested.
   (a) How interested I am
   (b) Despite of my interest
   (c) Interested as I am
   (d) Though interested I am

5. How could it be that this man, _____, could commit such heinous crime, not once but many times?
   (a) with his great moral intelligence
   (b) his great moral intelligence
   (c) he had his great moral intelligence
   (d) to have such great moral intelligence

6. _____ how beautiful she still is, she must have been quite cunning when she was young.
   (a) Consider
   (b) Considered
   (c) Considering
   (d) To consider

7. It is very difficult, _____ impossible, for a married woman to

get a job in India.
(a) if any (b) if ever (c) if so (d) if not

8. No matter how much intelligence a person may have, he cannot make wise choices unless he knows the facts _____ a problem.
(a) pertained (b) pertained to (c) pertaining (d) pertaining to

9. You might _____ advise me to give up my fortune as my argument.
(a) as well (b) as good (c) well (d) as well as

10. The room at the hotel _____, we went out to a restaurant just after the street lamps were lighted, and ate a comfortable and satisfactory dinner.
(a) to reserve (b) having reserved (c) reserving (d) being reserved

---

◎ **Collocation(연어)**

　　28. wage war 전쟁을 하다
　　29. watch one's language[mouth] 말조심하다
　　30. wear a frown 인상을 쓰다

◎ **표현연구**

화를 내지 마.
Don't fly off the handle. Don't hit the ceiling.
Don't raise the roof. Don't blow a gasket.
Don't blow up. Don't lose your temper.

◎ **신앙 명언**

매일 그리스도를 위해 살려면 매일 자신이 죽어야 한다.
Living daily for Christ requires dying daily to self.

실력문제 4회

* 다음 글의 빈칸에 들어갈 가장 적절한 표현을 고르시오.

1. Education is an admirable thing, but it is well to remember from time to time that nothing that is _____ can be taught.
   (a) worth knowing
   (b) worth to know
   (c) worthy knowing
   (d) worthy known

2. Mr. James was supposed to be there by now, so I think he'll be here _____ thirty minutes.
   (a) around
   (b) at nearby
   (c) in about
   (d) by at least

3. When he is with his friends he becomes so excited and talkative, _____ he remains mostly silent and subdued when he is with his wife.
   (a) when
   (b) whenever
   (c) whereof
   (d) whereas

4. Judging from his work on the walls, _____.
   (a) he would do with the interior
   (b) I had no idea what he would do with the interior
   (c) his work on the interior not being clear
   (d) no idea what he would do with the interior

5. Back when the telephone was a relatively new contraption, people often regarded it _____ important communications.
   (a) for too ephemeral as
   (b) too ephemeral as for
   (c) too as ephemeral for
   (d) as too ephemeral for

6. _____ become tomorrow's history as time slips by with frightening rapidity.
   (a) Headlines of today soon
   (b) As soon today's headlines
   (c) Today's headlines soon
   (d) As soon do today's headlines

7. _____ inner city schools are not doing a better job is that parents don't offer enough support.
   (a) It is the number one reason   (b) For the number one reason why
   (c) The number one reason why   (d) The number one reason is why

8. All our food products are completely _____ artificial flavorings and colorings.
   (a) free of   (b) nothing of   (c) lack from   (d) but from

9. He cared little for material goods and possessions, so that his own works _____ away for free.
   (a) often given were   (b) were given often
   (c) given often were   (d) were often given

10. The United Nations General Secretary urged the two sides to come back to the negotiation table, emphasizing the need to safeguard the _____ peace process at any cost.
    (a) threat   (b) threaten   (c) threatening   (d) threatened

---

◎ 신앙 명언

회개는 하나님과 동행하는 길을 열어 놓는다.
Repentance keeps the way clear in our walk with God.

◎ 신앙 명언

우리가 하나님의 능력에 의지할 때 우리의 약점은 축복이 된다.
Our weakness is a blessing when we lean God's strength.

◎ 신앙 명언

어제의 그늘 속에 살지 말고 오늘의 빛과 내일의 희망 속에 걸어가라.
Instead of living in the shadows of yesterday,
walk in the light of today and the hope of tomorrow.

문법 - Part III

실력문제 1회

* 다음 대화에서 어법상 틀리거나 어색한 부분을 고르시오.

1. (a) A: Is there anything else worth to watch?
   (b) B: I think there's a Western on
   (c) A: Do you mind if we watch it?
   (d) B: Well, I really wanted to see the baseball game.

2. (a) A: Are you insinuating that I'm no cultured?
   (b) B: I'm not insinuating anything. If the shoe fits, wear it.
   (c) A: Now, wait a minute! I've taken about all I'm going to take from you! What makes you so contrary?
   (d) B: I'm not contrary. I'm in a hurry. That's all.

3. (a) A: Hi, John! What's up! Long time no see.
   (b) B: I went to New York last week to visit my brother.
   (c) A: Oh, When have you got back from New York?
   (d) B: Just yesterday.

4. (a) A: Oh, no. Our car got stuck in the mud.
   (b) B: What are we supposed to do?
   (c) A: We must decide whether to wait for another car or to push it.
   (d) B: As far as I'm concerning, we'd better get out and push the car out of the mud.

5. (a) A: That's lovely ring you're wearing.
   (b) B: Thanks. I think it's pretty, too.
   (c) A: Where did you get it?
   (d) B: My boyfriend bought it me.

실력문제 2회

* 다음 대화에서 어법상 틀리거나 어색한 부분을 고르시오.

1. (a) A: Have you finished the work on my car?
   (b) B: I'm afraid not. We haven't got the parts yet.
   (c) A: Oh, that's nuisance. Do you think when it'll be ready?
   (d) B: Well, we are getting the parts in this morning. You'll be able to pick up the car tomorrow evening.

2. (a) A: Turn right at the next street.
   (b) B: OK. I think I'm getting better at turning now.
   (c) A: That was not bad, but there was a stop sign at that intersection.
   (d) B: You mean I must have stopped before I turned?

3. (a) A: All these new traffic laws are such a nuisance.
   (b) B: I agree.
   (c) A: In other hands, I guess they serve some useful purpose to society.
   (d) B: That's right. We should try to think positively.

4. (a) A: What do you do for a living?
   (b) B: I'm a receptionist at a downtown hotel.
   (c) A: Do you like it? I mean. isn't it kind of boring when you just sit the whole day away.
   (d) B: Actually, the hours is good and the money isn't that bad. To top it all, I'm my own boss.

5. (a) A: Those test questions were surprisingly easy.
   (b) B: Yes, but it is difficult to concentrate during such a long time.
   (c) A: Yes, any three-hour test is challenging.
   (d) B: I hope we both passed.

실력문제 3회

* 다음 대화에서 어법상 틀리거나 어색한 부분을 고르시오.

1. (a) A: I'd better leave right away.
   (b) B: What' the rush?
   (c) A: I should meet my advisor at eleven.
   (d) B: That's out of question. It's already eleven thirty.

2. (a) A: Get up. It's almost nine o'clock.
   (b) B: Why didn't you wake me up sooner?
   (c) A: You wouldn't get up when I did.
   (d) B: Do you want me to get fire?

3. (a) A: Can you tell me a little bit about yourself?
   (b) B: Gee, I don't know where to begin. What do you want to know?
   (c) A: Well, What are you doing?
   (d) B: I'm a mathematics teacher.

4. (a) A: Why the long face? Don't you like your new school?
   (b) B: No. Everyone was picking on me.
   (c) A: Never mind. Maybe it's because you are the new kid on the block. Cheer up, it'll get better.
   (d) B: I hope it.

5. (a) A: Could I take tomorrow off?
   (b) B: I don't think so.
   (c) A: I see, but the reason which I asked is that my husband's going into the hospital for an operation.
   (d) Oh, I understand. Well, in that case, I suppose you can.

실력문제 4회

* 다음 대화에서 어법상 틀리거나 어색한 부분을 고르시오.

1. (a) A: Sandy, you look great!
   (b) B: Thank you for saying so.
   (c) A: What happened! Did you lose weight or something?
   (d) B: Actually, I was in a diet and lost six pounds.

2. (a) A: Hey, Bill! Do you have a minute to talk with me?
   (b) B: Sure. What's on your mind?
   (c) A: I have to make a birthday card. I hope you can help me out for it.
   (d) B: I know that you are all thumbs.

3. (a) A: The doctor billed us for our annual check up last month.
   (b) B: Really? Our insurance is supposed to take care of that.
   (c) A: We'd better call our doctor and see if there's been some sort of mix-up.
   (d) B: Good idea. Let's set the bill aside until we get this straighten out.

4. (a) A: What happened to the patient?
   (b) B: We found him lying unconsciously in his bedroom.
   (c) A: He'll have to go to intensive care unit at once.
   (d) B: Can I see him?

5. (a) A: Do you want to go out for dinner tonight?
   (b) B: Tonight? I'm afraid I can't. I have to work late.
   (c) A: That's too bad.
   (d) B: Maybe we can go out for dinner some another time.

문법 - Part IV

실력문제 1회

* 다음 글에서 문법상 틀리거나 어색한 부분을 고르시오.

1. (a) Exercise is beneficial to your heart. (b) A 22-year study was conducted by doctors in California. (c) They found that people who work at physical jobs experience less heart attacks than other people. (d) These active people work all the time at moderate speeds.

2. (a) Many years ago everybody believed that the Earth to be flat. (b) If the Earth is round and you are standing in the United States, then a person standing in China must is not standing upside-down. (c) If the person in China is not standing upside-down, then the person in the United States is standing upside-down. (d) Thoughts like these made difficult for people to believe that the Earth was round.

3. (a) Hawaii composes of several islands. (b) The state is quite separate from the other U. S. states. (c) There is an interesting marine life that attracts many tourists to the state. (d) The cost of living is quite high.

4. (a) What is difficult to understand how people can complain about the economic conditions of the country and yet refuse to change their own habits. (b) According to recent statistics, most of the people in Korea still spend the same money they did before. (c) Have people forgotten so easily? (d) When are people going to learn that we all need to reduce and conserve if we are going to get out of this crisis?

5. (a) For the Japanese, a bath is not just a way to get clean. (b) It is also a way to relax and recover from a stressful day. (c) In Japan, people like to make very long, hot baths. (d) While they are in the bathtub, they like to listen to music or read books.

실력문제 2회

* 다음 글에서 문법상 틀리거나 어색한 부분을 고르시오.

1. (a) When confronted by a seeming irrational teenage son or daughter, the first step is to identify the specific problem. (b) Giving your teen a chance to give you all his reasons no matter how silly will help you get to the root of the problem. (c) More often than not the surface problem will only be an indication of a much deeper and perhaps quite different fundamental problem. (d) To be successful parents, use communication skills to get to the heart of the matter and keep your relations in good standing.

2. (a) For a child, learning takes a long time. (b) There are some quick bursts in learning and some periods of which progress is slow. (c) A child begins to speak sometimes around his or her first birthday. (d) By three, children know about 900 words and can use them in three- and four-word sentences.

3. (a) Products made from the new plastic include bottles used to hold shampoos or detergents. (b) When these are thrown away, they may be recycled, in other words, used again in the same form. (c) However, they may also be disposed in landfill sites, in which case, unlike current plastics, they are digested by bacteria in the soil and break down. (d) The oxidation products from the landfill sites and from other discarded bottles which have been burnt or have biodegraded are released slowly into the atmosphere.

4. (a) Ozone smog is created when carbon dioxide reacts with sunlight. (b) The result is smog-the air pollution that we can see and smell. (c) Too much ozone smog gives us headaches and makes difficult breathing. (d) One way to reduce ozone smog is to start using cleaner means of transportation.

5. (a) The giant panda bear is a favorite of children and animal-lovers throughout the world. (b) For many people, it also is symbolic of the sad situation for many other kinds of animals. (c) Though well known and loved, the panda is slowly dying out. (d) At present, there are only about 1,230 wild pandas leaving in the world.

◉ 신앙 명언

오직 하나님만이 아픈 마음의 공허함을 채울 수 있다.
Only God can fill the emptiness of an aching heart.

◉ 신앙 명언

우리 삶 가운데 하나님이 역사하심으로 인해 우리 가슴에 새 노래가 있다.
God's work in our life puts a new song in our heart.

◉ 신앙 명언

삶의 경주를 힘차게 끝마치기 위해서는 훈련이 필요하다.
In the race of life, it takes discipline to finish strong.

◉ 신앙 명언

하나님의 사랑이 닿지 않는 사람은 한 사람도 없다.
No one is beyond the reach of God's love

실력문제 3회

* 다음 글에서 문법상 틀리거나 어색한 부분을 고르시오.

1. (a) Dioxin, like plutonium, is an extremely poisonous substance. (b) An amount of either chemicals about the size of your fist is enough to kill all the people in the world. (c) The difference is that plutonium is still relatively rare, difficult to isolate, and well regulate. (d) On the other hand, Dioxin is found in many garden chemicals and easy to misuse.

2. (a) Mario slowly approached the doorway where Carmen stood. (b) His deliberate steps matched the pounding of the heart. (c) Hie eyes, flashing fire, fixed on her. (d) He stepped in front of her, her lips slightly opening as if he had something to say.

3. (a) Light travels very fast. (b) In thunderstorms we see a flash of lightening before we hear the thunder caused by the flash. (c) The light from the lightening reaches to us in almost no time at all. (d) It may take several seconds for the sound of the thunder to reach us.

4. (a) Video games have become an essential part of kid's life these days. (b) However, when it comes to the effects of video games on children, there is a double standard in the industry. (c) Publishers often trumpet educational games that help develop kid's learning skills. (d) Yet they discount arguments that violent games can have bad influence on behavior and attitude.

5. (a) Every people has his own way of gambling, and poker is an American tradition. (b) It is a card game that calls for skill, luck and a willingness of taking chances. (c) It was considered an important part of life in the wild west. (d) Many movies show tense conflicts or showdowns between cowboys at the poker table before a gunfight starts.

실력문제 4회

* 다음 글에서 문법상 틀리거나 어색한 부분을 고르시오.

1. (a) A mother mouse and her baby were running across a floor when they heard a noise, which a cat produced. (b) The mother mouse and her baby were frightened, but they stood still, and the mother called out in her loudest voice: "Bow Wow!" (c) The cat ran away. (d) Then the mother mouse turned to her baby and said, "Now, do you see, my child, how important is a second language?"

2. (a) Some salmon travel thousands of kilometers from the river where they were born. (b) Scientists think that salmon navigate in the sea by somehow sensing the magnetic field of the earth and the currents of the ocean. (c) They know that most salmon which they were hatched. (d) After reaching the coast, the salmon apparently remember the odor of their home stream and follow this scent.

3. (a) Hermes gave to a particularly pious worshipper a goose that laid golden eggs. (b) But the man was too impatient a man to wait for wealth to come in driblets, and thinking that the bird's inside must be solid gold he made haste to kill it. (c) Not only were his hopes disappointed, but he got no more golden eggs. (d) Because he found nothing in the goose but ordinary flesh and flood.

4. (a) Cartoons in the West have been associated with political and social matters for many years. (b) In wartime, for example, they proved to be an excellent way of spreading propaganda. (c) Nowadays cartoons are often used to make short, sharp comments on politics and government as well as on a variety of social matter. (d) In this way, the modern cartoon has become a very powerful force in influencing people in Europe and the United States.

5. (a) Following is the story of a movie that can make you understand what it was like to be a boy in a small U. S. town in the fifties. (b) One summer day four boys go off into the forest to look for another boy who has been missing for several days. (c) Through their exciting trip, they work together to help each other. (d) Their two-days trip leaves each of them with special memories.

◎ 표현연구
화를 내지 마.
Don't fly off the handle. Don't hit the ceiling.
Don't raise the roof. Don't blow a gasket.
Don't blow up. Don't lose your temper.

◎ 신앙 명언
예수님께서 우리를 걱정해 주시는지 의심이 가면 그의 눈물을 기억하라.
If you doubt that Jesus cares, remember His tears.

◎ 신앙 명언
회개는 하나님과 동행하는 길을 열어 놓는다.
Repentance keeps the way clear in our walk with God.

◎ 신앙 명언
우리가 하나님의 능력에 의지할 때 우리의 약점은 축복이 된다.
Our weakness is a blessing when we lean God's strength.

◎ 신앙 명언
적을 굴복시키는 가장 확실한 방법은 그를 친구로 만드는 것이다.
The best way to destroy your enemy is to make him your friend.

2. 어휘 - Part 1

실력문제 1회

* 다음 대화문의 빈칸에 들어갈 가장 적절한 표현을 고르시오.

1. A: What are we supposed to do for the next class?
   B: I'd like you to _____ over what's been covered so far.
   (a) go (b) move (c) turn (d) bring

2. A: Hello, May I speak to Judy?
   B: Please _____ for a minute. She'll be on the phone shortly.
   (a) hang loose (b) hang up (c) hang on (d) hang out

3. A: Harris, you look terrible. What's wrong?
   B: I've been sleeping less than four hours everyday this past week because I have four exams today and tomorrow. I feel like I'm on the _____ of a breakdown.
   (a) boundary (b) verge (c) limit (d) border

4. A: I heard that you've changed your job again.
   B: I just don't like to _____ to the same routine forever.
   (a) remain (b) stick (c) hold (d) linger

5. A: Did you ever meet her?
   B: I'm sure I've met her somewhere before, but I can't quite _____ her.
   (a) locate (b) remind (c) place (d) forget

6. A: What are you talking about? I don't get it.
   B: I've been talking for almost an hour and you still don't _____?
   (a) remember (b) trust me (c) have a say (d) get the picture

7. A: Can you fix my television?
   B: No, I don't have the _____ idea how to fix it.
   (a) shortest   (b) smallest   (c) tiniest   (d) slightest

8. A: What makes you so exciting?
   B: If I can write a clever verse about Velvety Soap, I'll win 5,000 dollars. Somehow, _____, I'm going to win.
   (a) as the crow flies   (b) by hook or by crook
   (c) up in the air   (d) down in the bumps

9. A: Did you pick up my coat from the dry cleaner?
   B: I'm sorry I forgot. It just _____ my mind.
   (a) slid   (b) split   (c) slipped   (d) shifted

10. A: What's the name of that song?
    B: I should know it. It's on the _____ of my tongue.
    (a) bottom   (b) back   (c) side   (d) tip

◉ 신앙 명언
인생의 폭풍우를 이기려면 만세 반석에 정박해야 한다.
To survive the storms of life, be anchored to the Rock of Ages.

◉ 신앙 명언
인간의 영혼은 용기를 주는 말로 인해 새로운 희망을 얻는다.
The human spirit can gain new hope
              from an encouraging word.

◉ 신앙 명언
네 정성을 다 쏟을 때 네 적은 것이 엄청난 것이 된다.
Your little is a lot when you give your all.

실력문제 2회

* 다음 대화문의 빈칸에 들어갈 가장 적절한 표현을 고르시오.

1. A: Can you help me _____ my new stereo system?
   B: Sure. That's easy for me.
   (a) build up   (b) take up   (c) hook up   (d) make up

2. A: Do you have to pick your friend up from work?
   B: Yes, again. I'm _____ up with going downtown every afternoon.
   (a) shut   (b) fed   (c) heated   (d) frozen

3. A: Did you hear that Tom and Judy had an argument?
   B: Really? they must have been _____ about something.
   (a) relieved   (b) thrilled   (c) upset   (d) appreciative

4. A: Why did you raise that question during the discussion?
   B: I didn't _____ the question. John did.
   (a) piece together   (b) set up   (c) bring up   (d) hustle out

5. A: How do you feel about coming back to work after two years' leave?
   B: I can't quite get into the _____ of it now, but I'm sure I'll be okay soon.
   (a) swing   (b) hang   (c) sling   (d) fall

6. A: I noticed nobody talks to Williams these days. What's that?
   B: Well, she kind of gets on everyone's _____.
   (a) shoulders   (b) minds   (c) ears   (d) nerves

7. A: What are we going to do about our charity program?
   B: Let's keep the ball _____. We're off to a good start, but we still need to collect more money.

(a) rolling   (b) bouncing   (c) throwing   (d) swinging

8. A: You look _____! What makes you depressed?
   B: Well...well, you know... I got fired yesterday.
   (a) white   (b) blue   (c) red   (d) yellow

9. A: Could you lend me one hundred dollars?
   B: I'm sorry, but I'm _____, too.
   (a) out   (b) crashed   (c) broke   (d) broken

10. A: Did you hear about the twenty-year-old year actress who married a sixty-year-old millionaire?
    B: Really? I bet she's a gold _____.
    (a) miner   (b) finder   (c) searcher   (d) digger

◎ 표현연구

인생에 성공하려면 참고 견디어야 해.
To succeed in life, you have to grin and bear it.

◎ 표현연구

그는 돈이 많다.
He has money to burn.
He has deep pocket.
He's rolling in dough.

◎ 표현연구

존은 보통 가난한 자들과 격이 없이 지낸다.
John usually rubs shoulders with the poor.

◎ 표현연구

전력을 다해라 그렇지 않으면 해고될 거야.
Buckle down or you'll be fired.

실력문제 3회

* 다음 대화문의 빈칸에 들어갈 가장 적절한 표현을 고르시오.

1. A: The manager is so _____.
   B: Yes. You have to give the answers he likes.
     (a) lenient   (b) picky   (c) upset   (d) humdrum

2. A: We've been discussing the issues for two hours.
   B: Yeah, It's getting late. Let's _____ it up for today.
     (a) add   (b) wrap   (c) call   (d) draw up

3. A: Do you think Jane can get a scholarship to Yale?
   B: She doesn't _____ a chance.
     (a) give me   (b) stand   (c) bring   (d) dismiss

4. A: Could you please _____ the noise down? I'm trying to relax.
   B: Sorry, I didn't realize we were talking so loud.
     (a) shut   (b) turn   (c) put   (d) hold

5. A: Have you heard Mr. Park was arrested for sexual assault?
   B: Of course. I know all the _____ of the case.
     (a) part and parcel   (b) odds and ends
     (c) give and take   (d) ins and outs

6. A: I can solve your problems.
   B: It's none of your business. Don't _____ your nose into my business.
     (a) hold   (b) jam   (c) pull   (d) poke

7. A: Cathy was showing off her _____ watch.
   B: Yeah. But it looked like the original.
     (a) authentic   (b) genuine   (c) counterfeit   (d) realistic

8. A: I'm going to my class reunion tonight.
   B: Class reunions are not my _____.
   (a) duck soup (b) cup of tea (c) rotten egg (d) order of the day

9. A: My car is almost out of gas.
   B: Let's make a U-turn here. I _____ a gas station one block back.
   (a) dropped (b) spotted (c) checked (d) traded

10. A: I'd like to send this package to the United Kingdom.
    B: Do you want to send it by airmail or _____ mail?
    (a) land (b) sea (c) surface (d) shipping

◉ 신앙 명언
곤경은 진정한 우정의 시금석이다.
Adversity is the test of true friendship.

◉ 신앙 명언
하나님께서 내미시는 징계의 손은 사랑의 손이다.
God's hand of discipline is a hand of love.

◉ 신앙 명언
어제의 그늘 속에 살지 말고 오늘의 빛과 내일의 희망 속에 걸어가라.
Instead of living in the shadows of yesterday,
walk in the light of today and the hope of tomorrow.

실력문제 4회

* 다음 대화문의 빈칸에 들어갈 가장 적절한 표현을 고르시오.

1. A: I heard that Roentgen _____ on his great discovery of X-rays quite by accident.
   B: You are such a well-informed person.
   (a) invented   (b) stumbled   (c) found   (d) looked

2. A: A new Japanese restaurant has just opened across the theatre.
   B: I could go _____ some Japanese food. Let's go there.
   (a) after   (b) by   (c) down   (d) for

3. A: My car didn't start. I had to walk home from the store.
   B: That's a _____ in the neck.
   (a) pain   (b) apple   (c) bother   (d) problem

4. A: How's Michael doing?
   B: He's fine. These days, he's really _____ on computer games.
   (a) booked   (b) held   (c) hooked   (d) reserved

5. A: Are you ready for the test tomorrow?
   B: No, I've got _____ in my stomach.
   (a) nerve   (b) anxiety   (c) butterflies   (d) bugs

6. A: I knew that England would beat Indonesia easily.
   B: Yes, the result of the game seemed to be _____.
   (a) out of contact   (b) fallen behind   (c) cut and dried   (d) taken up

7. A: It's so hot.
   B: Yeah, a cold water would really hit the _____.
   (a) road   (b) hay   (c) ceiling   (d) spot

8. A: Mr. Smith, Could you come to my house for dinner tomorrow

evening?

B: I'd love to, but I'm sorry I have a previous engagement. Will you give me a _____?

(a) break   (b) rain check   (c) session   (d) visitation

9. A: Your son's party caused enormous damage.

B: Don't get excited. I'll _____ all expenses.

(a) bill   (b) cover   (c) take   (d) get

10. A: Did you make an appointment?

B: I didn't know I needed one. She doesn't take _____?

(a) walk-ins   (b) interviews   (c) makeovers   (d) impromptu

---

◉ 이디엄

abide by 지키다
abound in ⋯이 풍부하다
account for 설명하다, ⋯의 원인이 되다, ⋯의 비율을 차지하다
adhere to ⋯에 들러붙다, ⋯을 고수하다
allow for ⋯을 고려하다
answer for 책임지다
ask for(something) 자초하다, 자업자득이다
ask out 남을 불러내다
ask (someone) in 초대하다
attend on 시중들다
attend to ⋯에 주의하다

어휘 - Part II

실력문제 1회

* 다음 글의 빈칸에 들어갈 가장 적절한 표현을 고르시오.

1. Many movie stars are having _____ surgery in order to look younger.
   (a) aesthetic   (b) plastic   (c) artistic   (d) heart

2. Please don't _____ in front of the children. I don't want them to learn such words.
   (a) speak   (b) exclaim   (c) protest   (d) swear

3. Sigmund Freud _____ that we all have a death instinct as well as a life instinct.
   (a) postulate   (b) proscribed   (c) preempted   (d) recapitulated

4. He _____ a lot and soaked his shirt with sweat after the excessive workout.
   (a) perspired   (b) respired   (c) expired   (d) inspired

5. Kimchi is a Korean traditional _____ cabbage that is very spicy.
   (a) fermented   (b) famished   (c) feeble   (d) grumpy

6. The detective _____ through old magazines to find more information about the suspect.
   (a) combed   (b) went   (c) got   (d) put

7. When Ann told Father the name of the new teacher, it _____ a bell, and Father said, "James Carson!"
   (a) pealed   (b) rang   (c) chimed   (d) tolled

8. The article claims that there is an actual decline in the tribe's per

capita protein ration as a result of the _____ of animal resources.

(a) depletion   (b) depiction   (c) deposition   (d) depreciation

9. To avoid contamination, surgeons _____ wash their hands before starting each operation.

(a) reluctantly   (b) scrupulously   (c) abjectly   (d) silently

10. Many modern advertisements are meant to _____ to the emotions of potential customers.

(a) appeal   (b) attest   (c) attribute   (d) addict

◉ 이디엄

back out 손을 떼다, 취소하다
back up 후원하다, 복사본을 뜨다, 뒤로 물러서다
beef up 강화하다
bear out 증명하다
black out 등화관제를 하다, 의식[시력]을 잃다
boil down to 도달하다, 결국 …이 되다
break down 고장나다, 쇠약해지다, 효력을 잃다
break out 갑자기 발생하다, 덮이다, 탈출하다
bring out 나타내다, 출판하다, 생산하다
bring up 기르다, 주의를 환기시키다
brush up on 공부를 다시 시작하다, 복습하다
buy it …을 택하다, …에 찬성하다
buy out 돈으로 사다, 매수하다

실력문제 2회

* 다음 글의 빈칸에 들어갈 가장 적절한 표현을 고르시오.

1. Members of the hiring committee expressed their _____ support during Monday's meeting for promoting Harrison to manager of Human Resources.
   (a) unanimous   (b) associated   (c) connected   (d) similar

2. Due to a substantial increase in employee _____, the company's gross earnings have risen tremendously, and all staff members will receive raises.
   (a) pursuance   (b) provocation   (c) productivity   (d) prosecution

3. The bus was so _____ with passengers that it was impossible for us to squeeze on board.
   (a) heavy   (b) covered   (c) busy   (d) packed

4. Our team was so good that we _____ three major prizes.
   (a) stole
   (b) were not even considered for
   (c) barely won
   (d) walked away with

5. The Internet, forerunner of a(an) _____ global web of digital communications, combines aspects of tele-communications and broadcasting.
   (a) assiduous   (b) superficial   (c) ubiquitous   (d) gregarious

6. Climbing up the mountain was so _____ that we had to take a long rest before starting down.
   (a) languid   (b) fastidious   (c) laborious   (d) insolent

7. Many American heroes are _____ in Arlington National Cemetery.
   (a) excavated   (b) torched   (c) defiled   (d) interred

8. Most undergraduates take four years to earn a degree, but some achieve it sooner by attending summer _____.
   (a) secession   (b) section   (c) sessions   (d) succession

9. Some psychologists claim it is not healthy to _____ one's emotions too much.
   (a) reprove   (b) reprehend   (c) repress   (d) reprieve

10. The pioneers had trouble growing crops in the _____ desert lands.
    (a) parched   (b) arable   (c) fertile   (d) aqueous

◎ 이디엄

call down 꾸짖다 요구하다,
call for 방문하다, 데리러 가다
carry out 실행하다
catch on 인기를 얻다, 이해하다
cheer up 격려하다, 기운을 내다
come by 획득하다, 방문하다
come off …이 되다, 성공하다, (단추가)떨어지다
come out 나오다, 지워지다, 드러나다
come up with 제안하다, 공급하다, 따라 잡다
cover for 대신해 주다
cut it rather fine 바싹 줄이다
cut no ice 아무 효과도 없다
cut short 짧게 하다, 간단히 말하다, 가로막다

실력문제 3회

* 다음 글의 빈칸에 들어갈 가장 적절한 표현을 고르시오.

1. They are supposed to _____ their things and move to another city before long.
   (a) pack   (b) rack   (c) sack   (d) lack

2. If you will put yourself in the customer's _____ , you may realize why the thing isn't selling.
   (a) moods   (b) mouth   (c) framework   (d) shoes

3. _____ extreme market fluctuations, I can assure you that this investment plan will help you build a safe yet profitable retirement fund.
   (a) Bar   (b) To bar   (c) Barring   (d) Barred

4. In accordance with a recently passed law, there will be a sales tax of five percent levied _____ all hotel rooms in this state as of January 1.
   (a) in   (b) on   (c) with   (d) over

5. The local paper reported this morning that Jean Stafford has _____ recalled a large shipment of its product, due to fears of contamination.
   (a) volubly   (b) visually   (c) voluntarily   (d) voraciously

6. Given her impulsive nature, Jane was inclined to come up with ideas _____.
   (a) still   (b) simultaneously   (c) hardly   (d) spontaneously

7. Arturo Toscanini once _____ a famous opera singer with a sarcastic remark that there were for him no stars except those in

the heavens.
(a) sided   (b) favored   (c) cowed   (d) screened

8. Please _____ receipt of this document by signing the enclosed form.
(a) send   (b) acknowledge   (c) know   (d) knowledge

9. Ms. Jane's suggestion motivated us to _____ our research into areas we previously had ignored.
(a) multiply   (b) dictate   (c) impress   (d) broaden

10. After the project was finished, she put _____ a transfer to the main office.
(a) in for   (b) up with   (c) back in   (d) over to

◉ 이디엄

dawn on 생각이 떠오르다
die down 사라져 버리다, 가라앉다
do a snow job 속이다
do up 손질하다, 고치다, 정돈하다
draw the line 한계를 정하다
dress down 호되게 꾸짖다, 때리다
drive a hard bargain 싼 값으로 사거나 팔다
drop out 낙오하다, 떠나다, 철수하다
dwell on 곰곰이 생각하다

실력문제 4회

* 다음 글의 빈칸에 가장 적절한 표현을 고르시오.

1. You will have to make a large _____ into your savings account to improve your credit record at this bank.
   (a) withdrawal   (b) contribution   (c) accumulation   (d) deposit

2. E-mail is virtually a(n) _____ method of getting information from one place to another at great speed.
   (a) shatterproof   (b) airproof   (c) foolproof   (d) childproof

3. I was amazed that she was _____ so soon after her accident.
   (a) free and easy   (b) neck and neck
   (c) up and about   (d) on pins and needles

4. The functions of the hands, eyes, and brain are so _____ that using the hands during early childhood helps to promote the child's entire perceptual development.
   (a) unalterable   (b) enigmatic   (c) intertwined   (d) regulated

5. _____ of harmful substances into the atmosphere is causing the protective ozone later to become depleted.
   (a) Prediction   (b) Preservation   (c) Trepidation   (d) Precipitation

6. If you don't _____ with the local traffic regulations, you may be fined or even jailed for up to a month.
   (a) go along   (b) obey   (c) comply   (d) seek

7. While I was waiting for coffee, the head waiter moved near to me bearing a large basket full of huge _____ peaches.
   (a) mouth-watering   (b) mind-boggling
   (c) eye-opening   (d) breath-taking

8. As I have already indicated, negotiation is not _____ process; there are levels and degrees of negotiation and in fact it is a continuum.
   (a) an ongoing
   (b) a wining-and-dining
   (c) a mud-slinging
   (d) an all-or-nothing

9. The world is not a get-rich-quick place; the traditional values of hard work and honesty still _____ in the long run.
   (a) luck out   (b) make do   (c) pay off   (d) hit the jackpot

10. In light of new evidence in this case, I think we can now _____ the list of suspects.
    (a) narrow down   (b) cut down   (c) cut out   (d) narrow out

◎ 이디엄

eat out 외식하다
egg (someone) on 다그치다, 부추기다, 선동하다
end up …로 끝내다
face down 용감히 맞서다
face the music 응보를 달게 받다
face up to 받아들이다
fall out 싸우다, 사이가 나쁘다
fall through 실패하다, 수포로 돌아가다
feed someone a line 속이다, 기만하다
feel for 동정하다, 더듬다
figure out 이해하다, 계산하다
fill out 채우다, 기입하다, 살찌다
freak out 정신을 잃다

3. 독해 - Part I

실력문제 1회

* 다음 글을 읽고 빈칸에 들어갈 가장 적절한 것을 고르시오.

1. Many people realize that hospitals are not all alike, but most believe the differences are a matter of size and overall quality. In fact, a hospital that excels in coronary bypass surgery may not be the best choice for cancer treatment. Most hospitals are not staffed or equipped to perform all procedures equally well. As with everything else in life, _____, and skills in medical procedures and surgery improve when they are done by experts who perform them frequently.

   (a) honesty is the best policy   (b) strike iron while it is hot
   (c) practice makes perfect   (d) actions speak louder than words

2. When people go online they are too trusting and native when it comes to personal information. However, they _____ online. Most share information that they would never give someone they met casually off-line. Would you tell the person standing next to you in the grocery store check-out line your address and phone number? Of course not, but it's no different than doing so in a chat room, often unknowingly.

   (a) can enjoy chatting with people
   (b) are more vulnerable than most realize
   (c) don't have to pay for the information they find
   (d) are less careful in expressing their opinions

3. Matter is made up of particles which are too small to see. The behavior of a collection of particles distinguishes one state of matter from another. Matter in the solid state has a definite, unchanging shape.

Matter in the liquid state has no definite shape and an unchanging volume. Matter in the gaseous state has neither definite shape nor definite volume. Matter can be converted from one state to another _____. If liquid water, for example, is cooled to its freezing point, it becomes a solid and if liquid water is heated, it becomes steam.

(a) in the state of liquid
(b) with the help of the particles
(c) by changing its temperature
(d) under a lot of pressure from outside

4. Women employees make real sacrifices and take great risks when they have children. In 82% of work situations where there is no labor union representation, pregnant workers are routinely fired. Others _____ when they come back to work after childbirth, losing seniority. Large numbers of new mothers fail to find affordable child care and are forced to take marginal jobs with short hours close to home.

(a) find it difficult to keep their position
(b) are redefined as new hires
(c) take a long time to get promoted
(d) are forced to resign

5. Divorce is never an easy issue, especially _____. Children caught in the middle of a divorce often need reassurance that despite the differences between Mom and Dad, both of their parents still love them. Children often assume that their parents will always stay together. When that sense of continuity is shaken, they fear what will happen to them, and who will take care of them. Children need to know that issues pertaining to their health, education, and shelter will be made with their best interest at heart. The most important thing you can do for your children it to tell them over and over that the divorce is between the two

parents who are having difficulties with each other, not between parents and children.

(a) if both parties do not agree to it
(b) once the separation period is over
(c) when children are involved
(d) since its procedures have become complicated

6. As a psychiatrist working with Vietnam veterans who suffer from severe Post-Traumatic Stress Disorder, I have observed how that unhealed combat trauma disables the basic social and cognitive capacities required for democratic participation. Loss of their participation in the democratic process is sad, but for Vietnam combat veterans with PTSD representing just around one-thousandth of the current American population, _____. But what would happen in a democracy where every citizen was a soldier or former soldier and warfare was more of less constant, as was the case in ancient Athens?

(a) it hardly threatens the process itself
(b) American democracy is seriously maimed by the loss
(c) politicians have been characteristically unmindful of it
(d) it is unfair for them to be left out

7. Now that I have a backpack, I can't believe I didn't get one ages ago! I got a planner from a former job, so it serves as a wallet, datebook, address book, and notepad. It's ok, but heavy. Don't know if I'll hang on to it when the year is over. I also always have a book, my work ID badge and office key, a small makeup case, and a cell phone. It comes in so handy when I'm doing errands and I can stuff all my purchases in it. _____.

(a) I will enjoy shopping again.
(b) And my hands are free!

(c) And it's incredibly light!
(d) Planners are really handy.

8. The earth's protective ozone layer will hit its all-time thinnest by 2000 or 2001, the World Meteorological Organization said Monday. Despite forecasts that international measures to halt the decline will help the layer improve by the middle of the next century, the ozone layer is at its most _____ stage now and things will get worse before they get any better, the WMO said. The ozone layer is protective fragile shield of gas that absorbs the harmful ultraviolet rays of sun but has been increasingly pierced by holes caused by man-made chemicals. The holes are blamed for causing skin cancer.

(a) inactive   (b) sophisticated   (c) strengthened   (d) vulnerable

9. In the late 19th century, defenders of business eagerly embraced the doctrine of Social Darwinism, which loosely adapted Charles Darwin's theory of "the origin of species" to the principles of "laissez." Human society had evolved naturally, the Social Darwinists reasoned, and any interference with existing institutions would only hold back progress and aid the weak. In a free society operating according to the principle of survival of the fittest, power would flow naturally to _____. Property holding and acquisition were therefore sacred rights, and wealth was a mark of well-deserved power and responsibility.

(a) the most progressive   (b) the most capable
(c) the most greedy   (d) the most reasonable

10. Testing language has traditionally taken the form of testing knowledge about language, usually the testing of knowledge of vocabulary and grammar. However, there is much more to being able to use language than knowledge about it. Dell Hymes proposed the concept of communicative competence. In communicative competence, he included not only the ability

to form correct sentences, but also the ability to use them at appropriate times. Since Hymes first proposed the idea in the early 1970's, it has been expanded considerably, and various types of competences have been proposed. However, the basic idea of communicative competence remains _____, both receptively and productively, in real situations.

(a) to be defined   (b) the ability to use language appropriately
(c) the same as ever   (d) difficult for students and teachers

> ◎ 이디엄
>
> get a head start 보다 일찍 시작하다
> get a kick out of 즐기다
> get a rise out of someone 놀리다, 약 올리다
> get down to …에 착수하다
> get even with 보복하다
> get into the swing of things 새로운 환경에 적응하다
> get it through one's head 이해하다, 믿다
> get the better of …을 이기다, 속이다
> give a wide berth to 피하다, 멀리하다
> give in 제출하다, 굴복하다, 무너지다
> go by 믿다, 의존하다
> go in for 참여하다, 즐기다
> go off the deep end 자제력을 잃다
> go through 겪다, 경험하다, 통과하다
> go under 굴복하다, 지다

실력문제 2회

1. Oversupplies of crude oil and recession fears sent world market prices to their lowest level in two years. Officials of the Organization of Petroleum Exporting Countries said they likely would vote _____ at their November 10 meeting, by cutting production by a million barrels a day. But the cartel's ability to stop the free fall is limited, since big non-OPEC producers Mexico, Russia, and Norway refuse to reduce exports.

    (a) to stop the energy crisis   (b) to limit their demand
    (c) to shore up prices   (d) to cut down product cost

2. Several factors influence the justice system's treatment of criminals. For one thing, the sex of offenders affects the severity of sentences. A woman is less likely to receive the death penalty than a man. Also, the court is more _____ to send a mother to prison than a father. Another factor in the treatment of offenders is their race. Nonwhites are awarded parole and probation less often. Finally, the age of offenders is considered in sentencing. Young offenders are given special treatment. And the elderly are given more lenient sentences.

    (a) willing   (b) reluctant   (c) loathsome   (d) favorable

3. After the endless rounds of holiday parties, with those ubiquitous canapes, dips and chips, lavish entrees and spectacular desserts, it's time to get back to a healthier way of eating. Even those who haven't overindulged will enjoy these simple, light meals. Luckily, healthy doesn't have to mean dull. The entrees we feature this month are as sustaining and delicious as they are imaginative, offering wonderful flavor with a minimum of fat. And because all the recipes are quick to prepare, they'll _____.

(a) gratify the palate of even the pickiest eaters
(b) help every type of weight watcher
(c) fit into the busiest of weekday schedules
(d) be of great help to those on a prescribed diet

4. In the 1950's and 1960's, when art was still considered a frivolous activity by Koreans struggling just to make ends meet, the Bank of Korea decided to support selected artists by purchasing their works. This was a rare move for a financial institute and it won great praise from the art community. _____, BOK's collection also grew, and now it boasts some 1800 artworks. Over 70 of these works will be presented at the Duksu Palace branch of the National Museum of Contemporary Art next month.

(a) When time passes and the economy improves
(b) While time passes and the economy improves
(c) As time passed and the economy improved
(d) As far as time and the economy are concerned

5. An official said the numbers show that "substantial progress" has been made in the fight against drunk driving. The agency listed several factors that contributed to the dramatic decline in drunk driving deaths. These factors included an increase in the legal drinking age, improved law enforcement, and increased public awareness of the problems _____ drinking and driving.

(a) associated with   (b) compared with
(c) disconnected to   (d) distinguished from

6. Cancer patients are occasionally seen in acupuncture clinics, and some of them respond favorably either to acupuncture or herbal treatment. Most patients, however, only resort to acupuncture at a late stage in their disease, and usually out of desperation. The majority of

these patients are above fifty and at a critical stage of their disease. Partly because of this, cancer patients who benefit from treatment usually experience only symptomatic relief, which, though very significant in some cases, is not enough to arrest or reverse the debilitation of the cancer. However, the efficacy of acupuncture treatment is quite amazing _____.

(a) in the case of older patients
(b) at the early stages of cancer
(c) in the face of other alternative treatments
(d) in spite of strong support

7. Some recent scientific, economic, and political research suggests that the curves for food demand and food supply will cross in a maximum of 60 years. By then, man's overpopulation, increasing pollution, and the diminishing food supply could _____.

(a) help man avoid extinction   (b) ensure man's survival
(c) make astounding achievements   (d) threaten to end human life

8. Every feeling of hardship is inseparable from the desire to escape from it; every idea of pleasure from the desire to enjoy it. All desires imply a want, and all wants are painful; hence our wretchedness consists in the disproportion between our desires and our powers. A conscious being _____ would be perfectly happy.

(a) who does not feel any hardship
(b) whose needs exceed his strength
(c) whose powers were equal to his desires
(d) whose desires were less than his powers

9. Analogy contributes to modern science by providing clues that may illuminate later discoveries, but analogy is also dangerous unless it is

applied with caution. It was once thought to provide positive demonstration of a fact. This led to many misleading ideas and false theories. However it seems clear and inviting, analogy _____.

(a) is really vague and murky
(b) never constitutes proof
(c) is not apt to lead to absurd results
(d) can never have value for an objective scientist

10. Dear Mr. Williams,

Dear We appreciate all of your hard work and great customer service. We have just been approved for our home mortgage that until recently was just a dream. It is nice knowing I do not have to be scared when dealing with credit issues. I also want to thank you for taking the time to teach us the pitfalls of the credit world. I can now _____ rather than just hope I am getting the best deal. We will make sure to recommend you to anyone who asks about your services.

(a) make an educated choice
(b) keep on with my research
(c) make my dream come true
(d) learn to be happy with what I have

◎ 이디엄

hand in 제출하다
hang in (there) 참고 견디다, 포기하지 않다
have an axe to grind 다른 속셈이 있다
have a way with …을 다루는 법을 알고 있다
have it in for …에게 원한을 품다
have words with …와 언쟁하다
head off 가로막다, 저지하다

실력문제 3회

1. The goal of psychoanalytic treatment itself has been defined as a simultaneous increase in the mobility of the id, in the tolerance of the superego, and in the synthesizing power of the ego. To the last point we add the suggestion that the analysis of the ego should include that of the individual's ego identity in relation to the historical changes which dominated his childhood milieu. For the individual's mastery over his neurosis begins when he is put in a position to accept the historical necessity which made him what he is. The individual feels free when he can choose to identify with his own ego identity and when he learns to apply that which is given to that which must be done. Only then can he derive ego strength from the coincidence of his one and life cycle with _____.

(a) the synthesizing power of the ego
(b) particular segments of human history
(c) a complete analysis of historical necessity
(d) the combination of the id and the superego

2. A surprisingly large number of people believe that English poses danger to traditional languages throughout the core English-speaking countries. This belief is almost comically inaccurate when one considers _____ Hindi-Urdu, Arabic, and Spanish, and when one considers the fact that the percentage of native speakers of English in the world's population has been shrinking for decades, and looks certain to shrink for decades more before leveling out.

(a) the enormous diversity of traditional languages such as
(b) the prodigious growth of languages like
(c) the most endangered tribal languages
(d) the obsessive and misinformed attention to

3. Fatness in America is a catastrophe. Obesity may knock tobacco out of the top spot as the leading cause of preventable deaths. _____ this, there should be an anti-fat rampage, targeting schools and discussing fast food. Specifically, schools should provide healthier food choices and make phys-ed classes mandatory for every grade. Moreover, there should be more walking trails in cities, and bosses should give their employees a chance to use them on company time.

(a) To encourage (b) To prevent
(c) To permit   (d) To prohibit

4. Perhaps the most interesting finding appeared in a recent study of _____ on a large number of ordinary people. While keeping a dog or cat as a pet, they had fewer health problems such as colds, headaches and stomachaches than they had before. Some doctors believe that the reason for this that the reduction in stress produced by pets strengthens the body's immune system through the action of chemicals released in the brain.

(a) the statistics of pet animals
(b) the strengths of having a pet
(c) the results of having a pet
(d) the effects of having a pet

5. Caesarian deliveries have risen so dramatically in the last decade that the procedure has stirred a nationwide medical controversy. Consumer groups charge that many C-sections are unnecessary and done to fit the convenience of the obstetrician's schedule. Physicians argue that wider use of Caesarians has helped lower maternal and _____ death rates in high-risk pregnancies.

(a) paternal   (b) infant   (c) adolescent   (d) untimely

6. By a strange combination of generosity and greed man protects the

weak in asylums and kills the strong in wars. By a strange combination of ingenuity and impotence he multiplies the basic necessities of life far beyond any possible need only to let millions _____ and unclothed for lack of efficient distribution.

(a) fall behind   (b) find shelter   (c) go hungry   (d) be happy

7. Those of us who have been occupied with biographies, as readers or as writers, know that to leave a great man and to face ourselves again, can give us something of a chill. But there are always quotations - that echo forever memorable sentences which assure the great man's immortality, and ours. _____, as we apply some Jeffersonian rhetoric to certain psychological insights of our day, this is how Jeffersonian elucidates this notion: "The times in which I have lived, and the scene is which I have been engaged, have required me to keep the mind too much in action to have leisure to study minutely its laws of action."

(a) In addition   (b) All together
(c) For example   (d) Thus increasingly

8. The patent system works best not for the inventor, but for a rich company that has the money to get good patent lawyers and fund litigation to protect a monopoly. It is not the person with a good idea who wins but _____. The game is further rigged by the fact that patent processing is not a sequential process, but high-speed race in which the well-connected and more aggressive win.

(a) the strong, muscular and stupid
(b) the clever, fast and rich
(c) the mean, cruel and wild
(d) the smart, neat and gentle

9. A barbarian is one who is crude, uncivilized, or lacking in culture. The ancient Greeks considered themselves far more civilized and advanced than any other peoples in the ancient world. To the Greeks, a barbarian was anyone who _____.

    (a) spoke Greek   (b) was not Greek
    (c) invaded Rome   (d) broke the law

10. In choosing a vacation spot, many of us look for a place that is quiet. But can you imagine a world without sounds? A famous explorer spent several weeks in Antarctica completely alone and away from all human sounds. Writing about the experience later, the explorer said that nothing was missed so much as the voices of friends and other familiar sounds. Such an experience gives one some insight into the _____.

    (a) need for solitude   (b) frozen countries
    (c) world of the deaf   (d) life of Eskimos

◎ 이디엄

hit on 우연히 만나다, 찾아내다
hit the books 학교 숙제를 하다, 예습하다
hit the nail on the head 핵심을 찌르다
hold good 유효하다
hold on 기다리다, 붙잡다, 계속하다
hold out 내밀다, 저항하다
hold over 계속하다, 연기하다

실력문제 4회

1. The constructivist theorists have heavily influenced contemporary educational practices. They construct the learning based on each student's perspective toward the learning, formulating the teaching and knowledge to be learned in a fashion relevant to the learner. In other words, each learner approaches the learning however he/she wants to. The constructivist theories imply that knowledge is constructed to accommodate the person. In contrast, _____ that there are universal truths out there and it's up to the learners to figure it out, to be enlightened.

   (a) the traditional educational practices reject the idea
   (b) contemporary learning theory contends
   (c) most classroom environments are now accepting
   (d) the old-fashioned way of teaching implies

2. Two or more people may own a piece of real property with equal privileges to use it as long as each lives. This kind of ownership is called joint tenancy. At the death of one of the owners, the property belongs to the surviving owners, although the deceased may have had heirs. The last survivor of the join tenancy _____.

   (a) must make a will   (b) is the executor of the estate
   (c) cannot sell the property   (d) becomes sole owner

3. The Church of England, or Anglican Church, is sometimes called the Establishment because it was establish by parliament as the official state church. The monarch must be a member of the church of England, but all other people in the country are free to choose their religion. In England there are Islamic mosques, Buddhist temples, Jewish synagogues, Roman Catholic churches, and churches of many Protestant denominations. The English have much _____.

(a) high church attendance (b) control by the Establishment
(c) fundamental faith (d) religious freedom

4. The public face of scientific genius tends to be old and graying. We think of Albert Einstein's disheveled hair, Charles Darwin's majestic beard, Isaac Newton's wrinkled visage - not to mention the balding luminaries who accept their Nobel Prizes each year. Yet the truth is that the breakthroughs that fire our imagination and change our lives are usually made by men and women who are still in their 30s or 40s - and that includes Einstein, Darwin, and Newton. It is no surprise indeed; younger scientists have invested less than their elders in _____. They question authority instinctively. They do not believe it when they are told that a new idea is crazy, so they are free to do the impossible.

(a) research findings of the past
(b) the intellectual dogma of the day
(c) innovative experimental data
(d) the disadvantages of advanced technology

5. We all need a certain amount of stress in our lives, but when it restricts our daily life it can become a problem and affect our health. We are all individuals, and what may be positive stress for one person might be negative for another. It is important, _____, that we learn to recognize our own capabilities and find ways of managing stressful events in our lives.

(a) therefore (b) for instance (c) for some reason (d) nonetheless

6. We generally chart the start of modern science as we know it from Francis Bacon. It is Bacon, writing in the first decades of the 17th century, who is usually credited with spelling out the principles of empirical science and the role that experiments should play in hypothesis testing. _____, however, is that, despite his enormous influence on

scientists from Newton onwards, Bacon never himself touched a test tube. He simply set the scene from his armchair and told scientists how they ought to proceed.

(a) The main point
(b) The great irony
(c) The most crucial
(d) The bottom line

7. Schools encourage parents not to push children beyond their ability. But in a Confucian society, education is the traditional path to higher social status. As a result, parents put enormous amounts of money to have their children tutored. However, once students get in, _____ is off. The work load is generally light. But if they want a job at one of the big companies, they'll have to work for it because unemployment for university graduates is now at 20 per cent.

(a) the education
(b) the schooling
(c) the pressure
(d) the inquiry

8. Although Japan produces little livestock, the Japanese people have an adequate protein diet because fish are so abundant. Japanese fisheries process more fish than the people can eat, so a substantial part of the fish products are _____.

(a) eaten   (b) caught   (c) nutritious   (d) exported

9. It is said that all cuisines are basically _____ cuisines. Throughout history, food has been transported across cultures. For example, the Chinese gave noodles to Europe and African slaves taught white Americans how to cultivate and cook rice. Some food experts assert that there is no such thing as authentic food.

(a) fusion   (b) uniformity   (c) eccentricity   (d) arrangement

10. The deserts seem unfriendly to all kinds of life. There is little

water or plant life, and scant protection from the strong sun. Yet there are many species of insects, reptiles, birds, and mammals in the deserts. The human race is so dependent upon water that we find it hard to understand how any animal life can exist without what seems to us an adequate water supply. They cannot; it is simply that what is adequate for the desert animals would be _____.

(a) inadequate for plants (b) scare on the desert
(c) wasted by humans   (d) inadequate for us

◉ 이디엄

keep at arm's length 멀리하다
keep close tabs on 주의하다, 감시하다
keep in touch with 연락하다
keep one's head 침착하다
keep under one's hat 비밀로 지키다, 말을 하지 않다
know better than to …할 이만큼 바보는 아니다
lay bare 폭로하다, 털어놓다
lay down 버리다, 계획하다, 규정하다
lay off 일시 해고하다
let down 실망시키다, 배반하다
live up to …에 부끄럽지 않은 생활을 하다
look out for 주의하다, 경계하다
look to A for B A에게 B를 바라다
lose heart 낙심하다, 실망하다
lose no time in …ing 곧 …하다
lose one's head 흥분하다, 이성을 잃다

독해 · Part II

실력문제 1회

* 다음 글을 읽고 질문에 가장 적절한 답을 고르시오.

1. What seems to be a single memory is actually a complex construction. Think of a hammer, and your brain hurriedly retrieves the tool's name, its appearance, its function, its heft and the sound of its clang, each extracted from a different region of the brain. The weakening of memory is in fact the failure to put together separate pieces of information stored in your brain. Many of us begin to experience the breakdown of that assembly process in our 20s — and that becomes downright worrisome when we reach our 50s.

Q. According to the passage, how can we define the weakening of memory?

(a) It is a process in which the brain cells deteriorate.
(b) It is the symptom of aging which debilitates people most.
(c) It is a process in which the brain fails to connect separate information.
(d) It is a symptom which aggravates most people in their twenties.

2. It is most important to leave college with some sort of certificate, but after that a lot is up to the individual to succeed in life. If the volition to make it to the top is there, then paper qualifications are not going to make much difference. How many CEOs and directors of large companies had college degrees in the past? A lot of them probably worked their way to the top from the shop floor. Since more people now struggle to earn a degree from a prestigious institution of higher learning, paper qualifications may seem to be of significance. I'm firmly convinced, however, that there

is a lot to be said about good sound experience and skills over diploma – a piece of paper.

   Q. Which of the following is the best title of the above passage?

     (a) Individual Efforts Lead to Success
     (b) Diploma-Not a Requirement for Success
     (c) From the Shop Floor to the for Success
     (d) College Education-a Must

3. The police are trying to apprehend two suspects who tried to make an illegal ATM withdrawal. This Sunday at approximately 12 a.m., two men aged 20-25 arrived at the Union Bank on Ocean Street and tried to gain access to the ATM machine in the foyer. Unable to gain access to the money compartment in their several attempts, the suspects became frustrated and fled. The police are offering rewards of up to $1,000 for information leading to an arrest.

   Q. which of the following is true about the suspects?

     (a) They had never committed crimes before.
     (b) They knew a lot about the bank and machines.
     (c) They were successful in obtaining money from the ATM.
     (d) They didn't succeed in what they had planned to do.

4. Average interest rates nationwide for ten-year and one-year adjustable rate mortgages dipped slightly this week, while rates for fifteen-year mortgages held steady. The rate on ten-year fixed rate mortgages went down to 7.16 percent from 7.17 percent. Fifteen-year mortgages remained unchanged at 6.48 percent.

   Q. Which of the following is the best title of the report?

     (a) Lenders Ask for a Steady Rate for Mortgages

(b) Fifteen-year Mortgages Remain Unchanged
(c) Interest Rates Nationwide at a Record 6.48 percent
(d) Mortgages Rates Slightly Lower

5. A realistic target for recycling mixed refuse is somewhere between 15 and 25 percent by weight, according to researchers at the Department of Trade and Industry's Warren Spring Laboratory. This proportion would include metals and perhaps some glass. Statistics compiled by researchers at the University of East Anglia show that we could almost halve the total weight of domestic waste going to landfill by a combination of 'collect' schemes (such as doorstep collections for newspapers), 'bring' schemes (such as bottle banks) and plants for extracting metals.

Q. Which of the following is true according to the above passage?

(a) A goal to reach 15 to 20% recycling may be too low.
(b) We may well raise the recycling rate up to 50 percent by weight.
(c) There may still be a more effective way of dealing with household garbage.
(d) A good suggestion for garbage disposal is being made by researchers.

6. The most widely used term in the psychological and applied linguistics literature is schema, a term that was coined as long ago as 1932 by the psychologist Bartlett in his classic study of how human memory works. Like frame theory, schema theory suggests that the knowledge we carry around in our heads is organized into interrelated patterns. These are constructed from all our previous experiences of a given aspect of the experiential world, and they enable us to make predictions about future experience.

Q. Which of the following can Not be inferred from the above passage?

(a) The term schema is somehow related to the mechanism of human memory.
(b) In frame theory, knowledge is thought to be organized into many patterns.
(c) In getting new knowledge, previous experiences have little, if any, influence.
(d) To understand a linguistic discourse, we use both linguistic and content knowledge.

7. The "expansion phase" in the business world encompasses both recovery and prosperity. During the period of recovery, old production facilities grow, and new ones are developed, bringing about new business along with expansion of the old ones. Because of the optimistic climate brought about by these developments, there is an increase in capital investments in machinery, as well as in the need for labor and raw materials. The expansion of one part of the economy has an echo effect in other areas. When the automobile industry thrives, for example, so does steel, glass and rubber production. The result is an ever- widening circle of prosperity.

Q: Which of the following is true according to the statement?

(a) When an economy is in a period of a revival, old industries thrive.
(b) When one industry increases production, others are phased out.
(c) When an economy is in a period of revival, old industries are changed into new ones.
(d) When one industry increases production, others centralize their activities.

8. Since such a drastic solution to pollution is impossible, we must employ determined public action. We can reduce pollution, even if we can't eliminate it altogether. But we must all do our part. Check your car to see if the pollution-control device is working. Reduce your use of electricity. Is air conditioning really necessary? Don't dump garbage or other waste on the land or in the water. Demand that government take firm action against polluters. We can have a clean world or we can do nothing. The choice is up to you.

Q: Which of the following is true according to the passage?

(a) Pollution should be controlled to run cars smoothly.
(b) Governments took determined action enough to prevent pollution.
(c) Strong determination to reduce pollution is required of individuals.
(d) We have no choice but to pollute the world.

9. The capitalist system is characterized by the private ownership of resources and the freedom of individuals to engage in the economic activities of their choice as a means for advancing their material well-being. Self-interest is the driving force of such an economy, and competition functions as a regulatory or control mechanism.

Capitalistic production is not organized in term of a government plan, but rather features the price system as a means of organizing and making effective the myriad of individual decisions which determine what is produced, the methods of production, and the sharing of output.

Q: Which of the following is the best title of the above passage?

(a) The Characteristics of a Modern Economy
(b) Various Types of Economic Systems
(c) Features of the Capitalist System
(d) The Shortcomings of the Capitalist System

10. Jerusalem was finally delivered. The first consideration of the Crusaders was how to keep it. In their great majority Crusaders decided that this would best be done with the creation of a feudal kingdom: a type of government the Crusaders were familiar with. A feudal kingdom would provide a centralized government, which would be capable of coordinating the defense of the newly acquired territory. Even though the idea was met with discontent by the clergy, who believed that the only proper government for the Holy City was an ecclesiastical one and that the civil ruler of the area should be subordinated to the clerical ruler, the imminent dangers to the newly acquired eastern territories were sufficient to convince most of the princes of the importance and necessity of a strong secular ruler.

Q: Which of the following is true according to the article?

(a) The Crusades believed that the proper government for Jerusalem was an ecclesiastical one.
(b) The clergy were contented that a feudal kingdom would be built in Jerusalem.
(c) Most of the princes believed the civil ruler of Jerusalem should be subordinated to the clerical ruler.
(d) The imminent dangers of the newly acquired eastern territories were considered very big by the Crusaders.

◎ 이디엄

make[pull] a face 얼굴을 찡그리다
make believe …인 체하다
make both ends meet 빚지지 않고 살아가다
make for …로 향해 가다, 공격하다, …에 기여하다
make good 성공하다, 보상하다, 수행하다
make head or tail of -를 이해하다

실력문제 2회

* 다음 글을 읽고 질문에 가장 적절한 답을 고르시오.

1. Watching things as they happen, the TV viewer is a part of events in a way new to man. And never is he so much a part of the whole as when things do not happen, for people will always prefer to look at something rather than nothing: between the plain wall and flickering commercial, the eyes will have the second. As hearth and fire were once center to the home, so now the television set is the center of modern man's being: all points of the room converge on its presence and the eye watches even as the mind dozes, much as our ancestors narcotized themselves with fire.

Q. Which of the following is Not true of the above passage?

(a) The TV viewer is most engaged when there are no special things happening.
(b) Our eyes choose to linger on the flickering commercial only for a moment before moving on.
(c) In the center of modern man's being are the narcotized fire-watchers.
(d) All modern TV viewers are irrecoverable couch potatoes in essence.

2. We're delighted to have you join exclusive group of Neil Platinum Card members. Here's your new card, along with information about some of the exceptional benefits reserved for you. Please sign the reverse side of your card right now and activate your card immediately, so you can use it at stores, restaurants, hotels, service stations and more. The Neil Platinum Card is welcome at more than 11 million locations worldwide.

Q: Which of the following is most likely to be presented after this passage?

(a) Steps to follow in order to activate the card
(b) Descriptions about the benefits card members enjoy
(c) List of locations abroad where the card is accepted
(d) Things the person should do before using the card

3. The core of science lies in basic research. Basic research seeks knowledge for its own sake, be it the understanding of the structure of atoms, the causes of earthquakes or dynamics of social interaction that occurs when two or more humans meet. Applied research aims at specific, practical problems. Result can be seen and enjoyed. More is spent on it than on basic research because the results are immediately practical. (The government spends only 7 percent of its research funds on basic research.)

Care must be taken that applied research not eliminate basic. Basic research is the ultimate key to a refined, improved technology.

Q: Which of the following can be inferred from the report?

(a) Basic research is a pure discipline because its results are totally unapplicable in the real world.
(b) Basic research is the key to specific and practical technology.
(c) The government enthusiastically supports basic research, but sometimes discourage scientists from research.
(d) The government earmarks most of the research funds for applied research.

4. The mystery of aging runs almost as deep as the mystery of life. During the past century, life expectancy has nearly doubled in developed countries, thanks to improvements in nutrition, sanitation and medical science. Yet the potential life span of a human being has not changed

significantly since the halawaka met the snake.

By the age of 50 every one of us, no matter how fit, will begin a slow decline in organ function and sensory acuity. And though some will enjoy another half century of robust health, our odds of living past 120 are virtually zero. Why, after being so exquisitely assembled, do we fall apart so predictably? Why do we outlive dogs, only to be outlived by turtles? And what are our prospects for catching up with them?

    Q: Which of the following is proper for the title of the above passage?

    (a) How long we and animals can live
    (b) The comparison between the life spans
    (c) The prospect for living past 120
    (d) How we grow old

5. For more than 15 years, virologists have believed human beings acquired the AIDS virus from a subspecies of chimpanzees. The new research narrows the microbe's place of origin to the region near the countries of Gabon, Equatorial Guinea and Cameroon, on the Atlantic Coast. The research sheds no light on the mystery of when or how the virus leaped the 'species barrier'. It may, however, shed light on more practical and clinically relevant questions. That is because preliminary evidence suggests the subspecies of chimpanzees does not become ill from the ancestral virus.

If further study proves that is case, the animals may help illuminate why the microbe is so deadly to their human cousins, who are 98 percent identical to them.

    Q: Which of the following is true of the new research in the report?

    (a) It discovered that the AIDS virus came from a subspecies of Chimpanzees

(b) It may shed light on the questions related to AIDS treatment
(c) It discovered how the virus leaped the species barrier
(d) It discovered why the microbe is so deadly to human beings

6. A few winters ago a dozen investigators independently reported figures on antihistamine pills. Each showed that a considerable percentage of colds cleared up after treatment. A great fuss ensued, at least in the advertisements, and a medical-product boom was on. It was based on an eternally springing hope and also a curious refusal to look past the statistics to a fact that has been known for a long time. As Henry G. Felsen, a humorist pointed out, proper medical treatment will cure a cold in seven days, but left to itself a cold will hang on for a week.

Q. What is most likely to be the fact that "has been known for a long time"?

(a) Antihistamine pill are quite effective.
(b) Statistics are always deceitful.
(c) No medicine cures a cold effectively.
(d) A cold will last for a week or seven days.

7. Though there certainly may be areas of friction in Israel between some ardently observant Jews and some equally ardent secular Jews, as described in your article "The Religious Wars", most Jewish Israelis feel and act as a single people; a family united by its religious heritage. Its members choose to observe its rules to a greater or lesser degree. The populace in Israel is not polarized, nor on the brink of a religious civil war.

Q: Which of the following is correct according to the passage?

(a) The portrayal of Jewish Israelis as a polarized people is erroneous.
(b) The Jews are single wherever they live.

(c) A religious civil war is on the brink of erupting in Israel.
(d) Ardently secular Jews refuse to observe religious rules.

8. Ensuring air craft are safe to fly depends on a crucial troika: the national regulatory authority, which grants airworthiness certificates; the aircraft manufacturer, which issues technical instructions for the maintenance, inspection and replacement of parts; and the airline, which is supposed to carry out the manufacturers' instructions. In the case of N73711, Aloha Airlines' maintenance procedures were seriously deficient. Its aircraft were overworked on short, island-hopping flights and were exposed to a corrosive salt atmosphere, yet its corrosion control program was inadequate.

Q : What is this passage mainly concerned with?

(a) Corrosion and metal fatigue
(b) Negligence of maintenance
(c) Multi-site damage
(d) Ever-aging fleet

9. Korea's remarkable rebound has led the way in East Asia, indeed worldwide, by recording a 10.7 percent economic growth rate last year. This rapid turnaround follow a tumultuous financial crisis that plunged the economy 6.7 percent in 1998. Despite the acute hardship, the financial crisis seem to have created opportunities to globalize the country through openness and reform. A government official says, "We learned the lesson that we can survive only when we offer the best possible goods and services to the world."

Q. Which of the following is Not true of the above passage?

(a) Koreans learned a lesson from an acute economic stringency.
(b) After a crisis, Korea globalized itself though openness and reform.

(c) Korea's economy recorded a negative growth rate during the recession.

(d) Korea recorded a remarkable economic growth rate after the recession.

10. Many animals are able to communicate with one another, although, of course, none of them can talk as we do. No animals actually use words, yet they have the means of communication. Take birds, for example; a hen with chicks gives a warning sound and all her chicks crouch down motionless, until the mother makes another call which then collects them together. Wild birds, when migrating at night, cry out; these cries may keep the birds together. If one of the migrating birds strayed, it could hear the others and return to the flock. We ourselves have more ways for communicating with one another than just by talking. Animals cannot talk, they use no words of sentences, but some of them do make noises corresponding to our exclamations of surprise and such.

Q. Which of the following is true according to the above passage?

(a) The modern means of communication by human beings has been learned from many animals such as chicks and migrating birds.

(b) The means of communication among beasts and birds is much more advanced than that of man.

(c) Although wild animals use no words they can send news to their fellows in a far-off land.

(d) In spite of having no which animals are able to communicate by some simple means of their own.

실력문제 3회

* 다음 글을 읽고 질문에 가장 적절한 답을 고르시오.

1. Unlike men, robots work in boring, dirty or unpleasant jobs without complaint or absence; They will drill holes or make sheet metal parts for weeks and tears at a time. Robots also work in job which are too dangerous over a long period of time for men, jobs which cause disease, or jobs in which frequent accidents occur with fumes or radiation. In addition, robots on the assembly line are more cost-effective than men; they can work 24 hours a day.

Q : Which of the following best summarizes the above passage?

(a) Robots can work without any breaks all day long.
(b) Robots are more obedient and cost-effective than men.
(c) Robots can prevent frequent accidents occurring with fumes or radiation.
(d) Robots can work in jobs too dangerous for people to do over a long period of time.

2. Scientists are stumped over how to clear the heavens of junk left from five decades of space travel and satellite launches. Although there has been some research on using lasers to change the orbit of small debris and on employing large foam balls that would encase and slow down speeding junk, these methods are not yet technically feasible. Therefore, scientists have focused their efforts on designing spacecraft that leave behind less waste, though that doesn't help clear the existing junk. Much research is yet needed to solve this problem.

Q. What is the main idea of the passage?

(a) Junk from space travel is increasing tremendously these days.

(b) It is important to develop a method to clear waste from space exploration.
(c) Recent models of space craft emit less waste than the old ones.
(d) Lasers have proven very effective in dealing with the junk problem.

3. Imagine life without siblings. There would be no bickering or living-room wrestling matches or hair-pulling. Forty-one percent of American families get to run single-child households. But for the rest, and for the increasing number of families that are blending stepchildren together, relationships among brothers and sisters are of paramount concern — as they should be. Indeed, positive sibling relationships can be a source of strength for life.

Q. What does the writer think about sibling relationship?

(a) Bad sibling relationships deteriorate with age.
(b) Step-siblings tend to have more conflicts with each other.
(c) Sibling rivalry is a major part of sibling relationship.
(d) Sibling relationships constitute one of important supports for life.

4. I agree with the U.S. position that the war against Colombian drug cartels must be raised another notch. It is unfortunate that Colombian President Andres Pastrana does not understand that he cannot negotiate peace with rebel forces from a position of weakness. These are ruthless individuals who do not obey the rules of law and honor, have no moral principles and are profiting handsomely from drug trafficking extortion and kidnapping. The President must maintain a close relationship with the military; it is the only force that can help him show the rebel groups that their conduct is dangerous.

JORGE PINZON
Bogota, Colombia

Q : Which of the following is the best title for the above letter?

(a) The Future of Colombia
(b) The U.S Position on Drug Trafficking
(c) What the Rebel Groups Want
(d) How to Deal with Drug Rebel

5. Approximately 16 percent of the total weight of a human body is protein. The protein myoglobin in muscle tissue stores oxygen and produces red color in meat. There are proteins in the saliva, gastric juices, and intestinal juices which digest food. The pituitary gland secretes a protein called human growth hormone, which regulates growth. Certain cells in the pancreas secrete insulin, a protein that regulates the amount of sugar in the blood.

Q: which of the following is the main point of the above passage?

(a) No other material constitutes more of the body than protein
(b) Proteins are responsible for some of the body's essential functions
(c) Proteins in different parts of the body have similar functions
(d) Cells containing more proteins work better than others having less

6. To : All employees
From : Personnel Office

As of September 1, 1999 True Con Inc. will be offering another health insurance carrier, Blue Cross of Boston. If you are interested in finding out more about the coverage provided by the new plan, please contact the personnel office. As a reminder, please make sure that all insurance forms for new of continuing policies are turned in by December 17, 1999. Paperwork not received by this date could delay the reimbursement of any claims subsequently submitted.

Q : Which of the following can be inferred from the notice?

(a) All employees will be fired if they don't meet a deadline.
(b) True Con employee would contact the personnel office to change health insurance.
(c) Paperwork submitted after a deadline can't be received.
(d) All the current health insurance carriers will be changed as of September 1, 1999.

7. Zaban is one of the most effective smoking cessation products on the market. Lozenges are more effective than Zaban, but they are only available in Great Britain. Unlike the patch or gum, Zaban is not a over-the-counter form of nicotine replacement therapy. It is actually an antidepressant that your doctor needs to prescribe. We are not sure exactly how it helps people quit.

Q : Which of the following is correct about Zaban?

(a) The way it works is not known.
(b) It is not available in Great Britain.
(c) When taken, it releases nicotine.
(d) It can be taken without a doctor's permission.

8. Barcelona-A group of nine mountaineers left for Nepal yesterday to clean up Mount Everest. Since the world's highest mountain was first climbed over 40 years ago, large amounts of garbage have been left on its slopes. The bodies of dead climbers have also been abandoned there. The Spanish expedition, assisted by 20 Sherpas, plans to collect an estimated 10 tons of garbage. The trash has been discarded by teams of mountaineers who have been climbing Mount Everest ever since it was first conquered by New Zealander Sir Edmund Hillary and Tenzing in 1953.

Q : Which of the following best summarizes the above newspaper article?

(a) Too much garbage has been thrown away along the valleys of

Himalaya.
(b) Mountain climbers should be more careful not to discard refuse.
(c) A Spanish expedition was on their way to clean up Mount Everest.
(d) The Spaniards are sallying forth for a springtime clean-up.

9. For older Americans, age segregation is most prevalent in nursing homes. Currently, 11.5 million elderly people in the United States are stuck in nursing homes. About one in five Americans will end up in such a home at some point in his or her life. The majority of these elderly persons enter nursing homes when their health is failing or they lack financial resources needed to live on their own. Entering a nursing home means becoming part of a total institution. Activities are determined solely by the institution and are rarely tailored to the individual preferences of residents, leaving them with no other way but to accept.

Q: What is the writer's attitude?

(a) reproachful   (b) astonished   (c) repentant   (d) confounded

10. Human beings are capable of thinking in two basic ways. Convergent thinking neatly and systematically tends toward an answer. Divergent thinking tends away from a center, perhaps in several directions at once, seeking avenues of inquiry rather than a particular destination. Scientists, on the whole, engage in convergent thinking, but it is divergent thinking that breaks with the past and leads to unpredictable conclusions.

Q : What is the main idea of the above passage?

(a) The systematic way of thinking
(b) Man's greatness as a thinker
(c) The character of divergent thinking
(d) The two ways of man's thinking

실력문제 4회

* 다음 글을 읽고 질문에 가장 적절한 답을 고르시오.

1. Under new guidelines distributed to all Minnesota motor vehicle agencies this week, driver's licenses will not be issued to any foreigner with a short-team visa. Drivers with out-of-state licenses will have to present at least one other valid form of identification to obtain a Minnesota license. Immigrants with visas authorizing them to remain in the country less than a year will have to use a driver's license from their homr country to drive in Minnesota. The new driver licensing rules are part of a national effort to crack down on false identification.

   Q : What is the main purpose of the new rules regarding driver's licenses?

   (a) To prevent immigrants from getting driver's licenses
   (b) To lower the rate of crime in Minnesota
   (c) To discourage immigration into Minnesota
   (d) To prevent possible misuse of driver's licenses

2. Carefully pack the appliance in a heavy, rigid cardboard box with plenty of newspapers on every side so it is snug in the box. All detachable parts, cords, etc. should be included with the appliance, securely packed so nothing is loose. Please pack carefully to avoid damage during shipment. Print clearly on the carton the name and address of the nearest service center and your name and return address. It is important that you include a letter with your name, the date and place you purchased the appliance, and a description of the fault requiring attention.

   Q : Which of the following can be inferred from the passage?

   (a) The appliance will be shipped a long distance.

(b) If the appliance is defective, it is the sender's fault.
(c) The appliance will be returned to the sender after inspection.
(d) The appliance is an expensive and newly purchased product.

3. French scientists said Friday they had found a way to genetically engineered animals to produce milk that can be easier to digest. They have only tested mice, but say if the same genetic changes can be made to cows, dairy farms can churn out easy-to-digest milk. "About 70 percent of all adults around the world have lactose intolearnce," Bernard Jost and colleagues at French Medical Institute said. They cannot digest lactose, a milk sugar. They get diarrhea, nausea, abdominal cramps and other uncomfortable symptoms. Jost's team said they inserted a rat gene into mice that causes them to pre-digest the milk before they secrete it. Most lactose-intolerant people lack an enzyme known as lactase phlorizinydrolase or LPH.

Q : Which of the following is true according to the report?

(a) Jost's team succeeded in testing cows in their experiment.
(b) Jost's team said that about 70 percent of dairy farms can produce easy-to-digest milk.
(c) Jost's team made mice that pre-digest the milk before they secrete it.
(d) Jost's team inserted a rat gene into cows to produce an enzyme.

4. All good detective fiction gives you a sharp sense of suspense. One could even say that suspense for its own sake is what detective aim at. A detective story can be crudely realized and bloody. Even though built on blood and bodies, no good detective story achieves its fame with such attractions; they are merely the pretense for a purely intellectual exercise of solving a puzzle and discovering the criminal. This is what draws one in and provides relaxation through its apparent opposite, namely, the

reader's competition with the detective in the quest of the probable right clue. The successful search itself is depicted in isolation from the rest of the story.

Q : Which of the following best summarizes the above passage?

(a) Suspense for its own sake is important in detective stories.
(b) Detective stories should be built on blood and bodies.
(c) Suspense is the most important element in detective stories.
(d) Readers should compete with detectives in the quest of suspense.

5. Seen aright, science is more than the instrument of man's increasing power and progress. It is also an instrument, the finest yet developed in the evolution of any species, for the malleable adaptation of man to his environment and the adjustment of his environment to man. If the human species is to remain successful, this instrument must be used more and more to control nature and the rate of social and technological change, as well as to promote it. In this sense, at least, science is far more than a new sense organ for comprehending the real relations of natural phenomena and the regularities we call "laws of nature." It is also man's means of adjustment to nature, man's instrument for the creation of an ideal environment.

Q : Which of the following is the best title for the above passage?

(a) The Primary Function of Science
(b) The Evolution of Human Species
(c) The Characters of Natural Laws
(d) The Relations of Natural Phenomena

6. I guess it is true that big and strong things are much less dangerous than small soft weak things. Nature (whatever that is) makes the small and weak reproduce faster. And that is not true of course. The ones that

did not reproduce faster than they died, disappeared. But how about little faults, little pains, little worries? The cosmic ulcer comes not from great concerns, from little irritations. And great things can kill a man, but if they do not he is strong and better for them. A man is destroyed by the duck nibblings of naggings, small bills, telephones (wrong number), athlete's foot, ragweed, the common cold, boredom. All of these are the negatives, the tiny frustrations, and no one is stronger than them.

Q : Which of the following would be the most appropriate title for the passage?

(a) The Danger of Small Things
(b) Nature and Man
(c) Little Things and Big Things
(d) The Cause of Man's Destruction

7. Cultures are ways of ordering space just as economies are. While they may coincide with the latter, they may also be distinguished from them: the cultural map and the economic map cannot simply be superimposed without anomaly, and this is after all only logical, if only because culture dates from even further back in time than the world economy, impressive though the life span of the latter may be. Culture is the oldest character in human history; economies succeed each other, political institution crumble, but civilization continues along its way. Rome fell in the fifth century AD, but the Church of Rome is still with us. When Hinduism stood up against Islamism in the eighteenth century, it opened up a vacuum into which the British conquest could insinuate itself, but the struggle between Hinduism and Islamism is still going on, whereas the British Raj ended over thirty years ago.

Q: Which of the following can be inferred in the above passage?

(a) Cultural maps are not easy to draw on the basis of economic ones.

(b) Cultural factors are essential to the study of the world economy.
(c) The decline of economy accelerated the fall of the Roman Empire.
(d) India exerted every effort to gain independence from the British.

8. We must stop measuring our standard of life by automobiles, production drives, and dollars of income. No standard of living is high when jobs become drudgery and hours dreary, when young men and women cannot afford a family, when children we walled off by brick from sod and sky. We must measure our education less by the amount of knowledge it instills in youthful minds than by the wisdom of living it creates. The amassment of knowledge is of negative value when it places business above family in the interests of men, and makes women consider careers ahead of children; when it instructs us in the magic that turns loose modern weapons without teaching us the human values to control them.

Q: What is the best title of the passage?

(a) Standard of Living of Today and Yesterday
(b) American Education
(c) The Negative Value of Knowledge
(d) New Social Ideals

9. The impulse to turn life into fun and games is the wellspring of sport. Humanity's penchant for play has been expressed in sports and games in every society and in every age. Boxing, for instance, spread throughout Africa's Nile Valley more than 6,000 years ago. Egyptian art depicts fencing as early as the 12th century B.C. And many modern court games trace their origins back to a centuries—old form of handball first played in monastery cloisters in Europe.

Q : Which of the following best summarizes the above passage?

(a) Many modern sports are out growths of daily tasks.
(b) No matter when and where they have lived, people have always enjoyed games.
(c) The cultural basis of the games we play developed in Africa and Egypt.
(d) Court games have been an international phenomenon throughout history.

10. Not all popular brands of cigarettes have the same tar and nicotine content. Those with filter tips have lower tar content than other brands. But there are ways to make smoking less hazardous. Cigarettes should not be smoked all the way down.

Smokers should take an annual physical check-up. Their physicians may include a lung function test, chest X-ray or a sputum test. smokers who give up cigarettes will feel better and breathe easier. Respiratory symptoms improve when smoking stops. The death rates of ex-smokers approach those of the nonsmokers.

Q: Which of the following is true according to the above article?

(a) A person who gives up smoking may gain weight rapidly for a short time
(b) Cellulose filters are more effective than any other filter
(c) Heavy smokers decrease their life spans by five years
(d) Smokers can improve their health if they stop smoking cigarettes

독해 · Part III

실력문제 1회

* 다음 글을 읽고 내용의 흐름상 어색한 부분을 고르시오.

1. The second shortcoming is the lack of an innovative workforce. (a) Although Asia is often praised for its "entrepreneurial" culture, this label lumps together two distinct traits: a desire to chase profits, and an ability to think up clever new ways. (b) Just as the virtual university has yet to supplant Oxford or Harvard, the virtual Silicon Valley is still no match for Palo Alto. (c) But they are often imitative opportunists. (d) Truly creative entrepreneurs are thin on the ground and, when they do appear, too many choose to migrate to America rather than stay at home.

2. The superego has two aspects which respond to "good and bad" deeds; rewards and punishments. (a) The positive aspect of the superego approves of unselfish acts that accord with the highest moral principles; this aspect is sometimes called the ego ideal. (b) The ego is concerned only with what the person can do, but the id is involved with that the person wants. (c) If we rescue a pig caught in the mud, even though we are in nice clothes, we experience a burst of personal pride. (d) It is the superego rewarding the ego, according to Freud.

3. A mirror is a great tool to enhance design. (a) It is easy to take care of and has the ability to do great tricks in expanding small spaces. (b) The owner could be working in the kitchen and still see the ocean view and the trees. (c) Someone considering a mirror for a room should take a piece into the room and see what it reflects. (d) A mirror, when you consider the costs of other objects that you're putting in a room, is comparatively inexpensive too.

4. Whether or not the fear of science-fiction food is realistic,

genetically engineered food has received a great deal of attention recently because many of these food products are now on the market. (a) Some people are concerned that these foods don't have the same taste or that they may cause people to become sick. (b) For example, trout genes are now used to produce longer-lasting tomatoes. (c) Yet, people who have allergies to fish may become ill from eating these tomatoes, if the trout gene has not been sufficiently sublimated in the gene-splicing process. (d) Trout genes made people like longer-lasting tomatoes because of their color, taste, and shelf life.

5. The Eskimos taught their children with great care. (a) The old stories were told in words which never changed, and the children had to retell them repeatedly until they knew them perfectly. (b) They learned the old Eskimo songs and dances which expressed their ideas about nature and the spirit world. (c) Old Eskimos have strong white teeth, but sweet food has harmed their children's teeth. (d) And most of all they earned the skills which they needed in order to survive in a harsh land— the skills which utilized every part of the native animals, birds and fish and the few plants and trees of the area.

◎ 이디엄

make no difference 중요하지 않다, 상관없다
make one's way 앞으로 나아가다, 성공하다
make out 이해하다, 성공하다, 작성하다, …인 체하다
make up 구성하다, 화해하다, 조작하다, 화장하다
make up for 보충하다, 보상하다
map out 계획하다
measure up 맞추어 나가다
meet (someone) halfway 타협하다
miss out on 기회를 놓치다(=miss the boat)
move heaven and earth to …하기 위해 전력을 다하다

실력문제 2회

* 다음 글을 읽고 내용의 흐름상 어색한 부분을 고르시오.

1. Chinese citizens can face harassment or prolonged detention in labor camps if they practice religion outside officially sponsored churches, the State Department says in a new reports on religious persecution around the world. (a) The report also cites credible reports of incidents of abuses of Buddhist monks and nuns in China, including Tibet. (b) China is one of 194 countries or territories examined in the report—the first of what will be an annual series on religious freedom. (c) The study was made available Wednesday to members of Congress and will be released to news organizations Thursday. (d) A free-market capitalist system cannot operate fully effectively unless all participants in the economy are given opportunities to achieve their best.

2. Since the appearance of the disease AIDS, people have been encouraged to use condoms as a means of practising safe sex and protecting themselves against AIDS and other diseases. (a) Condoms can be bought at a chemist's shop, or sometimes from a vending machine, e.g. in the rest rooms of a bar or pub. (b) People often joke about men being too embarrassed to ask for condoms in a shop, esp. if the assistant is a woman. (c) There are various generally-known names for condoms which include French letter, Rubber and Durex. (d) AIDS — acquired immune deficiency syndrome — was first reported in the United States in 1981 and has since become a major worldwide epidemic.

3. Keeping your blood pressure under control can seem like a huge challenge. Where do you start? (a) First, remember that hypertension can be successfully treated. (b) You should work with your health care provider to develop a treatment plan that makes sense for you. (c) Deciding on a treatment plan means evaluating a number of different

factors including your present health and whether you're on any other medications. (d) The higher your blood pressure is, the more likely it is hypertension is fatal to your life.

4. Salt in the soil may harm crops. Certain salt constituents alone can prove toxic to come plant varieties. (a) Also, high salt concentrations in the soil around plant roots may decrease the osmotic pressure, causing water to flow out of the plant to achieve equilibrium. (b) High salinity levels are often found in arid areas where intensive evaporation causes salt accumulation in soil. (c) In some cases, rather than destroying a crop, elevated salt levels may simply reduce crop yields and leave the plants prone to disease. (d) High salinity also can cause leaf tip and marginal leaf burn, bleaching, or defoliation.

5. Feeling depressed is not the same as experiencing 'clinical depression'. (a) Clinically significant levels of depression mean that the symptoms associated with depression (e.g. sadness, loss of interest in the things you enjoy) are so severe and persistent that they impair your ability to get through the day. (b) For people with clinical depression, the symptoms are relentless, appear to have no end, and do not go away in the face of happy events or good news. (c) When you feel these kinds of symptoms, you can count your blessings. (d) Clinical depression requires professional help.

◎ 이디엄

occur to 마음에 갑자기 떠오르다
pass away 죽다
pass for …으로 통하다
pass out 기절하다
pay respect for …에 경의를 표하다
pick on 괴롭히다

실력문제 3회

* 다음 글을 읽고 내용의 흐름상 어색한 부분을 고르시오.

1. The pattern of drug consumption is altering. (a) The average age of heroin addicts is rising in many countries. (b) Casual use seems to have fallen and heavy use has stabilized. (c) More American teenagers are using cannabis, but the number of youngsters experimenting with cocaine or heroin has stayed fairly steady. (d) The American heroin epidemic peaked around 1973, since then the number of new addicts has dropped back to the levels of the mid-1960s. / America's hideous crack epidemic has also long passed, and cocaine use has retreated from its 1970s peak. The likelihood of proceeding from cannabis to harder drugs such as cocaine or heroin has fallen consistently for a decade.

2. People often poke fun at progress, possibly because technology often presents new problems as it attempts to solve old ones. (a) Imagine what might happen to genes that have been genetically engineered in scientists' laboratories once they are released into the environment. (b) Most people will agree that more information is needed before we can be sure whether genetically engineered products will improve our lives. (c) The offshoot of introducing these genes could be terrifying : Some talk of the creation of human monsters, or Frankensteins. (d) In fact, there already exists genetically manipulated food that has been called "Frankenfood" by some.

3. The first music in the American colonies was church music. (a) In fact, the first book published in the American colonies was a psalm book. (b) The first composers in the colonies confined themselves to hymns and church music, both in the English and German settlements. (c) Perhaps America's greatest contribution to the world of music. (d) Many songs of course were brought from Europe by the colonists, and

although these were not often written down, they can still be heard, especially in isolated mountain settlements.

4. Environmentalists fear that biotechnology could transform nature. (a) For example, the genetic manipulation of animals is expanding rapidly. (b) Already fish like the carp have been genetically altered to grow faster. (c) The age of information will also be the age of biology. (d) Theoretically, scientists could insert into salmon genes that would alter their migration patterns, making it to catch the species in the oceans.

5. History has provided many examples of the destructive effects of ethnocentrism. (a) In ancient times, both the Romans in Europe and the Chinese in Asia viewed foreigners as barbarians. (b) The last dynasty of China was established by the Manchurians, who tried to harmonize with the Chinese. (c) In modern times, the German dictator Adolf Hitler argued that the Germans belonged to a superior race whose duty was to destroy "lesser races." (d) Acting on this ethnocentric idea, Hitler ordered the persecution of Jews, Gypsies, Slavs, and other groups whom he considered to be of "inferior races."

◎ 이디엄

pin down 명백하게 정의하다, 속박하다, 옴짝달싹 못하게 하다
play second fiddle to 남의 밑에 붙다
pull one's leg 놀리다
put down 줄이다, 적어두다, 진압하다
put one's foot into it 실언하다, 곤경에 빠지다
put one's life on the line 목숨을 걸다
put out (불을) 끄다, 출판하다
put through 성취하다, (전화를) 연결하다
put up 세우다, 짓다, 올리다

실력문제 4회

* 다음 글을 읽고 내용의 흐름상 어색한 부분을 고르시오.

1. The advertisement's image of women is artificial and can only be achieved artificially (even the "natural look" requires much preparation and expense). (a) Beauty is something that comes from without; more than one million dollars is spent every hour on cosmetics. (b) Desperate to conform to an ideal and impossible standard, many women go to great lengths to manipulate and change their faces and bodies. (c) The aspect of advertising most in need of analysis and change is the portrayal of working men. (d) A woman is conditioned to view her face as a mask and her body as an object constantly in need of alteration, improvement, and disguise.

2. Research shows that too much animal fat is bad for our health. (a) For example, since Americans eat a lot of meat, that have high rates of cancer and heart disease. (b) In contrast, since Koreans eat a large amount of grains and very little meat, they have very low rates of cancer and heart disease. (c) Unfortunately, as hamburgers, cola, and other foods high in fat become popular in Korea, the rates of heart disease and cancer are increasing here as well. (d) In fact, heart disease and cancer are the first and second most common causes of death in the U.S., representing about two in five deaths. Consequently, doctors advise people to eat more grains, fruit and vegetables, and to eat less meat.

3. Ultrasonic sound, which humans cannot hear, has many uses in medicine. (a) It is used to create sonograms, which are pictures of the body. (b) Doctors use sonograms to monitor the growth of an unborn baby inside its mother's uterus and to detect tumors, kidney stones, and heart disorders. (c) When deformities, tumors, or other problems are

detected, an immediate operation is needed. (d) Ultrasonic sound is also used in surgical procedures such as operating on nerves and shattering kidney stones.

4. You hurtle down the highway at 80 feet per second, four small patches of rubber providing your only contact with the pavement. (a) Two tone vehicles flash by within a few feet, driven by just about anybody who can pass an eye test. (b) Once in a while you ought to remind yourself: Traveling by car is the most dangerous thing that most of us noncombatants do. (c) Consider some of these items for your shopping list. (d) Better technology comes along every year to keep you and your family safer while driving, and the best time to get up-to-date is when you're shopping for a new car.

5. Why should language be vitally central to the acquisition of individual freedom? The first great discovery is the experience of aloneness. Aloneness is partially overcome through the senses. (a) To see something, to touch it, and finally to grasp it is the earliest expression of extending ourselves and overcoming our separateness. (b) Sound and language are then bridges to the not-me. (c) Language is the most natural and sophisticated form of self-extension. (d) The very heart of learning and the self-realizing process is language.

◎ 이디엄

raise a hue and cry 고함을 지르다
resort to 자주 드나들다, 호소하다
rub (someone) the wrong way 화나게 하다
rule out 제외하다, 배제하다
run down 쇠약해지다
run out of 바닥이 나다
run over 다시 검토하다, (차가 사람을) 치다

IV. 최종점검 문제

1. 문 법

Part I

* 다음 대화문의 빈칸에 가장 적절한 표현을 고르시오.(1-20)

1. A: I was wondering if you would be interested in buying my car.
   B: I would love _____, but I can't afford it.
   (a) buying   (b) to buy   (c) to   (d) to have bought

2. A: God, after all, he was a fraud. And no one knew that!
   B: If we _____ he was a fraud, we wouldn't trusted him.
   (a) have known   (b) knew   (c) know   (d) had known

3. A: _____ you didn't turn up at Dick's farewell party?
   B: Don't you know? He is the last man I want to see.
   (a) What if   (b) How come   (c) How about   (d) What about

4. A: What's on your mind?
   B: I'm considering the possibility _____ the school basketball team.
   (a) to join   (b) of joining   (c) that I will join   (d) for you to join

5. A: Judy, I'd like to take a trip over to the east coast this summer. How about you?
   B: Well, I am really thinking about an overseas trip. _____ it would cost?
   (a) How much do you think   (b) How many do you think
   (c) Do you think how much   (d) Do you think how many

6. A: Oh, it's getting rather late. I must be leaving now. Thank you for a most enjoyable evening.

B: Nice to _____ you. Take care.

(a) have met (b) having met (c) meet (d) meeting

7. A: That sounds like a pretty boring job.

    B: It _____. and I haven't eaten a single potato chip since I quit that potato inspection job.

    (a) was so (b) was sure (c) sure was (d) true was

8. A: Can you change some money for me?

    B: Certainly. _____ you wish to change?

    (a) What's like (b) What is it (c) What're ones (d) What could be

9. A: I can't believe that Dick got fired.

    B: I know. Who _____ that he would get pink-slipped?

    (a) would have thought it   (b) would have ever thought
    (c) have ever thought   (d) would have thought ever

10. A: I'd like to try on one of these dresses.

    B: I'll show you the fitting room. By the way, this is _____ style.

    (a) the last (b) the latest (c) the late (d) later

11. A: You've been so kind to me.

    B: If you get some problem, don't hesitate _____.

    (a) knowing me to last   (b) me to let know
    (c) letting me know   (d) to let me know

12. A: Would you tell Bill I'm really sorry I lost his book?

    B: Hadn't you _____?

    (a) better tell him yourself (b) yourself better tell him
    (c) tell him better yourself (d) better yourself tell him

13. A: Howard, how was your fishing trip?

    B: We _____ any fish this time.

    (a) didn't hardly catch   (b) hardly caught

(c) hardly not caught   (d) hardly didn't catch

14. A: Not again! We've _____ gas!
    B: Don't worry. We can call the Instant Car Service.
    (a) ran out of   (b) run out   (c) been running   (d) run out of

15. A: Are you going to the movies tonight?
    B: Yeah, by then I _____ my work.
    (a) will have finished   (b) finish   (c) will finish   (d) would finish

16. A: I can't write the English essay _____ that music on.
    B: Would you like me to turn it off?
    (a) with   (b) of   (c) in   (d) to

17. A: Why are they taking all the equipment away?
    B: The job _____, they are packing up to leave.
    (a) is done   (b) done   (c) was done   (d) having done

18. A: Did you go to Florida?
    B: No, but I wish _____ when I was in America; I hear it's a beautiful place.
    (a) we had gone   (b) that we go   (c) to have to go   (d) having gone

19. A: Don't you think I'll give it up. I know I can do it.
    B: Maybe you can. But the question is _____.
    (a) how long will it take   (b) to take it long
    (c) how long it will take   (d) taking it long

20. A: What do I need to do now?
    B: The company regulations require that you _____ a full statement of the accident.
    (a) submitting   (b) submission   (c) submit   (d) to submit

Part II

* 다음 글의 빈칸에 가장 적절한 표현을 고르시오.(21-40)

21. _____ I felt most frustrating was the fact that my application had been judged on the sole basis of my gender.
  (a) That   (b) Which   (c) What   (d) Where

22. Coming upon my own words, stolen and displayed in that book looking like a stranger at me, I was amused, flattered, chilled-and in a moment, simply _____.
  (a) painful   (b) painted   (c) pain   (d) painless

23. Signs in such public buildings as police stations _____ often in Spanish as well as in English, and many police officers study Spanish.
  (a) were written   (b) wrote   (c) have written   (d) writing

24. But finally we concluded that the nurses must have been the doctors as well _____ we could find no single official representative of the doctors there.
  (a) since   (b) whereas   (c) if   (d) and

25. The hordes of strangers moving into the city were what made it _____ so fast.
  (a) grow   (b) to grow   (c) growth   (d) growing

26. To compensate for the loss during this fiscal year, the company would have to _____.
  (a) cut severely costs   (b) severely cut costs
  (c) severely costs cut   (d) have severe cut costs

27. _____ when it started raining.

(a) No sooner had the game begun
(b) Scarcely the game had begun
(c) Hardly had the game begun
(d) As soon as the game had begun

28. Doctoral students who are preparing to take their qualifying examinations have been studying in the library every night _____ the last three months.
    (a) since   (b) before   (c) until   (d) for

29. We are saving aluminum cans, bottles, and other items _____.
    (a) to recycle (b) recycling   (c) to be recycled (d) being recycled

30. Lasers are now also used in high-speed printing and in the creation of three-dimensional images, _____.
    (a) called as holograms   (b) they are called holograms
    (c) called holograms   (d) being called as holograms

31. A revolt _____ meant the revival of a small Jewish state.
    (a) by the Maccabees in Palestine
    (b) is the Maccabees in Palestine
    (c) which the Maccabees in Palestine
    (d) has been the Maccabees in Palestine

32. Public pressure is towards more street lighting rather than less the reason is, of course, _____ people feel safer in well-lit streets.
    (a) how   (b) that   (c) when   (d) where

33. More than a third of Bangladesh _____ by monsoons.
    (a) has flooded (b) have flooded (c) was flooded (d) were flooded

34. _____ materials, such as emery, silica sand and quartz, are used in finishing rubber and plastic.

(a) Abrasion occurs in nature   (b) Naturalized abrasives occur
(c) Naturally occurring abrasive   (d) Natural occurrence of abrasion

35. Computer skills are necessary in _____ any profession, whereas many people refuse to learn these skills out of fear.
    (a) almost   (b) most   (c) mostly   (d) most of the

36. At last the doctor decided that he had no choice but _____ that the child be placed in foster care.
    (a) request   (b) to request   (c) requesting   (d) to be requested

37. The firm is not liable for damage resulting from circumstances _____ its control.
    (a) above   (b) inside   (c) around   (d) beyond

38. Dirty snow dampens reflections, increasing _____ that the snow absorbs.
    (a) amount of light and heat   (b) the amount of light and heat
    (c) that the amount of light and heat   (d) the amount of light and heat is

39. I heard some European Americans _____ exploitative Japanese merchants for ruining peaceful race relations for everyone else.
    (a) to rail for   (b) railing for   (c) to rail agains   (d) railing against

40. Your experience there cannot have been valuable, _____ you don't speak the language.
    (a) as if   (b) as for   (c) given that   (d) so that

Part III

* 다음 대화에서 어법상 틀리거나 어색한 부분을 고르시오.(41-45)

41. (a) A: You look pale. Is there anything the matter?
    (b) B: Well, I'm a little under the weather.
    (c) A: Another cold? Shall I get some medicine to you?
    (d) B: No, it's mostly in my stomach this time.

42. (a) A: What a surprise! You must be John!
    (b) B: That's right. Long time no see.
    (c) A: When was the last time we have seen each other?
    (d) B: Five years ago, perhaps?

43. (a) A: Did Judy pay you back the money you lent her?
    (b) B: With her small her salary, I doubt as she ever will.
    (c) A: I thought she'd got a raise.
    (d) B: Sha asked for it, but she didn't get it.

44. (a) A: I had a party last Saturday.
    (b) B: Are you going to have another one?
    (c) A: Absolutely, do you want to come?
    (d) B: Yes, I'd love to. Thanks for being invited.

45. (a) A: May I speak to Dr. Collins?
    (b) B: I'm sorry. He is out of town.
    (c) A: When will he be back? I need to discuss something with him.
    (d) B: You can call a week late.

※ 다음 글에서 문법상 틀리거나 어색한 부분을 고르시오.(46-50)

46. (a) Dental plaque constantly forms on your teeth. (b) By brushing at least twice a day and flossing, you will help minimize this plaque buildup. (c) In addition to homecare, we strongly recommend professional cleaning at least every 6 months. (d) Some individuals may require cleaning every 3 or 4 months depended on the amount of plaque buildup and on the present status of your gums.

47. (a) Every child inside is a hidden strength, an unknown ability, a hero waiting to be discovered. (b) In afterschool program, kids get involved in all kinds of activities. (c) Those activities help them realize they have the potential to do better and reach further than they ever imagined. (d) Let us know if you want an afterschool program in your area.

48. (a) In a bullfight, a piece of red cloth is used to attracting the attention of the bull. (b) When the bull charges, the man steps to one side and kills it by plunging a sword into its body. (c) Many people think that red objects make a bull angry. (d) However, a bull is really color-blinded.

49. (a) While the world of today is radically different from what it used to be only fifteen years ago, political science is slow to adapt. (b) Nation-state is no more the entity that makes policy choices in most case. (c) Yet political scientists are still reluctant to part with the idea of nation-state. (d) Challenged, or rather ignored, all evidence, they still believe nation states are units of political power.

50. (a) Experiments in genetic engineering have created important breakthrough in many areas. (b) They have led to cures for many diseases, the control of insect populations, and the improvement of food production. (c) However, most of these experiments are not foolproof. (d) Because no one knows for sure what negative consequences they could have.

2. 어휘

Part I

* 다음 대화문의 빈칸에 가장 적절한 표현을 고르시오.(1-25)

1. A: You're late again!
   B: I couldn't _____ it. My alarm didn't go off.
   (a) put   (b) help   (c) keep   (d) catch

2. A: Why do you hate him?
   B: I'm sick of his bossing us _____ like that. Who does he think he is?
   (a) around   (b) against   (c) with   (d) in

3. A: Can you _____ an eye on my house while I'm away?
   B: Sure, I'll be glad to.
   (a) catch   (b) hold   (c) keep   (d) have

4. A: _____
   B: Actually, I do. And this is a non-smoking section.
   (a) Did you kick the habit?
   (b) Do you mind if I smoke?
   (c) Can you give me a seat in the smoking section?
   (d) Second-hand smoke is worse than smoking, isn't it?

5. A: What's up? You look quite upset.
   B: A car nearly hit me. It was a close _____.
   (a) prevention   (b) call   (c) attention   (d) collusion

6. A: Let's get down to _____. What do you want?
   B: I want a vacation.
   (a) office   (b) business   (c) deal   (d) compact

7. A: What are you doing in _____ outfit? It's very cold today.
   B: I didn't know it was freezing.
   (a) haggard   (b) skimpy   (c) stinking   (d) sexy

8. A: What are you getting at?
   B: _____.
   (a) I'm arriving at that station   (b) I don't follow you
   (c) I didn't mean that   (d) Let me clarify

9. A: I feel so _____ by this sultry heat.
   B: Isn't it because you're skipping breakfast everyday in the name of losing weight?
   (a) elated   (b) energized   (c) enervated   (d) enchanted

10. A: Is the boss in?
    B: No, I'm afraid he's _____ on leave at the moment.
    (a) around   (b) about   (c) away   (d) over

11. A: I heard he was arrested for the demonstration.
    B: He's in hot water now. The police say they're going to _____ charges.
    (a) petition   (b) pledge   (c) press   (d) plead

12. A: According to the today's newspaper, many cars crashed into each other.
    B: Yes. The _____ happened in thick fog and caused traffic jam downtown.
    (a) pileup   (b) takeover   (c) blowup   (d) makeover

13. A: How can I meet the Governor?
    B: If you want to see the Governor, Mr. Root can pull _____ for you.
    (a) cords   (b) levers   (c) connections   (d) strings

14. A: I heard the news. Don't be down. I think you deserve a(n)_____.

B: Thanks. I hope the management thinks so, too.
(a) raise   (b) lift   (c) progress   (d) arousal

15. A: I have been waiting for you for a long time.
    B: I'm sorry for being late. I missed my keys. I had to look all _____ the apartment for them.
    (a) up   (b) down   (c) over   (d) aside

16. A: How did you get money for the project?
    B: The loan came in _____ just when we needed it.
    (a) hardly   (b) after   (c) late   (d) handy

17. A: He looked quite serious about his offer.
    B: Yes, I bet he had _____ intentions to help us.
    (a) suspicious   (b) malicious   (c) irrelevant   (d) genuine

18. A: Why did he quit his job?
    B: I guess he didn't get a _____ shake from this company.
    (a) prejudiced   (b) useful   (c) fair   (d) profitable

19. A: What happened? I thought you would make it.
    B: I tried my best, but I failed to pass _____.
    (a) muster   (b) courage   (c) trial   (d) ordeal

20. A: I don't know why, but the top seems to be really upset this morning.
    B: He is. We had better give him _____ today. He may take it out on us.
    (a) leave   (b) bargains   (c) room   (d) wages

21. A: The board members want to see the proposal tomorrow morning.
    B: I'll have our team _____ late tonight till they're completed it.
    (a) wake up   (b) watch out   (c) stay back   (d) stand up

22. A: I could take a later flight, but it would be rather inconvenient.
    B: To _____ you, we will give you a complementary ticket to fly anywhere in the United States.
    (a) pay   (b) return   (c) compensate   (d) grant

23. A: I wonder if I can buy some aspirin here.
    B: Sorry, we don't _____ medicine. You can go to the drugstore next door.
    (a) load   (b) lift   (c) contact   (d) carry

24. A: I thought you forgot our appointment.
    B: I'm really sorry I'm late. I was _____ up in traffic coming from Hyndai department store.
    (a) called   (b) held   (c) put   (d) get

25. A: I have heard Taiwan's earthquake caused an _____ amount of damage.
    B: Yeah. It's very unfortunate.
    (a) exorbitant   (b) exclusive   (c) exquisite   (d) extraneous

---

◉ 이디엄

see about ⋯에 유의하다, ⋯을 처리하다
see eye to eye with ⋯와 의견이 일치하다
see to it that ⋯에 주의하다, ⋯하도록 하다
serve (someone) right 당연한 취급을 하다, 그래 싸다
set aside 제쳐놓다, 저축하다
set out 시작하다, 작정하다, 설계하다
set store by ⋯을 중히 여기다
set up 설립하다, 개업하다, 제의하다
settle down 정착하다, 가라앉다

Part II

* 다음 글의 빈칸에 들어갈 가장 적절한 표현을 고르시오.(26-50)

26. If you fly with the same airline, you can _____ mileage points and use them to upgrade on future flights.
    (a) account   (b) assail   (c) accrue   (d) annex

27. In Moscow the economy was already slipping out of control. If the government responds to social pressures by printing new money, the result would be an acceleration into _____.
    (a) economic recovery   (b) economic bonanza
    (c) deflation   (d) hyperinflation

28. With an increasing number of always-on Net connections such as cable modems, _____ hackers could digitally sniff off the master locks to people's lives.
    (a) beneficial   (b) encouraging   (c) amicable   (d) malevolent

29. Online registration will not be available for several days _____ complications with our system.
    (a) as to   (b) due to   (c) in reference to   (d) except for

30. By relaxing the body and calming the mind, meditation seeks to alleviate the harmful effects of tension and stress-factors that are known to _____ a number of medical conditions.
    (a) aggravate   (b) preclude   (c) advance   (d) elude

31. I asked that janitor of our building to fix the leak in the roof, and he said he would _____ it today.
    (a) see to   (b) look at   (c) attend   (d) glimpse

32. If you don't get to _____ your hot temper, you're going to get

in hot water someday.

(a) check   (b) arrest   (c) lose   (d) express

33. Moving about is an _____ environment, at home or abroad, is often not unlike a voyage into the unknown and the uncharted. Yet these sallies into the new can become less fearsome if they are simply regarded as exercises in culture learning.

(a) intricate   (b) incessant   (c) unfeasible   (d) unfamiliar

34. Heart disease is a _____ condition so if your family has a history of suffering from heart attacks you had better schedule frequent checkups.

(a) hereditary   (b) chronic   (c) innate   (d) acquired

35. Contrary to the popular view, a democratic society is a place where are interests competing with each other; therefore, _____ cannot be attained automatically.

(a) disagreement   (b) consensus   (c) distraction   (d) agenda

36. The slow scientific progress in unraveling the link between farm practices and water pollution will continue to hamper innovation that could solve problems in _____ ways.

(a) burdensome   (b) cost-effective   (c) uninhibited   (d) tax-exempted

37. Unemployment has become the most serious problem during this _____ recession following the nation's financial crisis.

(a) frequent   (b) protracted   (c) rejuvenated   (d) elaborate

38. Many Japanese women seem to be _____ about the role they are expected to play in society as citizens.

(a) carnivorous   (b) ambivalent   (c) conspicuous   (d) ambidextrous

39. The growth of travel related industries has been _____ for a recent few years compared with other business sectors due to

steadily improving standards of living.
(a) prominent (b) tractable (c) lenient (d) impassive

40. Many countries have a law which states that adolescents under a certain age can't get married without the _____ of their parents.
(a) condition (b) connection (c) confession (d) consent

41. When the man bought the mansion, he did not know it was going to be such a _____ elephant.
(a) black (b) yellow (c) gray (d) white

42. The old carpenter _____ one inch off the door skillfully.
(a) planed (b) carried (c) shipped (d) trained

43. When a student completes his studies, he should, ideally, be able to make a _____ contribution to his country's social progress.
(a) superficial (b) substantial (c) subsidiary (d) superstitious

44. Children really hate appearing weak and have an obsession to _____ face before their friends.
(a) save (b) lose (c) keep (d) make

45. The world is not a get-rich-quick place; the traditional values of hard work and honesty still _____ in the last analysis.
(a) make do (b) pay off (c) luck out (d) hit the jackpot

46. Thanks to the Internet, it is now possible to _____ public reaction to political speeches even as the speeches are being made.
(a) gauge (b) grant (c) guarantee (d) grip

47. This kind of scientific paper requires a _____ style of writing rather than a redundant one.
(a) consistent (b) terse (c) logistical (d) tacit

48. The awareness of health risks and the prospect of parental punishment rarely seem to _____ middle and high school students from experimenting with cigarettes.
 (a) deter   (b) deepen   (c) deplore   (d) degrade

49. Despite her _____ appearance, she was chosen by the employer for a job which required neatness polish.
 (a) unkempt   (b) tidy   (c) alluring   (d) prepossessing

50. She's so _____ that I don't think she's going to pay for lunch.
 (a) stingy   (b) lavish   (c) rich   (d) extravagant

◉ 이디엄

show off 자랑하다, 과시하다
sit in on 참가하다
slack off 태만히 하다
stand by 지지하다, …를 편들다
stand a chance 가능성이 있다, 승산이 있다
stand for 대표하다, 지지하다, 참다
stand to reason …은 당연하다, 이치에 닿다
stand up to …에 맞서다
steer clear of …을 피하다
stick around 주변을 어슬렁거리다
stick to one's guns 자기의 주장을 고수하다
take a lot out of (someone) …를 지치게 하다
take (someone) by surprise 놀라게 하다, 기습을 하다
take down 내리다, 적다
take exception 화를 내다, 이의를 제기하다
take in 유숙시키다, 속이다
take issue with 대립하다, 논의하다

3. 독해

* 다음 글을 읽고 빈칸에 들어갈 가장 적절한 것을 고르시오.(1-16)

1. The traditional Puritan view of success held it that we had to work hard not primarily to make money but to make ourselves a better person. Success meant succeeding in achieving that moral purpose of self-improvement. Therefore, you had to make efforts to develop yourself, and if you were successful enough in doing that, _____ followed as a reward, as a by-product, so to speak. Man's duty to God, to fellow men, and to himself, was to work hard for its own sake, to be diligent in one's "calling."

(a) self confidence
(b) moral enhancement
(c) devoted vocation
(d) material gain

2. At first, expressive language arrives one word at a time, as early as by ten months for some children. By eighteen months, on average, a child has accumulated some fifty words, and from here the child's vocabulary grows at a fiery pace. Between the ages of two and six, children learn the meaning of some eight new words a day. By the time they enter school, they have a mind-boggling eleven thousand-word vocabulary. This vocabulary explosion is associated with an actual spurt in brain development. At each stage of language acquisition, there is _____ in different parts of the brain.

(a) a circular pattern
(b) an unexplained halt
(c) heightened activity
(d) slow regression

3. To ensure safe operation the plug must be inserted only into a standard power point which is effectively grounded through the normal

household writing. Extension cords used with the equipment must be correctly wired to provide connection to ground.

Incorrectly wired extension cords are a major cause of fatalities. The fact that the equipment operates satisfactorily does not imply that the power is grounded and that the installation is completely safe. _____, if in any doubt about the effective grounding of the power, consult a qualified electrician.

(a) For efficient operation (b) For saving power
(c) For your safety (d) For storage environment

4. The instinctive foundation of the intellectual life is curiosity, which is found among animals in its elementary form. Intelligence demands an alert curiosity, but it must be of a certain kind. The sort that leads village neighbors to try to peer through curtains after dark has no very high value. The widespread interest in gossip is inspired, not by love of knowledge, but by malice: no one gossip about other people's secret virtues, but only about their _____.

(a) well-known virtues (b) public malice
(c) secret vices (d) alert curiosity

5. "Business will account for 80 percent of Internet use and private users just 20 percent," a well-known technologist attending the economic forum here predicted Tuesday. Michael Dell. who runs Dell Corporation, made the forecast at a session on the "Future of the Internet." Microsoft president Bill Gates on Monday _____ high expectations about trading and banking in cyber-space. "Is everybody going to be shopping, banking there? It's just not realistic, it takes time for these things to happen," he said.

(a) dampened (b) bolstered (c) illuminated (d) solidified

6. The similarities between the wild world of ecology and the high-powered world of finance may seem few, but they have one thing in common: data, in large quantities. The difference is that, in ecology, the development of methods to extract meaningful trends from data has lagged behind the collection of the data themselves.

The result is that generations of ecologists tended to regard data collection as an end _____, and amassed heroic quantities of data with little idea of what should be done with them.

(a) for itself   (b) for themselves   (c) by itself   (d) in itself

7. Furnishing a home, like writing a book, is a(n) _____. People's tasted and needs tend to change. Rooms take on different purposes and functions. Furniture is rearranged, or discarded. New furniture comes in to replace the old.

(a) everlasting masterpiece   (b) soul-destroying process
(c) continual editing process   (d) endless headache

8. These days people tend to over-intellectualize their difficulties. In so doing they often turn simple practical matters into complex theoretical ones. _____, the problems can get completely out of their control, making people incapable of effective action.

(a) To make matters better   (b) On the contrary
(c) So far   (d) As a result

9. Deceptive paintwork is used to camouflage military installations, but clever painting alone does not hide the objects. If any painted objects throw a shadow, it can be detected by a field glass or camera lens. Consequently, camouflage or disguise of military installations must blend – by light, shade, and shape – into the landscape.

Gun emplacements on a flat surface must look flat; and, for jungle fighting, soldiers uniforms must be shaded to resemble _____.

(a) foliage   (b) wild animals   (c) flat surfaces   (d) the enemy

10. Italian cuisine has experienced increased popularity in recent years in Japan. But it was not just pasta and pizza which became household names. Sales of Espresso have also skyrocketed which has _____ increased demand for sophisticated home-use espresso machines. Their popularity is expected to grow as more restaurants and coffee shops include the European-style drink in their menus.

(a) excluded   (b) showed off   (c) participated in   (d) resulted in

11. Historical interpretation shape our image of the past and have an impact on future actions. Individuals often make decisions based on what they believe to be the historical purposes and goals of an institution. Given the variety and number of events that occur on any particular day, a historian can _____ about which events and combination of social activities he or she wishes to emphasize. Thus, two different historians can give differing interpretations to historical events yet remain accurate to historical fact.

(a) be vague   (b) be selective   (c) generalize   (d) falsify

12. Today we must abandon competence and secure cooperation. This must be a central fact in our considerations of international affairs; _____, we face certain disaster. Past thinking and methods did not succeed in preventing world wars. Future thinking must prevent wars.

(a) however   (b) otherwise   (c) nevertheless   (d) on the other hand

13. Primitive men thought that disease was caused by evil spirits which entered the body of the victim. They thought the only way to save a sick man was to drive the evil spirit out of his body. Several

methods were used. Usually the evil spirit was coaxed to come forth. If coaxing did not succeed, _____ was tried. In some cases tom-toms were beaten; in others the beating was done on the chest of the sick man. Usually the patient died before the evil spirit fled.

 (a) praying (b) magic (c) force (d) hypnotism

14. The most serious controversy to arise over intelligence tests has to do with the unresolved debate about whether heredity or environment has the greater influence on intelligence. Social scientists who hold that the environment has the stronger influence assail the tests for being racially and culturally biased. But those who believe that heredity is the dominant influence have used comparative test results to suggest genetic differences among the various races and ethnic groups. While the controversies have continued to rage, the continuity to be used. But now they are _____ used as the only basis for judging a child's intellectual performance and potential. This is because it is taken for granted that motivational and cultural factors also play a significant role in development.

 (a) still going to be (b) much less likely to be
 (c) more likely to be (d) forced to be

15. Kids and adults alike are told that we are running out of energy, minerals and other natural resources to recycle. this is sheer and utter nonsense. All facts and figures show energy and mineral reserves greatly increasing in amount and decreasing in price. Fear mongers use the tricky phrase "known reserves" which only counts the reserves available at current price levels. Oil, for example, in shale and deeper wells currently not cost productive to extract would be _____ should price levels increase to a certain level.

 (a) rather unnecessary (b) readily available

(c) very expensive   (d) completely worthless

16. Ever since the U.S. public began listening to radio soaps in the 1930s, cultural critics have explored the content, form, and popularity of daytime serials. Today, media critics take a variety of approaches. Some explore audience response and find that, depending on sex, race, or even nationality, people "decode" the same story in different ways. Others regard soaps as a kind of subversive form of popular culture that supports women's deepest grievances. Still others view the soap as a text and attempt to analyze it, much as _____.

(a) a literary critic dissects a work of literature
(b) a scientist conducts an experiment in the lab
(c) a journalist collects materials for his column
(d) an archeologist excavates an ancient civilization

◎ 이디엄

take no stock in …을 신용하지 않다
take on (성격을) 띠다, 고용하다
take to …이 좋아지다, 마음에 들다
take turns 번갈아 하다
tell on …에 영향을 미치다
throw up 토하다
tip off 비밀 정보를 제공하다
tone in with …와 조화하다
touch off 야기 시키다
turn down 거절하다, 줄이다, 소리를 낮추다
turn thumbs down on 불만을 나타내다
wallow one's pride 감정을 억누르다
wind up 끝마치다, 마무리 짓다
work out 결국 …이 되다, 해결하다

Part II

* 다음 글을 읽고 질문에 가장 적절한 답을 고르시오.(17-37)

17. The ancient Greeks knew that light could heal. They put sick patients in the sun to aid the curative process. But modern technology has dramatically increased the possibility of light, giving us lasers and light-activated drugs. Therapeutic light penetrates deep into the tissues and boosts the body's own natural healing processes. Researchers have shown that certain infrared wavelengths stimulate blood vessels, causing them to dilate, and increase circulation to the wounded area.

This stimulation improves the delivery of oxygen and nutrients as well as the removal of wastes, and so quickens the restoration of the damaged tissue.

Q. What is the passage mainly about?
(a) Modern medical technology
(b) Modern discovery of light
(c) Therapeutic power of light
(d) Stimulation and healing process

18. Several years ago, I spent a weekend with some friends in the country. Helen, my hostess, was seven months pregnant, and in the morning I would find her sitting alone in front of the fireplace, softly signing a beautiful lullaby to her unborn child.

After the birth of her son, Helen told me that same lullaby had a magical effect on him. No matter how hard the baby was crying, he would calm down when the song was sung. As a psychiatrist with a special interest in prenatal experiences, I was intrigued and wondered if a woman's actions could influence her unborn child. I began searching scientific literature for information that would help me understand the mind of the unborn.

Q. Which of the following would be the best title for the passage?

(a) On a special Hobby
(b) Spending a Weekend in the country
(c) The Great Achievement of a Psychiatrist
(d) The Secret life of the Unborn Child

19. After a 14-hour debate, the parliament of Australia's northern territory passed the world's first law what permits medically assisted voluntary euthanasia. Approved 15 to 10, the controversial bill allows the incurably sick to end their lives, provided that a physician and a psychiatrist determine the patient to be both terminally ill and sane.

Q. What will be an appropriate title of the above passage?

(a) Doctor's Right in Australia Strengthened
(b) Australia's First Abortion Bill Passed
(c) First Medical Examination Free in Australia
(d) Mercy Killing Allowed in Australia

20. Was it a carefully planned sabotage? Was it a man-made disaster caused by mechanical failure? Or was it simply hit by lightning? Did some lunatic shoot it from the sky? There are many stories and speculations about the Hindenburg tragedy, which marked the beginning and the end of transatlantic airships at the same time. Hindenburg, a 804-foot dirigible filled with over 7 million cubic feet of hydrogen, was a crowning achievement of the age. However, the explosion of the Hindenburg on May 6, 1937 changed the landscape for lighter-than-air crafts forever.

Q. According to the passage, what can be inferred about Hindenburg?

(a) There are many theories about the cause of its tragic explosion.

(b) It used a combination of hydrogen and nitrogen for fuel.
(c) The transatlantic airship industry flourished after its explosion.
(d) It crossed the Atlantic over 100 times by the year 1937.

21. Anyone experienced with depression and anxiety knows that these illnesses can be difficult to treat. In their treatment, two areas that have often been overlooked are hormonal causes and the link between biochemistry and the brain. Also depression and anxiety are also thought to underlie addictions, as people try some form of self-medication in order to feel better. Natural therapies are now popular because patients want to avoid the side effects of synthetic drugs. The key is to integrate natural and synthetic treatments optimizing the health of each patient.

Q. Which is correct according to the passage?

(a) Depression and anxiety might bring about drug addiction.
(b) Depression and anxiety are entirely due to hormone disorders.
(c) It is difficult to integrate natural and synthetic treatments.
(d) Natural therapies are more reliable than synthetic treatments.

22. Supermarket managers have all kinds of tricks to encourage people to spend more money. Their aim is to make customers go more slowly through the supermarket. They place colorful displays to surprising places to catch the customers' attention. They also make the corridors near the cash registers narrower.

Then a customer with a large shopping cart will get struck or have to slow down. In some supermarkets, the floor is even slightly uphill for people going toward the exits. Managers hope that when customers slow down, they will buy more.

Q. What would be the most suitable title for the above?

(a) The illusion of shopping paradise

(b) How to provide a better service in the supermarket
(c) A few tricks to detain a customer
(d) Slow down: a new marketing strategy of the supermarket.

23. Children are particularly susceptible to the effects of television because their minds are growing, developing, and learning much faster than those of adults. Whereas television could be used as an educational tool for children. more often simple entertaining cartoons with little or no educational value are shown.

Social scientists, teachers, and parents are troubled by the kinds of television programs children choose to watch. These groups of people are concerned about the media's impact on young children. They are worried about the effects of televised violence on society as well as commercials for sugarcoated food. Most importantly, however, they feel television is one factor that causes declining math and reading scores among schoolchildren. Because of the excessive time spent watching TV, children are spending less time reading and thinking independently.

Q. Which of the following is true according to the passage?

(a) Adults are more likely to be influenced by television than children.
(b) Social scientists are concerned about what children watch on TV.
(c) Schoolchildren can learn how to read scores from watching TV.
(d) Children who watch TV cannot read and think independently.

24. Children love cartoons. They can sit watching them for hours. And with today's cable cartoon channels, television offers one cartoon programs after another, twenty-four hours a day, seven days week. However, many of those television programs communicate a disturbing message: they suggest that the world is one big battlefield. In cartoon after cartoon, people and animals shoot, bomb, and blow one another up, without any serious or fatal consequences. Given the level of violence in our society

today, this is a dangerous message to be giving children.

Q. Which of the following is the best title of the above passage?

(a) The world Described by cartoons
(b) Serious Problems Raised by Television Programs
(c) the Reason Children Love Cartoons
(d) Cartoons- Dangerous Messages to Children

25. Manual laborers and desk jockeys alike are at risk of back pain, from mildly annoying to utterly incapacitating. Some experts speculate that humans are unusually vulnerable to backaches because of a flaw in our evolution. We may have figured out how to walk upright, but our spindly spines lack the strength to support our heavy heads. Strenuous activity can lead to injuries, but sitting around can be hard on your lower back, too.

Q. Which is correct according to the passage?

(a) Manual workers have more back pain than office workers.
(b) Inactivity is better for back pain.
(c) Back pain is easily curable.
(d) Humans are not fully suited to walking upright.

26. With a computer and fairly decent software, practically anyone can be an artist. They're already replacing breathing actors with computer simulations. Why not artists? By 2100, the idea of human artists may be so passé that experts of the 22nd century may wonder how we could have been so gauche as to rely on mere mortals to create fine works of art. Actually, as long as somebody can see things in a different way, artists will always exist. They just may use different media than before with which to express themselves.

Q : Which of the following would be the best title of the passage?

(a) Artists in the Future
(b) The Crisis of Human Artists
(c) The Computer: A New Type of Artist
(d) The Definition of the Artist

27. Prior to 1978, works were given 28 years of copyright protection, followed by the possibility of 28 more years, if application for renewal was made during the 28th year of the first term of protection. As of 1978, the renewal period for works still under copyright was extended to 47 years, and later an additional 20 years was added to this. Beginning in 1998, copyright holders were no longer required to apply for renewal. Copyright protection was automatically extended to 75 years, and later 95 years.

Q : Which of the following can be inferred from the passage?

(a) The copyright law has changed five times in total.
(b) Before 1998 copyright protection for a work was 28 years if not renewed.
(c) The copyright law was more beneficial to works prior to 1978.
(d) The minimum copyright protection period was 56 years.

28. The human brain responds to sudden fright by signaling the adrenal glands to release more adrenaline, also known as epinephrine, into the bloodstream. This substance, often called the 'fight or flight hormone', prepares the body for instant exertion. It makes the heart beat faster, stimulates the circulation, and relaxes the bronchial passages so they can send more air through the lungs. It can all happen very quickly because this is the body's life-preserving response to sudden danger.

Q: Which of the following is the best title for the above passage?

(a) The way the human body reacts to fear

(b) How does adrenaline get into the bloodstream?
(c) How to speed the heartbeat
(d) What stimulates circulation?

29. Win win policy refers to public policy that is capable of achieving both conservative and liberal goals simultaneously. Examples could be given from any field of public policy, such as economic, social, environmental, legal, or political policy. Win win policies should be distinguished from compromises, where both sides partially retreat from achieving their goals in order to obtain an agreement. Win win policy is sometimes referred to as super optimizing policy. The concept of win win means all major sides win, but the concept of winning can be ambiguous. If each side does some winning and some losing, that is sometimes called a win win solution, but it is really a traditional compromise with a glorifying name.

Q: Which of the following best summarizes the above passage?

(a) Win win policy is distinguished from compromise and means all major sides win
(b) Win win policy is as important as compromise in politics
(c) The concept of win win policy is a very ambiguous concept
(d) Win win policies can be applied to any field of public policy

30. The sweat house was used to treat many illnesses, and in cases of fever where sweating was desirable, this treatment proved very helpful. The sweat house was a dirt-covered hut in which a fire was kept burning. When a feverish person entered, the single door would be closed tight. The person would remain in the hut and endure the stifling heat for as long as possible. Then, this person would run outside and complete the treatment by leaping into the nearest lake or stream.

Q: Which of the following is the best title for the above passage?

(a) What is a Sweat House?
(b) How to Construct Sweat House
(c) How to Cure Feverish Patients
(d) The Effect of Sweat Houses on Fever Treatment

31. The land we walk on, the air we breathe, and the water we drink are slowly being poisoned by the waste we create. In the process of producing and consuming material goods, our society generates mountains of waste. Household wastes are often discarded with little regard for their harmful effects. As a result, we are now facing waste problems in proportions beyond imagination. We dispose of our waste by storing, dumping, burying or burning it. But it does not go away, and will most certainly come back to haunt both us and future generations, whose problems may be greatly magnified because of our failure to handle waste appropriately.

Q: Which of the following can be inferred from the above passage?

(a) We must bury our waste instead of dumping or burning it.
(b) The best way to eliminate the waste problem is to prevent it in.
(c) Industrial toxic wastes are more harmful than household wastes.
(d) Reducing waste is a less effective solution than recycling and reusing

32. We all think freedom is important, but when push comes to shove, it's not our top concern. Those who stand up for liberty by criticizing government action during times of crisis will always be a persecuted minority in this country. They face derision and mockery because they speak up when they are supposed to be silent, point out error when there is supposed to unity. Without them, however, our country would not be the free nation it is today. Today's civil libertarians can be counted among those who stood up for freedom for all of us in spite of popular opinion.

Q : Which of the following is true about civil libertarians?

(a) When things get difficult, freedom is not their top concern.
(b) They represent the main stream of our society.
(c) They work hard to unite our country during times of crisis.
(d) During times of crisis they sometimes criticize government.

33. The government was accused of keeping communities in the dark and trying to make boat people an election issue yesterday after it announced three new immigration detention centers would be built. The Rimmer Army Barracks, which housed Kosovo refugees, will be set up as a center to house up to 1,000 asylum seekers. TPK Management, whose contract is up at the end of the year, will manage the new centers. The Immigration Minister, Mr. Smith, yesterday blamed the long delays in moving people from detention centers on Labor's continued refusal to pass a bill banning access to court appeals and on the difficulty the government has had in deporting people who arrived without documentation. "What we're saying is mandatory detention will not be unwound regardless of numbers," said Mr. Smith.

Q : Which of the following is correct according to the article?

(a) Labor is against the construction of the new immigration detention centers.
(b) The new centers will help the government deport people without documentation.
(c) There will be no change in management regarding detention in the centers to be added.
(d) The new immigration detention centers are intended to help asylum seekers.

34. While the euro is certain to define what Europe is, it also will underscore what it is not. Euroland will have a single currency, a central

bank and a common monetary policy, but it will still be led by 11 distinct economies. It will have a central banker, but 11 finance ministers. Monetary union will tightly mesh the Euroland countries economically, but it will not create a budgetary or political superstructure to oversee them. And while 11 nations can agree on the creation of the euro, they have shown very little unanimity on what policy to pursue in Iraq or closer to home, Kosovo province. A common foreign policy remains distant dream.

Q: Which of the following best summarizes the above passage?

(a) The euro does not mean the political or economical unification.
(b) The euro will solve the political and economic discord in Europe.
(c) The euro will encourage the political and economical independence of European countries.
(d) The euro will unite the Euroland countries economically

35. Since the 1980s, mental health experts have known that the shorter days of fall and winter can bring on the blues. Studies show that winter depression is caused by a death of daylight. Summer depression, on the other hand, seems more closely tied to heat than to light. The effects of heat can be like depression. You lose motivation, you sit around a lot, you're not engaged in things, it can interfere with your sleep. Summer depression may be an extreme expression of the body's normal physiological response to heat.

Q: Which of the following is true according to the article?

(a) Winter depression is related to the length of day.
(b) Summer depression is the body's normal response to light.
(c) The symptoms of winter depression include sleeplessness.
(d) A person with summer depression suffers from headaches.

36. Catching a cloud might seem as tricky a task as trying to bottle

a rainbow. But the residents of Caleta Chungungo, a mountain village in one of the driest regions of northern Chile, have found a way of doing it. They are able to wring water from an otherwise stingy sky by trapping it in nets. Unlike its neighbors in the surrounding valleys, Caleta gets little relief from nearby rivers carrying water from the Andes to the sea. Even worse, the town lies in the path of the Pacific anticyclone.

    Q : Which of the following can be inferred from the above passage?

      (a) Someone once tried to catch a rainbow in vain.
      (b) It is practically impossible for human beings to make the skies rain.
      (c) Chileans have had a hard time fighting off drought.
      (d) Water had to be shipped in from afar before the cloud-capture system was developed.

37. This site should work on most browsers, although it is written with Netscape as the priority browser. The major topic pages are all headed with a navigation graphic. However, if you wish to follow all the topics in sequence, use the buttons at the bottom of each page to navigate through the site. Side excursions on this site always have link buttons back to the major topic under study. To avoid getting lost in space it is always a good idea to open a new window when you link to remote sites.

    Q. Which of the following is not true according to the above passage?

      (a) Netscape will probably work best on this web site.
      (b) The site was made to work using any browser.
      (c) After a side excursion, it is easy to return to the main topic.
      (d) Buttons at the bottom of the page allow you to explore topics in sequence.

* 다음 글을 읽고 내용의 흐름상 어색한 부분을 고르시오.(38-40)

38. You know life's gift to you is your body. Your thanks in return is to take the best care of it you can. (a) Give it a chance to function at its highest level, unimpeded by toxic waste and weight; let your body shine. (b) It does not want to be overweight, it wants to have the shape that you know it can have. (c) All you have to do is facilitate its natural processes, and you can start to experience the joys of a body you will be proud of. (d) Enjoy yourself as you consider the disappearance of the slender body you know has been locked inside you all this time.

39. In astronomy the heliocentric theory advanced by Copernicus in the sixteenth century was just the beginning. (a) In 1632, Galileo published a book defending the heliocentric concept and ridiculing supporters of traditional geocentric theory. (b) But the church brought Galileo before the Inquisition and he was sentenced to perpetual house arrest. (c) Despite a public recantation, Galileo is reported to have had the last word- "And yet it does move." (d) Heliocentric theory raised many difficulties, notably when observation of planetary orbits did not confirm Copernicus' belief.

40. Even in a marriage that is fundamentally fine, we may have to live with a certain amount of loneliness. (a) No two people match perfectly. (b) Parts of ourselves may be understood by the person we had hoped would be our soul mate. (c) There's nothing my husband can do that will ever get me to share his mania for professional football. (d) There's nothing I can do that will make him love the poems of Yeats.

제3부

해 설

유형별 문제 분석

제1부 PRE-TEST

II. 틀린 부분 찾기

실력문제 1회

1. 선행사가 사물(world)이므로 whom→ which. 관계대명사에 밑줄이 그어져 있으면 주의해서 보아야 한다. count for much 중요하다.

    ✍(해석) 그가 섬기던 신이나 보존했던 학문도 은퇴한 세상에서 중요하지 않았다. **정답 ④**

2. finish는 동명사를 목적어로 취하는 동사이므로 ② to read→ reading. 동명사를 목적어로 취하는 동사는 <MEGAFEPS>로 기억하면 된다. M(mind 싫어하다, 꺼리다), E(enjoy 즐기다), G(give up 포기하다), A(avoid 피하다), F(finish 끝내다), E(escape, evade 피하다), P(postpone, put off 연기하다), S(suggest 제안하다) 등이다.

    ✍(해석) 내가 신문을 다 읽어서 신문에 보도된 끔찍한 사고에 관하여 생각하기 시작 했다. **정답 ②**

3. both뒤에는 복수명사가 와야 하므로 ① both→ mutual(상호간의, 공통의). convert 바꾸다, 개종시키다, 환산하다. currency 유통, 통화 invoice 송장.

    ✍(해석) 상호 합의 하에 가격은 송장을 보낸 날짜에 공시된 환율에 따라 다른 통화로 환산할 수도 있다. **정답 ①**

4. plan은 to 부정사를 목적어로 취하므로 ② to improved→to improve. in (the) light of -을 고려하여(=considering). cutback 축소, 삭감(=reduction). fare 요금.

✍(해석) 경제적 위축을 고려해 많은 항공사들이 보다 저렴한 항공료에 안락한 서비스를 개선시키려고 계획을 세우고 있다. **정답 ②**

5. 전치사 다음에는 명사, 동명사, 대명사(목적격)가 와야 하므로 ④ to learn→ learning. financial 재정의, 회계의(=fiscal, pecuniary, monetary).
✍(해석) 당신이 선택하는 회계 컨설턴트는 당신의 업종에 대한 지식이 있어야 하고 당신의 회사에 관해 더 많이 배우려는 관심을 가져야 한다. **정답 ④**

6. 전치사 뒤에는 명사가 와야 하므로 ③ cave draw→ cave drawing(동굴 벽화).
✍(해석) 가장 훌륭한 몇 개의 동굴 벽화와 그림들이 프랑스에서 발견되었다. **정답 ③**

7. call의 구문을 묻는 문제이다. call A B(A를 B로 부르다)를 수동태로 고치면 A is called B의 형태이다. 따라서 ③에서 as를 없애야 한다. [참고] A를 B로 간주하다: regard A as B=look upon A as B= think of A as B= consider A B
✍(해석) 19세기의 가장 유명한 소프라노인 제니 린드는 "스웨덴 의 나이팅게일"이라고 불리웠다. **정답 ③**

8. 접속사 that이하는 완전한 문장이 와야 하므로 ④ that→ what. What은 문장에서 주어, 목적어, 보어의 역할을 한다.
✍(해석) 그 충돌 사고에서 살아 남은 사람은 없었고, 당국에 의하면 충돌의 원인이 무엇인지 아직도 단서를 찾지 못하고 있다고 한다. **정답 ④**

9. 비교하는 대상이 같아야 한다. '수'를 비교하고 있으므로 ④ girl students→ that of girl students. (해 석) 심지어 초등학교 수준에서도 특히 시골 지역에서는 남학생 수가 여학생수를 훨씬 능가하고 있다. **정답 ③**

10. 선행사가 단수이므로 ④ try to→ tries to. (해석) 집단치료는 집단 구성원들 간에 도움을 줄 수 있는 상호작용을 촉진하고 고무시키는 치료사의 인도에 따라 여러 명의 의뢰인을 동시에 치료하는 것을 가리킨다. **정답 ④**

11. smash를 수식해야 하므로 ③ bad→badly smash (해석) 현재로서 공

식적인 목표는 밀로소비치의 군사력을 현저히 무력화시켜 코소보 해방군과 코소보 마을에 자행되고 있는 인종 살육(genccidal을 더 이상 계속할 수 없게 하는 것이다. **정답 ③**

12. 전치사 뒤에 명사, 동명사가 오는데 목적어(color)가 있으므로 ④ change→ changing.
✍(해석) 북미에서는 카멜레온이라는 이름은 색깔을 바꿀 수 있는 여러 종류의 도마뱀들에게 보통 주어진다. **정답 ④**

13. 복합명사의 첫 번째 명사는 형용사적으로 쓰여 단수로 써야 하므로 ① oceans→ ocean. iceberg 빙산.
✍(해석) 바람과 해류는 빙산을 근원지로부터 수천 킬로미터 이동시킨다. **정답 ①**

14. 명사 definition(정의)을 수식하는 형용사가 와야 하므로 ④ not→ no. not은 부사이고, no는 형용사라는 것에 주의할 것.
✍(해석) 대부분의 사람들이 민속음악의 개념을 일반적으로 이해한다고 할지라도, 간단하고 널리 수용되는 정의가 내려지지 않았다. **정답 ④**

15. 전치사구(of the ocean)에 의해 수식을 받으므로 명사(surface)앞에 정관사가 들어가야 한다. ③ below surface→ below the surface. penetrate 관통하다(=pierce), 간파하다(=discern)
✍(해석) 태양 빛은 바다 표면 아래로 수 백미터만 침투할 수 있다. **정답 ③**

16. <형용사+ enough to+ 동사>의 구문을 묻는 문제이므로 ②에서 too를 없애야 한다. too-to 구문이 아닌 것에 주의할 것. drought 가뭄
✍(해석) 가뭄은 물의 순환에 심각한 불균형을 야기 시킬 만큼 오랫동안 건조한 날씨가 계속되는 기간이다. **정답 ②**

17. which 이하를 분석해 보면 타동사 made에 목적어가 없으므로 수동태가 되어야 한다. 따라서 ④ which made→ which was made. 타동사가 자동사가 되는 것이 수동태이다. 다시 말하면 타동사인데 목적어가 없으면 수동태이다.

✍(해석) 미국의 면적은 1803년 루이지애나를 매입한 결과로 두 배가 되었다. **정답 ④**

18. 타동사 modify(변경하다, 완화하다)의 동명사인 modifying 뒤에 목적어가 와야 하므로 ③ the distribute→ the distribution. 명사는 주어, 목적어, 보어, 동격의 역할을 한다. 또한 관사 뒤에는 명사가 와야 하므로 ③이 틀린 것을 알 수 있다.
✍(해석) 구름은 지구표면과 대기권 안에서 태양열을 분배하는데 변화를 주는 매우 중요한 기능을 수행한다. **정답 ③**

19. 형용사 dry를 수식해야 하므로 ④ complete→ completely. part 지역(=area, region)
✍(해석) 어떤 사막지역들은 수개월 또는 심지어 수년간 강수량이 없다고 할지라도, 완전히 건조해지지는 않는다. **정답 ④**

20. <정관사+형용사+명사>의 어순이므로 ② centrally→ central. govern 다스리다(=rule), 억제하다(=restrain), 지배하다(=guide). function 작용하다(=work), 역할을 하다(=be used) (해석) 신체의 중앙통제기관으로서 뇌는 신체의 다른 기관의 기능을 지배한다. **정답 ②**

실력문제 2회

1. <형용사+명사>의 어순이므로 ④ resourceful→ resource. (해석) 대부분의 사람들이 기름 혹은 물이 세계에서 가장 소중한 천연 자원이라고 주장할 때, 막 패러는 생명을 유지할 수 있는 미래를 위한 가장 필수적인 자원이 사실상 지식이라는 것을 믿었다. **정답 ④**

2. 조동사 뒤에는 동사 원형이 와야 하므로 ① took place→ take place. summit 정상(=top), 절정(=acme), (국가의) 정상급 commodity 상품(=goods, merchandise) (해석) 지식과 정보가 귀중한 상품이 된 정보사회의 급속한 발전을 이미 목격한 새로운 세기에 정상이 생길 것이다. **정답 ①**

3. deal은 자동사로 의미상 with와 함께 쓴다. ② deal the→ deal with

the. deal with 거래하다, 대처하다 casualties 사상자들 authorities 당국

✎(해석) 존 박 사는 당국의 어떤 도움도 없이 그와 조수들이 지친 때문에 생긴 사상자들을 돌볼 수 있을지 우려를 나타냈다. **정답 ②**

4. 선행사(aspects)와 관계대명사 뒤에 나오는 동사의 수가 일치해야 하므로 ② needs→ need.

✎(해석) 더 토론할 필요가 있는 그 문제의 모든 양상들이 다음 정규 회의에서 다루어질 것이다. **정답 ②**

5. for 이하가 <공연 내내>의 뜻이므로 ④ performers→ performance. 사람 명사와 사물명사를 구별하는 것에 주의할 것.

✎(해석) 우리는 타운젠드 홀에서 열린 음악회를 매우 즐겼지만, 개인적인 문제 때문에 공연 내내 머물지 못했다. **정답 ④**

6. <사역동사(let)+ 목적어+ 원형동사> 구문이므로 ② to know→know.

✎(해석) 만약 당신이 얼마나 많은 부수가 필요한가를 출판부에 미리 알려 준다면, 그들은 며칠 정도면 그것들을 입수할 수 있게 해 줄 것이다. **정답 ②**

7. <as(접속사)+주어+동사> 구문과 recommend(추천하다, 권고하다)가 타동사인데 목적어가 없고 뒤에 by가 있는 것에 주의할 것. 따라서 as이하는 'as it is recommended by'로 써야 하고 'it is'는 생략할 수 있다. 그러므로 ④ recommendation→ recommended. cleaning agent 세척제.

✎(해석) 이 세척제가 제조업자에 의해 추천된 물질에 사용된다면 가장 효과가 있을 것이다. **정답 ④**

8. by는 완료를 the end of next month는 미래를 표시하므로, 주절의 동사는 미래완료가 와야 한다. ② has doubled→will has doubled.

✎(해석) 현재의 추세로 미루어 본다면 데이터 전송 속도는 다음 달 말까지 두 배가 될 것이다. **정답 ②**

9. ①에는 주어진 문장의 동사(is)의 주어가 되면서, 목적어(customer service)를 동반하므로 동명사가 와야 한다. ① Improve→ Improving.

✎(해석) 고객 서비스를 개선시키는 것이 회사 업무를 향상시키고 운영

비를 줄이는데 핵심적인 것이다. **정답 ①**

10. 주어와 동사가 의미가 통하지 않는다. shower는 '소나기로 적시다'의 뜻이므로 ① showers→ shows.
✍(해석) 한 독자적인 여론조사가 보여주는 바에 따르면 토마스가 현재 그 주에서 가장 인기 있는 정치가라고 한다. **정답 ①**

11. < 주어+ 타동사+ it + 보어(형용사, 명사)+ for 의미상 주어+ to 동사> 구문을 묻는 문제이다. it는 가목적어, to이하는 진목적어이다. 이 구문에서 타동사로 사용되는 것에는 make, find, believe, think 등이 있다. ② makes possible→ makes it possible. payroll tax 근로소득세
✍(해석) 새로운 컴퓨터 기술로 인해 누구나 근로소득세를 비교적 쉽게 계산할 수 있게 되었다. **정답 ②**

12. find의 목적보어로서 동사가 올 수 없으므로 ② run→ running. keep[hold] pace with …와 보조를 맞추다, …에 뒤지지 않다.
✍(해석) 한국 시장을 책임진 경영진들은 기회를 놓치지 않고 정부의 정책과 보조를 맞추어 경영하는 것이 어렵게 되었다. **정답 ②**

13. before가 접속사이므로 뒤에 <주어+동사>가 와야 한다. 따라서 ④ presenting→ presented. board 이사회.
✍(해석) 그가 보고서에 최종 수정을 가한 몇 시간 후에 그것을 이사회에 보고했다. **정답 ④**

14. to 부정사가 명사구(a good point)를 수식하는 형용사적 용법이므로 ② to emphasis→ to emphasize. emphasis 강조. emphasize 강조하다 (=stress, underline, underscore)
✍(해석) 대부분의 소규모 출판사들이 실패하는 분야가 마케팅과 유통이므로 그것을 강조하는 것이 아마도 장점이 될 것이다. **정답 ②**

15. 주어가 사람일 때 과거분사를, 주어가 사물일 때 현재 분사를 사용한다. (Ex) I am interested in this book.= This book is interesting to me. tired 피곤한, 지친 tiring 지루한, 지치게 하는 ④ tiring→tired

✍(해석) 톰은 휴식 없이 14시간을 일한 후에 매우 피곤하게 느꼈다. **정답 ④**

16. <be+과거분사>형태가 와야 하므로 ② be withhold→ be withheld. withhold 보류하다(=keep), 억제하다(=hold back) delinquent 직무에 태만한, 비행의, 체납의 [참고] juvenile delinquency 청소년 범죄.

✍(해석) 그 고객이 체납액에 대한 우리의 통지에 만족스럽게 답변할 때까지 서비스가 보류될 것이다. **정답 ②**

17. 주절에 제안, 주장, 명령, 요구, 결정, 권고 등의 뜻을 가진 동사, 형용사, 명사가 있을 경우 that절에서는 동사원형을 쓰거나 조동사 should를 쓴다. 주절에 쓰이는 동사는 다음과 같다. 즉 insist, urge, order, suggest, propose, advise, demand, request, require, ask, recommend, decide 등이다. 그런데 incorporate는 구체화하다(=embody)는 뜻을 가진 타동사이고, 뒤에 목적어가 없으므로 수동태가 되어야 한다. 그래서 ③ incorporates→ (should) be incorporated.

✍(해석) 위원회는 새로운 정책을 회사 전체에 구체화할 것을 제안했다. **정답 ③**

18. discuss(토론하다)가 타동사인데 목적어가 없으므로 수동태가 되어야 한다. 또한 as가 접속사이므로 ① discussing→ discussed. 본문을 그대로 쓰면 As it was discussed가 되는데, it was가 생략되어 있다.

✍(해석) 토의된 대로 위원회 지도자들은 그들의 지역에서 일어나고 있는 것에 관하여 5분씩 보고할 것이다. **정답 ①**

19. < be subject to+ 명사상당어구>를 묻는 문제이다. 따라서 ④ taxable→ tax. be subject to ⋯을 받다, ⋯되기 쉽다.

✍(해석) 각 나라마다 세금이 부과되는 모든 부동산의 가치를 정하는 부동산 감정사가 있다. **정답 ④**

20. 전치사 뒤에는 명사, 동명사, 대명사(목적격)가 온다. misuse(오용하다)가 타동사이므로 동명사가 오면 뒤에 목적어가 와야 한다. 그런데 전치사 of 가 뒤에 왔으므로 ④ misusing→ misuse. warranty 보증서. damage 손해, 피해(=injury, harm), 손해 배상금

✍(해석) 이 보증서에는 정상적인 부품들의 소모나 제품의 오용 때문에

생긴 손해는 포함되지 않는다. **정답 ④**

실력문제 3회

1. 수의 일치에 관한 문제이다. 본문은 <There be+명사(주어)>구문의 변형인데, many reasons가 복수이므로 ① remains→ remain.
✍(해석) 아랍 국가들과 이스라엘 사이에 존재하는 적대감에 많은 이유들이 남아 있다. **정답 ①**

2. <use A to-동사>구문을 묻는 문제이다. 본문에서 A(목적어)에 해당되는 부분은 관계대명사 which로 갔으므로 ④ to making→ to make.
✍(해석) 드라 베가의 최상의 그림들이 위장된 테이프와 함께 만들어지는데, 그는 그것을 사용해 장사 그림들을 만든다. **정답 ④**

3. 조동사 뒤에는 동사 원형이 와야 한다. amaze(놀라게 하다)가 타동사인 데 목적어가 없으므로 수동태가 되어야 한다. 따라서 ③ you'll amazed → you'll be amazed.
✍(해석) 어떤 일요일 아침이라도 주택 지구에 가면, 오전 9시에 125번가의 장면에 놀랄 것이다. **정답 ③**

4. amount to(…에 달하다)로 보아 Within이하의 구는 추가적인 개념을 표현하고 있으므로 ① within→ with. considerable 상당한(=sizable, much or large).
✍(해석) 사원들이 적립하는 퇴직금에 회사가 같은 금액을 내고 있어서, 퇴직적립금은 곧 상당한 액수에 달할 수 있을 것이다. **정답 ①**

5. 뒤에 시간이 나오므로 ④ beside→ during. during office hours 근무시간 중. stern 엄한, 단호한(=severe, strict).
✍(해석) 많은 회사들이 근무시간 중 개인 용도로 이메일이나 인터넷을 사용하는 직원들에게 단호한 징계 조치를 취하고 있다. **정답 ④**

6. apply to(적용하다)와 apply for(신청하다, 지원하다)의 차이를 묻는

문제이다. ② to grant→for grant. grant money 보조금.

✎(해석) 암연구소는 여러 제약회사가 제공하는 보조금을 신청했다.
정답 ②

7. suitable for(…에 적합한)의 어법을 묻는 문제이므로 ③ in→ for. * 단어를 기억할 때는 <동사+전치사>, <명사+전치사>, <형용사+전치사>를 묶어 암기해 두는 것이 시험에 유익하다. [예] addicted to(…에 중독된), adequate for(…에 충분한), adjacent to(…에 인접한), bad at(…을 못하는), brilliant at(…가 뛰어난) 등. ventilation 통풍

✎(해석) 스키복은 종종 너무 끼거나 행동하기 불편하고 통풍을 막기 때문에 등산복으로는 부적합하다. **정답 ③**

8. enroll A in B(A를 B에 등록시키다)를 묻는 문제이므로 ② from your → in your.

✎(해석) 당신이 귀사의 네 명을 등록시키면 다섯 번째 사람은 무료로 보낼 수 있다. **정답 ②**

9. 주절과 종속절이 상반되는 내용이므로, 종속절에 양보를 나타내는 접속사가 와야 한다. 따라서 ④ so→ though. expert 익숙한, 노련한(=very skillful)

✎(해석) 이 훈련 세미나는 비록 당신이 노련한 연설가는 아니라고 할지라도 훌륭한 발표회를 하는 방법을 가르쳐 줄 것이다. **정답 ④**

10. <so A that 주어+동사>구문을 묻는 문제이므로 ② while→ that. nervous 초조한, 긴장한(=emotionally tense, restless; uneasy)

✎(해석) 화이트 씨는 너무나 긴장해서 다른 서류철을 자신의 가방에 넣었다. **정답 ②**

11. 콤마 앞뒤의 내용이 대조를 이루므로 역접을 나타내는 등위접속사가 와야 한다. 따라서 ③ although→ yet. chores 잡일.

✎(해석) 노트북 컴퓨터는 쉽게 운반할 수 있을 만큼 작지만, 데스크탑 컴퓨터와 같은 일을 처리할 정도로 강력하다. **정답 ③**

12. 틀린 부분 찾기 문제나 문법적인 빈 칸 채우기 문제를 풀 때는 첫째,

주어와 동사를 찾아야 한다. 둘째, 수, 시제, 인칭, 격을 체크하는 것이 좋다. 이 두 가지만 확인해도 정답을 알 수 있는 문제가 종종 출제된다. 본문의 주어는 proposal이므로 ③ were→ was. semiconductor 반도체

✎(해석) 반도체 디자인을 향상시키기 위한 다른 야심 있는 제안을 연구 개발팀이 내놓았다. **정답 ③**

13. 대명사가 무엇을 받는가 하는 것을 반드시 확인해야 한다. 본문의 he는 Consultants를 받으므로 ③ he→ they.

✎(해석) 비록 컨설턴트들이 최종 결정을 내리는 경우는 좀처럼 없지만, 그들이 사원 모집과 선발에 점점 더 관여하고 있다. **정답 ③**

14. <현재완료+since+과거>를 묻는 문제이므로 ④ in→ since. 'in 1995'은 과거시제와 어울린다.

✎(해석) 나는 비록 4개월 동안 휴직을 했다고 할지라도, 1995년 이래로 제너럴 일렉트릭스에서 일하고 있다. **정답 ④**

15. <소유격+명사>이므로 ④ vulnerable→ vulnerability. vulnerable 상하기 쉬운, 공격받기 쉬운(=open to, or easily hurt by, criticism or attack) plug in(into) 플러그를 꽂다. peripheral 주변의, 말초의, 주변 장치.

✎(해석) 전화선이나 다른 주변 장치를 컴퓨터에 연결하면 전력 문제에 취약성이 커진다. **정답 ④**

16. Once(접속사)이하 media까지 종속절이고, 주절의 주어는 the company's advertising이고 동사는 improved이다. ③에는 동사를 수식하는 부사가 와야 하므로 ③ dramatic→ dramatically. once(접) …하자마자, 일단 …하면. take over 인계 받다, 떠맡다

✎(해석) 홍보 대행사에서 미디어와의 접촉을 떠맡자, 그 회사의 광고가 극적으로 개선되었다. **정답 ③**

17. 본문 내용상 운동 전후를 비교하고 있으므로 ② much efficiently→ more efficiently.

✎(해석) 규칙적으로 에어로빅을 하면 심장 박동을 더 효율적으로 되고 개인의 활력이 증진된다. **정답 ②**

18. 유사 단어의 뜻을 묻는 문제가 가끔 출제된다. 본문은 disposal과 disposable의 차이를 묻고 있다. disposal 처분, 양도, 배치 disposable(종종 복수) 일회용물품. 따라서 ③ disposal→ disposables.

✍(해석) 환경론자들은 접시나 냅킨과 같은 일회용 가정용품들의 사용을 말린다. **정답 ③**

19. complement 보충하다, 보어 compliment 칭찬하다, 축하하다, 증정하다. 본문의 내용상 ① complemented→ complimented.

✍(해석) 그는 일을 잘 했다고 칭찬을 받았다. [참고] You did a good job= You made it. 잘 했어. **정답 ①**

20. 혼동되는 형용사를 구별하는 문제이다. respectful 정중한, 공손한 respective 각각의 respectable 존경할만한, 훌륭한, 상당한. 본문의 내용상 ③ respectful→ respective.

✍(해석) 회장은 각 부서가 능력껏 최선을 다해 각각의 업무를 해야 한다고 특별히 언급했다. **정답 ③**

실력문제 4회

1. 관계대명사 문제는 첫째, 선행사의 유무를 보아야 한다. 선행사가 있는 경우에는 who, which, that 등의 관계대명사를 쓴다. 선행사가 없는 경우에는 what이나 복합 관계 대명사(관계대명사+ever)를 사용한다. 둘째, 관계대명사의 격을 체크해야 한다. <소유격+ 명사>, <주격+동사>, <목적격+주어>라는 것을 기억하자. 본문에서는 that이 선행사가 없으므로 ④ that→ what. what절은 문장에서 주어, 목적어, 보어의 역할을 한다. 타동사 promise의 목적어가 없는데, what이 목적어 역할을 하는 것이다.

✍(해석) 내가 사장에게 말하고 싶은 한 가지는 그가 약속을 너무 자주 잊는다는 것이다. **정답 ④**

2. besides는 전치사와 부사밖에 없으므로 일단 ②가 틀렸다는 것을 알 수 있다. 선행사가 있고, 타동사 apply(…을 …에 적용하다)의 목적어가 없

으므로 ② besides→ which.
   ✍(해석) 워크샵에서는 개인과 조직의 학습에 적용할 학습방식의 중요성을 탐구한다.. **정답 ②**

3. 선행사가 앞 문장 전체이며, 계속적 용법으로 쓰여야 하므로 ③ what → which.
   ✍(해석) 새 주택의 건축이 지난 6개월 동안 꾸준하게 감소했는데, 이것은 경제에 나쁜 신호이다. **정답 ③**

4. which이하는 타동사 acknowledged(인정했다)의 목적어(명사절)로 완전한 문장이므로 ② which→ that.
   ✍(해석) 목재 산업의 대표자는 수요가 증가함에 따라 경질 목재의 가격이 계속해서 오를 것을 인정했다. **정답 ②**

5. whatever(=anything that)와 any가 겹치므로 ② any를 없애야 한다.
   ✍(해석) 기업 상장에 있어서, 회사들은 수상할 것은 무엇이든지 포함해야 한다. **정답 ②**

6. <the+비교급…, the+비교급…>구문을 묻는 문제이다. ② fast→ the faster.
   ✍(해석) 사태가 불안정하면 할수록, 사태가 급변하면 할수록, 다중 선택의 가능성을 살려 놓는다는 것은 가치 있는 일이다. **정답 ②**

7. 전치사 of의 목적어로 명사가 오고 등위접속사 and 다음에도 명사가 와야 한다(병렬법). 따라서 ④ intimidate→ intimidation.
   ✍(해석) 그 변호사는 아첨과 위협의 적절한 결합을 사용하여 그 증인을 반대심문 했다. **정답 ④**

8. 영향의 뜻인 impact 뒤에는 on이 오므로 ③ at→ on.
   ✍(해석) 독일 마르크화의 강세는 수입 증가와 인플레이션에 가장 큰 영향을 미치고 있다. **정답 ③**

9. and의 앞뒤에는 같은 형태가 와야 하므로 ② plant→ plants. further 촉진시키다(=give aid to; promote)

✎(해석) 해양식물과 동물, 그리고 그들의 생태학적 관계를 연구하는 해양생물학은 수산업의 효과적인 발전을 촉진시켰다. **정답 ②**

10. conclusion과 어울리는 동사는 reach이므로 ② do→ reach. reach a conclusion 결론에 도달하다. premises 전제 inference 추론
✎(해석) 주어진 전제로부터 논리적 추론에 의해 결론에 도달하는 추리 방법을 연역법이라고 한다. **정답 ②**

11. 주어가 동시에 그 문장의 목적어가 될 때는 재귀대명사를 써야 하므로 ④ them→ themselves.
✎(해석) 우리의 장난감들은 아이들의 안전을 마음에 두고 제작되며, 장난감의 부품들이 분리가 될 때 아기들을 위험으로 몰아넣는다는 것을 알고 있다. **정답 ④**

12. 본문의 의미상 ③ use away→ use up. use up 고갈시키다(=exhaust, deplete).
✎(해석) 과학자들과 경제학자들은 인간이 결코 지상의 모든 광물자원을 고갈시킬 수 없다고 믿는다. **정답 ③**

13. <another+단수명사>가 되어야 하므로 ③ people→ person.
✎(해석) 개인 수표와 같은 양도성증서는 보통 배서에 의해 타인에게 양도될 수 있다. **정답 ③**

14. 본문의 의미상 ③ explorer(탐험가)→ exploration(탐험).
✎(해석) 배핀만은 인도에 무역로를 찾고 있었던 유럽인들에 의한 북미의 탐험에 중요한 역할을 하였다. **정답 ③**

15. 접속사 before뒤에 <주어+동사>가 오고, revise(개정하다)와 replace(대치하다)가 타동사인데 목적어가 없으므로 수동태가 되어야 한다. ④ it drastically→ it is drastically. life expectancy 수명(=expectation of life; life span) approximately 약(=about, some, estimated)
✎(해석) 과학적 원리는 약 10년의 수명을 가진 후에 그것이 보다 더 새로운 정보에 의해 전격적으로 개정되거나 대치되는 것으로 추산된다. **정답 ④**

16. 콤마와 콤마사이에 들어가는 것은 부사구나 명사구이다. 본문에서는 부사구가 들어가야 하므로 ① the same→ like.

✎(해석) 전파는 광파 처럼 1초에 186,282마일의 일정한 속도로 움직인다.
정답 ①

17. 문장에 술어동사가 하나만 있어야 하므로 ③ is concerned→ concerned. 분사 concerned가 the body of law를 수식함. define A as B. A를 B로 정의 하다.

✎(해석) 항공법은 직접 간접적으로 민간항공과 관련되는 법체계로 정의 된다. 정답 ③

18. deposit(침전시키다)는 타동사인데 목적어가 없으므로 ④ deposit→ are deposited. dirt 흙(=earth, soil)

✎(해석) 빙하가 녹음에 따라 바위, 표석, 나무, 그리고 다량의 흙이 침전 된다. 정답 ④

19. A-words(a-로 시작하는 형용사)는 서술적으로 쓰이므로 ③ alike→ same. A-words를 다음과 같이 기억하자. [혼자 살면서 자다가 깨면 무서운 줄 알아야지 수줍어하기는] - alone, alive, asleep, awake, afraid, aware, ashamed 등이다.

✎(해석) 신체는 아침부터 저녁까지 같은 온도에 머무르지 않는다. 정답 ③

20. <various(다양한)+복수명사>이므로 ① option→options. fiscal year 회계년도

✎(해석) 우리 제조 부서의 구조조정을 위한 다양한 선택 사항들이 개설 되었지만, 어떤 것도 다음 회계년도 종료 시까지는 마무리짓지 않을 것이다.
정답 ①

III. 어휘력 문제

실력문제 1회

1. inadequate 부족한(=insufficient, scanty, meager, deficient) downfall 낙하, 몰락(=a sudden fail, comedown, ruin, destruction), 쏟아짐(=a heavy fall) ① substantial 실제의 (=material, actual, visible, real, true), 상당한 (=ample, abundant, plentiful, large), 내용이 있는(=strong, solid), 중요한 (=important) ② inconsequential 중요하지 않은(=of no consequence) ④ proper 적당한, 적절한(=suitable, appropriate, fitting, fit, adequate, pertinent, relevant, apt, apropos, to the point)
   ✎(해석) 필요한 군사 무기가 충분하게 공급되지 않았기 때문에 마침내 히틀러 군대들이 패망하게 되었다. **정답 ③**

2. relinquish 그만 두다, 버리다, 포기하다(=give up, let go, resign, abandon, renounce, surrender, give in, yield, capitulate) ① change 바꾸다 (=vary, alter, modify, transform), 환전하다, 교환하다(=exchange) ③ increase 증가하다(=add to, augment, enlarge, multiply, extend, expand, step up, jack up) ④ protect 보호하다, 막다(=defend, guard, shelter, shield, screen)
   ✎(해석) 우리는 한국 시민으로서 우리의 권리들을 포기해서는 안 된다. **정답 ②**

3. verify 입증하다, 확증하다(=prove, turn out, confirm, corroborate, substantiate) ① confirm 확실하게 하다, 확증하다, 확인하다(=ratify, sanction, validate, approve, endorse) ② withdraw 물러나게 하다(=take back, remove, retract, recall, retreat, shrink) ③ repeat 반복하다(=iterate, recite, reiterate) ④ modify 수정하다, 수식하다
   ✎(해석) 그 하원의원은 앞선 그의 성명을 확인할 것을 요구받았다. **정답 ①**

4. extricate 구해 내다, 해방하다(=set free, disentangle, liberate, relieve, disengage, free) ① rankle 쑤시다(=fester, irritate, gall, pain) ② remove

옮기다, 벗다, 제거하다(=abolish, eliminate, get rid of, do away with, discard, exterminate, wipe out, blot out, erase, efface, eradicate, dispose of, uproot, obliterate) ③ vaunt 자랑하다(=boast, brag, vapor, talk big, take pride in, pride oneself on, be proud of, put on airs) ④ scrutinize 자세히 조사하다(=examine closely, inspect, investigate, look into)
✐(해석) 그 농부는 가시 철조망으로부터 그 개를 구했다. **정답 ②**

5. allegiance 충성(=loyalty, fidelity, faithfulness) ① disloyalty 불충, 불성실 ② judgment 판단(=deciding), 판결(=a legal decision) ③ sedition 치안방해, 선동(=agitation, incitement, insurgence, disloyalty)
✐(해석) 날마다 수백만 명의 어린이들이 "성조기와 그 국기가 상징하는 미국에 대한 충성을 맹세한다." **정답 ④**

6. pertinent 적절한, 요령 있는(=relevant, apposite, applicable, apt) ① imaginative 상상적인 ② unrealistic 비현실적인 ③ relevant 관련된, 적절한(=pertinent, fitting, apposite, apropos, germane, appropriate) ④ controversial 논쟁의, 쟁점이 되는(=subject to controversy, debatable)
✐(해석) 그 작가가 그의 소설을 변경한 이유는 매우 적절한 것이다. **정답 ③**

7. portray 묘사하다, 그리다(=describe, depict, depicture, delineate, limn) ① rehabilitate 복구하다, 회복하다(=restore, reinstate, reestablish) ② impeach 탄핵하다, 비난하다, 고소하다(=accuse, charge, indict, arraign, censure, cite, impute, try) ③ vitiate 손상시키다 (=spoil, impair, corrupt, pervert), 더럽히다(=adulterate, invalidate)
✐(해석) 그녀는 그 도시를 아라비아해에 있는 맨하탄과 헐리웃의 혼합으로 묘사했다. **정답 ④**

8. absolve 용서하다(=set free, relieve, forgive, shrive), 사면하다(=acquit, pardon) ① exonerate 무죄임을 입증하다, 면제하다(= exculpate, free, clear, absolve, acquit) ② console 위로하다, 위문하다(=comfort, solace, hearten, sympathize with) ③ reprove 비난하다(=admonish, blame, censure, rebuke, chide, criticize)

✎(해석) 소년이 아버지의 책상 서랍에서 약간의 돈을 훔쳤다고 고백했을 때 그 목사는 소년을 용서해 주었다. **정답** ①

9. antipathy 반감, 혐오(= feeling against; aversion; distaste; repugnance; dislike) ① sympathy 동정, 공감(=compassion) ② empathy 감정이입 ④ antipode 정반대의 사물

✎(해석) 나는 관대하려고 노력하지만 더럽고 단정치 못한 사람들에게는 혐오감을 느낀다. **정답** ③

10. abrogate 취소하다, 폐지하다(=revoke, cancel, call off, annul, nullify, repeal, retract) ① establish 설립하다(=found, institute, set up), 확립하다(=confirm, fix, settle, secure, set), 제정하다(=ordain, appoint, enact) ③ abscond 도망하다(=steal off and hide; depart secretly; flee; decamp, bolt) ④ assimilate 동화하다, 동일하게 하다(=digest, absorb; incorporate, merge)

✎(해석)만약 노동조합들이 그들의 전통적인 역할을 폐지한다면, 그들은 비난 받을 것이다. **정답** ②

11. belligerent 호전적인(=warlike, combative, bellicose, hostile, pugnacious, quarrelsome, trigger-happy, hawkish) ① courageous 용감한(=brave, valiant, valorous, gallant, intrepid, plucky, chivalrous, daring, bold, audacious, fearless, dauntless, undaunted) ② cowardly 비겁한(=timid, timorous, dastardly, shy, craven, fearful, frightened, scared, chicken-hearted) ③ hostile 적대적인(=unfriendly, antagonistic) ④ stupid 우둔한, 바보의 (=foolish, obtuse, dull, slow-witted)

✎(해석) 당신의 호전적인 태도로 인해 인기가 없는 요인이 되는 경우가 자주 있다. **정답** ③

12. benevolent 친절한, 자비로운(=kind; charitable) ① considerable 중요한(=important), 상당한(=much or large, sizable) ③ miserable 비참한(=wretched, forlorn, doleful), 비열한(=mean, paltry) ④ inventive 발명의, 재주 있는

✎(해석) 자비로운 고용주는 종업원의 복지에 진실한 관심을 가지고 있다.

정답 ②

13. conciliate 화해시키다, 달래다, 조정하다(=pacify; propitiate; mediate) ① mediate 중재하다, 조정하다(=intercede, arbitrate) ② meditate 깊이 생각하다(=ponder, muse, speculate, contemplate, brood over, deliberate) ③ commence 시작하다(=initiate, originate, introduce, inaugurate, set out, take the first step, launch) ④ consecrate 신성하게 하다(=sanctify, hallow) (해석) 이 시점에서 노동자와 경영자의 의견을 조정하기는 어렵다. **정답 ①**

14. contravene 위반하다, 반박하다(=violate, go against; contradict) ① approve 승인하다, 찬성하다(=support, ratify, endorse) ② concede 양보하다(=consent, yield, give in, assent) ③ manifest 명시하다(=show, reveal, display, evidence, bring forward), 증명하다(=demonstrate) ④ gainsay 부정하다(=deny), 반박하다(=contradict)
✐(해석) 검열관의 도덕성에 이의를 제기하려니 부끄럽고, 그의 권위에 반박하려니 두려워서, 그 작가가 취한 일차적인 반응은 검열을 피하자는 것이었다. **정답 ④**

15. demented 미친, 발광한(=out of [down from] one's mind; mad; insane; deranged) ① incessant 끊임없는(=constant, unceasing) ② irrelevant 부적당한(=not pertinent; not to the point) ③ insoluble 용해되지 않는
✐(해석) 누가 이것을 했던지 간에 그는 미쳤음에 틀림없다. 멀쩡한 사람이 그런 식으로 행동했을 리가 없기 때문이다. **정답 ④**

16. discreet 사려 깊은, 신중한(=judicious, sagacious, prudent, wary, alert, circumspect, cautious, careful, watchful, heedful, vigilant) ① intelligent 이성 있는, 총명한(=clever, wise) ② violent 격렬한, 난폭한(=vehement, boisterous, impetuous, rampart, wild) ③ copious 풍부한(=plentiful, abundant)
✐(해석) 네가 한 밤중쯤에 그에게 전화를 건 것은 신중하지 못했다. **정답 ④**

17. efface 지우다, 삭제하다, 말살하다(=erase, delete, obliterate, expunge, strike, cancel, blot, wipe out, eradicate, root out, uproot, get rid of, do away with, remove, abolish) ② effective 효과적인(=efficacious, effectual, potent)

③ grope 손으로 더듬다(=feel, fumble) ④ stash 간수하다, 숨기다(=put or hide away)
✎(해석) 전쟁의 상처들은 그 사건 동안에 지워졌다. **정답 ①**

18. exasperate 화나게 하다(=infuriate, enrage, incense, anger, vex, provoke, annoy, roil, nettle, peeve) ① coax 설득하다, 달래다, 어르다(=cajole, inveigle, wheedle, persuade, urge) ② deceive 속이다(=take in, cheat, defraud, swindle, hoax, trick, impose on) ③ frighten 놀라게 하다(=scare)
✎(해석) 아비들아 너희 자녀를 노엽게 하지말고 주의 교훈으로 양육하라. **정답 ④**

19. forebear 조상(=ancestor, antecedent, progenitor, forefather) ② descendant 후손(=offspring, posterity, scion) ③ dictator 독재자(=arbiter, autocrat, monocrat, despot) ④ forecast 예상(=prediction, foretelling, prophecy, presage, portent)
✎(해석) 존 에프 케네디의 조상들은 아일랜드에서 미국으로 이민을 왔다. **정답 ①**

20. heterogeneous 이종의, 이질의(=diverse, mixed, conglomerate, varied; unlike, dissimilar) ① homogeneous 동종의, 동질의(=similar) ② varied 다양한(=various), 변화된(=changed, altered) ③ congested 넘치는(=overfilled, clogged), 북적거리는(=crowded, jammed, crammed), 충혈된 ④ intractable 다루기 어려운(=unmanageable; obstinate, perverse; refractory, rebellious)
✎(해석) 많은 다른 종족 집단들과 문화집단들이 대도시의 이질적인 주민 내에서 발견된다. **정답 ②**

실력문제 2회

1. demolish 부수다, 파괴하다(=tear down, destroy, raze, level, ruin, wreck, wipe out) ① abandon 버리다, 포기하다(=relinquish, resign, give up, forgo, surrender, waive, desert, forsake, discard, throw up, wash one's hands of) ③ ostracize 추방하다(=banish, exclude, bar, blackball, outcast) ④ rant 고함치다(=rave, fume, rail, rage, scold, nag)
　✎(해석) 철거반원이 그 낡은 건물을 허는데 며칠이 걸렸다. **정답 ②**

2. prolific 다산의(=fruitful, fecund, productive, fertile) ① traumatic 외상성의, 외상약 trauma 외상(=a bodily injury or shock), 충격(=an emotional shock) ② saturate 적시다(=soak, drench, impregnate, imbue) ③ native 출생지의, 토착의, 타고난(=indigenous, innate, inherent, aboriginal, endemic, natal, natural)
　✎(해석) 가장 놀라운 특징은 그녀가 어린 나이인데도 그렇게 많은 작품을 쓴 작가였다는 것이다. **정답 ④**

3. bedrock 기반(=foundation, bottom, base), 암반 ① impasse 난국, 곤경(=deadlock, blind alley, dead end, standstill, standoff, cessation, bottleneck, stalemate) ② perspective 관점(=standpoint, point of view, viewpoint) ③ prejudice 선입관, 편견(=bias, preoccupation, partiality, unfairness, predilection, prepossession)
　✎(해석) 심리분석이 의존하는 기반은 무의식에 대한 확신이다. **정답 ④**

4. tenable 공격에 견딜 수 있는, 유지할 수 있는, 주장할 수 있는 ① tenuous 얇은(=slender, fine, thin), 빈약한(=flimsy, unsubstantial), 희박한(=rare, rarefied) ② warrantable 증거가 될 수 있는 ③ redundant 과다한(=excessive, superfluous), 장황한(=wordy, bombastic, verbose) ④ tolerable 참을 수 있는(=endurable), 꽤 좋은(=fairly good, passable)
　✎(해석) 그의 많은 동료들은 결국 아인슈타인의 이론이 조리 있는 것이라는데 동의했다. **정답 ②**

5. meek 유순한, 순종하는(=submissive, spiritless, yielding, acquiescent, patient and mild) ① practical 실질적인, 쓸모있는(=pragmatical, useful, operative, effective) ② aggressive 공격적인(=hostile, quarrelsome, bold and active, enterprising) ④ patient 인내심 있는(=enduring, persevering), 근면한(=diligent)
✎(해석) 경기장에서 퇴장하라는 명령을 받고 두 명의 여학생만 항의했다. 나머지는 너무 양순해서 불평을 하지 않았다. **정답 ③**

6. elastic 탄력 있는(=tensile, resilient, extensible, ductile) ① indispensable 필요 불가결한(=vital, needful, necessary, essential, required) ② flexible 구부리기 쉬운, 유순한, 융통성이 있는(=pliant, limber, lithe, supple, adaptable) ③ invariable 불변의(=unvarying, constant, steady) ④ portable 들고 다닐 수 있는, 휴대용의(=transportable, movable, carryable)
✎(해석) 고무는 우리 일상 생활에서 가장 융통성이 많은 재료들 중 하나이다. **정답 ②**

7. gallant 용감한(=brave, courageous, bold), 친절한, 화려한 ① obedient 온순한, 순종하는(=acquiescent, complying, compliant, tractable, docile, submissive, pliant) ③ pertinent 적절한, 관계 있는(=relevant, apposite, applicable) ④ courtly 예의 바른(=dignified, elegant)
✎(해석) 그 장교는 여자에 대한 태도가 친절했다. **정답 ②**

8. solemnly 장엄하게, 진지하게(=gravely, seriously) ① slowly 천천히(=unhurriedly, deliberately, at a snail's pace ② cautiously 주의 깊게(=carefully) ③ somberly 침울하게, 진지하게 somber 어두운, 우울(=gloomy, dark, sad, dismal, leaden, depressing) ④ weakly 병약한(=sickly), 약한(=feeble)
✎(해석) 오늘날까지도 타이타닉호의 침몰을 이야기할 때, 생존자들은 그들의 시련을 진지하게 말하는 경향이 있다. **정답 ③**

9. pert 버릇없는, 건방진(=impudent, impertinent, saucy, flippant; bold, forward) saucy 뻔뻔스런, 건방진, 멋진(=smart, chic, piquant) ① recessive

퇴행의, 열성의(=receding, receding, regressive, retrogressive) ② oblivious 잘 잊는(=forgetful) ④ nimble 민첩한, 재치 있는(=active, supple, agile, brisk, lively, sprightly, spry, alert, quick)
✍(해석) 윌리암의 건방지고 뻔뻔스러운 말이 항상 그의 아내를 괴롭혔다.
정답 ③

10. dissent 의견이 다르다(=differ in opinion, disagree, object) ① concur 동시에 일어나다(=coincide), 동의하다(=agree) ② resent 분개하다(=be indignant, enrage), 원망하다 ③ consent 동의하다, 승낙하다(=assent, concede, comply with, accede) ④ opposite 마주보는, 반대의(=set against; in a contrary direction; entirely different; exactly contrary)
✍(해석) 그 수정안을 승인하는 투표는 결코 만장일치는 아니었다. 6명의 회원은 반대했다. **정답 ④**

11. fragile 깨지기 쉬운, 약한(=easily broken, breakable, fragile, weak, infirm, frail, brittle, delicate) ① light 가벼운, 민첩한, 경솔한(=rash, frivolous, thoughtless, flippant) ③ temporary 일시적인, 임시의 (=impermanent, irregular, seasonal, provisional, momentary, fleeting, transitory) ④ priceless 귀중한(=invaluable, precious; inestimable value)
✍(해석) 손잡이가 약해서 너무 많은 압력을 가하면 쉽게 부러질 것이다. **정답 ②**

12. discrepancy 차이, 불일치, 어긋남(=difference; disagreement; variation; inconsistency) ① discretion 분별, 조심(=prudence), 자유 재량 ② discredit 치욕(=disgrace), 불신용 ④ discomfort 불안, 곤란(=uneasiness, distress, annoyance, embarrassment, hardship)
✍(해석) 80명의 학생들이 댄스 파티에 참석했는데 단지 74매의 입장권만 입구에서 걷혔다. 이 차이를 설명할 수 있겠니? **정답 ③**

13. enchant 마법에 걸리게 하다, 황홀하게 하다, 매혹하다(=cast a spell over, hypnotize, enamor, bewitch; enrapture; charm, attract, captivate, fascinate) ② embarrass 당황하게 하다, 곤란하게 하다(=disconcert, discomfit, nonplus, bother, abash, encumber, trouble, hamper, complicate, perplex)

③ imprison 투옥하다(=lock up, detain, hold, jail, incarcerate) ④ impute -에 돌리다, 전가하다(=attribute, ascribe)
✎(해석) 이 사건에서 그가 매료된 것은 사기로 시작하여 살인으로 끝난 절차의 교묘함에 있었다. **정답 ①**

14. prevalent 널리 행해지는, 유행의(=widespread, predominant, prominent, prevailing, preponderant, current, rife) ② justify 정당화하다(=exonerate, excuse, warrant, vindicate, acquit, absolve) justified by faith 이신칭의, 이신득의 ④ proper 적당한(=suitable, pertinent, appropriate, fit, apropos, relevant), 정말의, 고유의
✎(해석) 정치가들에 의한 비윤리적인 행동들이 요즈음 더 널리 행해졌다. **정답 ①**

15. pressing 절박한, 긴급한(=urgent, imminent, emergent, exigent, critical) ① pressure 압력, 압박, 강제력, 영향력(=compelling force or influence) ③ perverse 외고집의(=stubborn, obstinate, obdurate, wayward; cross, petulant), 모순된(=contrary) ④ consequential 당연한(=consequent), 거드름 피우는(=self-important)
✎(해석) 새로운 지구촌은 많은 긴급한 문제들에 직면해 있다. **정답 ②**

16. genuine 참된, 진짜인(=true, real, authentic, sincere, unaffected) ① perfect 완전한(=complete, flawless, sheer, utter), 이상적인(=ideal) ② imitate 모방하다, 본뜨다(=mimic, reproduce, resemble) ④ valuable 귀중한(=precious, costly; worthy, meritorious)
✎(해석) 쥬디는 인조털 코트를 입고 있었는데, 모두 진자 표범가죽으로 만든 것이라고 생각했다. **정답 ③**

17. heyday 전성기, 절정기(=golden age, prime) ③ initiation 개시, 착수, 입회(=commencement; admission) ④ decline 감소
✎(해석) 증기 철도는 19세기에 전성기였다. **정답 ②**

18. impromptu 즉석의, 즉흥적인(=extemporaneous, extempore, offhand, improvised, unpremeditated, spontaneous) ② informative 정보를 주는, 유

익힌(=instructive) ③ expressive 표현적인

✍(해석) 그의 청중들은 그런 철저한 발표가 즉각적인 연설에서 행해질 수 있다는 것에 놀랐다. **정답 ④**

19. complicated 복잡한(=not simple or easy; intricate, complex, tangled, entangled, byzantine, involved, enigmatic, composite) ① coarse 거친, 조잡한, 천박한(=rough, uncouth, rude, crude, crass, low, vulgar, gross, common, unrefined) ② lengthy 장황한(=talkative, verbose, loquacious, chatty, wordy, prolix, garrulous, long-winded) ③ obsolete 사라진, 구식의(=no longer in use, out of date, extinct, antiquated)

✍(해석) 졸업에 대한 요구조건 가운데 일부가 복잡하게 보이면, 지도교수님을 만나세요. **정답 ④**

20. misgiving 불안한 느낌, 의심이나 염려, 걱정, 불안(=uneasy feeling; feeling of doubt or suspicion; foreboding; lack of confidence) ① confidence 신뢰(=trust, reliance), 확신 (=assurance) ② misconduct 비행(=improper behavior) ④ coolness 서늘함, 냉담, 침착(=calmness, indifference)

✍(해석) 아빠는 엄마가 운전을 하면 불안해하지 않는데, 엄마가 운전을 뛰어나게 잘하기 때문이다. **정답 ③**

실력문제 3회

1. outlandish 이상스러운, 이국적인(=strange, bizarre, eccentric, odd, foreign, grotesque, queer, fantastic) ① jolly 유쾌한, 즐거운(=joyous, frolicsome, mirthful, buoyant, elated) ② liable 책임 있는, -하기 쉬운(=subject, open to, apt to, exposed to) ③ rustic 시골의(=rural), 소박한(=simple or artless), 거칠게 만든(=rough or uncouth)

✍(해석) 가장 무도회는 사람들이 아주 이상한 복장을 하고 오기 때문에 항상 재미있다. **정답 ④**

2. infraction 위반(=violation) ① discrepancy 차이, 불일치[참조; 실력문제 2회 12번] ③ urgent 긴급한[참조; 실력문제 2회 15번] ④ revolt 반역

(=uprising, rebellion, insurgence, insurrection, mutiny, sedition), 반감 (=disgust)

✍(해석) 대통령은 지난 몇 개월 동안에 심각한 위반으로 비난을 받아 왔다. **정답 ②**

3. shallow 얕은(=not deep), 천박한(=lacking depth of character, intellect ② deep 심오한(=abstruse), 진지한(=serious, profound), 통렬한(=intense) ④ windy 바람이 부는, 수다스러운

✍(해석) 그 해안은 우리가 생각하는 만큼 낮지 않았다. **정답 ③**

4. impetus 힘, 기세, 자극. 기동력(=force, motivation, stimulus, momentum) ① impiety 불경, 불효(=lack of reverence for God; disrespect) ② timidity 겁 많음, 수줍음(=shyness) ③ incentive 자극(=stimulus), 동기(=motive), 의욕 ④ distortion 왜곡(=twist)

✍(해석) 그것들을 발전시키기 위하여 일단 상업적인 자극이 가해지면, 그 제품들은 빠르게 개선되어야 한다. **정답 ③**

5. enterprising 기업적인, 모험적인(=energetic, venturesome, adventurous; eager, ambitious, pushing) ① vigorous 원기 있는, 힘센(=active, strong, energetic, vital) ② reluctant 마지못한(=unwilling) ③ suspicious 의심 깊은, 수상한(=doubtful, dubious) ④ entertaining 즐거운, 재미있는(=interesting and pleasurable; amusing)

✍(해석) 일부 기업적인 부부들은 일주일 중의 작업기간에 총 10시간 이상을 일한다. 그러나 이런 속도는 이국적인 휴가나 비싼 헬스클럽에 의하여 완화된다. **정답 ①**

6. interrogate 질문하다, 심문하다(=examine, inquire, hear, try, grill) ① chase 추격하다(=pursue), 사냥하다(=hunt), 쫓아내다(=drive away) ② praise 칭찬하다(=acclaim, approve, commend, extol, eulogize, applaud), 찬미하다(=glorify, laud) ④ intermingle 혼합하다(=mix, mingle, blend)

✍(해석) 그들은 정치적 시위에 관하여 약 20시간 동안 심문을 받았다고 말했다. **정답 ③**

7. stiff 빳빳한(=rigid, firm), 끈기있는(=not fluid; thick), 곤란한(=harsh), 어려운(=difficult) 부자연스러운(=awkward), 비싼(=high) ① sticky 끈적거리는(=glutinous) ③ dense 짙은(=thick), 우둔한(=stupid) ④ woven 짜여진
✐(해석) 껄껄하고 빳빳한 섬유인 삼은 덥고 온화한 기후에서 자라는 식물에서 나온다. **정답 ②**

8. tiny 아주 작은(=very small, minute, miniature, minuscule, diminutive, wee) ① indefinite 불명확한, 막연한(=vague, not certain, unsure) ② variable 변하기 쉬운(=changeable, inconstant) ④ intangible 만질 수 없는(=untouchable)
✐(해석) 중성자는 매우 작기 때문에 1평방 인치를 덮는데 1조 개가 필요하다. **정답 ③**

9. cut down 베어 넘어뜨리다, 줄이다(=reduce, decrease, diminish, lessen, slim down) ② appease 달래다, 진정시키다(=mollify, pacify, moderate, soothe), 채우다(=satisfy, slake) ③ increase 증가하다(=augment, add to, enlarge, extend) ④ appreciate 진가를 인정하다(=esteem, prize, value), 올바르게 인식하다(=comprehend), 감상하다, 감사하다
✐(해석) 의사는 내가 탄수화물의 소비를 줄이라고 말했다. **정답 ①**

10. enervate 약화시키다(=weaken, devitalize, unnerve, emasculate, debilitate, enfeeble, effeminate) ① avenge 보복하다(=revenge, retaliate, strike back, requite, pay back, take an eye for an eye or a pound of flesh) ② avert 돌리다(=keep off, turn aside, ward off, turn away), 피하다(=prevent) ④ cripple 병신으로 만들다(=lame), 무능하게 하다(=disable, impair)
✐(해석) 그의 반대자의 공격에 대한 권리가 젊은 정치가를 약하게 만들었다. **정답 ③**

11. torpid 무기력한(=lethargic, dormant), 느린(=dull, sluggish, inert, unmoving) ② energetic 정력적인, 힘센(=potent, powerful) ③ delightful 매우 기쁜, 유쾌한(=pleasing, enjoyable, charming, attractive, alluring) ④

harmonious 조화한

✍(해석) 힘든 레슬링 시합 후 나는 한때 완전히 무기력한 상태가 되어 있었다. **정답 ①**

12. meticulous 소심한, 꼼꼼한(=fastidious, precise, scrupulous) ① kind 친절한(=gentle, tender; sympathetic; mild; friendly, obliging, benign; solicitous; lenient) ② ambitious 야심 있는 ③ tedious 지루한(=wearisome, wearing, dry, dry-as-dust, boring, tiresome, irksome, monotonous, prosy, uninteresting) ④ scrupulous 양심적인(=consciously honest), 세심한(=careful of details; precise)

✍(해석) 그 은행에 새로 고용된 직원이 꼼꼼한 것으로 알려져 있다. **정답 ④**

13. immense 광대한(=vast, tremendous, huge, enormous, colossal; gigantic, mammoth, infinite), 훌륭한(=splendid) ① beautiful 아름다운 ② unsettled 정하지 않은, 일정치 않은 ④ immediate 즉시의(=prompt, instant, present), 직접의(=direct)

✍(해석) 카우보이 영화는 전통적으로 광대하게 펼쳐진 험준한 지역의 장면으로 시작된다. **정답 ③**

14. obstacle 장애(물)(=impediment, hurdle, barrier, hindrance, obstruction, snag, barrage) ① factor 요인(=component, element, part, constituent, ingredient) ③ occurrence 발생, 사건(=event, incident) ④ phenomenon 현상, 경이(=wonder)

✍(해석) 인체가 외부물질을 거부하는 경향은 성공적인 조직이식에 주된 장애가 된다. **정답 ②**

15. flourish 번성하다(=prosper, thrive, flower, bloom, blossom, burgeon), 휘두르다(=wield) ① perish 죽다(=expire, die, crumble, be destroyed or ruined), 몹시 괴로워하다 ② discourage 낙심시키다(=depress, dishearten, dismay), 방해하다(=dissuade, deter)

✍(해석) 오페라는 혁명 10년 동안에 프랑스에서 번성했어야 했다. **정답 ③**

16. preposterous 터무니없는(=absurd, fatuous, inane, ludicrous, ridiculous,

outrageous, asinine) ① primordial 원래의(=primitive, fundamental, original) ② prosperous 번성하는(=thriving), 순조로운 ④ outstanding 현저한 (=prominent, eminent, remarkable, conspicuous, striking, salient, noticeable, exceptional)
✍(해석) 지각에 대한 그의 변명이 너무 터무니없어서 모든 사람이 웃었다.
정답 ③

17. proficiency 숙달, 기술(=skill) ① excavation 발굴(=digging out) ② labor 노동, 노력 ④ experiment 실험.
✍(해석) 비버는 복잡한 집과 댐을 만들기 위하여 공학기술을 사용한다.
정답 ③

18. override 무시하다, 짓밟다, 무효로 하다(=disregard; annul; supercede) ① reside 살다, 거주하다(=live, dwell, abide, lodge) ② annul 취소하다 (=cancel, call off, repeal, retract, revoke, nullify, rescind, quash), 제거하다 ③ drench 흠뻑 물에 적시다(=soak, douse, souse, wet, saturate) ④establish 설립하다(=found, institute, set up), 취임시키다, 확립하다(=confirm, fix)
✍(해석) 자신의 행복을 추구하기 위해 타인의 행복을 짓밟아서는 안 된다.
정답 ②

19. profuse 풍부한(=abundant, plentiful, copious), 아낌없는(=generous), 낭비하는(=extravagant, wasteful) ① gratuitous 무료의(=free, gratis), 이유 없는(=baseless, uncalled for, unwarranted) ② robust 강건한(=vigorous, healthy, lusty, strong, sturdy, stalwart), 확고한 ③ persistent 완고한 (=constant, steadfast)
✍(해석) 북미는 포도가 매우 풍부하게 재배되고, 많은 종류가 존재하기 때문에 천연 포도밭으로 불려진다. 정답 ③

20. stupor 무감각, 마비, 망연자실(=lethargy, torpor, apathy, coma, daze, numbness, trance) ① responsibility 책임, 의무 ② anger 노여움 ③ resentment 분개, 원한 ④ aspiration 포부, 열망(=longing)
✍(해석) 나의 시선이 돌아서는 그녀의 걸음걸이를 따라 가고 있을 때, 망연자실감 때문에 나는 짓눌렸다. 정답 ③

실력문제 4회

1. recurrent 재발하는, 정기적으로 일어나는 ① periodic 주기적인(=recurrent, cyclic, intermittent, epochal) ② perennial 사철을 통한, 다년생의, 영구한(=enduring, lasting, endless, persistent) ③ prolonged 연장된 ④ unacceptable 받아들일 수 없는

✍(해석) 그가 주기적으로 회의에 빠진 것이 모든 사람에게 큰 뉴스거리였다. **정답 ①**

2. adapt 적응시키다(=adjust, suit, fit), 각색하다(=modify) ① refrain 그만 두다, 삼가다(=abstain, cease, desist, forbear) ② adopt 채용하다, 양자로 삼다(=embrace, take to oneself, assume, borrow; foster, give a home to, accept as one's own) ③ flee 달아나다, 도망하다(=decamp, run away, fly, abscond)

✍(해석) 인간은 환경에 적응하는 신비한 능력을 가지고 있다. **정답 ④**

3. deplete 비우다(=drain, empty), 고갈시키다(=use up, exhaust) ① disprove -의 반증을 들다, 논박하다(=refute, confute) ② exhaust 다 써버리다, 피폐시키다(=tire out, wear out) ③ malinger 꾀병을 부리다 ④ appease 달래다, 진정시키다(=pacify, quiet, soothe)

✍(해석) 일단 물이 없어지면 탐험가들은 희망을 포기해야만 했다. **정답 ②**

4. parsimony 인색(=stinginess, miserliness) ① charisma 천부적 재능 ② affection 애정(=love, attachment), 병(=disease) ④ retribution 보복, 징벌(=compensation, redress, reprisal, reciprocation, nemesis, amends)

✍(해석) 그의 인색함은 영화계에서 전설적인 것이었다. **정답 ③**

5. sheer 완전한(=absolute, utter), 얇은(=very thin; transparent), 순수한(=mere, simple) ① latent 숨어 있는, 잠복성의(=hidden, concealed) ② absolute 완전한(=complete, perfect, thorough, entire, total), 전제의(=despotic, autocratic) ③ potential 가능한 (=possible), 잠재하는(=dormant, latent) ④ ambiguous 애매한(=vague, obscure, equivocal, uncertain)

✍(해석) 많은 청중이 완전한 지루함 때문에 나갔다. **정답 ②**

6. incumbent 의지하는, 의무로서 지워지는, 현직의 ① obligatory 의무로서 부과하는, 강제적인(=mandatory, compelling) ② reasonable 합리적인 ③ submissive 순종하는(=obedient), 유순한(=yielding, docile) ④ superfluous 불필요한, 여분의(=unnecessary, needless, excessive)
 ✍(해석) 프랭크는 그의 소홀로 인해 빚어진 피해에 대해 보상을 하는 것이 당연한 의무라고 느꼈다. **정답 ①**

7. drive a person up a wall 사람을 화나게 하다. ① enrage 화나게 하다(=infuriate) ② enervate 기운을 빼앗다(=weaken) ④ diffident 자신 없는, 수줍은(=shy)
 ✍(해석) 수업 중에 볼펜을 똑딱거리는 학생들은 나를 화나게 한다. **정답 ①**

8. vehement 맹렬한, 열광적인(=violent, furious, hot; forcible, forceful; impetuous, excited, passionate; fervent) ② weird 신비로운, 기묘한(=uncanny, eerie, mysterious, ghostly) ③ absurd 어리석은, 불합리한 ④ onerous 성가신, 부담스러운(=burdensome, oppressive)
 ✍(해석) 그는 그 주의 남은 날 동안 맹렬한 항거를 계속했다. **정답 ①**

9. shrink 오그라들다(=contract), 줄다(=lessen), 겁내다(=draw back; flinch) ② fade 시들다 (=languish, wither, shrivel), 사라지다(=vanish, disappear), (색이)바래다(=pale, dim, bleach, whiten) ③ unravel 풀다(=ravel, untwine, untwist, disentangle, untangle), 해결하다(=develop, explain, unfold) ④ contract 계약하다, (병에)걸리다(=get or incur), 수축시키다(=reduce in size, shrink), 줄이다(=shorten)
 ✍(해석) 양모는 뜨거운 물에 담그면 오그라드는 경향이 있다. **정답 ④**

10. prescient 미리 아는, 선견지명이 있는(=prophetic) ① pliable 유순한, 융통성이 있는(=plastic, ductile, malleable, flexible, supple, limber, yielding, docile, tractable, obedient, compliant, submissive) ② intractable 다루기 힘든(=unmanageable), 고집스러운(=obstinate, stubborn, obdurate, perverse, wayward, headstrong) ④ keen 날카로운(=sharp, cutting, piercing, stinging,

nippy), 격렬한, 열심인(=eager, enthusiastic, ardent)
✎(해석) 아마도 1년 전 미리 알고 있던 서방국가들이 현재의 전쟁을 막기 위해 병력을 주둔시킬 수도 있었다. **정답 ③**

11. disseminate 퍼뜨리다, 보급시키다(=disperse, diffuse, distribute, scatter, spread) ① record 기록하다(=register, put down, write down, jot down) ② discount 할인하다 ③ obtain 얻다(=come by, get by, acquire, land)
✎(해석) 국립과학재단은 과학자원에 관계되는 정보를 보급시킨다. **정답 ④**

12. discord 불일치(=disagreement), 부조화(=disharmony) ① compromise 타협(=settlement) ③ disillusion 환멸 ④ anxiety 걱정(=worry, uneasiness), 열망(=an eager desire)
✎(해석) 인접해 있는 방에 매우 다른 장식구도를 쓴다는 것은 스타일에 있어서의 부조화와 통일성의 결여를 초래할 수도 있다. **정답 ②**

13. harmful 유해한(=injurious, detrimental, poisonous, deleterious, pernicious, noxious, noisome) ② prodigious 거대한(=immense, enormous, huge, vast, gargantuan, mammoth, gigantic) ③ intrusive 침입적인, 방해하는 ④ mordant 비꼬는, 신랄한(=caustic, sarcastic)
✎(해석) 어떤 박테리아는 유익한 반면, 다른 것들은 병을 일으킨다는 점에서 유해하다. **정답 ①**

14. ubiquitously 무소부재하게, 어디서나(=omnipresently) ① contradictorily 모순되게 ③ arbitrarily 마음대로
✎(해석) 이 시점에서 우리는 이러한 이례적인 결정의 중심에 표현되지 않은 채로 남아 있는 우리 문화의 근본적이며 무소부재한 가정들을 접하게 된다. **정답 ②**

15. philanthropic 박애의(=humanitarian), 자선의 ① profligate 방탕한(=wanton, reckless, intemperate), 낭비하는(=wasteful, extravagant prodigal) ② governmental 정부의 ④ multinational 다국적의
✎(해석) 포드재단은 세계에서 가장 부유한 박애단체 중 하나이다. **정답 ③**

16. drawback 결점(=disadvantage, weakness, shortcoming, fault, failing, defect, foible) ① property 재산, 소유, 본질 ② addictive 첨가제 ④ disparity상이(=difference), 부등(=inequality), 불균형
✍(해석) 많은 순수한 금속들이 너무 연하고, 너무 쉽게 녹이 슬거나 어떤 다른 결점을 가지고 있기 때문에 거의 쓸모가 없다. 정답 ③

17. nuts and bolts (기계의) 작동부, (사물의)요점(=the working or moving parts of a machine; the basic elements or practical aspects of something)
✍(해석) 그 연사는 그 나라에 새로운 전화 시스템을 가설하기 위한 그의 계획의 요점을 설명했다. 정답 ④

18. the ins and outs 세부, 곡절, 자초지종(=all the details and intricacies)
✍(해석) 조지는 그 사건의 모든 세부사항을 알았다. 정답 ③

19. germane 밀접한 관계가 있는, 적절한(=pertinent, relevant) ② immaterial 비물질적인, 무형의, 영적인(=spiritual), 중요하지 않은(=unimportant) ③ essential 필수적인 (=indispensable) ④ vague 막연한, 모호한(=indefinite; not sharp, certain, or precise)
✍(해석) 우리는 핵 발생연료들이 토론에 적절하지 않았기 때문에 그것들이 가진 문제를 배제시켰다. 정답 ①

20. indefatigable 지치지 않는(=untiring, tireless) sinew 건(=tendon), 완력(=muscular power, strength) ① courageous 용감한(=brave, valorous) ② excellent 탁월한(=very good; of very high quality) ③ defiant 도전적인, 반항적인(=rebellious)
✍(해석) 그는 매우 근육질이고 정력적이고, 세계에서 가장 지칠 줄 모르는 사냥꾼이자 덫을 놓는 사람이었다. 정답 ④

Ⅳ 문장 완성형

실력문제 1회

1. '재정적 손실'과 어울리는 형용사를 고르면 된다. ② massive 크고 무거운, 대량의 ④ realistic 현실주의의, 현실적인, 사실주의의
    ✍(해석) 미국 항공사는 9월 11일 공격이후 2001년에 대량의 재정 손실을 게시했고, 올해 다시 여전히 수입이 약하다. **정답 ②**

2. <between A and B>에 유의하면 답을 고를 수 있다. ① connection 연결, 관계, 거래처
    ✍(해석) 테러 집단들과 중동의 폭격 간에 관계가 있다는 새로운 보고가 있었다. **정답 ①**

3. 문제해결의 키는 before이하의 '파업에 들어가기 전에'이다. 따라서 정답은 ① negotiate '협상하다(=settle), 협정하다'가 된다. ② stipulate 규정하다(=specify) ③ reciprocate 교환하다(=exchange), 보답하다(=repay) ④ correlate 상호 연관시키다
    ✍(해석) 노사는 그들이 파업에 들어가기 전에 협상 할 수 있기를 희망한다. **정답 ①**

4. 문제해결의 키는 noisy(시끄러운)에 있다. and로 연결된 빈칸에는 부정적인 뜻이 들어와야 하므로 ② raucous가 정답이 된다. ② raucous 목쉰, 귀에 거슬리는(=hoarse, grating, rasping, harsh, strident, loud and rowdy) ① rapturous 열광적인 ③ ravenous 게걸스럽게 먹는, 굶주린(=rapacious, greedy, voracious, gluttonous) ④ rigorous 엄한, 가혹한 (=austere, severe, uncompromising, rigid, resolute, stiff, strict, exacting, firm)
    ✍(해석) 밥은 현대음악보다는 고전음악을 더 좋아한다. 그는 현대음악은 시끄럽고 귀에 거슬린다고 말한다. **정답 ②**

5. 'we have been split in two'으로 보아 빈칸에는 ① cut가 들어간다. ③ diverge 분기하다, 갈라지다(=branch off), 빗나가다(=deflect, digress, divert) ④ activate 활동적으로 하다

✎(해석) 인간 정신의 의식과 무의식 사이에 있는 연락선은 모두 단절되어져서 우리는 두 부분으로 나뉘어져 왔다. **정답 ①**

6. ② laborious 어려운(=difficult), 힘든(=hard-working) ③ monotonous 단조로운

✎(해석) 인간은 도전적인 일을 할 기회를 필요로 한다. 나는 단순히 반복적인 판에 박힌 많은 일들을 이런 범주에 포함시키지 않는다. 나는 단조로운 일에 흥미가 없다. **정답 ③**

7. 문제해결의 키는 'an excellent person'에 있다. 훌륭한 인재가 되려면 능력이 있어야 하므로 빈칸에는 ① competence가 들어가야 한다. ① competence 능력(=capability, capacity), 적성(=fitness, proficiency), 자산(=means, resources, wealth) ② complacency 만족(=contentment), 자기만족(=self-satisfaction, smugness) ③ compensation 보상 ④ compunction 양심의 가책, 회한(=remorse, self-reproach, regret, contrition, penitence)

✎(해석) 그의 능력과 경험 때문에 그는 이 직업에 훌륭한 인재가 되었다. **정답 ①**

8. rice와 관련되어 사용할 수 있는 단어는 ② allot(할당하다) 이다. ① entreat 간청하다(=request, crave, beseech, implore, pray, supplicate, plead, solicit) ② allot 할당하다(=grant, assign, share, distribute) ③ resolve 결심하다(=determine, make up one's mind, decide) ④ detach 분리하다(=separate, disconnect, sever)

✎(해석) 식량이 거의 없었기 때문에 각 가족마다 1파운드의 쌀만이 할당되었다. **정답 ②**

9. 'he was either lazy or inefficient'로 보아 빈칸에는 ② fault가 와야 한다.

✎(해석) 국가의 천연 자원 덕분에 모든 미국인이 아주 최근까지는, 자기 아버지보다 돈을 더 많이 벌 것이라고 합리적으로 기대할 수 있었다. 그래서 만일 돈을 적게 번다면, 그 잘못은 자신의 것임에 틀림이 없었다. 그 이유는 그가 게으르거나 무능했기 때문이었다. **정답 ②**

10. 빈칸에는 문장의 내용상 ④ passionate(열정적인)가 들어가야 한다. ① erratic 산만한, 변덕스러운(=irregular, random), 엉뚱한(=eccentric, queer) ② frustrated 실망한, 욕구불만의 frustrate 좌절시키다(=discourage, baffle, upset, cripple), 방해하다 ③ irregular 불규칙한(=uneven, not straight, not uniform), 불법의

✎(해석) 그 연사는 열정적인 연설로 침묵하고 있는 청중의 감정을 고조시키려고 노력했다. **정답 ④**

11. 문맥상 빈칸에는 move(움직이다)의 동의어가 들어가야 한다. ① arouse 깨우다, 자극하다(=rouse, awaken, stir, excite, stimulate, whet) ② budge 움직이다(=move, shift), 바꾸다(=alter, change) ③ dodge 피하다 (=avoid, escape, shun, eschew, elude, evade) ④ provoke 화나게 하다 (=anger, irritate), 불러일으키다(=excite, stir up, evoke)

✎(해석) 존과 밥은 그 큰 바위를 움직이려고 했으나 움직일 수 없었다. **정답 ②**

12. 빈칸에는 그가 한 말을 이해할 수 없는 이유가 들어가야 한다. ① master 지배하다(=conquer, subdue, rule), 숙달하다(=become proficient in, gain mastery in) ② mumble 중얼거리다, 웅얼거리다(=murmur, mutter) ③ molest 괴롭히다(=disturb, annoy, vex, pester, harass) ④ ridicule 비웃다, 조롱하다(=deride, mock, make fun of, make sport of, make an ass of, make a donkey of, jeer, scoff, scorn, sneer, poke fun at)

✎(해석) 그는 항상 중얼거리기 때문에 우리는 그가 말한 것을 이해할 수 없다. **정답 ②**

13. 빈칸 뒤에 'and tough times(불경기)'와 어울리는 것은 ④ recession (경기후퇴, 침체)이다. ① prosperity 호황 ② plateau 고원(경기) ③ boom 벼락경기, 급격한 증가

✎(해석) 마케팅 담당자들은 언제나 입술 연지에서 란제리에 이르는 모든 것을 팔기 위해서 예쁜 얼굴과 완전한 몸매를 이용해 왔으나, 경기후퇴와 광고업계의 불경기로 인해 수퍼모델들이 몇 안 되는 신뢰할 만한 판매

도구의 하나가 되었다. **정답 ④**

14. 빈칸 뒤에 'individual liberty'(개인적 자유)와 어울리는 것은 ② haven (안식처, 피난처, 항구)이다. ① anomaly 비정상(=abnormality) ③ shambles 도살장(=slaughterhouse), 혼란(=disorder) ④ inferno 지옥(=hell, hades, Gehena Tophet, pandemonium)

✍(해석) 컬럼버스의 여행은 전 세계 사람들에게 이제는 개인적 자유의 상징과 안식처가 된 민주주의의 대담한 실험 끝에 미국을 낳은 긴 과정의 첫 단계였다. **정답 ②**

15. turn to A for B (A에게 B를 의지하다)를 묻는 문제이다.
✍(해석) 그 계획에 재정지원을 하기 위해서 그들은 필요한 기금을 위해 대중에게 의지해야만 한다. **정답 ②**

16. 빈칸 뒤에 나오는 'the unwholesome old ways'와 어울리는 동사를 고르면 된다. ① reinforce 강화하다, 보강하다(=strengthen, support, buttress, replenish) ② continue 계속하다(=last, keep on, go on) ③ replace 제자리에 놓다. …에 대신하다 (=put back, supplant, supercede, substitute) ④ reinstate 회복하다(=restore, reinstall, rehabilitate)

✍(해석) 그들의 개혁운동의 궁극적인 목표가 획일적일 수 없지만, 건전하지 못한 낡은 방식들을 대신할 수많은 다양한 요소들로 구성되어야 한다. **정답 ③**

17. but으로 보아 빈칸에는 부정적인 의미의 단어가 들어가고, 'talks too much'는 결점이 될 수 있으므로 정답은 ④ failing이 된다. ④ failing 단점, 결점(=fault, weakness, drawback, shortcoming, defect, demerit, foible, disadvantage, blemish, imperfection) ① crime 죄(=sin), 범죄(=vice) ② deviation 일탈, 탈선(=change, deflection, alteration, swerving, warp, refraction, diversion, digression, divergence) ③ mistake 잘못, 착오(=error, blunder, slip, misunderstanding)

✍(해석) 쥬디는 멋진 소녀이지만 하나의 큰 결점이 있는데, 그것은 말을 너무 많이 하는 것이다. **정답 ④**

18. and 뒤의 내용으로 보아 빈칸에는 '유효한'의 뜻을 가진 'in force'가 들어간다. ① affect …에 영향을 미치다(=influence, have an effect/impact on), 감동시키다(=move, touch) ② force 힘(=strength, power), 폭력(=violence), 설득력, 효과(=effectiveness), 무력(=military power) ③ void 공간(=an empty space), 공허감(=a feeling of emptiness) ④ effective 유효한(=efficient, efficacious, in effect), 실제 동원할 수 있는(=operative), 눈에 띄는 (=impressive)

✍(해석) 부시는 바그다드(이라크)에 대한 경제제재는 유효하고 역사는 압제자를 제거하는 방식이 있다고 말한 것에 불과하다. **정답 ②**

19. let grass grow under one's feet 게으르다, 시간을 낭비하다(=be idle, be lazy, waste time)

✍(해석) 게으르지 말아라. 너는 좀 더 빨리 일하는 것을 배워야 한다. **정답 ③**

20. 빈칸에는 의미상 '편협한'의 뜻을 가진 단어가 와야 한다. ① emotional 감정적인 ② broadminded 마음이 넓은 ③ tolerant 관대한(=generous, lenient, understanding, receptive, sophisticated) ④ intolerant 편협한(=dogmatic, narrow, bigoted, prejudiced, biased)

✍(해석) 사람이 너무 편협해서 모든 사람은 평등하며 우리는 민족, 피부색, 주의를 문제 삼지 않아야 한다는 것을 믿도록 하는 것은 어려울 것이다. **정답 ④**

실력문제 2회

1. 'barely'(거의 -않다)의 뜻에 유의하면, 빈칸에 들어가는 단어를 고를 수 있다. ① heavy 무거운, 곤란한, 슬픈, 격렬한 ② intermittent 간헐적인(=periodic)

✍(해석) 비가 간헐적으로 와서 우리가 길을 따라 내려갈 때 머리에 거의 맞지 않았다. **정답 ②**

2. Since이하의 부사절의 내용에 유의하면, 빈칸에 들어가는 단어를 고를

수 있다. ① dismay 낙담케 하다, 당황케 하다(=discourage; embarrass) ② apathetic 무관심한(=indifferent) ③ composed 가라앉은(=sedate) ④ enrapture 황홀하게 하다(=transport, entrance, enchant), -을 기뻐 날뛰게 하다(=fill with delight; bewitch)
✍(해석) 그 학생이 그의 프로젝트에 관하여 열심히 일하지 않았기 때문에, 그가 수상했다는 것을 알고서 매우 기뻤다. **정답 ④**

3. 빈칸에는 의미상 '술취한'의 뜻을 가진 단어가 와야 한다. ② undeniable 부정할 수 없는, 훌륭한(=excellent) ③ intoxicated 술 취한, 흥분한 ④ overexcited 지나치게 흥분한
✍(해석) 조사가 보여준 바에 따르면 그 운전사는 사고 당시에 술에 취했다는 것이다. **정답 ③**

4. 빈칸에는 의미상 '들을 수 있는'의 뜻을 가진 단어가 와야 한다. ① fragile 부서지기 쉬운(=breakable, brittle, delicate, frail) ② audible 들을 수 있는 ④ decrepit 노쇠한(=old, feeble, senile, on one's last leg, doddering), 낡은(=shaky, delapidated, broken-down)
✍(해석) 그는 너무 부드럽게 말해서 그의 목소리는 정말로 들리지 않았다. **정답 ②**

5. 빈칸에는 의미상 '유능한'의 뜻을 가진 단어가 와야 한다.① compatible 양립할 수 있는, 모순 없는(=consistent), 조화로운 (=harmonious) ③ conspicuous 눈에 잘 띄는(=prominent, notable, eminent, outstanding, striking, salient, remarkable, noticeable) ④ competent 유능한(=capable), 충분한(=adequate, sufficient)
✍(해석) 나는 존슨이 그의 새 직업에 성공하지 못할 것이라고 생각한다. 왜냐하면 그는 그런 형태의 일에 유능하지 못하기 때문이다. **정답 ④**

6. 내용상 법률용어가 들어가야 하므로 ② complicity(공모, 연루, 공범)가 답이 된다. ① simulation 가장(=pretense), 흉내, 시뮬레이션, 모의실험[훈련] ③ exuberance 무성, 풍부(=profusion) ④ contingency 우연성(=chance), 사고(=accident)

☞(해석) 그 방화범이 검사에 의해 심문 받을 때, 범죄에 있어 공범을 부인했다. **정답** ②

7. 빈칸에는 의미상 '유죄판결'의 뜻을 가진 단어가 와야 한다. ① verdict 평결, 판정 ② sentence 판결, 선고 ③ conviction 유죄판결, 확신 ④ acquittal 석방, 변제
☞(해석) 밥의 증언이 없다면 뇌물의 증거가 부족하여 재판에서 유죄판결이 불가능하다. **정답** ③

8. 내용상 빈칸에는 '요약된', '간략한'의 뜻을 가진 단어가 와야 한다. ① investigative 조사의, 연구적인 ② predominant 우세한 ③ insular섬의, 고립한 insular account 편협한 사고 ④ synoptic 개요의
☞(해석) 대중 매체가 제공하는 엄청난 정보량에 압도당하여 우리는 뉴스를 손쉽게 소화할 수 있는 요약된 설명을 원하게 된다. **정답** ④

9. 'as it were'(말하자면)에 유의하면 빈칸에 attract의 동의어가 들어간다. ① affect …에게 영향을 미치다 ② tempt 유혹하다. ④ hypnotize 최면을 걸다.
☞(해석) 나는 오랫동안 광고판에 시선을 고정했다. 그 흰 공백이 내 눈을 매혹하고, 마치 내 뇌를 유혹하는 듯 했다. 나는 그것을 읽으려고 노력했지만, 결국 허사였다. **정답** ②

10. 빈칸에는 의미상 '중화하다'의 뜻을 가진 단어가 와야 한다. ① contradict 부정하다, 모순 되다 ② counteract …에 거슬리다, 중화하다 ③ frustrate 좌절시키다, 무효로 하다 ④ deprecate 비난하다, 반대하다
☞(해석) 불안한 사람들은 자신이 처한 실제 상황을 숙고할 수 없고, 그에 따른 계획도 세울 수 없게 된다. 불안감과 서로에게 집착함으로 그 불안감을 중화하고, 가능한 일상적 삶의 방식을 유지함으로써 불안감의 상처를 줄이려는 희망은 많은 사람들을 무능하게 만들었다. **정답** ②

11. 'not the festive mood'에 힌트가 나와 있다. ① senility 노쇠, 노망 ② capriciousness 변덕스러움 ③ insanity 광기 ④ solemnity 엄숙, 장엄, 의식(=rite, ceremony)

✍(해석) 기대했던 대로의 축제의 분위기가 아니라, 압제적인 엄숙함이 그 모임의 분위기를 특징지었다. **정답 ④**

12. 'because of their frankness'에 힌트가 나와 있다. ① sarcastic 빈정거리는(=scornful, contemptuous, withering, cynical, satiric, ironical, sardonic) ② sadistic 가학적인(=perverted, twisted; cruel, brutal, fiendish; malicious, pernicious) ③ digressive 본론을 떠난, 지엽적인 ④ ingenuous 솔직한, 소박한, 순진한(=frank, open, candid; simple, naive, artless; trusting, unsuspecting)
✍(해석) 그의 꾸밈없는 비평은 솔직함 때문에 당혹스러울 경우가 자주 있다. **정답 ④**

13. ① recumbent 드러누운, 기댄(=lying down; reclining) ② redundant 과다한, 장황한(=excessive, superfluous; wordy) ③ resonant 울려 퍼지는, 공명하(=resounding; intensifying sound; vibrant, sonorous) ④ reticent 과묵한(=disinclined to speak; taciturn)
✍(해석) 제인은 우리에게 말하려 하지 않았다. 왜냐하면 그녀는 수줍고 과묵하기 때문이다. **정답 ④**

14. ④frail 허약한(=weak, feeble, delicate, infirm) ① faint 희미한(=indistinct), 막연한(=vague), (마음이)약한, 어지러운(=giddy) ②sinew 질긴(=tough), 억센 근육을 가진 ③ flimsy (재료가) 가볍고 얄팍한(=light and thin), (물체가) 손상되기 쉬운(=easily injured and destroyed)
✍(해석) 그 노인은 오랜 질병 후에 돌풍이 불면 날아갈지도 모를 만큼 너무 야위고 허약해 보였다. **정답 ④**

15. 빈칸에는 glaucoma(녹내장) 으로 보아, '말초의'라는 뜻을 가진 단어가 와야 한다. ① peripatetic 소요학파의, 걸어 다니는(=walking or moving about; itinerant) ② peripheral 주변의, 말초의 ③ periphrastic 완곡한 ④ ocular 시각상의
✍(해석) 녹내장 환자들은 그들의 말초 시력이 손상되었으며 정면에서 직접이 아니면 물체를 더 이상 볼 수 없다는 것을 안다. **정답 ②**

16. 빈칸에는 의미상 '저조한'의 뜻을 가진 단어가 와야 한다. ① sustain 떠받치다, 지지하다(=support, bolster, buttress) ③ depress 내려 누르다, 쇠약하게 하다 ④ stabilize 안정시키다.

✍(해석) 출생율과 그 나라의 발달 정도는 역비례의 관계가 있는 것처럼 보인다. 즉 산업 상의 발전과 과학적인 발전 도시화 과정, 더 나아가서는 생활수준의 향상의 정도가 크면 클수록 그 나라의 출생률은 그 만큼 저조한 경향이 있다. **정답 ③**

17. 빈칸에는 의미상 '화나다'의 뜻을 가진 단어가 와야 한다. ① degenerate 타락하다(=demoralize, degrade, fall away) ② exasperate 노하게 하다 (=irritate, provoke), 악화시키다(=aggravate) ③ consummate 뛰어난 (=superb), 완전한(=complete) ④ expend 쓰다, 소모하다(=spend; use up)

✍(해석) 선생은 그 학생들에게 여분의 일을 주었다. 왜냐하면 그녀는 강의실에서 모든 소음과 잡담에 화가 났기 때문이다. **정답 ②**

18. 빈칸에는 의미상 '본래의'의 뜻을 가진 단어가 와야 한다. ① incoherent 모순 된, 조리가 없는 ② inherent 본래의, 고유의(=essential, innate, natural, intrinsic, built-in) ③ incessant 끊임없는 (=unceasing, constant, ceaseless) ④ incredible 믿을 수 없는(=unbelievable)

✍(해석) 언론의 자유는 민주주의에 있어 고유의 권리이다. **정답 ②**

19. ③ dwindle 작아지다, 감소하다(=shrink) ④ expand 확장하다, 넓어지다(=enlarge)

✍(해석) 명목상의 임금이 하락할지 모르지만 관세장벽의 제거가 물가수준에 더 큰 폭의 하락을 초래할 것이고 그 결과 실질적인 임금이 상승할 것이다. **정답 ①**

20. ① retard 지연시키다 ② rebuke 비난하다 ③ retreat 철수하다, 은퇴하다(=withdraw, retire) ④ retain 보유하다(=hold, keep)

✍(해석) 명백하게도 긴 가뭄은 이 나무의 성장을 뒤지게 한다. **정답 ①**

실력문제 3회

1. ① in view of …을 고려하여, …이 보이는 곳에 ② in spite of …에도 불구하고(=despite, with all, after all, for all, notwithstanding, in the face of) ③ regardless of …에 관계없이(=without regard to, irrespective of) ④ in terms of …에 의하여, …의 관점으로
☞(해석) 하나님 앞과 산 자와 죽은 자를 심판하실 그리스도 예수 앞에서 그의 나타나실 것과 그의 나라를 두고 엄히 명하노니(딤후4:1) **정답 ①**

2. ① controversial 논쟁의 ② unheralded 포고 없는 ③ easygoing 태평한 ④ prolific 생산력 있는(=fertile, fruitful, productive), 다작의
☞(해석) 은퇴할 때까지 57권의 책을 저술해서 그가 금세기의 가장 다작인 신학자들 중 하나로 간주되는 것은 당연하다. **정답 ④**

3. ① appraise 평가하다(=estimate, assess, evaluate, rate) ② glamorize 매력적으로 만들다, 미화하다 launch 진수하다, 시작하다 ③ portray 묘사하다(=describe, depict) strengthen 강화하다 ④ expose 노출하다, 드러내다 condemn 비난하다, 형을 선고하다(=sentence)
☞(해석) 흑인들에 대한 불공평함을 효과적으로 묘사한 소설 '톰 아저씨의 오두막집'은 반노예운동을 강화하는데 중요한 영향을 주었다. **정답 ③**

4. ① intercede 조정하나, 중재하다 ② publish 발표하다, 출판하다 ③ decipher 풀다 ④ unveil 폭로하다
☞(해석) 간첩들은 그 비밀암호가 풀리지 않는다는 것을 알아냈다. **정답 ③**

5. ③ psycho 정신병의, 전신 의학의 ③ lunatic 미친(=insane) lunatic asylum 정신병원 ④ fantastic 공상적인, 괴이한
☞(해석) 병원, 감옥 그리고 정신병원은 사람들이 가기를 두려워하는 곳이다. **정답 ③**

6. ① intractable 다루기 힘든, 고집 센(=obstinate, stubborn, obdurate, perverse, wayward) ② suspicious 수상한(=doubtful, dubious) ③ obsequious

아부하는, 아첨하는(=servile) ④ antagonistic 반대하는, 대립하는, 적대적인 (=hostile)

✎(해석) 그는 그의 상사가 제안하는 것은 무엇이나 사려 깊은 생각 없이 받아들이기 때문에, 우리 회사에서 가장 아부하는 사람으로 간주되었다. **정답 ③**

7. ① intensive 강렬한, 집중적인 ② homogeneous 동종의 ③ systematic 체계적인 ④ varied 다양한(=various, a variety of, assorted, miscellaneous, sundry)

✎(해석) 많은 교육자들은 학생들의 능력 범위는 제한을 받기 때문에 같은 수준의 학생들을 하나의 그 그룹으로 형성하는 것이 교육을 항상 시킬 것이라고 주장했다. **정답 ②**

8. ① fascinate 매혹하다 ② redeem 만회하다(=regain), 메꾸다(=offset), 상환하다, 속죄하다 ③ illuminate 조명하다 ④ ratify 비준하다, 확증하다 (=endorse, corroborate, confirm)

✎(해석) 그녀의 목소리가 매력이 있어서 변변찮은 외모를 만회했다. **정답 ②**

9. ① retrieve 회수하다, 회복하다(=recover, bring back) ② recall 소환하다, 취소하다(=revoke, call off, cancel, annul, nullify) ③ reprieve 형집행을 유예하다, 일시 구제하다 ④ restrict 한정하다, 제한하다(=limit)

✎(해석) 어떤 인공물도 지금까지 타이타닉의 난파로부터 회수되지 않았다. **정답 ①**

10. ① snugly 기분 좋게, 따스하게 ② stealthily 은밀하게 stealthy 은밀한, 남몰래 하는(=covert, secret, privy, surreptitious, furtive) ③ modestly 겸손하게, 알맞게 ④ moodily 우울하게

✎(해석) 그가 따라가는 사람에게 보이기를 원치 않았기에, 그는 은밀하게 움직였다. **정답 ②**

11. ② define 정의하다 ③ evaluate 평가하다 ④ contrast 대조하다

✎(해석) 만약 당신이 에세이 시험 문제에 답하는 것에 차이점을 강조하

고자 한다면, 문제의 키워드는 대조하는 것이다. **정답 ④**

12. ② ameliorate 개선하다(=improve, better) ③ impair 손상시키다 (=injure) ④ enhance 향상시키다, 올리다(=elevate, raise, hoist, heighten)
✍(해석) 흡연은 당신의 건강을 해칠 수 있다. **정답 ③**

13. ① insightful 통찰력이 있는 ② incongruous 조화되지 않는(=unsuitable, inappropriate) ③ prosperous 번성하는(=thriving, flowering, flourishing) ④ appropriate 적당한 (=proper, suitable, pertinent, relevant)
✍(해석) 당신의 부적절한 말들은 토론을 어지럽혔다. **정답 ②**

14. <spend+시간+V-ing>구문을 묻는 문제이다. ① overcome 극복하다 (=get over, tide over, surmount, conquer, subdue, defeat, overthrow) ② recuperate 회복하다(=recover, come back, pull through, convalescence, rally, get well, make one's comeback)
✍(해석) 그는 그 문제에 관하여 공개 성명을 하기 전에 회복하는 데 보다 많은 시간을 보낼 것이다. **정답 ②**

15. 'the clergy condemned it'(성직자가 그것을 비난하였다)와 어울리는 것이 빈칸에 들어가면 된다. ① adventurous 모험을 좋아하는, 모험적인 ② arrogant 거만한(=domineering, autocratic, sneering, proud, haughty, insolent) ③ decent 상당한 신분의, 점잖은(=decorous, chaste) ④ impious 불경한, 신앙심 없는(=unholy, godless, irreligious, blasphemous, sacrilegious)
✍(해석) 벤자민 프랭클린이 피뢰침을 발명했을 때, 성직자들은 그것을 신의 의지를 좌절시키려는 불경한 시도로 비난하였다. **정답 ④**

16. 'as we learn to breathe or to walk'에서 빈칸에 들어갈 단어의 힌트를 얻을 수 있다. ① initiation 개시(=commencement, inauguration), 가입 (=admittance, introduction) ② record 기록, 경력, 성적 ③ analogy 유추 by analogy 유추하여(=analogically, by parity of reasoning) ④ instinct 본능 (=drive), 직감(=sense), 직관(=intuition)
✍(해석) 우리는 숨쉬고 걷는 것을 배우듯이 본능적으로 문장구성을 배우지는 않는다. 우리는 기억에서 문장을 반복하고 유추하여 문장을 바꾼다.

정답 ③

17. ① crude 천연 그대로의(=raw, unrefined, unprepared), 미숙한(=rudimentary, underdeveloped), 불완전한(=incomplete) ② manual 손의, 손으로 하는 ③ congenial 같은 성질의, 알맞은, 성미에 맞는(=agreeable, pleasing) ④ indigenous 고유의, 토착의(=innate, inborn, inherent, natural, native)

✍(해석) 태권도는 한국에서 발전된 고유의 스포츠 중의 하나이다. **정답 ④**

18. ① be up to 감당할 수 있다, …의 의무이다 ② be in for 겪다, 당하다 ③ be open to 개방되다, …의 여지가 있다, …을 받기 쉽다(=be exposed to, be vulnerable to, be susceptible to) ④ be content with 만족하다(=be satisfied with)

✍(해석) 주저하지 말고 당신의 생각을 제시해 주세요. 우리는 어떤 제안에도 항상 개방되어 있어요. **정답 ③**

19. ① repel 물리치다(=drive or force back, reject) ② permeate 침투하다(=penetrate, pervade, saturate) ③ measure 측정하다 ④ intrigue 음모를 꾸미다(=plot, conspire), 흥미를 끌다(=arouse)

✍(해석) 무시간이라는 개념은 처음부터 역설적이다. 왜냐하면 성인의 의식은 기간에 대한 인식으로 침투되기 때문이다. **정답 ②**

20. ① resentful 분개하는, 원망하는 ② prudent 분별 있는(=wary) ③ outright 철저한(=downright), 솔직한(=straightforward), 분명한 ④ insulting 모욕하는

✍(해석) 미온적인 수락은 분명한 거절보다 훨씬 더 당혹스럽다. **정답 ③**

실력문제 4회

1. '양보'를 나타내는 구문이므로, 앞뒤 빈칸에는 대조적인 뜻의 단어가 들어가야 한다.

✍(해석) 예수는 그의 가르침들 속에 있는 진리를 발견한 제자들에 의해

존경을 받았다고 할지라도, 그의 가르침들은 유대 지도자들에게는 위협이 되었다. **정답 ②**

2. 'intolerant'(참을 수 없는, 편협한), 'his strange behavior'로 보아 빈칸에 들어갈 단어를 고를 수 있다. ① revere 숭배하다, 존경하다(=respect, esteem, adore, venerate, look up to) ② shun 피하다(=avoid, eschew, help, escape) ③ contradict 반대하다, 모순 되다 ④ tolerate 참다(=stand, bear, put up with, endure, persevere)
✍(해석) 이 교수는 편협한 경우가 자주 있었다. 더구나 그의 이상한 행동 때문에 그의 대부분의 지기들은 가능할 때는 언제나 그를 피했다. **정답 ②**

3. 'instead of' 앞뒤에는 대조의 뜻이 들어가야 한다. tear down 헐다(=demolish)
✍(해석) 역사적인 중요성을 가진 건물들이 지금 허물지 않고 세워지고 있다. **정답 ①**

4. distinguish A from B (A와 B를 구별하다). 빈칸에는 'genuine'(진짜의)의 반대말이 와야 한다. ① authentic 진정한, 믿을 만한(=genuine, real, true) ② contraband 밀수, 밀수품(=smuggled goods) ③ counterpart 대응하는 것, 서로 비슷한 것[사람] ④ counterfeit 가짜의, 위조의(=forged; false, pretended, sham)
✍(해석) 은행 창구 직원은 10달러짜리 진짜 돈과 가짜 돈을 쉽게 구별할 수 있다. **정답 ④**

5. 빈칸에 들어갈 단어의 힌트는 'as a symbol of strength'이다. ① brilliant 빛나는, 화려한 ② splendid 훌륭한(=shining, brilliant), 굉장한(=magnificent, gorgeous), 멋진(=fine) ③ staunch 충실한(=steadfast, loyal), 견고한(=strong, steady, solid), 방수의(=seaworthy) ④ starveling 굶주린, 빈약한
✍(해석) 북미의 동부 지역에서 오동나무는 그 목재의 견고한 성질 때문에 어디에서나 힘의 상징으로 여겨진다. **정답 ③**

6. ① come up with …에 따라잡다, 제안하다(=arise) ② come down on 호통치다, 꾸짖다(=scold severely) ③ come into force 시행되다 ④ come to terms with 화해하다, 받아들이다(=accept)
✎(해석) 그는 오래지 않아 설득력 있는 사례를 제안했다. **정답 ①**

7. ① callous 냉담한(=insensitive, indifferent) ② arduous 힘 드는 (=laborious), 끈기 있는(=strenuous, energetic) ③ callow 미성숙한 (=immature) ④ ardent 열심 있는
✎(해석) 미성숙한 젊은이는 성인으로서 행동해야 할 바에 대해 경험이나 지식이 매우 적다. **정답 ③**

8. ① animosity 악의, 증오(=ill will, animus; violent hatred) ③ affinity 인척(관계), 친근성, 좋아함(=kinship; sympathy; liking; attraction) ④ equanimity 균형, 침착, 냉정(=emotional balance; composure; calmness)
✎(해석) 급우간의 우정관계는 종종 가정에 대한 충성심만큼 강하다. **정답 ③**

9. ① arbitrary 자의적인, 제멋대로의(=capricious; absolute, despotic) ② egregious 지독한, 얼토당토않은(=flagrant, notorious) ③ exemplary 본보기의 ④ aimless 목적이 없는 (=purposeless, pointless, rambling)
✎(해석) 그와 같은 지독한 범죄에는 어떤 벌도 심한 것이 아니다. 그 범죄의 극악무도함을 이해하는 것이 거의 불가능하다. **정답 ②**

10. ① extraordinary 비범한(=exceptional) ② collaborative 협력하는 (=cooperative) ③ brilliant 빛나는, 훌륭한(=shining, distinguished) ④ persistent 완고한, 부단한 (=persevering, continuing)
✎(해석) 그 집단의 구성원들은 개인으로서 매우 유능한 일을 했지만, 가장 좋은 결과를 낳았던 것은 그들의 협력이었다. **정답 ②**

11. ① hyperbole 과장(법), 과장어구 ② in detail 상세하게(=at length) ③ mischance 불운, 재난(=bad luck)
✎(해석) 만일 어떤 사람이 항상 과장해서 말한다면, 다른 사람들이 그가 한 말의 어떤 부분을 그대로 받아들일 위험은 거의 없다. **정답 ①**

12. ② credibility gap 언행 불일치, 불신감, 단절(감) ③ cooperation 협력
✍(해석) 얼마간의 타협할 수 없는 신념과 얼마간의 채워지지 않은 기대, 그리고 결혼이 사람들의 내면에서 그들의 가장 좋은 것뿐만 아니라 가장 추악한 특징들도 불러낸다는 사실을 가정할 때, 어떠한 부부라도 서로 협력을 해야만 한다. **정답 ③**

13. journeyman (도제 수습을 마친) 장인 ① automatically 자동적으로 ③ judiciously 분별력 있게, 현명하게(=wisely)
✍(해석) 엄밀히 말해서, 우리의 제안은 개인이 능력과 업적을 성취했을 때 그들이 자동적으로 장인의 지위에 오르도록, 충분한 장인 수준의 지위들을 설정하자는 것이다. **정답 ①**

14. ③ depletion 고갈, 소모 appalling 소름이 끼치는, 무시무시한(=dreadful), 지독한 ④ disintegration 분해, 붕괴, 분열
✍(해석) 식민지들의 건설의 결과로 천연자원의 급속하고 부주의한 소모와 지독한 인간의 고통을 초래했다. **정답 ③**

15. ① complimentary 칭찬하는 prestige 위신, 명성 ② jaded 지칠 대로 지친, 물린(=tired, satiated) ③ ephemeral 순간적인, 덧없는(=short-lived, transitory) eternity 영원성 ④ gauche 어색한, 서투른(=awkward, tactless)
✍(해석) 어떤 철학자들은 영원성의 관점에서 볼 때 인간의 생애는 덧없는 것이라고 생각한다. 만물의 거대한 계획안에서 인간의 존재는 생각만큼 중요하지 않아 보이는 것이다. **정답 ③**

16. ① flight 도피, restoration 회복 ② fascination 매혹, deterioration 악화 ③ rejection 거절, vogue 유행(=mode, fashion) ④ censure 비난, 공격 dissolution 분해, 해소, 해산
✍(해석) 가족에 대한 평가가 현저하게 변하고 있다. 가족을 가치 있고 안정된 제도로 일반적으로 인정하던 것에서, 와해가 임박하고 환영할 만큼 억압적이고 파탄한 제도로서 널리 공격받게 된 것이다. **정답 ④**

17. 'With him telling untruths is as frequent and customary an activity as'에서 빈칸에 들어갈 단어의 힌트를 얻을 수 있다. ① notorious 악명 높

은 (=infamous, arrant, flagrant) ② inveterate 뿌리 깊은, 만성의(=deep-rooted, deep-seated, chronic, confirmed, established, ingrained, habitual, hardened) ③ incorrigible 교정할 수 없는(=irreclaimable, abandoned, beyond redemption) ④ consummate 완전한, 유능한, 극도의(=complete, perfect, finished, absolute; sheer, unmitigated; profound, intense)

✍(해석) 그는 고착되고 뿌리 깊은 습관의 희생자이다. 그에게는 거짓말을 하는 것이 아침에 양치를 하거나 조반으로 토스트나 커피를 주문하는 것처럼 빈번하고 관습적인 행동이다. 그러면 그는 상습적인 거짓말쟁이다. **정답 ②**

18. 'forget their differences'에서 빈칸에 들어갈 어구의 힌트를 얻을 수 있다. ① pull up 빼다, 끌어올리다, 세우다 ② pull through 극복하다(=get over) ③ pull together 협력하다(=collaborate, cooperate, concur, come into line) ④ pull out 뽑다, 철수하다(=depart, withdraw)

✍(해석) 만약 그들이 견해차를 잊기만 하고 협력한다면, 그들이 선거에 이길 가능성이 있을지도 모른다. **정답 ③**

19. Bohemian 자유분방한 ① decadence 퇴폐성 strict 엄격한, 정확한 ② promiscuity 난잡, 혼음 ③ sexism 성 차별주의 ④ licentiousness 방탕

✍(해석) 그의 성에 대한 자유분방한 태도는 개방적이라고 해야 한다. 그는 혼음의 옹호자가 아니라, 타인들의 행동에 대하여 관용적인 태도를 주장하는 것이다. **정답 ②**

20. itinerant 순회하는(=wandering) songster 가수, 시인(=minstrel) ① rascal 불량배 ② nomadic herdsman 방랑하는 목자 ④ wandering minstrel 방랑하는 음유시인

✍(해석) 어린 귀뚜라미는 걱정 없이 방랑하는 시인이다. 귀뚜라미는 영원한 집을 구하지 않는다. 한 개의 돌이나 잎새 하나가 안식처로 충분하다. 귀뚜라미는 길가에서 먹이를 먹는다. 곤충의 세계에서 귀뚜라미는 방랑하는 음유 시인이다. **정답 ④**

V. 어법

실력문제 1회

1. 문장을 분석할 때는 항상 주어와 동사를 체크하는 것이 우선이다. 빈칸에는 술어동사가 들어가야 하므로 ③이 정답이 된다.
   ✍(해석) 사회개혁가인 제인 아담스는 1912년 미국 진보당 형성에 중요한 역할을 했다. **정답** ③

2. 빈칸에는 the areas를 수식하는 형용사절이 들어가야 하므로 ①이 정답이 된다. ①은 where they are built로 쓸 수 있다
   ✍(해석) 댐은 건설되는 지역에 매우 도움을 줄 수 있다. **정답** ①

3. 빈칸에는 <주어+동사>가 들어가야 하므로 ③이 정답이 된다. fire extinguisher 소화기
   ✍(해석) 소화기는 산소의 불을 냉각시키거나 제거하여 작용하는데, 대부분은 두 가지 기능을 모두 수행한다. **정답** ③

4. 병행구조의 문제이다. by의 목적어로 동명사가 와야 하므로 ③이 정답이 된다. 즉 <동명사, 동명사, and 동명사>의 형태가 되어야 한다. solicit 간청하다(=appeal), 권유하다
   ✍(해석) 태어나면서부터 아기 쏙독새는 어미새 앞으로 걸어가, 다가서 어미 새의 부리를 쪼며 먹이를 구한다. **정답** ③

5. < A, 주어+동사(완전한 문장)>의 형태에서 A에 들어가는 것은 부사(구,절)[분사구문]와 명사구(동격)이다. 본문에서는 부사구인 ①이 정답이다. 연결사(접속사나 관계사)가 없으므로 ②, ④는 답에서 제외된다.
   ✍(해석) 들개는 고양이처럼 매우 예민한 시각, 청각, 그리고 후각을 가지고 있다. **정답** ①

6. 빈칸에는 be동사의 보어가 와야 한다. 보어가 될 수 있는 것은 명사(구, 절)와 형용사이다. 그런데 관계대명사 that의 선행사가 필요하므로 명사구인 ①이 정답이 된다. core value 핵심가치

✍(해석) 사회제도란 그 구성원들의 행동을 그 집단의 핵심가치로 이끌어내는 사회관계의 복잡한 네트워크이다. **정답** ①

7. 빈칸에는 전치사의 목적어인 명사구가 와야 하므로 ①이 정답이 된다. 전치사 뒤에 [부사+형용사+명사]의 어순도 기억하자. ④는 어순이 틀린다. 부사 easily가 명사 metals를 수식 할 수 없다. plating 도금 corrode 부식하다(=eat into; wear away)

✍(해석) 모든 카드뮴의 약 75%가 철과 강철같이 쉽게 부식되는 금속들의 카드뮴 도금에 사용된다. **정답** ①

8. 본문의 술어동사가 is indicated 이다. 따라서 빈칸에는 명사절을 이끄는 접속사가 들어와야 한다. What절은 문장에서 주어, 목적어, 보어의 역할을 한다. 반면에 that절 이하는 완전한 문장이 온다. 그러므로 정답은 ④가 된다. [예문] I didn't know what she said. what이 타동사 said의 목적어 역할을 한다. I think that he is honest. alchemy 연금술

✍(해석) 점성술뿐만 아니라 연금술도 사고의 기본적인 측면으로 간주될 수 있다는 것이 그들의 명백한 보편성에 의해 나타난다. **정답** ④

9. 빈칸에는 <종속접속사+주어+동사>의 형태가 오거나, 분사구문이 와야 하므로(5번 해설 참조) ②가 정답이 된다.

✍(해석) 래그타임(재즈의 일종)음악은 미국의 남부 및 중서부에서 시작되어 1890년대에 고전적인 형식에 도달했다. **정답** ②

10. < the+비교급 __A__ , the+비교급 __B__ >구문에서는 A와 B가 병행구조를 이루어야 하므로 ③이 정답이 된다. shrub 관목

✍(해석) 관목은 키우기에 힘이 들면 들수록 그 값은 그만큼 더 비싸다. **정답** ③

11. 빈칸에는 내용상 '양보'를 나타내는 어구가 와야 한다. tremor 떨림, 흔들거림, 미진

✍(해석) 근처에서 약한 지진이 일어났다는 놀라운 보고에도 불구하고, 노동자들은 건물의 기초를 놓기 시작했다. **정답** ③

12. 빈칸에는 looked를 수식하는 부사가 와야 한다. look뒤에는 동명사가 올 수 없다. 또한 to-부정사가 오는 경우는 '예상하다'의 뜻으로 사용될 경우에 한정된다.
 ✍(해석) 조디는 높이 솟아있는 신들을 탐색하듯이 보았다. 봉우리 들이 연이어 있었고, 그 끝에는 바다가 있었다. **정답 ③**

13. 빈칸에는 'Good things'를 수식하는 어구가 와야 한다. enjoy는 타동사인데 목적어가 없으므로 과거분사형이 되어야 한다.
 ✍(해석) 오랫동안 향유되어온 좋은 것들은 쉽게 포기될 수 없다. **정답 ②**

14. <know+의문사+to-부정사>구문을 묻는 문제이다. 'know+동명사/부정사'는 쓸 수 없다.
 ✍(해석) 컴퓨터를 사용하는 방법을 아는 것이 더 중요해지고 있다. **정답 ④**

15. 빈칸에는 의미상 앞에 나온 문장 전체를 대신하는 단수 대명사가 와야 한다.
 ✍(해석) 개구리가 바구니에서 도망가서 어린 소녀들이 모두 비명을 질렀다. **정답 ③**

16. <However/No matter how+ 형용사+주어+동사>의 어순을 묻는 문제이다.
 ✍(해석) 사막이 아무리 건조하다 할지라도, 반드시 가치 없는 것은 아니다.
 정답 ①

17. <despite+명사상당어구>를 묻는 문제이다. 빈칸에는 명사상당어구이면서, 문맥상 부정어가 와야 한다.
 ✍(해석) 그 날 저녁 이전에는 적절하게 소개를 받은 적이 없다고 할지라도, 벤슨 박사와 나는 사실 몇 년 동안 알고 지내서, 길에서 만나면 각자의 명성을 알지 못하면서도 인사를 했다. **정답 ④**

18. ①, ③ read over[through] 통독하다 ② read out[loud] 음독하다 ④ read into …의 뜻으로 해석하다
 ✍(해석) 이 진술이 의미하는 것은 쓰여져 있는 그대로이다. 다른 뜻으로

해석하려고 노력하지 마라. **정답 ④**

19. 빈칸에는 의미상 '양보'를 나타내는 표현이 와야 한다. ③ Much as it concerned the public= Though it concerned the public much. ② as far as…까지, …하는 한[에서는] ④ as long as …하는 동안, …하기만 하면
✍(해석) 비록 오염문제가 대중들이 많이 관심을 가지고 있다 할지라도, 정부는 그 문제를 해결하는데 충분히 응하지 않았다. **정답 ③**

20. 분사, 동명사, 부정사의 부정(not)은 그 앞에 쓴다. 주절의 시제보다 앞선 것을 나타낼 때는 완료형(having+과거분사)을 쓴다. (해석) 전에 그를 만난 적이 없어서 나는 그를 모른다. **정답 ②**

실력문제 2회

1. <부사절, 주어+동사>구문이므로 빈칸에는 부사절이 들어가면 된다. allow는 다음의 세 가지 구문을 취한다. 첫째, allow+목적어+to-부정사 둘째, be allowed to+부정사 셋째, allow+V-ing(동명사). 따라서 정답은 ①이 된다.
✍(해석) 우유가 따뜻한 곳에 있을 때는 신맛이 난다. 왜냐하면 박테리아가 있어서 유당을 산으로 바꾸기 때문이다. **정답 ①**

2. 'if it is exposed'에서 it is(주어와 be동사)가 생략될 수 있다. be exposed to …에 노출되다, …에 접하게 되다.
✍(해석) 순수 나프타는 불꽃에 접하게 되면 높은 폭발성을 가진다. **정답 ②**

3. 빈칸에는 clouds(명사)를 수식하는 관계대명사, 현재분사, 과거분사 등이 와야 한다. 본문에서는 뒤에 shield(타동사)의 목적어가 있으므로, 빈칸에는 관계대명사 주격과 동사가 들어가야 한다.
✍(해석) 금성은 그 혹성의 표면을 볼 수 없도록 차단하는 두껍고 불투명한 구름으로 영원하게 덮여 있다. **정답 ④**

4. 빈칸에는 be동사의 보어로 형용사나 명사가 와야 한다. 그런데 빈칸 뒤에 관계대명사 절이 오기 때문에, 빈칸에는 관계대명사의 선행사인 명사

가 와야 한다. subsidy 보조금 viable 실행 가능한(=workable)
☞(해석) 에타놀 세금 보조금은 원래 대체 연료가 경제적으로 실행 가능하도록 하기 위한 임시 조치였다. **정답 ④**

5. 빈칸에는 <주어+동사>가 와야 한다. gauge 측정하다(=measure), 판단하다(=judge), 평가하다. 어법 문제를 풀 때는 우선 주어와 동사를 확인하고, 다음에 수, 시제, 인칭, 격 등을 체크하는 것이 좋다.
☞(해석) 경제학자들은 자유 시장에서 판매되는 재화와 용역의 가격에 대한 측정치인 국민총생산(GNP)에 의하여 경제 활동을 측정한다. **정답 ③**

6. <have+목적어(사람)+원형동사>구문을 묻는 문제이다.
☞(해석) 샘씨는 조수에게 의사록을 받아쓰게 하여 참석자들에게 나누어 줄 것이다. **정답 ①**

7. 병치법(Parallelism)의 문제이다. A, B, and C의 구조에서 A, B, C는 같은 형태가 와야 한다. A와 B에 동사가 왔기 때문에, C도 동사가 와야 한다. 등위접속사의 앞뒤가 구조가 같아야 한다. 등위접속사는 <BOYFANS>로 기억할 것. 즉 'but, or, yet, for, and, nor, so'이다.
☞(해석) 벌목인부, 즉 나무꾼은 숲에서 나무를 베고, 톱질하여, 통나무로 만들어 제재소로 가져간다. **정답 ②**

8. 본문은 완전한 문장이므로 빈칸에는 주어인 'Sunburn'과 동격이 되는 명사상당어구가 와야 한다.
☞(해석) 피부가 따갑고 붉어지는 경우인 햇볕에 타는 것은 열 때문이 아니라 자외선 때문이다. **정답 ④**

9. 빈칸에는 부사절을 이끄는 접속사가 들어가야 한다. '주어+동사'가 있는 문장이 연결되려면 접속사, 관계대명사, 그리고 분사구문이 필요하다.
☞(해석) 모든 벚나무는 꽃이 피면 매우 아름답지만, 어떤 종류는 품질이 낮은 열매를 맺기 때문에 꽃을 목적으로 재배된다. **정답 ①**

10. <make+목적어+목적 보어>구문을 묻는 문제이다. make는 목적보어로 형용사, 과거분사, 명사, 동사원형 등이 올 수 있다.

✍(해석) 고금을 통해서 사람들은 일을 보다 쉽게 할 수 있는 수천 가지의 연장과 기계, 기술을 발명해 왔다. **정답 ②**

11. 'whether A or B'에서 A와 B는 형태가 같아야 한다. A가 to-부정사이므로, B도 to-부정사가 와야 한다.
✍(해석) 잡지 발행인들은 수익을 올리기 위해 정기 구독료를 올릴 것인지 아니면 광고를 실을 것인지 선택해야 한다. **정답 ①**

12. 빈칸 뒤에는 완전한 문장이 왔으므로, 빈칸에는 'It be ~that' 구문이 와야 한다.
✍(해석) 첫 번째 빙하기가 시작되기 전에 살았던 자바원인이 인간과 닮은 최초의 유인원이었다고 일반적으로 믿어진다. **정답 ①**

13. 빈칸에는 'the one'을 수식하는 형용사절(관계사절)이 와야 한다.
✍(해석) 모든 곡식 중 쌀이 그 어느 곡물보다 많은 사람들의 식량이 되고 있는 것이다. **정답 ④**

14. bring(타동사)의 목적어가 없으므로, 빈칸에는 bring의 수동태가 와야 한다.
✍(해석) 기술이 발전함에 따라 태양의 거대한 에너지가 우리의 손이 닿는 곳으로 들어오고 있다. **정답 ④**

15. 빈칸에는 <접속사+주어>가 와야 한다. ②는 명사절을 이끄는 접속사이므로 답에서 제외된다.
✍(해석) 가설이 검증되지 못한다면 타당하다고 결론을 내릴 수 없지만 그 가설을 계속해서 사용할 수 있다. **정답 ①**

16. 빈칸에는 that절(형용사절)의 수식을 받는 명사가 와야 하고, that절에 의해 한정되므로 정관가 the가 필요하다.
✍(해석) 식량의 분배를 결정했던 규정들이 초기 문화의 발달에 영향을 준 것으로 추정된다. **정답 ④**

17. <주어+동사+not-either>, <neither+동사+주어>의 어순을 묻는 문제이다.

✍(해석) 캐나다는 미국 시민들이 입국하는데 여권을 요구하지 않는데, 그것은 멕시코도 마찬가지이다. **정답 ②**

18. 빈칸에는 타동사 plan(…을 계획하다)의 목적어가 없고, 연결장치(접속사, 관계사)가 필요하다. 따라서 빈칸에는 선행사를 포함한 관계대명사 what이 와야 한다.
✍(해석) 경쟁력을 유지하기 위해서 펄 회사는 가까운 미래에 그들의 경쟁자들이 무엇을 계획하고 있는지 인식해야만 한다. **정답 ②**

19. way와 the company사이에 접속사 that이 생략되어 있다. 타동사 manage(-을 경영하다) 의 목적어가 없으므로, 빈칸에는 수동형이 와야 한다.
✍(해석) 전반적인 재정 상황의 개선은 그 회사와 자회사들이 경영되어지는 방법에 변화가 없다면 불가능하다. **정답 ④**

20. exception은 전치사 with를 동반한다. with the exception of (…을 제외 하고)를 기억하자.
✍(해석) 몇 가지 예외가 있지만, 대부분의 사업가들은 사 업 척 해가 어렵다는 것을 알게 될 것이다. **정답 ②**

실력문제 3회

1. 빈칸에는 부사상당어구(부사구, 부사절)나 명사상당어구(명사구, 명사절)가 와야 한다. 본문의 빈칸에는 주어(Thomas Paine)와 동격이 되는 명사구가 와야 한다.
✍(해석) 그의 시절에 가장 독자가 많았던 작가인 토마스 페인은 칭찬과 미움을 함께 불러일으켰다. **정답 ③**

2. 빈칸에는 의미상 현재진행형이 와야 한다.
✍(해석) 사람들이 실온보다 낮은 체온을 가질 때, 열이 몸속으로 계속 흘러 들어온다. **정답 ④**

3. <not only A but also B (A뿐만 아니라 B도)>구문을 묻는 문제이다.

✍(해석) 선글라스는 눈을 보호해줄 뿐만 아니라 피부에 주름이 생기는 것을 막아준다. **정답 ③**

4. 빈칸에는 <동사+명사>의 형태가 와야 한다.
✍(해석) 바람과 물은 재생 가능한 에너지 원천이다. 그러나 단지 아주 작은 양의 전력만을 생산할 뿐이다. **정답 ③**

5. 본문의 동사가 is이므로, 그 앞에는 명사절이 와야 한다. 명사절을 이끄는 것은 that, what, whatever 등이 있는데, 빈칸에는 명사(description)를 수식하는 형용사가 와야 한다. 형용사가 될 수 있는 것은 what과 whatever이다.
✍(해석) 발라드에 무엇이 묘사되든지 그것은 간결하며 전통적이다. **정답 ④**

6. 빈칸에는 marl의 동격 또는 marl을 설명해 주는 관계사절이 올 수 있는데, 본문에서는 동격으로 명사구가 들어간다.
✍(해석) 상업용 비료가 대중화 되기 전에, 농부들은 일종의 점토혼합물인 이회토를 비료로 사용하였다. **정답 ①**

7. 본문의 주어는 'The role'이고, 동사는 'cannot be denied'이다. 빈칸에는 주어를 수식하는 형용사절(관계사절)이 와야 한다.
✍(해석) 그 지역 사회를 형성하는데 있어 계곡의 독특한 지세가 해 온 역할을 부인할 수 없다. **정답 ②**

8. 빈칸에는 be 동사의 보어로 형용사인 과거분사가 온다.
✍(해석) 뉴턴의 물리학은 우주가 강력하고 합리적인 창조자에 의해 창조되었기 때문에 근본적으로 논리적이라는 신념에 근거하고 있었다. **정답 ①**

9. 빈칸에는 전치사(on)의 목적어로 명사구가 와야 한다. 'of most materials'가 'surfaces'를 한정하므로 정관사 the가 붙어야 한다.
✍(해석) 사상균과 곰팡이는 대부분의 물질 표면에서 자랄 수 있는 균류이다. **정답 ③**

10. 빈칸 앞은 완전한 문장이므로, 빈칸에는 부사상당어구가 와야 한다.

✍(해석) 대가족의 이점들은 도시화된 사회에서 더 이상 분명하지 않다. **정답 ④**

11. 동명사(matching)를 수식할 수 있는 것은 부사이다.
✍(해석) 당신이 찾고 있는 물건의 구체적 내역을 보내 주시면, 우리가 당신의 조건을 가장 잘 충족시키는 상품을 제공하는 회사들의 목록을 보내드리겠습니다. **정답 ①**

12. 'by the time he retires'(그가 은퇴할 때까지)는 시간을 나타내는 부사절로, 빈칸에는 미래완료 시제가 와야 한다.
✍(해석) 윌리엄스는 그가 은퇴할 때까지, 교수회의 의장으로 15년간 일한 것이 된다. **정답 ④**

13. 빈칸 뒤에 명사구가 왔으므로, 빈칸에는 전치사가 와야 한다.
(해석) 해리슨이 지금 하고 있는 약간의 색깔 조정 작업을 제외하고는, 이 안내책자는 인쇄 준비가 되었다. **정답 ③**

14. <most of+the+복수명사>를 묻는 문제이다.
✍(해석) 이 가격대의 대부분 의 다른 자동차와는 달리 '카메라'는 최첨단의 컴퓨터 운항 체제를 갖추었다. **정답 ③**

15. 빈칸 뒤에 목적어(its selection)가 있으므로, 빈칸에는 동명사인 ② ensuring이 와야 한다. readily 쉽게(=easily), 기꺼이(=willingly)
✍(해석) 컴퓨터 회사는 정부에 의해 제안된 이익이 되는 계약에 대한 선택권을 보장하는 조건에 기꺼이 동의했다. **정답 ②**

16. <so+형용사/부사+동사+주어+that>구문을 묻는 문제이다. 이것은 주부가 길어서 주어와 동사의 어순을 도치시킨 것이다.
✍(해석) 중국 승려의 손에서 나오는 힘이 너무 엄청나서 그 힘으로 어른도 그 자리로부터 들어올리는 것으로 알려졌다. **정답 ①**

17. <지각동사(see)+목적어+원형동사/현재분사>구문을 묻는 문제이다.
✍(해석) 그 선생은 곁눈으로 누군가가 다른 학생에게 쪽지를 넘겨주는 것을 보았다. **정답 ①**

18. come[get] to grips with 열심히 노력하다(=struggle), 이해하다 (=understand), 맞붙다(=get hold of)

✐(해석) 마침내 대처여사는 새로운 경제 현실을 이해하지 못했기 때문에 일자리에서 물러났다. **정답** ②

19. 빈칸에는 의미상 '이유'를 나타내는 접속사가 와야 한다.

✐(해석) 이 주제에 대해서는 아주 명확한 것이면 말할 수 있기 때문에 오랜 세월 동안 연구하고 실험하는 것이 필요할 것이다. **정답** ③

20. crave for 간절히 구하다(=ask for earnestly), 갈망하다(=long for eagerly)

✐(해석) 사랑을 마음속 깊이 갈망함에도 불구하고, 거의 모든 다른 일들이 사랑보다 더 중요한 것으로 간주된다. 우리는 거의 모든 힘을 성공, 명성, 돈, 권력 등과 같은 목표를 성취하는 방법을 배우는데 사용하며, 거의 아무도 사랑의 기술을 배우지 않는다. **정답** ④

실력문제 4회

1. 빈칸에는 be동사의 보어로 형용사나 명사가 와야 한다. 그런데 빈칸 뒤에 for 이하와 연결이 되는 것은 ④ all that was required 이다.

✐(해석) 만약에 두뇌의 이중 신호가 인간 의식에 필수적인 전부라면, 컴퓨터도 인식 능력을 얻어서 자신만의 이성을 소유할 수 있는 가능성이 있을 것이다. **정답** ④

2. 본문의 동사가 'is'이므로 동사가 있는 ①, ③, ④가 답에서 제외된다. 빈 칸에는 명사구나 명사절이 와야 한다.

✐(해석) 모래 숲 속의 식물이 넓게 자리를 잡은 것은 토양 속에 이용 가능한 영양소의 낮은 수준 때문이다. **정답** ②

3. 여기서 from은 원인이나 이유를 나타내는 '- 때문에, -로 인하여'의 뜻이다. (예) suffer from gout 통풍을 앓다 die from wound 상처로 인하여 죽다.

✍(해석) 알렉산더 플레밍이 페니실린을 발견하기 전에, 많은 사람들이 단순한 병균 감염으로 죽었다. **정답 ②**

4. 빈칸에는 타동사(have)의 목적어인 명사구가 와야 한다.
✍(해석) 액체와 기체는 명확한 형체가 없기 때문에, 그것들은 용기에서 자유롭게 흐른다. **정답 ④**

5. 의미상 빈칸에는 '쌀을 제외한'의 뜻이 와야 한다. except to나 excepting의 사용을 피할 것. ③ but for(=without)뒤에는 가정법이 온다. ④ excepting은 전치사로 대개 문두 또는 not이나 without뒤에서 쓰이며, '…을 빼고, …을 제외하면'의 뜻이다.
✍(해석) 쌀을 제외한 모든 곡물들은 미국의 대초원에서 재배된다. **정답 ①**

6. 콤마 앞에는 부사상당어구나 명사상당어구가 와야 한다. 따라서 ①은 답에서 제외된다. <When+주어+동사>가 되어야 하므로 ②, ③도 답에서 제외된다. while 동시에(=at the same time)
✍(해석) 뉴잉글랜드에서 영어선생이었던 웹스터가 영어 사전을 썼다. **정답 ④**

7. 빈칸에는 triangle을 수식하는 형용사구/절이 와야 하고, 선행사와 관계사절의 동사와 수의 일치가 되어야 한다.
✍(해석) 정삼각형은 세 변이 길이와 각도가 같은 삼각형이다. **정답 ③**

8. <be used to+동명사: -에 익숙해져 있다>를 묻는 문제이다. 'used to+동사원형'은 과거의 습관을 나타내며 '-하곤 했다'의 뜻이다.
✍(해석) 대부분이 유럽인들 과는 달리 미국인들은 매일 아침 한 사발의 곡물 식품을 먹는데 익숙해져 있다. **정답 ③**

9. prior 앞의, 이전의(=earlier; previous) prior to …에 앞서, 먼저 (=before in time)
✍(해석) 인슐린을 발견하기 전에 당뇨병을 치료하는 것이 불가능했다. **정답 ①**

10. <부사구/부사절+조동사+주어+동사>이 어순을 묻는 문제이다. 본문

에서 빈칸 앞이 부사절이다. 따라서 정답은 ②가 된다.

✎(해석) 한 학생이 대수학을 정통해서야 비로소 기하학, 삼각법, 그리고 물리학의 원리들을 이해하기 시작 할 수 있다. **정답 ②**

11. 빈칸에는 conclusion과 동격인 that절이 와야 한다.

✎(해석) 빛이 색으로 이루어져 있다는 것에 기초를 둔 인상주의 화가들은 그림자가 실제로 검은색이 아니라는 결론에 도달했다. **정답 ④**

12. <consider+동명사>를 묻는 문제이다.

✎(해석) 서부 캐나다 사람들은 나머지 주들에서 분리되는 것을 고려해 왔다. **정답 ④**

13. 의문사가 문중에 있을 때의 어순은 <의문사+주어+동사>이다.

✎(해석) 오늘날의 정교한 망원경조차도, 어떤 물체가 얼마나 멀리 있는지 정확하게 말할 수 없다. **정답 ①**

14. 원급의 비교는 'as-as구문'을 쓴다. those는 수식어와 함께 '…한 것[사람]들'의 뜻으로 사용된다.

✎(해석) 볼펜 제조업자들은 우주선에 사용되는 것들만큼 정확한 치수로 작업한다. **정답 ①**

15. 본문은 so-that구문이고, 품사끼리의 어순은 <부사+형용사+관사+명사>이다.

✎(해석) 이제 텔레비전은 많은 사람들의 삶에 너무 중요한 역할을 하므로, 그것이 좋은 것인지 나쁜 것인지를 결정하려고 애쓰는 것이 필수적이다. **정답 ③**

16. 타동사 break가 목적어가 없으므로, 빈칸에는 수동형이 와야 한다.

✎(해석) 우리는 우리 선수들에 의해 세 개의 전국기록이 갱신되는 것을 보는 스릴을 가졌다. **정답 ③**

17. 제안, 주장, 요구, 명령, 추천 등의 동사(suggest, propose, insist, persist, request, require, ask, command, order, recommend), 명사, 동명사가 이끄는 that절의 동사는 should가 생략된 동사원형을 써야 한다.

✍(해석) 상임 기술자는 비록 통신망이 지금까지는 문제가 없기는 할지라도, 다시 설치되어야 한다고 주장한다. **정답** ①

18. 빈칸에는 문맥의 의미상 '그렇지 않으면'의 뜻인 'or'이 와야 한다. hand in 제출하다 (해석) 병 때문에 결근한 직원들은 사장에게 진단서를 제출해야만 한다. 그렇지 않으면 빠진 시간을 보충해야 한다. **정답** ②

19. 빈칸에는 burst(급격한 증가, 폭발)와 어울리는 ② electricity(전기)가 와야 한다. ① electrics 전등, 전기 설비 ③ electrical 전기에 관한, 전기의 ④ electronic 전자의
✍(해석) 폭풍 때문에 일어난 전기의 급격한 증가는 우리의 컴퓨터 시스템은 어떤 영향도 끼치지 않았다. **정답** ②

20. be faced with …에 직면하다. face 직면하다(=confront) deficit 적자(=a red ink)
✍(해석) 1990년대에 구축된 거대한 예산 적자에 직면하여 대통령은 더 많은 직업을 창출하고 큰 산업을 민영화하기로 결정했다. **정답** ③

VI. 장문독해

실력문제 1회

1-5. 테러범들의 세균 무기에 대항하는 방어력을 증강시키기 위해서 우리는 때가 늦었지만 백신을 제조하고 있고, 국민 보건의 필요성에 대해 경각심을 가지고 있다. 그것에 더하여 정부와 민간단체들은 자가 면역 반응을 촉발시키지 않고 신체의 타고난 면역 체계 능력을 확장시키는 방법들에 대한 기본적인 연구의 지원을 증가시키고 있다. 2년 전에 나는 질병통제 연구소의 한 직원에게 우리가 모든 병원균들에 대한 "만능 백신"의 꿈을 언제 성취할 수 있느냐고 물었다. 그는 손을 흔들면서 "아마 50년이 지나면" 이라고 말했다. 그는 내가 기자인 것을 눈치 채고서, 그것을 25년까지 줄여서 말했다. 현재 압력을 받고 과학자들은 여러 종류의 질병과 싸우는 "다기능

백신들"을 추구하고 있으며, 이 세대에 그것을 볼 수도 있다. 위기로부터 예기치 않았던 용맹이 나타난다. 그리고 오늘의 생물학전의 위협으로부터 내일의 전염병의 정복이 올 수도 있다.

germ arsenal 세균 무기 belated 때늦은(=too late, overdue) immune system 면역체계 trigger 촉발시키다, 시작케 하다(=activate, prompt) autoimmune response 자가 면역 반응 pathogens 병원균 multivalent 다원자가(多原子價)의, 다면적 가치를 지닌

(정답) 1. (b) 2. (d) 3. (d) 4. (b) 5. (b)

6-8. 금주운동은 아마도 모든 개혁 운동 중에서 가장 널리 퍼진 것이었을 것이다. 1810년 조사는 대략 14,000개의 증류소가 매년 2500만 갤런의 알콜을 생산한다고 보고했다. 7백만 명이 넘는 과도한 음주가들이 있는 "음주 공화국"은 모든 남성과 여성, 아이들 일인당-맥주, 와인, 사과주를 포함시키지 않고도- 연간 3갤론 이상의 술을 생산했다. 그리고 이 조사자들은 틀림없이 몇 개의 증류소를 빠뜨렸을 것이다. 미국을 여행했던 영국의 개혁가 윌리엄 코베트는 1819년에 사람들은 "와인이나 알콜을 마실 것을 요구받지 않고는 좀처럼 누군가의 집에 들어가기 어렵다. 심지어 아침에도" 라고 말했다. 금주운동은 수많은 주장에 기초하고 있다. 가장 처음에 "십자가의 군사들"은 비난받지 않는 삶을 살아야 한다는 종교적인 요구가 있었다. 다른 사람들은 술에 취한 노동자들이 경제에 미치는 영향을 강조했다. 역동적인 새로운 경제-공장과 철도가 꽉 짜여진 스케줄로 가동되는-에서는 술에 취해 있는 것이 단순 농업 경제에서 그랬던 것보다 훨씬 더 큰 문제가 되었다. 인도주의자들은 음주와 가난 사이의 관계를 강조했다. 그 운동에서 주장하는 것들 중 많은 부분이 무고한 엄마와 아이들이 겪게 되는 고통에 그 초점을 맞추었다. "금주의 아들들"에서 나온 소책자에서는 "음주는 가족을 괴롭히는 거의 모든 악의(직접 또는 간접적인) 원인이다"라고 언급하기도 했다. 1883년에 그 연합단체는 미국금주연합이 형성되었던 필라델피아에서 국가 회의를 소집했다. 그러나 그 회의는 내부적인 긴장들을 드러냈다. 목표가 완화인지 혹은 절대 금주인지, 그리고 만일 후자의 경우라면 단지 독한 술로부터의 금주인지 아니면 와인이나 사과주, 맥주까지도 포함되는가? 그 운동이 권고 정도에서 진행되어야 하는가? 혹은 법에 의해서 진

행되어야 하는가? 그 시대의 대부분의 운동처럼 금주 운동에도 모든 타협을 거부하는 일단의 완벽주의자들이 있었고, 그들은 알콜 음료의 거래는 도덕적으로 잘못된 것이고 법에 의해 금지되어야 한다는 결의안을 통과시켰다. 1836년 봄 정기회의에서 그 연합 단체는 모든 알콜 음료의 금주-대신에 온건주의자들로 하여금 그 운동을 그만두게 하는 값비싼 승리-를 요구했다. 그러나 1830년과 1860년 사이에 그 금주 운동은 미국의 일인당 알콜 소비량을 급격하게 감소시켰다.

   crusade 십자군, 개혁운동. temperance crusade 금주운동(=crusade against alcohol). distillery 증류소, 증류주 제조소(=still). sottish 술고래의. tipple 알코올 음료, 독주, 조금씩 습관적으로 마시다. abstinence 절제, 자제 (=temperance, moderation), 금식, 금주

  (정답) 6. (d) 7. (a) 8. (c)

  9-13. 텔레비전이 이 나라(미국)의 가정에 들어오게 되었을 때, 암울한 분위기의 예언이 만연해 있었다. 이것은 독서의 종말을 의미하는 것이었고, 책은 최후의 운명을 맞이하였다. 지금까지 무슨 일이 일어났는가? 텔레비전의 전반적인 내용에 대한 쌓여 가는 불만족, 책 판매량의 꾸준한 증가 등이다. 순수한 시각적 매체의 거대한 잠재능력을 과소평가 하지 말아야 한다. 영화, 텔레비전, 그리고 심지어 사진은 결국 그것들에게서 발견될 모든 용도에 아직 적용되지 않았다. 그럼에도 불구하고 그것들이 책을 대신할 것인지 그리고 책을 단순한 과거의 것으로 취급되게 만들 것인지는 의심스럽다. 매우 고상한 기능이 아니라고 할지라도 가장 가치 있는 것들 중에 하나의 도구로서 책의 중요성을 깨닫는 가장 간단한 방법은 우리가 사전이나 백과사전이 없다면 어떻게 일을 처리해 나가는지를 상상하는 것이다. 사실 책으로서 책의 유용함은 한정되어 있으며, 세계의 많은 실용적인 작업이 다른 도구에 의해 잘 교육되고 있다. 그래도 유용함이라는 제한된 범위 내에서 우리가 도구로서 사용하는 책은 더 새로운 커뮤니케이션 형태에서 결핍된 이점을 가지고 있다. 책은 계속 다시 연구될 수 있으며, 우리는 그것이 제공하는 것을 많은 방해물에도 불구하고, 우리가 원하고 필요한 만큼 천천히 취급할 수 있다. 우리는 우리가 가는 곳이면 어디든지 책을 가지고 갈 수 있으며, 다른 사람에게 불편함이나 방해를 주지 않고 그것들을 사용할

수 있다.
[clue] 'according to the passage'라는 어구가 나오면 내용을 묻는 문제이다. 이런 문제는 설문지를 먼저 읽고 본문에 들어가는 것이 좋다.

(정답) 9. (a) 10. (d) 11. (a) 12. (d) 13. (b)

14-18. 우리는 엔비시의 탐 브러커의 조수가 분말 가루가 안에 들어 있던 협박 편지를 개봉한 후 탄저균 양성 반응을 보였다는 것을 알았다. 바로 그 순간에 뉴스 룸에 다른 편지가 분말을 비처럼 뿌린 후 뉴욕 타임즈에 있는 사람들이 대피되었다. 이 편지의 주소는 생물학 테러 전문가인 주디스 밀러 앞으로 보내진 것이었다. 초기 검사에서 탄저균의 조짐을 보이지는 않았지만, 그 위협은 여전히 실제적이고 교활한 것처럼 보인다. 당신은 메신저들을 쏠 필요가 없었고, 단지 그들을 죽도록 겁나게 만들기만 하면 되었다. 그 이유는 공포도 마찬가지로 전염성이 있기 때문이다. 그것은 공기와 전선을 통해서 확산이 되고, 시장을 감염시키고, 전체 산업을 파괴시키며 집에 있는 피해자들은 잠자리에서 이불을 뒤집어 쓴 채로 있게 된다. 그리고 최악의 경우는 무서운 일들이 그렇게 많고, 짓궂은 장난도 그렇게 많기 때문에 여러 면에서 우리들 자신까지도 공포에 눌리고 있었다.

anthrax 탄저균 evacuate 대피하다, 철수시키다(=remove, deplete, vacate) lay waste to 파괴하다(=destroy) hoax 짓궂은 장난

(정답) 14. (b) 15. (c) 16. (c) 17. (d) 18. (a)

19-20. 비록 20세기 그림에서 지금까지 논의되었던 세 가지 경향이 조각에서도 역시 발견된다 할지라도, 그 유사성이 지나치게 강조되어서는 안 된다. 그림이 더 풍부하고 더 대담했었던 반면에, 미술 형태로서 그것의 리더십이 도전을 받지 않은 채로 남아있지 않았고, 조각이 다른 경로로 따라오는 일이 자주 있었다.

[clue] 20. 본문 마지막 문장의 'different'가 문제에서 'independently of'로 표현된 것을 유의해야 한다. 이것은 영어의 다양성(variety) 때문이라고 볼 수 있다. 독해를 할 때, 'A'라는 단어가 'A$_1$→ A$_2$→ A$_3$→ A$_4$'로 동의어가 흘러가는 것에 주목해야 한다.

(정답) 19. (a) 20. (d)

실력문제 2회

1-3. 세계 인구의 폭발적인 증가는 인간의 번식력의 돌연한 증가에 의해 야기되지 않았고, 아마도 세계의 어느 지역에서의 출생율의 증가에 기인한 것도 아니다. 그것은 의학의 발전과 그 결과로 출산율이 높은 지역에서 사망률의 감소에 의해 거의 전적으로 야기되었다. 이것은 생물학적인 관심도 있다. 자연은 과잉이 성공이라는 것을 모토로 삼고 인간을 포함해 생명체의 능력에 제한 없이 생산한다면, 생명체는 그것이 존재할 수 있는 세계 모든 지역을 머지않아 차지할 것이다.

fertility 다산, 비옥(=fruitfulness), 번식력 excess 초과, 과잉(=surplus, lavishness)

(정답) 1. (c) 2. (a) 3. (d)

4-7. 모든 사회적 동물들은 의사전달방법이 필요하다. 그들은 그것을 사용해 정보를 교환하거나 질서 있는 사회를 유지한다. 인간은 다양한 방법으로 의사전달을 한다. 그 방법들 중 하나는 몸짓이다. 인간들은 윙크를 하거나, 손뼉을 치거나, 휘파람을 불거나, 미소를 짓거나 웃음으로써 동의를 표한다. 그들은 엄지손가락을 땅으로 향하게 하거나, 혓바닥을 입 밖으로 내서 흔들거나, 손가락으로 코를 잡고 코를 풀거나, 눈살을 찌푸림으로 반대 표시를 한다. 그들은 손가락으로 지적함으로써 방향을 나타내고, 종종 손을 벌려서 크기를 표시한다.

(정답) 4. (c) 5. (b) 6. (d) 7. (a)

8-12. 기술적인 성공의 시대에 생명구조가 종종 그것의 인공적인 모방물과 비교가 안 될 정도로 더 효과적이라는 사실을 우리는 때때로 상기한다. 박쥐의 음파조직이 이 견해에 대한 가장 좋은 예이다. 그것은 인간에 의해 고안된 레이더나 음파탐지기보다 수 억 배 더 효과적이고 예민하다. 물론 박쥐는 약 5천만년 동안 진화하여 그들의 음파 조직을 정교화해 왔다. 반향 위치탐색에 대한 그들의 생리학적 구조는 이런 모든 축척된 경험에 근거했기에, 우리의 철저한 연구와 분석을 받을만한 가치가 있다.
박쥐의 반향 위치 탐색의 정확도를 측정하기 위하여 우리는 먼저 그것에 의존도를 고려해야만 한다. 음파 때문에 곤충을 먹는 박쥐는 시력이 없이 잘 지낼 수 있다. 이것은 18세기 후반에 이탈리아 박물학자 라자로 스팔라자니 에 의해 수행된 실험에 의해 훌륭히 증명되었다. 그는 종탑에서 몇 마리 박쥐를 잡아, 그것들의 눈을 가리고 야외로 풀어주었다. 이렇게 눈을 가리운 박쥐들 중 네 마리는 종탑으로 돌아오는 길을 발견한 후에 다시 잡혔고, 그들의 위의 내용물을 검사했을 때 스팔라자니는 그들이 날아다니는 곤충을 잡아 잔뜩 먹을 수 있다는 사실을 알아냈다. 우리는 이 실험으로부터 곤충들이 사람이 들을 수 있는 소리를 내지 않을 때조차도 박쥐들은 어둠 속에서 곤충들을 쉽게 발견한다는 사실을 알게 된다. 박쥐는 한 시간 내에 부드러운 몸과 조용한 비행을 하는 나방이나 모기를 수백 마리를 잡을 것이다. 박쥐는 심지어 공중으로 던져진 조약돌이나 솜을 뭉친 모양의 공도 발견해 추적할 수 있다.

 sonar 수중 음파 탐지 contrive 고안하다, 연구하다(=devise), 설계하다(=design), 꾸미다 accumulate 모으다, 축적하다(=amass, hoard, pile up) emit 내뿜다, 방사하다(=give out, send out, give forth, discharge) gnat 각다귀, 영 모기(=mosquito)

 (정답) 8. (b) 9. (a) 10. (d) 11. (c) 12. (b)

 13-15. 컴퓨터 기술이 점점 발전하게 됨에 따라 걱정거리가 될 새로운 질병이 있다. 컴퓨터를 방해하도록 고안된 컴퓨터 "바이러스" 프로그램이 회사와 가정 및 대학의 컴퓨터를 감염시키고 있다. 이들 바이러스는 생물학적 전염과 매우 흡사하게 빠른 속도로 번져서 감염된 체제에 혼란을 일으킨다. 이 바이러스는 다른 프로그램에 몰래 붙어서 파일을 삭제하거나 변질시킨다. 이 손상은 컴퓨터의 시계를 사용함으로써 일반적으로 가동된다. 그렇게 되면 실행되는 모든 프로그램은 전화선을 통해 확산되는 프로그램을 포함하여 바이러스에 노출될 것이다. 바이러스 침투의 사고들이 증가하기 때문에 업체와 기관들은 소프트웨어를 공유하는 것에 대해 경계하고 있다. 면역 프로그램이 개발됨에 따라 안전방침이 증가될 필요가 있다.

 sabotage 파괴하다, 방해하다 contagion 감염, 전염병 delete 삭제하다, 지우다(=erase, take out, cross out, blot out, strike out, expunge) execute 실행하다, 수행하다(=perform, carry out) wary 조심성 있는, 신중한

(=cautious, careful, heedful, alert, circumspect, discreet, prudent, vigilant) immunity 면제, 면역

(정답) 13. (d) 14. (b) 15. (c)

16-20. 그럼에도 불구하고 성실하고 진지한 비판가들에 의해 미국문화의 좋지 못한 상황에 관한 입심 좋은 비난의 소리가 있어서, 나는 그 반대의 증거를 몇 가지 제시하려고 한다. 사람들은 이런 비판가에게 어떠한 국가도 상류층의 고급문화를 일상생활의 구조 속에 완전하게 통합시키지 못했음을 상기하게 된다. 셰익스피어 나라 영국의 지나간 영광을 회고하는 사람들의 갈망하는 기억 속에는 곰 놀리기가 셰익스피어의 어느 공연보다도 더 인기가 있었던 것은 좀처럼 상기되지 않는다. 유배날리스가 '건전한 신체에 건강한 정신'을 선언함을 본 로마에서 트라잔 황제에게 기원 후 106년에 오천 쌍 가량의 검투사들이 죽음의 시합으로 데시아의 데스발러스에 대한 승리를 축하하는 것을 볼 수 있었음을 누가 기억하려 하겠는가? 그리고 이것을 즐거움의 명분이라고 하겠는가?

voluble 입심 좋은(=talkative). hue and cry 심한 비난, 추적의 고함소리. abysmal 심연의(=not measurable), 지독히 나쁜(=very bad). haute culture 고급 문화. warp and woof 기초, 기틀. moon 멍하니 바라보다[보내다]. bearbaiting 곰 놀리기. gladiator 검투사

(정답) 16. (b) 17. (b) 18. (b) 19. (b) 20. (c)

실력문제 3회

1-3. 20세기에는 과학과 정치는 물론 철학과 문학에서도 막강한 책들이 나왔다. 그러나 이 시대가 전문화 시대이다 보니 이런 책들에 담긴 영향력 있는 사상들이 전문가들을 위한 논문이나 문헌에서 먼저 주창되거나 언급된 다음에야 보통 사람에게 전해지는 것을 흔히 본다. 대중적인 잡지의 기사들과 번역 작품들은 맨 나중에 나온다. 과학이 우리 세계에 영향을 끼쳐왔다는 것은 부정할 수 없다. 그러나 과학적인 언어를 보통 사람의 언어로 옮긴 책이 없었더라면 그 진보는 크지 않고 미미했을 것이다. 이제 무대는 일찍이 세계에 선보였던 가장 강력한 책들 중 일부를 위해 펼쳐져 있다. 이

제 책은 인간이 이 지구상에서 살아남으려면 반드시 개발되어야 할 것으로 과학이 나타내 주는 단일 세계의 삶에 이르는 길을 인간이 모색하도록 도울 필요가 있다.

stride 큰 걸음, 전진 minuscule 매우 작은(=very small)

(정답) 1. (d)　2. (b)　3. (b)

4-8. 두뇌의 뒤쪽으로 관심을 돌려보면, 히포캠퍼스는 50-90세의 나이에 그 크기의 약 20퍼센트를 잃어버릴 수 있다. 이 작은 해마 모양의 구조는 기억을 다시 찾을 뿐 아니라 형성시키는 데도 결정적인 역할을 한다. 정상적인 노화 과정 속에서 신경 전달 물질인 아세틸클로린의 히포캠퍼스 내에서의 수준은 떨어진다. 아세틸클로린은 뉴론이 의사소통을 하는 수단인 분자들 중 하나이기 때문에 히포캠퍼스 내에서 이것이 희소하다는 것은 "그렇지 않다면 건강한 노인들에게서 기억력 상실을 가장 잘 설명해 줄 수 있는 것 중 하나다"라고 휄리는 말한다. 그러면 건강하지 못한 노인들에게는 어떤가? (검시를 통한 경우를 제외하고는) 알츠하이머병을 진단할 수 있는 분명한 방법은 없다. 그러나 소규모 지적 상태 검사라고 불려지는 점검은 근사하게 추적할 수 있다. 이것은 예를 들어 오늘 날짜와 올해의 연수를 묻는다. 그리고 100부터 거꾸로 7씩 차이를 두고 세어 내려오도록 하기도 하고, 방금 몇 분전에 말했던 물체 세 가지의 이름을 떠올리게 해보거나, '눈을 감으세요'와 같은 문장을 읽어 주고 그대로 따라 해보도록 하거나 기타 단순한 임무들을 할 수 있도록 하기도 한다. 이 테스트에서 성적이 낮고, 지명들을 혼동하거나, 주도적이지 못하거나, 친구들을 알아보지 못하는 문제들이 함께 발생하면, 약속을 잊어버리는 경우보다도 알츠하이머병을 예상하는 데 있어 적중할 확률이 더 높다.

retrieve 되찾다, 회복하다(=recover), 만회하다. memory deficit 기억력 상실. autopsy 검시(=postmortem). presage 예언하다(=foretell, predict, prophesy, forecast, portend), 전조가 되다, 전조, 예감(=omen). cerebritis 뇌염. frontal lobe 전엽. cerebral 대뇌의, 뇌의. dissection 해부, 분석.

(정답) 4. (b)　5. (c)　6. (c)　7. (d)　8. (b)

9-13. 선택의 전쟁과 필연의 전쟁이 있다. 베트남전, 코소보전, 심지어 걸프전이 선택의 전쟁이었다. 이런 전쟁들에서는 원칙, 이념, 지정학 혹은

때로는 순수한 인도주의라는 이유로 싸우게 되었다. 결국 우리는 수동적인 태도로 인해 대가를 지불할 수도 있다. 그러나 우리는 전쟁을 할 필요가 없다. 필연의 전쟁은 사느냐 죽느냐의 싸움이요, 그 속에서 조국의 안전과 안보가 위험에 처해진다. 대 테러전쟁이 그런 전쟁이다. 2차 세계대전도 마찬가지이다. 50년이란 세월은 긴 휴식 시간이다. 그리고 그것이 드러나고 있다. 그런 전쟁을 벌이는 습관은 위축되어 버렸다. 우리가 이런 필연의 전쟁을 벌이기 위해 동원해 왔던 언어가 선택의 전쟁의 언어이다. 그래서 도덕적 고민에 무거운 부담이 되고, 우리 미국인들이 얼마나 섬세하고 분별력 있고, 관용적이고 민감한 사람들인가를 증명하는 일에 강박관념을 가지고 관계를 맺고 있다.

at stake 위험한(=at risk, in danger) wage a war 전쟁을 벌이다 atrophy 위축하다, 쇠약해지다(=degenerate, weaken, wither) freighted with …이 부담되는(=burdened with)

(정답) 9. (c) 10. (d) 11. (d) 12. (d) 13. (b)

14-16. 수세기 동안 우리는 어떤 축복들, 예를 들어, 그 앞에서는 부자와 가난한 자가 동등한 안정된 법과 그 법 테두리에서 우리가 임대한 것을 믿을 수 있는 자유, 그리고 궁극적인 권력을 보통 사람에게 주는 정부체제들을 누려 왔다. 우리는 인내와 이성적인 타협, 그리고 자유롭게 표현되는 여론에 의해 살아 왔고, 더구나 매우 훌륭하게 살아 왔다. 그러나 우리는 이런 축복들을 우리가 숨쉬는 공기처럼 당연히 여기게 되었다. 그것들은 너무나 익숙해졌기 때문에 우리에게는 모두 매력을 잃었다. 실제로 그 축복들에 대해 어느 정도 비판적이고 경멸하는 것이 지성인의 한 특징이 된 것이다. 젊은이들은 정치에 있어서 진보적 정신을 비웃고, 자유토론, 인내 그리고 협상의 가치를 의문시함으로서 싸구려 명성을 얻었다.

compromise 타협, 화해(=settlement, concession, middle term, bargain, covenant) contemptuous 얕보는, 경멸하는(=scornful, disdainful, supercilious, haughty, derisive) sneer 비웃다, 냉소하다(=jeer, taunt, scoff, deride, flout, mock, ridicule, disdain, decry, belittle, slight, lampoon, laugh at, give the raspberry)

(정답) 14. (d) 15. (b) 16. (a)

17-20. 유명한 뮤지컬 비극인 '웨스트 사이드 스토리'는 셰익스피어의 희곡 '로미오와 쥴리엣'에 등장하는 몬테규와 캐플릿 집안을 서로 싸우는 거리의 두 갱 집단인 제트파와 샤크파로 바꾼 것이다. 제트파는 미국으로 새로 이주한 푸에르토리코인들이고, 샤크파는 뉴욕 토박이들이다. 극의 배경은 1950년대 초반으로, 당시는 대도시 갱들의 싸움으로 이들이 다치거나 죽기도 했다. 제롬 로빈스의 탄탄한 안무로 구성된 극의 줄거리는 푸에르토리코인인 마리아가 토니를 사랑한다는 내용이다. 토니는 두 집단의 싸움을 말리려다가 마리아의 오빠를 살해하게 되고 결국은 자살하게 된다. 레너드 번스타인의 탁월한 음악 외에도 이 무대를 통해 브로드웨이에 데뷔한 스테판 손다임은 작사에 놀라운 재능을 보였다. '웨스트 사이드 스토리'는 1957년 9월 26일에 처음으로 공연되었다. 이것은 734회 공연되었으며, 10개월간 순회공연을 한 뒤 뉴욕으로 돌아와 246회의 연장 공연을 했다. 1961년에는 영화로 제작되었으며, 1980년에는 뉴욕 리바이벌 공연이 성공적으로 이루어졌다.

feud 불화, 다툼(=contention, strife, bickering, conflict, rancor, grudge, revenge, vendetta), 반목하다, 서로 다투다(=quarrel, struggle) warfare 전쟁, 투쟁(=military operations, hostilities, combat, conflict) choreograph 안무하다 tour 순회하다

(정답) 17. (b) 18. (b) 19. (d) 20. (a)

실력문제 4회

1-4. 철학은 명상과 같은, 현상들의 개관을 전제로 한다; 그리고 자신의 개관을 위해서, 철학자는 행동에 참가하지 않으면서, 관객으로 남아 있어야만 한다. 즉 그는, 경기를 보는 관객처럼, 활동무대 바깥에서 그것을 지켜봐야만 한다. 그러나 철학자의 현세에 대한 명상이 요구하는 객관적인 판단은, 비록 그것이 용이하다 하더라도, 공간적인 간격만으로 이끌어져서는 안 된다. 다시 말하면, 사건들로부터 물러서서 숙고하는 시간인 시간적인 간격도 똑같이 필수적이다. 그가 침착한 관객이자 냉철한 참가자로서 삶 속에서 사람들을 지배하는 열정들을 인정하고, 그러한 열정들을 불러일으키는 동기 혹은 관념들을 파악할 수 있게 하기 위함이다. 실용적이고 개인적인 이

해관계로부터 정신적으로 초연한, 이처럼 뒤로 물러선 태도를 통해, 그는 현상들을 개관하고 개괄할 수 있는 것이다.
(정답) 1. (d) 2. (a) 3. (d) 4. (b)

5-9. 여러 사회에서 공통된 유형이 인습적인 행동규칙의 주기적인 완화를 제공해 준다. 어떤 사회에서는 이와 같은 일이 모든 성의 장벽을 낮추는 정도에까지 이르며, 심지어는 근친상간의 금기를 이완하는 데까지 이른다. 또 어떤 사회에서는 단지 축제, 음주 혹은 다른 여러 형태의 오락을 곁들인 무용이 있을 수도 있다. 우리는 그런 활동에 상응하는 것을 우리의 할로인 파티, 가면무도회, 가장무도회, 그리고 마디글라스에서 볼 수 있다. 몇몇 사회는 의식절차를 갖춘 농탕질과 농담이라든가, 아니면 익살, 상스러운 장난 혹은 이야기, 그리고 다른 그 비슷한 활동이 허용되고 심지어는 부추겨지는 행사들을 제공한다. 재담꾼과 어릿광대는 여러 사회에서 흔히 보이는 인물이다. 그들의 억제되지 않은 행동으로 그들은 사회적으로 억눌린 원한과 적대감에 대해 대리의 배출구를 제공하는 것이다.
buffoonery 익살. ribald trick 상스러운 장난. jester 재담꾼.
(정답) 5. (c) 6. (c) 7. (d) 8. (d) 9. (c)

10-12. 때로는 가만히 앉아 남의 이야기를 듣는 것이 매우 어려울 때가 있다. 여기에는 기본적인 세 가지 이유가 있다. 첫째, 사람들은 관계가 있건 없건 간에 자신의 생각과 욕구로 너무나 분주하다. 그래서 사람들의 90퍼센트가 말을 하는 사람이고, 불과 10퍼센트만이 듣는 사람이다. 둘째, 어떤 사람들은 자기중심적이다. 이런 사람들은 다른 사람이 하는 말을 듣는 대신, 그 다음에 자신이 얘기하기 위해 그 사람의 말이 끝나기를 기다릴 뿐이다. 자신의 생각을 정리하느라고 남의 말을 잘 듣지 못하는 것이다. 셋째, 말하는 사람의 동기나 성격상의 특징을 분석하느라 역시 그 사람이 하는 말을 듣지 못하는 사람도 있다.
(정답) 10. (c) 11. (c) 12. (a)

13-17. 불행은 친구를 사랑한다(낙심한 사람들은 그렇지 않은 사람들보다 더 감정적으로 의지가 되는 것을 구하기 쉽다). 그러나 친구는 분명하게 불행을 사랑하지 않는다. 1976년에 심리학자인 제임스 코네가 미이애미 대학교에 있을 때, 45명의 여대생들에게 20분간 전화로 그 중 일부는 낙심한

여성들과 이야기를 하도록 하였다.-학생들은 그것에 대해 알지 못했다고 할지라도. 나중에 학생들은 낙심한 여성들과 시간을 보내는 것이 다른 나머지 사람들에 비해 거의 재미가 없었다고 지적했다. 이와 같은 반응은 행복하지 않은 사람들 사이에 너무나 평범한 악순환의 일부이다. 그들의 행동은 그들이 필요로 하는 의지가 되고 수용해 주는 바로 그 사람들을 쫓아 버리게 되고, 그 때문에 그들의 우울증을 더욱 악화시키고 의지할 욕구를 더욱 강렬하게 만든다. 다른 사람들이 그들을 부정적으로 바라본다고 우울한 사람들이 말했을 때, 그들이 옳다는 것이 당연하다는 것을 제시하기 때문에 이런 결과들은 또한 중요하다.

(정답) 13. (b) 14. (d) 15. (a) 16. (d) 17. (b)

18-20. 제트기 엔진과 로켓 엔진은 뉴턴의 제3법칙 원리에 따라 작동하지만, 제트기 엔진은 연료를 연소할 때 공기로부터 산소를 얻고, 로켓 엔진은 직접 산소를 지니고 다녀야 한다는 점에서 다르다. 강한 압력 하에서 한 방향으로 방출되는 가스는 엔진에 반대방향으로 추진력을 가한다. 뉴턴의 제3 법칙에 따르면, 작용에는 그와 동등하고 상반되는 반작용이 있다. 이 원리는 고무풍선을 불어 날리는 것으로 설명할 수 있다. 공기가 반대 방향으로 빠져 나가면서 풍선이 앞으로 움직이는 것이다.

(정답) 18. (a) 19. (b) 20. (d)

VII. 종합문제

1. 최종점검 문제

1. 'such as volcanic eruptions'(화산폭발과 같은)와 어울리는 단어가 빈칸에 들어가야 한다. (a) optimistic 낙관적인 (b) comfortable 안락한 (c) joyous 즐거운 (d) catastrophic 재난의, 재앙의(=disastrous, calamitous)
(해석) 고대인들에게 신화는 종종 화산폭발과 같은 재난적인 사건을 설명하기 위한 시도였다. **정답 (d)**

2. (a) erudition 학식, 박학. arbiter 중재자(=arbitrator, umpire, referee,

mediator, judge) (b) pomposity 호화, 거만. censor 검열관 (c) conspirator 공모자 (d) contribution 기여. moralist 도덕가
✍(해석) 그의 학식이 대단해서 그는 미술과 음악에 관한 모든 분쟁의 중재자가 되었다. **정답 (a)**

3. 'employees become machine attendants'(직원들이 기계의 수행원이 된다)로 미루어 보아 빈칸에는 '비인간화'가 와야 한다. frustration 욕구불만
✍(해석) 새로운 사무실은 합리화된다. 즉 기계가 사용되고, 직원들이 기계의 수행원이 된다. 업무는 개인적인 것이 아니고 공장에서처럼 집단적이다. 서로 교환 가능하고 신속하게 대체할 수 있는 사무원들로 표준화되어 있다. 비인간화의 지점까지 전문화되어 있다. **정답 (b)**

4. (a) anachronistic 시대착오적인(=anachronic) (b) synchronous 동시에 일어나는(=simultaneous) (c) chronic 만성의, 상습적인(=habitual, confirmed, consistent, settled, inveterate, rooted) (d) incongruous 조화되지 않은, 부적절한(=unsuitable, inappropriate)
✍(해석) 상습적인 거짓말쟁이는 끊임없이 지속적으로 계속해서 거짓말을 하고, 고질병 환자는 거의 언제나 아프고, 심한 흡연가는 니코틴에 변치 않고 탐닉하는 사람이다. **정답 (c)**

5. induce 유발하다. (a) biographic 전기의 (b) sadistic 가학성의 (c) soporific 최면의, 졸리는(=sedative, soothing, lethargic, torpid, sluggish), 최면제 (d) bombastic 과장한, 허풍떠는
✍(해석) 몹시 아픈 사람에게 최면을 유발할 방법을 찾아서 현대 연구자들은 원시인들이 버렸던 많은 최면의 합성물을 분석해 왔다. **정답 (c)**

6. break into 침입하다(=burst into, crash in) acquit 방면하다, 해제하다(=clear, release) assault 공격하다(=aggress, assail, attack, come[swoop/descend] down on) (a) retaliate 보복하다(=avenge, revenge, retort, requite, return, repay) (b) excuse 용서하다, 변명하다(=pardon, condone, forgive, exonerate, absolve, acquit, exempt) (c) sympathize 동정하다(=feel for, sorrow for, condole, commiserate) (d) behave 행동하다(=act, bear

oneself, conduct oneself)

✎(해석) 강도가 내 집에 침입하여 내가 그를 때려눕히면 법률은 나를 무죄로 할 것이고, 내가 신체적으로 공격을 받는다면 합리적인 폭력으로 보복을 허용할 것이다. **정답 (a)**

7. (a) loot 약탈하다(=plunder, pillage, ransack, despoil, sack, deprecate, maraud, freeboot) (b) micturate 방뇨하다, 오줌누다(=urinate) (c) cherish 소중히 하다, 품다(=hold dear; cling to, hold to, nurture) (d) supplicate 간청하다, 탄원하다(=entreat, petition, beseech)

✎(해석) 토양표본이 보여준 바에 따르면 강도들이 약 2000년 전에 무덤에 침입하여 금과 은이 포함되어 있는 것이면 무엇이든지 약탈한 후에 버렸다는 것이다. **정답 (a)**

8. rank 분류하다, 평가하다, 자리잡다 juvenile delinquency 청소년 비행 epidemic 유행성의, 만연한(=infectious, contagious) (a) aspiration 포부, 열망, 호흡 (b) reputation 평판, 명성 (d) benevolence 자비심, 박애, 자선(=kindness, charity)

✎(해석) 범죄는 대부분의 미국인들의 마음속에서 제일의 문제로 자리잡는다. 일부의 사람들은 청소년 비행이 만연해 있다고들 한다. **정답 (c)**

9. (a) tamed 길들여진(=tame, domestic, domesticated) recollect 회상하다(=remember, recall, bring to mind, look back on) (b) evolve 전개하다, 진화시키다(=develop gradually; unfold) (c) extinct 꺼진(=extinguished, quenched), 멸종된(=exterminated, obsolete, died out, passed away, dead, gone) (d) salient 현저한, 두드러진(=outstanding, prominent, striking, conspicuous) appreciate 평가하다, 감상하다, 감사하다

✎(해석) 멸종위기에 놓인 종들이 멸종되어 가는 것을 막아 후손들이 동물계의 큰 다양성을 즐길 수 있도록 하는 것이 국제 야생동물 보존 위원회의 과업이다. **정답 (c)**

10. (a) deter 단념시키다, 막다(=restrain, hinder, discourage) deter A from B (A로 하여금 B하지 못하게 하다)에 주의할 것. '금지'의 뜻을 나타

내는 동사 뒤에는 전치사 from이 온다는 것을 기억하자. (예) keep, prevent, hinder, ban, bar, prohibit, inhibit, abstain, refrain 등이 있다. (b) deepen 깊게 하다, 진하게 하다 (c) deplore 비탄하다(=lament, mourn, grieve), 후회하다 (d) degrade 낮추다, 저하시키다, 타락시키다

✍(해석) 건강에 해가 된다는 인식과 부모에게 벌을 받게 될 예상에도 불구하고, 중학교와 고등학교 학생들이 담배를 피우려는 것을 거의 막지 못하는 것 같다.
정답 (a)

11. 의미상 '-하는 한'의 뜻을 가진 접속사가 들어가야 한다. (a) in case that -의 경우를 생각하여, 만일 -라면(=if) (d) as long as -하는 한(=if only), -하는 동안(=while) (해석) 우리의 신형 복사기는 가능한 한 자주 유지 보수가 이루어진다면 계속하여 사용자에게 좋은 서비스를 제공할 것이다. **정답 (d)**

12. 'the next two weeks'라는 미래를 표시하는 부사구가 있으므로 (a), (b)는 답에서 제외된다. 의미상 본문은 '의무'를 나타내므로 (c)가 답이 된다.
✍(해석) 최근에 사고가 증가하고 있으므로 앞으로 2주에 걸쳐 안전 검사가 강화 되어야 할 것이다. **정답 (c)**

13. 빈칸에는 접속사가 들어가야 하므로 (c)가 답이 된다. 'unless they are accompanied'에서 'they are'가 생략되었다. (b) without는 전치사이므로 'without being accompanied'가 되어야 한다.
✍(해석) 마케팅 제안서는 사실 분석 자료가 첨부되지 않는다면 기획부로 제출되어서는 안 된다. **정답 (c)**

14. lock은 '보관하다'의 뜻을 가진 타동사인데 뒤에 목적어가 없으므로 수동태가 되어야 한다.
✍(해석) 민감한 성격의 데이터들은 항상 특별 보관함에 보관되어야 한다.
정답 (b)

15. 빈칸에서 concert까지 부사구가 되어야 하므로 빈칸에는 전치사가

들어가야 한다. 따라서 (c)가 답이 된다. (c) unlike -과 다른(=different from)

✍(해석) 폭우 때문에 참석자가 없었던 작년의 야외 음악회와는 달리, 올해의 음악회는 많은 군중을 끌어들일 것으로 예상된다. **정답 (c)**

16. 빈칸에는 be동사의 보어이면서, as--as구문이므로 형용사역할을 하는 분사가 들어가야 한다. 그런데 주어가 사물(headlines)이므로 (b)가 답이 된다. (예문) I'm interested in this book.(주어가 사람: 과거분사) This book is interesting to me.(주어가 사물: 현재분사)

✍(해석) 진행 중인 노동쟁의의 조기 해결에 관한 오늘 신문의 표제들은 이사들이 바라던 것만큼 고무적이지 못했다. **정답 (b)**

17. 빈칸 앞에 선행사가 없으므로 관계대명사가 있는 (c), (d)는 답에서 제외된다. and 앞뒤로 같은 구조가 와야 하고, 의미상으로 보아도 (b)가 답이 된다.

✍(해석) 재생 자원들은 규칙적으로 자연 과정에 의해 보충이 되어, 끝없이 공급되기 때문에 그렇게 부른다. **정답 (b)**

18. 본문의 동사가 'is'이므로 (a)는 답에서 제외된다. 타동사 compare가 목적어가 없으므로 빈칸에는 과거분사가 와야 한다.

✍(해석) 용량 요소는 발전소가 최대 용량으로 가동되었을 때 생산될 수 있는 양과 비교하여 발전소가 실제로 생산하는 에너지의 양이다. **정답 (b)**

19. they 바로 앞에는 접속사가 와야 하며, 빈칸에는 be동사의 보어로서 형용사가 있어야 하므로 (c)가 답이 된다.

✍(해석) 류머티즘과 기관지염, 소화계 질병은 한 때 그랬던 것만큼 그렇게 유행하지 않는다. **정답 (c)**

20. 'would have arrived'로 보아서 본문은 가정법 과거완료이다. 따라서 빈칸 뒤에 'if+주어 +had+과거분사'가 와야 한다. if I had not been detained= had I not been detained(if가 생략되면 도치된다)

✍(해석) 마지막 순간에 예상치 않았던 전화로 붙들리지 않았더라면 약속한 시간 정각에 도착했을 것이다. **정답 (d)**

21. comparable뒤에는 to나 with가 온다. comparable to(필적하는), comparable with(비교되는)의 뜻이다. (d) comparable of→ comparable to that of. 여기서 that=the expense이다.

✐(해석) 올해 남은 기간 동안 차를 임대하는 비용은 좋은 중고차를 구입하는 비용과 필적할 것이다. **정답 (d)**

22. 시간이나 조건을 나타내는 부사절은 현재가 미래를, 현재완료가 미래완료를 대신하므로 (c) will have discovered→ have discovered.

✐(해석) 나는 네가 형이 있는 곳을 찾아야 비로소 안심할 것이라는 것을 안다. **정답 (c)**

23. 분사구문이 과거분사로 시작 되는가 현재분사로 시작되는가 하는 문제가 자주 출제된다. 분별하는 방법은 첫째, 타동사(draw)뒤에 목적어가 있으면 현재분사, 없으면 과거분사이다. 둘째, 주절의 주어(investors)와 분사의 관계가 능동이면 현재분사, 수동이면 과거분사이다. 따라서 (a) drawing → drawn. flee달아나다(=escape, run away), 물러가다(=withdraw), 사라지다(=vanish) falter 비틀거리다(=stumble), 중얼거리다(=stammer), 주춤하다(=waver)

✐(해석) 고성장과 금리로 인해 폴란드에 의해 끌렸던 투자자들은 이제 성장이 주춤하고 채무가 늘어나면서 폴란드에서 물러가고 있다. **정답 (a)**

24. 본문의 주어는 inmates, 동사는 contend이다. 한 문장에 동사가 두 개 있을 수 없으므로 (a)return→ returning. inmate 재소자 stigma 치욕, 반점, 흔적(=blemish, birthmark, brand, blot, stain, reproach) ex-convict 전과자

✐(해석) 외부세계로 돌아가는 재소자들은 전과자라는 흔적, 즉 사회라는 더 큰 울타리에 성공적으로 적응하는데 있어서의 장애물과 싸운다. **정답 (a)**

25. 동사의 패턴(문장 5형식)에 관한 문제라고 볼 수 있다. 동사가 나오면 몇 가지를 체크해야 한다. 첫째, 자동사인가 타동사인가를 체크한다. 자동사는 수동태가 될 수 없다는 것을 기억할 필요가 있다. 타동사 뒤에는 전치사가 올 수 없다는 것에도 주의해야 한다. 둘째, 문장의 5형식 중 몇 형식

에 속하는 동사(동사의 구문)인가를 체크한다. 셋째, 동사의 수의 일치를 체크한다. 끝으로, 동사의 시제를 체크한다. remain은 자동사이므로 수동태가 될 수 없다. (c) to be remained→ to remain.

✍(해석) 경제적으로 볼 때 동아시아지역의 역동성은 1960년대와 1970년대 초기의 고도 성장률이 반복될 수는 없겠지만 여전할 것으로 기대된다.
정답 (c)

26. Parallelism(병행구조)을 묻는 문제이다. 등위접속사 and 앞뒤의 구조가 같아야 하므로 (d) appreciation→ be appreciated.

✍(해석) 모든 음악은 표현과 설계라는 두 가지 요소로 구성된다. 표현은 부정확하고 주관적이며, 개인적이고 본능적인 방식으로 향유될 수 있다. 한편 설계는 정확하고, 이해와 감상을 위해 객관적으로 분석되어야만 한다.
정답 (d)

27. object는 두 가지 구문으로 쓰인다. (1) object to+(동)명사 (2) object+that절. 따라서 ① object to→ object.

✍(해석) 이 연구 분야에는 사람들이 거의 없기 때문에 위와 같은 법칙들이 무의미하다고 반대할 수도 있으나, 사실은 그렇지 않다. **정답 ①**

28. <It is necessary[essential/ important/ imperative/ natural/ compulsory/ rational] that +주어+(should)+동사원형>을 묻는 문제이다. (a) is not→ not be.

✍(해석) 형성된 물질이 불안정하게 되어 원래 성분으로 분해 되는 지점까지 온도를 올리지 않는 것이 중요하다. **정답 (a)**

29. <dissuade A from B>(A를 설득하여 B하지 못하게 하다). (a) to be seated→ from being seated.

✍(해석) 김 의원을 설득하여 앉지 못하게 하면서 외교문제위원회 위원장은 그에게 그의 계획을 망쳐놓지 말라고 요청했다. **정답 (a)**

30. what이하가 완전한 문장을 이루고 있으므로 (c) what→ that.

✍(해석) 인간이 어떻게 서로 다른지, 그리고 다른 동물 종들과는 어떻게 다른가를 연구하는 것을 자신의 임무로 삼고 있는 인류학자들은 모든 공동체가 자신들을 독특하게 인간적이라고 생각하고 있다는 사실을 알려줄 것

이다. 정답 (c)

31. crack down on 단속하다, …을 엄하게 다스리다(=enforce laws or rules strictly: require full obedience to a rule) (a) do a double take 놀라서 다시 보다, 갑자기 이해하다(=look again in surprise; suddenly understand what is seen or said) (b) do good 착한 일을 하다, 효력이 있다, 도움이 되다 (c) hit and run 사람을 치고 달아나다.

✐(해석) 경찰은 미성년자들에게 술을 판매하는 것을 단속했다. 정답 (d)

32. bigotry 편협한 신앙, 완고 (b) conflict 갈등 (c) ritual 의식 (d) prejudice 편견, 선입견(=bias, preoccupation, partiality, predilection)

✐(해석) 종교적 편견에 대한 어떤 적개심은 전혀 놀라운 것이 아니다. 정답 (d)

33. cadaverous 시체 같은, 파랗게 질린(=pale, ghastly) (c) ghastly 무시무시한, 유령 같은, 기분 나쁜(=horrible, frightful; ghostlike, pale; very bad or unpleasant)

✐(해석) 그 시련 후에 그는 창백한 모습이었지만, 아직도 살아 있었다. 정답 (c)

34. go home 급소를 깊이 찌르다(=hit the target). (a) fold up 반듯하게 접다, 망하다, 파산하다(=collapse, fail) (c) mislead 잘못 인도하다 (d) ambiguous 애매한

✐(해석) 존은 토론에 능숙한 사람이었고, 그의 계산된 풍자는 정곡을 찔렀다. 그의 상대방은 그 공격에 얼굴이 빨개졌다. 정답 (b)

35. vulnerable 상처 입기 쉬운, 취약성[약점]이 있는 (a) futile 효과 없는, 무익한(=useless) (b) feasible 실행할 수 있는, 가능한(=possible; likely, probable) (c) likable 좋아하는, 마음에 드는(=attractive, pleasant, genial) (d) susceptible 영향을 받기 쉬운(=easily influenced or affected by)

✐(해석) 가정 밖에서는 일자리가 부족해서, 여성들은 불황에 더 영향을 받기 쉽다. 정답 (d)

36. insulated 고립된, 격리된(=isolated, detached) (a) indifferent 무관심

한, 냉담한(=apathetic, callous, unfeeling) (b) sophisticated 순진하지 않은, 복잡한(=not simple, naive; worldly-wise or knowledgable, subtle; highly complex or developed) (d) saturated 스며든, 흠뻑 젖은, 가득한(=soaked; filled)

✎(해석) 포유동물에 있어서 태아는 바깥 세계와 더 고립되어 있다. 그러나 어미의 생리적인 상태에는 물론 더 직접적으로 의존한다. **정답 (c)**

37. boil down to 결국 …으로 되다(=end up, wind up, reduce itself to, come down to) (b) pile up 쌓이다, 축적하다(=heap up, accumulate, amass, hoard) (c) pick up 들어 올리다(=take up, lift), 회복하다(=recover), 태우다, 속도를 내다(=gain; speed up) (d) turn up 나타나다(=appear, emerge)

✎(해석) 그 모든 문제는 결국 노사간의 세력다툼으로 끝이 났다. **정답 (a)**

38. acrimonious 신랄한(=bitter, resentful, cynical) (a) crazed 발광한 (b) cunning 교활한, 간사한(=sly, crafty, foxy, tricky, wily, insidious) (c) confused 혼동된 (d) bitter 쓴, 지독한(=severe, rigorous), 괴로운(=painful)

✎(해석) 우리는 그녀의 신랄한 비평을 무시하려고 애를 썼으나, 그것은 상당한 자제력을 요하는 것이었다. **정답 (d)**

39. inscrutability 불가사의(=untraceability, enigma, insolubility, mystery) (a) thoughtfulness 사려 깊음 (c) intensity 강도, 세기 (d) improbability 있을 것 같지 않은 일

✎(해석) 그러나 내가 숨어 있는 곳을 알아내지 못할 것이라고 확신해서, 나는 전혀 당황하지 않았다. **정답 (b)**

40. luminous 반짝이는, 빛나는(=bright, shining, brilliant, glowing, lustrous, radiant) (b) diminutive 작은, 소형의(=very small; tiny) (c) immense 거대한(=very large; huge; vast) (d) ravishing 매혹적인(=captivating, enchanting)

✎(해석) 세기말에는 연간 수입이 30억 달러라는 전망이 네이다의 빛나는 눈앞에서 춤추고 있다. **정답 (a)**

2. 최종 독해

1-4. 이 나라에 복권 게임의 수가 늘어나고 있는 것에 대한 나의 우려를 표현하고 싶다. 내가 이런 종류의 도박을 반대하는 데에는 몇 가지 이유들이 있다. 첫째로, 복권 게임을 운영하는 사람들이 사람들로부터 상당한 액수의 돈을 걷어가고 있는데, 그들 대부분은 나이가 들어 그렇게 돈을 돌릴 여유가 없는 사람들이다. 예를 들어 우리 아래 동네 노부부는 지난 주 복권을 사는데 20달러 이상을 썼는데, 그들은 사회보장연금 수표로 겨우 연명한다. 둘째로, 원칙적으로 나는 도박에 반대하지 않지만, 이 특별한 종류의 복권 게임을 하는 사람 편에서 아무런 기술도 필요하지 않기 때문에 특히 지성인들에게 불쾌감을 준다. 끝으로, 복권을 파는 곳들은 종종 그렇지 않으면 조용할 동네에 달갑지 않은 사람들을 끌어들인다. 결론적으로 나는 모든 종류의 복권 게임을 폐지할 것을 건의하고 싶다.

 meager 빈약한, 아주 적은(=poor, not full or rich; inadequate, scanty) offensive 불쾌한(=nasty, disgustful) sprawl 쭉 펴다(=spread out)

 정답 1. (d)　2. (c)　3. (b)　4. (c)

5-7.
 언론을 언론이 아닌 것이 되어 주길 기대해서는 안 된다. 언론에 대해 문학비평가들은 문학적이지 못하다고 비난하고, 역사가들은 역사적 정확성이 없다고 비난하며, 법관들은 증거의 법칙에 의거한 사실을 동원하지 않는다고 비난한다. 그러나 언론은 문학도, 역사도, 법도 아니다. 그것은 몹시 서둘러 모은 사건들에 대한 도망치는 듯한 기록 외에는 별것이 아닐 때가 대부분이다. 사실은 많은 뉴스들이 일어난 일에 대한 가설이다. 물론 과학도 일어난 것에 대한 가설로 이루어진다. 물론 과학은 가설로 작업하면서 오류가 발견 될 때 그 가설들은 삭제해 나가며, 실수로 인해 인명의 대가를 치른다 해도 대개는 별 비난 없이 그렇게 한다. 과학적 정확성을 주장하지 않는 언론은 그 실수가 쉽게 용서되지 않는다. 모두가 인정하듯 언론은 이따금씩 정신없이 새로운 소식을 탐하는 사람들의 구미를 맞추면서 종종 불충분한 정보를 가지고 서둘러 활자화한다. 이상적인 사회라면 절대적 확신에 도달할 때까지는 아무 것도 활자화하지 말라고 요구할 수 있을 것이다. 그러나 그런 사회는 사건의 궁극적 결과를 기다리는 동안 우리네 언론의 오류가 그와 비교해 볼 때 진실의 모범으로 보일 정도로 풍문과 불안과 거짓으로 가득 차게 될 것이다.

　marshal 정돈하다, 안내하다(=arrange in order; guide). fleeing 달아나는 듯한, 서두르는. at bottom 본심은, 사실은, 근본적으로(는). admittedly 일반적으로 인정하듯이, 확실히. be rife with …로 가득하다(=be full of)

　정답 5. (b)　6. (a)　7. (c)

8-10.
　프랑켄슈타인 이야기는 원래의 의도와 원래의 타당성을 뛰어넘는 생존능력을 가지고 있다. 자신이 창조한 괴물에 대해 죄책감이 시달리는 겁먹은 과학자의 상은 첫 원자폭탄의 폭발과 더불어 이론에 머물기를 그만두었다. 실제적인 폭탄 제조와 그 결과를 가져온 이론적 작업에 참여했던 젊고 이상적인 사람들 중 일부의 혐오감은 이제 조심스러워지고 미리 경고를 받아 그들의 연구의 윤리적이며 사회적이고 정치적인 의미를 고려해 보려고 애를 쓰는 과학자들에게 분명한 영향을 주었다. 그들은 심지어 일부 연구가 과연 행해져야 되는지 의구심을 갖기도 했다. "당위"의 문제들이 심각하기 대두되면서 윤리학이 도입되었고 "도덕의 우위에 있는 과학"이나 "가치와 무관한 과학"에 대한 전통적 환상 중 일부가 흔들리기 시작하고 있다.

　viability 생존 능력 guilt-ridden 죄책감에 시달리는 revulsion 혐오감(=disgust)

　정답 8. (d)　9. (b)　10. (d)

해설 · 2부 총신·장신 신학대학원 TEPS 문제분석

III. 실력 문제
1. 문법 - Part I

실력문제 1회

1. discuss는 타동사이므로 전치사를 동반할 수 없다. discuss=talk over.
   (해석) A: 누군가를 만나려고 기다리고 있나요?
          B: 존과 의논할 긴급한 업무가 있어요.
   정답 (a)

2. <talk A into+V-ing>(A를 설득하여 -하게 하다) 구문을 묻는 문제이다.
   (해석) A: 톰이 너와 함께 뉴욕에 갈거니?
          B: 그를 설득해서 나와 함께 가게 할 수 없어.
   정답 (c)

3. 'hear'가 지각동사이므로 목적보어가 동사원형 또는 V-ing가 와야 한다.
   (해석) A: 오늘 아침에 왜 그렇게 늦었니?
          B: 정말 죄송해요. 자명종이 울리는 소리를 못 들었어요.
   정답 (c)

4. 빈칸에는 'make up my mind'의 목적어가 와야 하므로 (b)가 답이 된다.
   (해석) A: 여기서 무엇을 주문해야 할지 결정을 못했어요.
          B: 피자를 드시는 것이 어때요? 이 곳은 치즈피자를 잘 해요.
   정답 (b)

5. 타동사구 put off(연기하다)의 목적어가 없으므로 수동형을 써야 하고,

문맥상 미래이다. put off 연기하다(=postpone, delay, defer, procrastinate, hold over, adjourn)

 ✍(해석) A: 오는 금요일에 만나기로 되어 있지?
    B: 그래, 하지만 사장이 아직도 감기에 걸려서 연기 될 거야.
 정답 (c)

6. I'm flattered 과찬입니다.
 ✍(해석) A: 제인, 오늘밤 아름다워 보이는데요.
    B: 과찬의 말씀 입니다.
 정답 (c)

7. 문맥의 의미상 빈칸에는 '-할 필요가 없다'(don't have to, don't need to)는 표현이 와야 한다.
 ✍(해석) A: 지금 당장 집에 전화해야 하나요?
    B: 아니, 그럴 필요가 없어.
 정답 (d)

8. 혼합가정법 구문을 묻는 문제이다. 혼합가정법 구문은 "If+주어+had+과거분사.. , 주어 +would[should/might/could]+동사원형.. "이다. 조건절은 과거의 일을(직설법 과거, 가정법 과거완료), 주절은 현재의 일을(직설법 현재, 가정법 과거) 나타낸다. 주로 현재나 과거를 표시하는 부사구가 힌트이다
 ✍(해석) A: 요즘 우리가 위험에 처해 있어.
    B: 만약 당신이 내 말을 들었더라면 우리는 지금 위험하지 않았을 텐데.
 정답 (d)

9. in case (…하는 경우에 대비하여)이하는 조건을 표시하는 부사절이므로 현재 시제가 와야 한다.
 ✍(해석) A: 오늘 일기 예보가 어떠니?
    B: 비가 올 경우에 대여 우산을 가져 가.
 정답 (a)

제3부 PRE-TEST와 TEPS 문제에 대한 해설 및 해답 317

10. 빈칸에는 make의 목적어로 what이 와야 한다.
&(해석) A: 무슨 일이 있었니?
　　　　B: 그래, 해리스가 나에게 더 이상 말하지 않아 어찌해야 할 지를 모르겠어.
정답 (b)

실력문제 2회

1. hope뒤에는 <hope+that절, hope+to-동사>로 써야 한다. 'hope+목적어 +to-동사/V-ing'는 쓸 수 없다.
&(해석) A: 메리가 어제 밤 회의에 참석했니?
　　　　B: 아니, 하지만 그녀가 오기를 바랬는데.
정답 (d)

2. Once(일단 -하면)가 접속사이므로 빈칸에는 <주어+동사>가 와야 한다.
&(해석) A: 당신이 머지않아 새 아파트에 이사 온다고 들었어.
　　　　B: 일단 수선이 끝나면 즉시 이사할 거야.
정답 (b)

3. if Tom is not more fluent than Jack=if not more so.
&(해석) A: 영어의 유창함에 있어 탐과 잭을 비교하면 어떠니?
　　　　B: 탐이 잭보다 더 유창하지 않을지라도, 잭만큼 유창하다.
정답 (b)

4. recall+V-ing(동명사)이고, 타동사 inform(알리다) 뒤에 목적어가 없으므로 수동태가 와야 한다.
&(해석) A: 그 새로운 규칙에 대해서 알고 있지?
　　　　B: 아니. 그 규칙에 대해 들어본 기억이 없어.
정답 (d)

5. <with+명사구+분사>구문을 묻는 문제이다. 명사구와 분사의 관계가 능동이면 현재분사, 수동이면 과거분사를 쓴다.
&(해석) A: 제인은 30분 동안 눈을 감은 채 앉아 있어.

B: 아마도 어제 밤에 한숨도 못 잔 것 같아.
정답 (d)

6. <동사+대명사+부사>를 묻는 문제이다.
   ✍(해석) A: 도와 드릴까요?
   　　　　 B: 코리아헤럴드 한 부를 찾고 있어요. 여기서 그것을 구할 수 있어요?
   정답 (b)

7. <spend+시간+V-ing>을 묻는 문제이다. try to+동사(-하려고 노력하다). try+V-ing(시험 삼아 -하다)
   ✍(해석) A: 오늘 아침 왜 그렇게 늦었니?
   　　　　 B: 차를 잡는데 20분 이상 걸렸어.
   정답 (d)

8. 'could have caught'로 보아 가정법 과거완료이다. <If only+가정법>이므로, 빈칸에는 'had+과거분사'가 와야 한다.
   ✍(해석) A: 좀 더 일찍 집에서 출발했으면 좋겠는데! 그러면 기차를 탈 수 있었을 텐데.
   　　　　 B: 지금 그런 말을 해도 소용없어.
   정답 (a)

9. <in spite of/despite+명사, 대명사, 동명사>, <in spite of the fact that/despite the fact that+주어+동사>를 묻는 문제이다. (d) besides 전치사로 '…외에, …을 제외하고', 부사로 '그 위에, 게다가'의 뜻이다.
   ✍(해석) A: 너의 팀이 하이킹을 못 갈 줄 알았어.
   　　　　 B: 비록 날씨가 도와주지는 않았지만, 여하튼 하이킹을 갔어.
   정답 (c)

10. 빈칸 뒤에 문장이 나오므로 (a), (b)는 답에서 제외된다. 선행사가 없으므로 (c)도 답에서 제외된다. 빈칸에는 hear의 목적어로 명사절을 이끄는 접속사 that이 와야 한다.
    ✍(해석) A: 올해 연말 보너스가 없다는 것을 들었어?

B: 나는 놀라지 않아. 많은 회사들도 마찬가지야.
정답 (c)

실력문제 3회

1. 빈칸에는 'in stock'(재고가 있는)에서 stock이 생략되고, 전치사적 부사 'in'이 와야 한다.
   ✍(해석) A: 플로피 디스크가 있는지 전화합니다.
      B: 재고가 있는지 확인해 보겠습니다.
   정답 (d)

2. '…로 돌아가는 길'의 표현은 'one's way back to'이다.
   ✍(해석) A: 어제 길을 잃었다고 들었어요.
      B: 예, 박물관에 갔다가 호텔로 돌아가는 길을 못 찾았어요.
   정답(c)

3. <do nothing but+동사원형>(-하기만 한다)을 묻는 문제이다.
   ✍(해석) A: 그녀가 왜 직장을 그만 두었는지 아니?
      B: 아니. 그녀가 여기 있는 동안 내내 불평하기만 했어.
   정답 (d)

4. <as if+가정법>을 묻는 문제이다. 본문에서는 빈칸 이하가 'as if I had deceived you'이 된다.
   ✍(해석) A: 나는 너를 더 이상 믿을 수 없어. 네가 전체 이야기를 날조했잖아.
      B: 왜 너는 내가 너를 속였던 것처럼 말하니?
   정답 (c)

5. 빈칸에는 '어떻게 해서든지'의 뜻인 somehow가 와야 한다. (b) by the way 그런데 (c) in a way 어느 점에서는, 다소 in one's own way 일종
   ✍(해석) A: 그것을 테니스장에 옮겨줄 수 있니?
      B: 어떻게 해서든지 내가 거기에 갈 거야.
   정답 (a)

6. <quite[rather]+a(n)+형용사+명사>의 어순을 묻는 문제이다.
   ✎(해석) A: 폴락의 작품이라는 것을 모른다고 할지라도, 저는 이 그림이 좋아요.
          B: 대단한 볼거리네요. 그가 그렇게 다작을 했는지 몰랐어요.
   정답 (b)

7. <be busy+(in)+V-ing>구문(-하느라고 바쁘다)을 묻는 문제이다.
   ✎(해석) A: 네 형이 어떻게 지내니? 잠시 동안 못 보았어.
          B: 그는 잘 지내지만 논문을 쓰느라고 바빠.
   정답 (d)

8. <such(형용사)+명사+as>, <so(부사)+형용사+as>를 묻는 문제이다.
   ✎(해석) A: 돈을 좀 빌릴 수 있니?
          B: 너에게 돈을 빌려 줄 만큼 내가 그렇게 바보는 아니야.
   정답 (a)

9. <How come+주어+동사?>(왜 -하니)를 묻는 문제이다. (b) What about+V-ing=How about+V-ing=What do you say to+V-ing …하는 것이 어때?
   ✎(해석) A: 차가 고장 나서 집까지 내내 걸어 왔어.
          B: 왜 버스를 타지 않았니?
   정답 (a)

10. <Nor+조동사+주어+동사>의 어순을 묻는 문제이다.
    ✎(해석) A: 술을 많이 마시니?
           B: 많이 못 해. 그러고 싶지도 않아.
    정답 (c)

실력문제 4회

1. <break A of B> 구문을 묻는 문제이다.
   ✎(해석) A: 담배를 많이 피우니?

B: 그래. 이 습관을 끊어야 해.
정답 (d)

2. <부정어+what(so)ever>(=never)를 묻는 문제이다.
   (해석) A: 그는 수학 공부를 어떻게 하니?
          B: 그는 결코 수학에 재능이 없어.
정답 (a)

3. 라틴어에서 온 형용사의 비교급은 to를 쓴다. (예) prefer, preferable, senior, junior, superior, inferior
   ✍(해석) A: 구두시험을 월요일이나 수요일간에 선택을 해야만 해. 네 생각은 어떠니?
          B: 글쎄, 나로서는 수요일이 월요일보다 더 좋아.
정답 (d)

4. < be in the middle of+V-ing>(…하는 중이다)구문을 묻는 문제이다.
   ✍(해석) A: 조가 전화했을 때 너는 무엇을 하고 있었니?
          B: 요리를 하려고 하고 있었어.
정답 (c)

5. What gives you that idea?=What makes you think so?=Why do you think so?
   ✍(해석) A: 그녀가 그를 싫어하는 것 같아.
          B: 왜 너는 그렇게 생각하니?
정답 (b)

6. 빈칸에는 The man을 수식하는 형용사구나 형용사절이 와야 한다. 따라서 (d)는 답에서 제외된다. '착용'을 뜻하는 'in'을 묻는 문제이다. (예) dressed in black suit[brown boots, uniform, wedding ring] (a) 'having the brown suit on'으로 고쳐야 한다.
   ✍(해석) A: 윌리암스가 누구야?
          B: 갈색 신사복을 입고 있는 남자가 그 사람이야.
정답 (b)

7. <what do you say to+V-ing?>(-하는 것이 어때?)를 묻는 문제이다.
    ✍(해석) A: 나가서 한 잔 하는 것이 어때?
           B: 좋은 생각이지
    정답 (d)

8. resemble은 세 가지를 기억해 두는 것이 좋다. (1) 뒤에 전치사가 못 온다(타동사이므로). (2) 진행형을 못 쓴다(상태를 표시하므로) (3) 수동태를 못 쓴다.
    ✍(해석) A: 그는 어떻게 생겼니?
           B: 아버지를 매우 닮았어.
    정답 (d)

9. <should have+과거분사>는 과거에 이루지 못한 사실에 대한 후회를 나타낸다.
    ✍(해석) A: 나는 오늘 아침에 너무 졸려.
           B: 너는 지난밤에 좀 더 일찍 잠자리에 들었으면 좋았을 걸.
    정답 (c)

10. 빈칸에는 의미상 whatever가 와야 한다. whatever I say 내가 무슨 말을 하던지
    ✍(해석) A: 그를 꼬셔서 클럽에 가입시키려고 애쓰는 것이 너무 어려워.
           B: 맞아. 내가 무슨 말을 하던지 그는 항상 반대할 무언가를 가지고 있어.
    정답 (d)

◉ 문법 · Part II

실력문제 1회

1. <devote oneself to+V-ing>(-에 몰두하다)를 묻는 문제이다.
    ✍(해석) 시인들은 그들의 영감을 단어들로 옮기는데 몰두한다. **정답** (a)

2. 목적어가 없고, 주어(the story)와 수동 관계에 있으므로 빈칸에는 과거분사가 와야 한다.
✎(해석) 유머러스한 어조로 쓰여져서 그 이야기는 즉시 독자의 주목을 끌었다. **정답 (b)**

3. would have died로 보아 본문은 가정법 과거완료이다. 따라서 If절에 'had+과거분사'가 와야 한다. If the cell had become...=Had the cell become..
✎(해석) 만약 세포가 완전하게 차단된다면, 그 환자는 죽게 될 텐데. **정답 (b)**

4. <have+사람+원형동사>를 묻는 문제이다. would는 기대를 나타낸다. 'Do to others'와 병행되는 것에도 힌트가 있다.
✎(해석) 황금률은 "다른 사람들이 네게 하기를 원하는 대로 다른 사람들에게 행하라"는 것이다. **정답 (c)**

5. get mad at …에게 화를 내다. get mad about …에 대해 화를 내다.
✎(해석) 나는 그가 그녀에게 그 전과 같이 화를 낸 것을 결코 보지 못했다 **정답 (d)**

6. 빈칸에는 대동사 does가 와야 한다. as yours does=as your system seems odd.
✎(해석) 나는 당신의 체제가 우리에게 이상한 것처럼 우리들의 체제가 당신에게 이상한 것처럼 보인다고 믿는다. **정답 (d)**

7. 빈칸에는 우선 동사가 와야 하므로 (b), (d)는 답에서 제외된다. to-동사와 maintain, increase와 병행된다.
✎(해석) 농업 경제학자들은 농작물의 질을 개선시키고, 토양의 질을 유지하며, 논밭의 생산량을 증가시키기 위해 일한다. **정답 (c)**

8. Enclosed please find …을 동봉하였으니 받아주시기 바랍니다.
✎(해석) 저희 학교 소책자와 지원양식을 동봉하였으니 받아주시기 바랍

니다. **정답 (b)**

9. pending 미정의(=not yet decided), …때까지는(=until) pend 매달리다, 미해결인 채로 있다
✍(해석) 바바라는 상임의장이 선출될 때까지 그 회의를 진행하기로 동의했다. **정답 (c)**

10. 빈칸에는 의미상 '비정상적인 성장을 거듭 한다'는 뜻을 나타내는 복수를 써야 한다. (b) growing은 동명사로서 복수형을 쓸 수 없다. (c) grown-up 성인
✍(해석) 암은 체세포가 종양이라 불리는 비정상적인 성장을 거듭하면서 통제할 수 없게 증식할 때 일어난다. **정답 (d)**

실력문제 2회

1. 빈칸 앞에 완전한 문장이 왔으므로, 빈칸에는 부사구, 부사절, 분사구문이 올 수 있다. 본문에서는 분사구문인 (d)가 정답이 된다.
✍(해석) 과학자들은 비정상적인 유전자를 결정하기를 희망한다. 그 다음에 가능하면 유전자 자체를 이용하여 질병 치료법을 개발하기를 원한다.
정답 (d)

2. 본문의 주어는 A black asphalt road, 동사는 grows이다. 따라서 빈칸에 관계대명사절이 들어가야 하며, 선행사가 사물이므로 which를 써야 한다.
✍(해석) 검은 아스팔트 도로는 햇볕을 가릴 수 있는 것이 아무 것도 없기 때문에 여름에는 매우 뜨겁게 된다. **정답 (d)**

3. give의 목적어가 없고, advice와 빈칸의 관계가 수동이므로 빈칸에는 과거분사가 온다.
✍(해석) 그에게 준 모든 충고는 무시되었다. 그는 들으려고도 하지 않았다.
정답 (c)

4. <be able to+동사원형>이므로 빈칸에는 동사원형이 와야 한다. (c)

access 입수하다, 이용하다(=get data from, or add data to, a database)
　✎(해석) 오늘날 사업의 장에서 당신이 필요할 때, 필요한 곳에 모든 형태의 커뮤니케이션을 이용할 수 있다는 것이 필수적이다. **정답 (c)**

5. <appear+to-동사>이므로 (d)는 답에서 제외된다. start는 자동사이므로 수동태가 될 수 없어서 (b)도 답에서 제외된다. when이하의 'spread'가 과거로 술어동사 'appears'보다 한 시제 앞서므로, 빈칸에는 완료부정사 (appears to have started)가 와야 한다.
　✎(해석) 가까운 인가에서 발생한 화재가 강한 바람을 등에 업고 메마른 땅을 통해 퍼져 나갔을 때 산불이 시작된 것 같다. **정답 (a)**

6. not even …조차도 아니다. out of breath(형용사구)로 보어의 역할을 하므로 맨 끝에 와야 한다. out of breath 숨을 헐떡이며(=breathless, panting)
　✎(해석) 탐은 매우 건강해. 막 6마일을 달리고도 숨도 헐떡이지 않아.
정답 (b)

7. <be+to-동사>는 '예정, 의무, 가능, 운명, 의도'를 나타낸다. 본문에서는 예정을 표시한다. 타동사(hold 개최하다)의 목적어가 없으므로 수동태가 와야 한다. be held 열리다
　✎(해석) 언론의 발표에 의하면 다음달 여기서 두 번째 연례 시상식 행사가 열릴 예정이다. **정답 (d)**

8. 표현을 묻는 문제이다. left no stone unturned 모든 조치를 다 취하다.
　(해석) 재정적 상황이 너무 절망적이어서 그는 모든 조치를 다 취했다.
정답 (a)

9. 주절에 있는 명사형 suggestion이 있으므로 that절에서는 동사원형이 와야 한다. should를 넣을 수 있다. parole 가석방하다 in the custody of … 의 보관[보호]하에 be sentenced to death 사형을 선고받다
　✎(해석) 그 죄수가 사형을 선고받아야 한다는 제안에 재판관이 동의했다.
정답 (d)

10. might not have been으로 보아 본문은 가정법 과거완료 구문이다. 빈칸에는 if절이 들어가야 한다. 여기서는 if it had not been for=had it not been for=but for(…이 없었더라면) 중에 하나가 들어가야 한다.
　✍(해석) 논쟁의 여지가 있는 수필을 감히 출판한 엘리자벳 피보디가 없었더라면, "시민 불복종의 의무에 관하여"라는 도로의 영향이 그렇게 광범위하게 미치지 못했을 것이다. **정답 (c)**

실력문제 3회

1. <tell+목적어+to-동사>구문을 묻는 문제이다. 같은 구문을 쓰는 동사는 advise, ask, beg, want, like, order, teach, allow, compel, force, oblige, enable, persuade 등이다. (c) refrain A from+V-ing(A가 …하지 못하게 하다)
　✍(해석) 환자가 잠이 들었기 때문에 그 의사는 우리에게 병실에 들어가지 말라고 말했다. **정답 (b)**

2. given…=when you consider[take into account] 당신이 …를 고려했을 때
　✍(해석) 존의 미래에 관한 불확실성을 고려했을 때, 나는 다른 선택이 거의 없었다. **정답 (b)**

3. 빈칸에는 동사가 와야 하므로 (a), (b)는 답에서 제외된다. '구성되다'의 표현: comprise, comprize, be comprised[comprized] of, be composed of, be constituted of, consist of
　✍(해석) 특별 내각 위원회는 딕, 윌리암스, 토니 뉴우톤으로 구성되었다.
　정답 (d)

4. 양보구문을 묻는 문제이다. Though I am interested=Interested as I am.
　✍(해석) 비록 내가 물리적 우주에 관심이 있을지라도, 내가 관심을 가지고 있는 것은 바로 인간, 인간의 사랑과 미움, 그의 고귀한 업적과 실패이다. **정답 (a)**

5. 빈칸에는 동격(명사구), 부사구가 올 수 있는데, 본문에서는 동격인 (b)는 의미상 들어갈 수 없다. 따라서 빈칸에는 부사구인 (a)가 답이 된다.

✍(해석) 높은 도덕적 지성을 가진 이 남자가 어떻게 그렇게 잔인한 범죄를, 그것도 한 번이 아니고 여러 번 저지를 수 있었을까? **정답 (a)**

6. 분사구문에서 주절의 주어(she)와 동사의 관계가 능동 관계이고, 뒤에 목적어가 있기 때문에 빈칸에는 (c) considering이 와야 한다.
✍(해석) 아직도 그녀가 얼마나 아름다운 것을 고려해 보면, 젊었을 때는 매우 아름다웠음에 틀림없다. **정답 (c)**

7. '불가능하지는 않더라도'의 표현은 'if not impossible'이다. [참고] few, if any(있다고 해도 거의 없다). seldom, if ever(있다 해도 거의 드물다)
✍(해석) 인도에서 결혼한 여자가 직업을 가지는 것은 불가능하지는 않더라도 매우 어렵다. **정답 (d)**

8. pertain은 자동사이므로 전치사(to)가 붙고, 명사를 수식할 때 현재분사 형태를 취한다. pertain to 속하다, 관계하다
✍(해석) 사람이 아무리 많은 지식을 가지고 있다 할지라도, 문제에 관계된 사실들을 알지 못한다면 현명한 선택을 할 수 없다. **정답 (d)**

9. might as well A as B (B하는 것보다 A하는 것이 낫다) You might as well throw money away as spend it in gambling.(도박에 돈을 쓸 바에야 버리는 편이 낫다)
✍(해석) 당신은 나의 주장을 포기하라고 권고할 바에야 나의 재산을 포기하라고 권고하는 것이 낫다. **정답 (a)**

10. 콤마 앞에 분사구문이 와야 하고, 타동사 reserve(예약하다)의 목적어가 없으므로 수동태가 되어야 하므로 답은 (d) being reserved가 된다. 본문을 분사구문으로 다르게 표현하면 Having reserved the rooms at the hotel이 된다.
✍(해석) 호텔에 방을 예약하고서 우리는 가로등이 켜진 직후에 식당으로 가서 편안하고 만족스러운 저녁을 먹었다. **정답 (d)**

실력문제 4회

1. be worth+V-ing …할 가치가 있다(=be worthwhile to-동사, be worthy of+V-ing)
✎(해석) 교육이란 훌륭한 것이지만, 가끔 알 가치가 있는 어떤 것도 가르칠 수 없는 것임을 기억하는 것이 좋다. 정답 (a)

2. 빈칸에는 시간의 경과를 나타내는 in이 와야 한다. (a) around thirty minutes 약 30 분 (b) nearby 가까이의 (d) by는 행동의 완료를 나타낸다
✎(해석) 제임스는 지금쯤 거기에 있기로 되어 있다. 그래서 약 30 분만 있으면 여기에 올 것으로 생각된다. **정답 (c)**

3. 문맥상 빈칸에는 '대조'의 뜻을 가진 whereas(반면에)가 와야 한다.
✎(해석) 친구와 함께 있을 때는 매우 흥분하고 말이 많지만, 반면에 그는 자기 아내와 있을 때는 대부분 조용하고 차분하다. **정답 (d)**

4. 빈칸에는 Judging from의 의미상 주어로 사람 주어가 와야 한다. (a)는 의미상 답에서 제외된다.
✎(해석) 그가 외벽 작업을 한 것으로 판단해 보면, 나는 그가 내장을 어떻게 할지 모르겠다. **해답 (b)**

5. <too+형용사+for+명사>(너무나 …해서 …할 수 없다)구문을 묻는 문제이다.
A를 B로 간주하다: regard A as B=think of A as B=look upon A as B
✎(해석) 전화기가 비교적 새로운 고안물이었던 과거에, 사람들은 그것이 중요한 커뮤니케이션을 하기에는 너무 순간적인 것을 간주하는 경우가 자주 있었다. **정답 (d)**

6. 빈칸에는 주어가 와야 하므로 (b), (d)는 답에서 제외된다. 오늘의 소유격은 today's이다.
✎(해석) 오늘의 기사 제목은 무서운 속도로 시간이 흘러감에 따라 내일

이 역사가 된다. **정답 (c)**

7. 본문은 빈칸에서 better job까지가 주부, is가 동사, that절이 보어인 문장이다. 따라서 동사가 있는 (a), (d)는 답에서 제외된다. 빈칸에는 주어가 될 수 있는 명사구가 와야 하므로 (b)도 답에서 제외된다.
✎(해석) 도심의 학교들이 더 좋은 성적을 내지 못하는 제일의 이유는 부모들이 충분한 지원을 하지 않는 것에 있다.
정답 (c)

8. 빈칸에는 의미상 '…이 없는'의 뜻인 free of가 와야 한다. (a) free of[from]=without. (b) nothing of 조금도 …이 없는[아닌] He is nothing of a poet 그에게는 조금도 시인다운 데가 없다.
✎(해석) 우리가 만드는 모든 식품은 인공조미료와 색소가 전혀 없다.
정답 (a)

9. <조동사+부사+본동사>의 어순을 묻는 문제이다.
✎(해석) 그는 물질적 이득이나 소유에 관심이 없었기 때문에 자신의 작품들을 공짜로 주는 일이 자주 있었다. **정답 (d)**

10. 빈칸에는 peace process를 수식하는 형용사가 와야 하므로 (a), (b)는 답에서 제외된다. 의미상 '위협받고 있는'의 뜻을 가진 (d) threatened가 답이다.
✎(해석) 유엔 사무총장은 어떤 비용을 치르더라도 위협받고 있는 평화 협상을 지속해야 할 필요성을 강조하며, 양측을 촉구해서 협상 테이블로 돌아오라고 했다. **정답 (d)**

◉ 문법 · Part III

실력문제 1회

1. Part Ⅱ [실력문제 4회] 1번 해설을 참고할 것.
✎(해석) (a) A: 다른 볼 만한 것이 뭐 있니?

(b) B: 서부 영화를 상영하고 있는 것 같아.
(c) A: 그것을 보아도 괜찮니?
(d) B: 글쎄, 나는 야구를 정말로 보고 싶었어.
정답 (a) to watch→ watching.

2. no는 형용사이고 not은 부사인 것에 주의할 것.
✍(해석) (a) A: 내가 교양이 없다는 것을 빗대는 것이니?
(b) B: 나는 빗댄 것이 전혀 없어. 신발이 맞으면 신으라는 것이지.
(c) A: 잠깐만 기다려! 나도 참을 만큼 참았어! 왜 그렇게 반대로 나오는 거야?
(d) B: 반대로 나오는 것이 아니야. 나는 급해. 그것뿐이야.
정답 (a) I'm no cultured→ I'm not cultured.

3. 분명한 때를 나타내는 부사는 현재완료와 함께 쓸 수 없다.
✍(해석) (a) A: 안녕, 존! 무슨 일이 있니? 오래 간만이야.
(b) B: 지난주에 형 집에 가려고 뉴욕에 갔어.
(c) A: 언제 뉴욕에서 돌아왔니?
(d) B: 어제 막 돌아왔지.
정답 (c) have you got back→ did you get back.

4. So[As] far as I'm concerned=As for me=For my part (나로서는, 내 생각에는).
✍(해석) (a) A: 이런, 우리 차가 진흙에 빠졌어요.
(b) B: 어떻게 해야 하지요?
(c) A: 다른 차를 기다리던지 내려서 밀던지 해야지요.
(d) B: 나로서는, 우리가 내려서 차를 진흙에서 꺼내는 것이 좋을 것 같아요.
정답 (d) concerning→ concerned.

5. '나에게 그것을 사 주다'의 표현: buy me it=buy it for me.
✍(해석) (a) A: 네가 끼고 있는 반지가 정말 예쁘구나.
(b) B: 고마워. 나도 역시 그렇게 생각해.

(c) A: 어디서 샀니?
(d) B: 내 남자 친구가 사 주었어.

정답 (d) My boyfriend bought it me→ My boyfriend bought it to me.

실력문제 2회

1. <의문사+do you think+주어+동사>구문이다. 이런 형태를 취하는 동사는 think류 동사로 believe, suppose, imagine, guess 등이며, Yes나 No로 대답 할 수 없다. [참고] 'Do you know+주어+동사'구문과 비교해서 기억할 것.
✍(해석)(a) A: 내 차 다 고쳤나요?
(b) B: 못 고쳤어요. 아직 부품을 못 구했어요.
(c) A: 아, 그거 골치 아픈 일이군요. 언제 준비될 것 같은가요?
(d) B: 글쎄요. 오늘 오전에 부품을 구할 것입니다. 내일 저녁에 이 차를 가져갈 수 있어요.

정답 (c) Do you think when it'll be ready?→ When do you think it'll be ready?

2. 과거에 이루지 못한 사실에 대한 후회는 <should have+과거분사>를 쓴다.
✍(해석)(a) A: 다음 도로에서 우회전 해.
(b) B: 좋아. 내가 회전하는 솜씨가 좋아지고 있는 것 같아.
(c) A: 나쁘지는 않았지만, 아까 네 거리에서 정지 신호였어.
(d) B: 회전하기 전에 정지했어야 했다는 말이지?

정답 (d) must→ should.

3. on the other hand 반면에(=from the opposed point of view)
✍(해석)(a) A: 이 모든 새 교통 법규들이 매우 귀찮아.
(b) B: 나도 그래요.
(c) A: 반면에 그것들이 사회의 유익한 목적에 도움이 되는 것 같아.
(d) B: 맞아요. 적극적으로 생각해야겠지요.

정답 (c) In other hands→ On the other hand.

4. '시간이 좋다'의 표현: The hours are good. kind of 다소(=rather) to

top it all 게다가

    ✍(해석) (a) A: 무슨 일을 하시나요?

           (b) B: 시내 호텔에서 응접을 맡고 있어요.

           (c) A: 그것을 좋아하세요? 내 말은 하루 온 종일 앉아서 보내자면 좀 지루하지 않아요?

           (d) B: 사실은 시간이 좋고 수입도 그렇게 나쁘지 않아요. 게다가 상관하는 사람도 없어요.

    정답 (d) the hours is good→ the hours are good.

5. <for+불특정한 기간>이 온다. (예) for a long time, for a week <during+특정한 기간이 온다. (예) during last winter, during Christmas

    ✍(해석) (a) A: 그 시험 문제들은 놀라우리 만큼 쉬웠어.

           (b) B: 그래. 하지만 그처럼 오랜 시간 동안 집중하는 것은 어려워.

           (c) A: 맞아. 세 시간 짜리 시험은 어떤 것이라도 힘들어.

           (d) B: 우리 모두 합격했으면 좋겠다.

    정답 (b) during→ for

실력문제 3회

1. out of question 틀림없이, 분명히(=clearly) out of the question 불가능한(=impossible)

    ✍(해석) (a) A: 즉시 떠나는 것이 좋겠어요.

           (b) B: 뭐가 그렇게 바빠요?

           (c) A: 10시에 지도교수를 만나야 해요.

           (d) B: 그것은 불가능해요. 이미 10시 30분이에요.

    정답 (d) out of question→ out of the question.

2. '해고되다'의 표현: get fired[sacked]; be fired; be dismissed[discharged]; be dropped from the pay-roll

    ✍(해석) (a) A: 일어나. 거의 9시야.

           (b) B: 나를 좀 더 일찍 깨우지 그랬어요.

(c) A: 내가 깨울 때 일어나지 않았어.

(d) B: 내가 해고되기를 원하니?

정답 (d) get fire→ get fired.

3. '직업이 무엇입니까?'의 표현: What do you do (for a living)?; What's your occupation[job/ line]?; What business are you in?; What kind work are you?

✐(해석)(a) A: 당신에 관해서 좀 말해 줄 수 있어요?

(b) B: 어디에서부터 시작할지 모르겠어요. 무엇을 알고 싶으세요?

(c) A: 글쎄요, 직업이 무엇이지요?

(d) B: 수학 선생이에요.

정답 (c) What are you doing?→ What do you do (for a living)?

4. I hope that it'll get better=I hope so.

✐(해석)(a) A: 왜 우울하니? 새 학교가 마음에 안 들어?

(b) B: 예. 모두 나를 괴롭혀요.

(c) A: 걱정하지 마. 아마도 새로 전학 왔기 때문일 거야. 기운을 내, 좋아질 거야.

(d) B: 저도 그러길 바래요.

정답 (d) I hope it.→ I hope so.

5. 선행사 the reason 다음에 관계부사 why 또는 for which(전치사+관계대명사=관계부사를 써야 한다.

✐(해석)(a) A: 내일 하루 쉬어도 될까요?

(b) B: 안될 것 같은데요.

(c) A: 알아요, 하지만 내가 부탁하는 이유는 남편이 수술을 하러 병원에 갑니다.

(d) B: 이해가 갑니다. 그렇다면 그렇게 해도 될 것 같아요.

정답 (c) the reason which→ the reason why 또는 the reason for which.

실력문제 4회

1. '다이어트를 하다'의 표현: be on a diet. lose weight 살을 빼다 gain weight 살이 찌다

&(해석)(a) A: 샌디야, 좋아 보이는구나!
　　　　(b) B: 그래? 그렇게 말해줘서 고마워.
　　　　(c) A: 무슨 일이니? 살을 뺀 거야?
　　　　(d) B: 사실은 다이어트해서 5파운드를 뺐어.
　　정답 (d) in a diet→ on a diet.

2. '…가 …하는 것을 돕다'의 표현: help+사람+out with+사물. What's on your mind? 무슨 생각을 하나요? be all thumbs 손재주가 없다(=be clumsy)

&(해석)(a) A: 안녕, 빌! 나와 이야기할 시간 좀 있니?
　　　　(b) B: 물론이지. 무슨 일이야?
　　　　(c) A: 생일카드를 만들어야 해. 네가 그것을 도와주길 바래.
　　　　(d) B: 네가 손재주가 없는 것을 내가 알아.
　　정답 (c) help me out for it→ help me out with it.

3. <get+사물+과거분사>, <get+사람+to-동사>구문을 묻는 문제이다. mix-up 혼란, 혼전(=confusion; tangle) straighten out 해결하다, 똑바르게 하다, 정리하다(=correct a mistake; put right for use or action; reform)

&(해석)(a) A: 의사가 지난 달 우리가 연례 검진 받은 청구서를 보냈어.
　　　　(b) B: 정말로? 우리 보험으로 해결하기로 되어 있는데.
　　　　(c) A: 의사에게 전화를 걸어 다소 혼동이 있었는지 알아보는 것이 좋겠어.
　　　　(d) B: 좋은 생각이야. 이 문제를 해결 할 때까지 청구서의 지불을 미루자.
　　정답 (d) straighten→ straightened.

4. '…에 있다'는 뜻인 lie는 2형식 동사(불완전자동사)이므로 보어가 와야 한다. 보어가 될 수 있는 것은 명사와 형용사이다. intensive care unit 중환자실

&(해석)(a) A: 환자에게 무슨 일이 생겼어요?

(b) B: 그가 침대에서 의식을 잃은 것을 발견했어요.
(c) A: 그는 즉시 중환자실로 가야만 해요.
(d) B: 그를 볼 수 있나요?

정답 (b) unconsciously→ unconscious.

5. another는 some, other가 수식할 수 없다. 'another+단수명사'도 기억하자.
✍(해석)(a) A: 오늘밤에 저녁 외식하러 가고 싶나요?
(b) B: 오늘밤 에요? 못할 것 같아요. 늦게까지 일해야 하거든요.
(c) A: 안 됐군요.
(d) B: 아마 다음 기회에 저녁 식사하러 갈 수 있겠지요.

정답 (d) some another time→ another time 또는 some other time.

◉ 문법 · Part Ⅳ

실력문제 1회

1. ✍(해석) (a) 운동은 심장에 유익하다. (b) 캘리포니아의 의사들이 22년 동안 연구를 했다. (c) 그들은 육체노동에 종사하는 사람들이 다른 사람들보다 심장마비를 덜 겪는다는 것을 발견했다. (d) 이 활동적인 사람들은 적절한 속도로 항상 일한다.
뒤에 복수명사가 왔으므로 양의 개념(less)을 쓸 수 없다.

정답 (c) less→ fewer.

2. ✍(해석) (a) 오래 전에 많은 사람들은 지구가 둥글다고 믿었다. (b) 만일 지구가 둥글고 어떤 사람이 미국에 서 있다면, 중국에 서 있는 사람은 거꾸로 서 있어야 한다. (c) 만일 중국에 있는 사람이 거꾸로 서 있지 않다면, 미국에 있는 사람이 거꾸로 서 있는 셈이다. (d) 이와 같은 생각 때문에 사람들이 지구가 둥글다고 믿기 어렵게 만들었다.
<타동사+it+형용사/명사+for+의미상 주어+to-동사>구문을 묻는 문제이다. 여기서 it는 가목적어이다. 이와 같이 쓰이는 동사에는 make, find, think, believe 등이 있다.

정답 (d) made difficult for people→ made it difficult for people.

3. ✍(해석) (a) 하와이는 여러 개의 섬으로 구성되어 있다. (b) 이 주는 다른 미국 주들과는 상당히 떨어져 있다. (c) 그 주에는 많은 관광객들을 이끄는 흥미로운 해양생활이 있다. (d) 생활비는 매우 비싸다.

'-로 구성되어 있다'의 표현: be composed of, be made up of, consist of, comprise

정답 (a) composes of→ is composed of.

4. ✍(해석) (a) 이해하기 어려운 것은 국민들이 어떻게 나라의 경제적 사정을 불평하면서도 자신들의 습관을 변화하지 않으려는가 하는 것이다. (b) 최근 통계에 의하면, 대부분의 한국인들이 여전히 전과 같이 소비한다는 것이다. (c) 사람들이 너무 쉽게 잊어버린 것일까? (d) 이 위기에서 벗어나기 위해서 아끼고 절약해야 한다는 것을 언제 알게 될까?

본문의 주어는 What is difficult to understand이고, how people can 이하가 보어이므로 동사 is가 빠져 있다.

정답 (a) What is difficult to understand how→ What is difficult to understand is how.

5. ✍(해석) (a) 일본인들에게 목욕은 몸을 깨끗이 하는 방법만은 아니다. (b) 그것은 피곤한 긴장이 많은 하루의 피로를 풀어주고 몸을 회복시키는 방법이 기도 하다. (c) 일본인들은 매우 오랫동안 온수목욕하기를 좋아한다. (d) 욕조에 있을 때 그들은 음악을 듣거나 책읽기를 좋아한다.

'목욕하다'의 표현: take a bath; bathe

정답 (c) make→ take.

실력문제 2회

1. ✍(해석) (a) 외관상 분별없는 십대 아들이나 딸과 대면하게 됐을 때의 첫 번째 조치는 그 특정 문제를 인식하는 것이다. (b) 아무리 형편없는 이유가 할지라도 당신의 아이들에게 그들의 모든 구실들을 당신에게 털어놓을 기회를 주는 것은 문제의 근원에 다가서는 데 도움이 될 것이다. (c) 표면적

인 문제들은 좀더 깊은 내적인 문제에 대한 지표가 될 뿐만 아니라 기본적인 문제의 지표가 된다. (d) 성공적인 부모가 되기 위해서는 문제의 핵심에 접근하는 대화기술을 사용하고 좋은 관계를 유지시켜야 한다.

<관사+부사+형용사+명사>의 어순을 묻는 문제이다.

정답 (a) a seeming irrational teenage son→ a seemingly irrational teenage son.

2. ✍(해석) (a) 어린아이에게 언어를 배우는 것은 시간이 오래 걸리는 일이다. (b) 갑자기 말문이 터질 수도 있고 학습속도가 느려지는 기간도 있다. (c) 어린아이는 첫돌 무렵에 말을 하기 시작한다. (d) 세 살이 되면 어린아이들은 900단어를 알고 그 단어들을 써서 서너 단어로 된 문장을 말할 수 있다.

<전치사+관계대명사>의 용법을 묻는 문제이다. '-동안'을 나타내는 전치사는 during이다.

정답 (b) of→ during.

3. ✍(해석) (a) 새 플라스틱으로 만들어진 제품들은 샴푸나 세제를 담는 병들이 포함된다. (b) 이런 병들이 버려지면 재활용, 즉 같은 형태로 다시 사용할 수 있다. (c) 그러나, 그것들이 매립지에 버려질 수도 있는데 이럴 경우 현재의 플라스틱과는 달리 그것들은 흙 속에서 세균에 의해 소화되어 썩어 없어진다. (d) 매립지와 태우거나 생물학적으로 부패시킨 다른 폐기 용기들로부터 나온 산화물들은 대기 중에 서서히 방출된다.

dispose of (…을 제거하다)는 동사구가 수동태가 되면 be disposed of가 된다.

정답 (c) be disposed in→ be disposed of.

4. ✍(해석) (a) 이산화탄소가 태양 빛과 반응할 때 오존 스모그가 생긴다. (b) 그 결과는 스모그 즉 우리가 보고 냄새 맡을 수 있는 공기 오염이다. (c) 너무 지나친 오존 스모그는 두통을 가져오고 호흡을 어렵게 한다. (d) 오존 스모그를 줄이는 한 가지 길은 수송이라는 세탁 수단을 사용하기 시작하는 것이다.

본문에서 make는 5형식 동사로 쓰였다. 5형식은 <주어+동사+목적어+목적보어>이다.

정답 (c) makes difficult breathing→ makes breathing difficult.

5. ✍(해석) (a) 자이언트 팬더는 전 세계적으로 어린이들과 동물 애호가들의 사랑을 받는다. (b) 많은 사람들에게 그것은 또한 다른 많은 종류의 동물들이 처한 슬픈 상황을 상징한다. (c) 비록 잘 알려져 있고 사랑을 받고는 있지만, 팬더는 천천히 멸종되어 가고 있다. (d) 현재 전 세계에 남아 있는 야생 팬더는 약 1,230마리에 불과하다.

타동사(leave: 남기다)가 뒤에 목적어가 없으면 과거분사를 써야 한다.

정답 (d) leaving→ left.

실력문제 3회

1. ✍(해석) (a) 다이옥신은 플루토늄과 마찬가지로 매우 유해한 물질이다. (b) 두 물질 다 주먹만한 크기의 양만으로도 전 세계 인구를 죽이기에 충분하다. (c) 차이점은 플루토늄이 아직 까지 상대적으로 드물고, 분리해 내기가 어려우며 잘 통제되고 있다는 점이다. (d) 반면에 다이옥신은 원예용 화학물질에서 많이 발견되고 있으며 오용하기가 쉽다.

<either+단수명사>를 묻는 문제이다.

정답 (b) chemicals→ chemical.

2. ✍(해석) (a) 마리오는 칼멘이 서 있는 현관으로 서서히 접근했다. (b) 그의 조심스러운 발걸음은 가슴이 뛰는 것과 어울렸다. (c) 그의 눈은 반짝이는 불처럼 그녀에게 고정되었다. (d) 무엇인가를 말하려는 것처럼, 그는 입술을 다소 벌린 채로 그녀 앞에 섰다.

타동사 open이 목적어가 없고, her lips와의 관계가 수동이므로 과거분사가 와야 한다.

정답 (d) opening→ opened.

3. ✍(해석) (a) 빛은 매우 빠르게 이동한다. (b) 우리는 뇌우가 있을 때마다 섬광에 의해서 생긴 천둥소리를 듣기 전에 번갯불을 본다. (c) 번갯불에서 나온 빛은 거의 즉각적으로 우리에게 도달한다. (d) 천둥소리가 우리에게 도달하는데 수초가 걸릴 수도 있다.

절대 3형식 동사(절대타동사) 즉 뒤에 전치사가 오면 틀리는 동사를 기억하자.

(예) approach, accompany, attend, address, await, challenge, enter inhabit, escape, marry, mention, resemble, join, phone, discuss, contact, kiss, survive, greet, obey, reach.

정답 (c) reaches to→ reach.

4. ✍(해석) (a) 비디오게임은 요즈음 아이들의 삶의 중요한 부분이 되어 왔다. (b) 그러나 아이들에 대한 비디오게임의 영향에 관해 생각해 볼 때, 비디오 산업에 이중적인 기준이 있다. (c) 제작자들은 아이들의 학습 기술을 개발하는데 도움을 주는 교육적 게임을 보급하는 일이 자주 있다. (d) 그러나 그들은 폭력성 게임들이 행동과 태도에 나쁜 영향을 미칠 수 있다는 논의를 무시한다.

'영향을 미치다'의 표현: have an influence[effect/ impact] on; affect; impinge on. trumpet 포고하다(=proclaim loudly), 퍼뜨리다 discount 무시하다(=disregard)

정답 (d) have bad influence on→ have a bad influence on.

5. ✍(해석) (a) 민족마다 제 나름의 도박하는 방식이 있는데 포커는 미국의 전통이다. (b) 이것은 기술과 운, 그리고 기꺼이 모험을 거는 정신을 요구하는 카드 게임이다. (c) 옛 서부에서는 이것이 중요한 삶의 일부로 생각되었다. (d) 많은 영화들은 총싸움이 나기 전에 포커테이블에 있던 카우보이들 사이에 긴장된 갈등의 순간들이나 마지막 패를 보이는 장면들을 보여 준다.

<willingness/willing+to-동사>구문을 묻는 문제이다. 명사나 형용사 뒤에 오는 전치사나 부정사를 기억할 필요가 있다. 동격을 표현할 때 쓰는 명사 (동격명사)도 알아야 한다. <동격명사+of/that절>의 구문을 쓴다. (예) ① 가능명사:possibility, probability ② 희망명사: hope, intention ③ 사고명사: idea, thought, notion ④ 입증명사: proof, evidence. <decide[tend/plan/offer]+to-동사>구문과 그 동사의 명사형도 같은 구문을 쓴다. 즉 decision/tendency/plan도 뒤에 'to-동사'가 온다. take chances 모험을 하다 showdown (포커에서) 손에 든 패를 전부 보임, 결판, 공개

정답 (b) willingness of taking chances→ willingness to take chances.

실력문제 4회

1. ✎(해석) (a) 엄마 쥐와 아기 쥐가 마루를 가로질러 달리고 있다가 고양이가 내는 소리를 들었다. (b) 엄마 쥐와 아기 쥐는 몹시 놀랐으나, 움직이지 않고 있었다. 엄마 쥐가 큰 소리로 "멍멍" 하고 외쳤다. (c) 그 고양이는 도망을 쳤다. (d) 그런 후 엄마 쥐가 아기 쥐를 향해 돌아서서 "자, 아가야, 제 2 외국어가 얼마나 중요한지 알겠지?"라고 말했다.

see의 목적어로 how이하의 절이 왔으므로, how이하는 간접의문문이다. 간접의문문의 어 은 <의문사+주어+동사>이다.

정답 (d) how important is a second language→ how important a second language is.

2. ✎(해석) (a) 어떤 연어들은 그들이 태어난 강으로부터 수천 킬로미터를 여행한다. (b) 과학자들은 연어가 지구의 자기장과 해류를 감지함으로써 바다 속을 항해한다고 생각한다. (c) 그들은 대부분의 연어가 알을 낳기 위해 그들이 부화됐던 강으로 되돌아온다는 것을 알고 있다. (d) 연안에 도착한 후 연어는 고향의 강 냄새를 분명하게 기억하고 그 냄새를 따라 간다.

관계대명사가 있는 문장은 반드시 체크할 필요가 있다. 본문의 (c)에서 which이하가 완전한 문장이므로, which앞에 전치사 in이 와야 한다.

spawn 알을 낳다, 산란하다(=produce or deposit eggs, sperm, or young)
odor 냄새(=a smell; scant; aroma)

정답 (c) which→ in which.

3. ✎(해석) (a) 헤르메스 신이 매우 경건한 숭배자에게 황금 알을 낳는 거위 한 마리를 주었다. (b) 그러나 그 사람은 너무 성급한 나머지 조금씩 생겨나는 재물을 기다릴 수가 없었다. 그리하여 거위의 뱃속은 틀림없이 순금으로 되어있을 것이라고 생각하고는 서둘러 거위를 죽였다. (c) 그의 희망은 사라져 버렸고 뿐만 아니라 그는 더 이상 황금 알을 얻지 못했다. (d) 왜냐하면 그는 거위의 뱃속에서 평범한 고깃덩어리와 핏덩이 외에는 아무것도 발견하지 못했기 때문이다.

because는 이유를 나타내는 부사절을 이끄는 종속접속사이므로 주절이

있어야 한다. for는 이유를 나타내는 등위접속사이다. by[in] driblets 조금씩
정답 (d) Because→ For.

4. ✍(해석) (a) 서구의 만화는 오랜 동안 정치, 사회적인 문제와 연관을 맺어왔다. (b) 예컨대, 전시에는 만화가 훌륭한 선전을 퍼뜨리는 도구임이 입증되기도 했다. (c) 오늘날 만화는 다양한 사회 문제들뿐만 아니라 정치와 정부에 대한 예리한 논평들을 하는데 쓰여 지는 일이 자주 있다. (d) 이런 방법으로 현대의 만화는 유럽과 미국에서 사람들에게 영향을 주는 매우 강력한 힘이 되어 왔다.
<a variety of+복수명사>를 묻는 문제이다. a variety of 다양한(=various, assorted)
정답 (c) social matter→ social matters.

5. ✍(해석) (a) 다음은 1950년대 미국의 조그마한 도시에서 소년으로 살아간다는 것이 어떤 것이었나를 이해할 수 있게 해 주는 영화의 이야기이다. (b) 어느 여름 날 네 명의 소년이 며칠 동안 사라졌던 한 소년을 찾기 위해서 숲으로 들어간다. (c) 흥분되는 여행을 통해 소년들은 힘을 합해 서로를 돕는다. (d) 이틀간의 여행으로 소년들 각자에게 특별한 추억이 생긴다.
'명사+명사'에서 앞의 명사는 형용사적으로 사용되어 단수로 써야 한다.
go off 출발하다(=leave, depart), 도망치다(=flee), 죽다(=die), 발사[폭발]되다(=explode, blow up, discharge, blast, set off, detonate), 실신[기절]하다(=faint, lose consciousness, swoon)
정답 (d) two-days trip→ two-day trip.

● 2. 어휘- Part I

실력문제 1회

1. ✍(해석) A: 다음 수업을 대비해서 무엇을 할까요?
B: 지금까지 했던 것을 복습하는 것이 좋겠다.
(a) go over 복습하다(=review, brush up, runover, rehearse), 검사하다

(=examine, inspect, look into, investigate, check up on) (c) turn over 뒤집다(=upset turn down, overthrow, overturn, capsize), 양도하다(=transfer, hand over, make over, give away, deliver, bequeath), 위임하다(=delegate, entrust), 숙고하다(=think over, meditate, ponder, reflect on, dwell on, mull over, deliberate, muse, speculate, contemplate) 정답 (a) go

2. ✎(해석) A: 여보세요, 주디 좀 바꿔 주세요.
 B: 잠시만 기다리세요. 금방 바꿔 드리지요.
 (c) hang on <전화를> 끊지 않고 기다리다, 일을 끈기 있게 하다(=listen attentively; hold on; go on; persist; persevere; stick it out; stand out) (a) hang loose 축 처지다, 차분히 있다 (b) hang up 전화를 끊다, 걸다 지체시키다(=end a telephone call; ring off; put the phone down; put on a hanger, hook, etc.; delay) (d) hang out 시간을 보내다(=spend much time)
 정답 (c) hang on

3. ✎(해석) A: 해리스, 안 돼 보여. 무슨 문제가 있니?
 B: 어제와 오늘에 네 과목 시험이 있어서 지난 주 매일 네 시간도 못 잤어. 막 아플 것 같아.
 on the verge[point, brink, edge, threshold] of 막-하려고 하다.
 breakdown 고장, 몰락, 쇠약(=a failure of health) (a) boundary 경계, 한계(=limit) (d) border 가장자리, 경계(=edge; margin)
 정답 (b) verge

4. ✎(해석) A: 네가 다시 직업을 바꾸었다고 들었어.
 B: 영원히 같은 일상적인 일에 집착하고 싶지 않아.
 (b) stick to …에 달라붙다, …에 집착하다, …을 고집하다(=cling to, adhere to, hold to, cleave to, attach to; persist in, insist on) (d) linger 남아 있다, 꾸물거리다
 정답 (b) stick

5. ✎(해석) A: 그녀를 만난 적이 있어요?
 B: 전에 어디에서 만나본 것이 확실해요. 하지만 기억이 안 나요.

(a) locate 위치를 …에 정하다, 알아내다(=find out) (c) place 확인하다, 기억해 내다(=recognize; identify)
정답 (c) place

6. ☞(해석) A: 무슨 소리를 하는 거야? 나는 이해가 안 돼.
B: 내가 거의 한 시간 동안 말했는데도 아직도 이해가 안 되니?
'이해가 되니?'의 표현: Do you understand?; Do you follow me?; Do you get it?; Do you get the picture?; Are you with me? (c) have a say 참견하다
정답 (d) get the picture

7. ☞(해석) A: 내 텔레비전을 고칠 수 있나요?
B: 어떻게 고치는지 전혀 모르겠는데요.
'전혀 모르겠다'의 표현: I don't have the vaguest[faintest/ slightest] idea.; I'm clueless ; I don't have a clue.
정답 (d) slightest

8. ☞(해석) A: 왜 너는 그렇게 흥분하니?
B: 벨베티 비누에 대하여 멋있는 시구를 지으면 오천 달러를 타지. 여하튼 무슨 짓을 해서라도 내가 타려고 해.
(b) by hook or by crook 무슨 짓을 해서라도, 어떻게 해서라도(=by any means, honest or dishonest; in any way necessary) (a) as the crow flies 직선거리로(=in a straight, direct line; by the most direct way; along a straight line between two places) (c) up in the air 미정의(=in midair, in limbo, not settled, uncertain, undecided), 흥분하여, 화나서(=in great anger or excitement) (d) down in the bumps 풀이 죽어, 기가 죽어(=down in the mouth, depressed, sad or discouraged, gloomy, dejected)
정답 (b) by hook or crook

9. ☞(해석) A: 세탁소에서 내 코트를 가져 왔나요?
B: 잊어버려서 미안해요. 깜빡했어요.
slip one's mind[memory] 잊어버리다(=forget) (a) slid: slide(미끄러지

다)의 과거, 과거분사 (b) split 쪼개다, 분열시키다(=separate; break or tear apart; disunite) (d) shift 이동시키다, 방향을 바꾸다, 꾸려나가다(=get along)

정답 (c) slipped

10. ✍(해석) A: 그 노래 제목이 무엇이지요?
B: 제가 제목을 아는 것일 텐데요. 혀끝에서 뱅뱅 돌고 기억이안 나는군요.

on[at] the tip of one's tongue 하마터면 말이 나올 뻔하여, 말이 입 끝에서 뱅뱅 돌 뿐 생각이 안 나(=almost spoken; at th point of being said: almost remembered; at the point where one can almost say it but cannot because it is forgotten) from the bottom of the[one's] heart 충심으로, 진심으로(=with all one's heart; with great feeling; sincerely)

정답 (d) tip

실력문제 2회

1. ✍(해석) A: 새 입체 음향 시스템을 조립하는 것을 도와줄 수 있어요?
B: 물론이지요. 그것은 내게 쉬운 일이지요.

(c) hook up 조립하다(=connect) (a) build up 확립하다, 증진시키다 (b) take up 차지하다(=occupy, cover), 집어 올리다(=raise, lift, pick up), 태우다, 싣다(=load), 시작하다, 맡다(=assume), 공부하다(=study) (d) make up 구성하다(=constitute, form), 조립하다(=put together, construct), 편찬하다 (=compile), 꾸며내다(=invent, fabricate, forge), 보충하다(=compensate for, make good), 중재하다(=come to terms, become reconciled, compromise), 화장하다(=put on cosmetics, make one's toilet)

정답 (c) hook up

2. ✍(해석) A: 직장에서 당신 친구를 자동차로 데리러 가야 하나요?
B: 네, 또 가야 합니다. 매일 오후에 시내 중심가를 간다는 것은 지긋지긋하군요.

'진절머리가 나다'의 표현: I'm fed up with it[him].; I've sick and tired of it.; I've had enough (of it).; I've had it up to here. (a) shut up 잠그다, 감금하다, 간수하다, 입을 다물다

정답 (b) fed

3. ✍(해석) A: 탐과 주디가 싸웠다는 걸 들었니?
B: 그래? 그 애들은 무언가 정말로 화가 났음에 틀림없어.
대화의 의미상 빈칸에는 '화가 난'의 뜻을 가진 (d)가 들어가야 한다.
(d) upset 뒤집힌, 타도된, 엉망인(=tipped over; overthrown, defeated; disturbed, disordered) (a) relieve 경감하다, 안도케 하다, 구제하다, 돋보이게 하다(=ease; free from; give or bring aid to) (b) appreciative 감상적인, 감사하고 (c) thrill 감동[감격, 흥분]시키다, 떨게 하다(=quiver, tremble), 오싹하다

정답 (d) upset

4. ✍(해석) A: 당신은 왜 토론 중에 그 질문을 제기했지요?
B: 내가 제기하지 않았어요. 존이 했지요.
(c) bring up 양육하다(=raise, rear, educate), 내놓다(=raise, introduce, produce, advance, bring forward), 토하다(=vomit, throw up) (a) piece together …을 잇다, 종합하다 (b) set up 세우다(=erect, put up), 설립하다(=establish, found, organize, institute, inaugurate), 건설[조립]하다(=construct; assemble, put together) (d) hustle out 서둘러 만들어 내다 (=crank out, hammer out)

정답 (c) bring

5. ✍(해석) A: 2년의 휴가 후 일터로 돌아온 것에 관해 어떻게 생각해?
B: 지금 일에 적응하여 리듬을 익힐 수 없지만, 곧 괜찮아 질 거야.
get into the swing of …에 적응하여 리듬을 익히다.
get[have/see] the hang of …의 요령을 터득하다, …을 이해하다 (=learn[have] the knack of; understand the meaning or idea of) (c) sling 투석기, 장난감 고무총(=slingshot)

정답 (a) swing

6. ✍(해석) A: 요즈음 아무도 윌리암스와 말하지 않는 것을 알아. 왜 그러지?
　　　　　 B: 글쎄, 그녀는 모든 사람을 좀 짜증나게 해.
get on one's nerves …의 신경을 건드리다, …을 신경질 나게 하다, …을 안달 나게 하다(=give one the nerves; make one irritable[nervous])
정답 (d) nerves

7. ✍(해석) A: 자선 프로그램에 관하여 무엇을 하려고 하나요?
　　　　　 B: 계속해서 추진합시다. 잘 시작했지만 더 많은 돈을 아직도 모금해야 해요.
keep the ball rolling 계속해서 추진하다(=keep up an activity or action).
(b) bounce 튀다, 급히 움직이다, 부도나다
정답 (a) rolling

8. ✍(해석) A: 너 우울해 보이는데! 우울한 이유가 무엇이니?
　　　　　 B: 글쎄, 나 어제 해고당했어.
빈칸에는 문맥상 '우울한'의 뜻을 가진 'blue'가 와야 한다.
(b) blued 우울한(=gloomy, melancholy). feel blue 우울하다 (a) white 창백한(=pale, wan) (c) red 불그스름한 (d) yellow 겁 많은, 비겁한(=cowardly)
정답 (b) blue

9. ✍(해석) A: 백 달러 빌려줄 수 있니?
　　　　　 B: 미안하지만, 나도 무일푼이야.
(c) broke 무일푼으로, 파산하여(=having little or no money; bankrupt; penniless). dead[stone, stony] broke 완전히 파산하여. go broke 무일푼이 되다, 파산하다 (a) I'm out 나는 빠지겠어. (b) crashed 만취한 (d) broken 부서진, 낙담한, 파괴된
정답 (c) broke

10. ✍(해석) A: 60세의 백만장자와 결혼한 20세의 여배우에 관해 들었나요?
　　　　　　 B: 그래? 그녀는 남자를 우려먹는 여자가 확실해.
a gold digger 금광꾼, 남자를 우려먹는 여자. (a) miner 광부
정답 (d) digger

실력문제 3회

1. ✍(해석) A: 관리자가 너무 까다로워요.
   B: 예. 당신은 그가 좋아하는 대답을 해야 해요.
   (b) picky 법석대는, 까다로운(=overly fastidious; fussy; choosy) (a) lenient 관대한(=generous, broad-minded, magnanimous) (d) humdrum 평범한, 단조로운(=dull; monotonous)
   정답 (b) picky

2. ✍(해석) A: 두 시간 동안 그 문제를 토론해 왔어요.
   B: 예, 늦었어요. 오늘은 끝내지요.
   (b) wrap up 포장하다, 마치다, …을 요약하다(=bundle up; finish; conclude; settle) (a) add up 이치[조리]에 맞다, 이해되다, 결국 …의 뜻이 되다(to)(=come to the correct amount; make sense) (c) call up 전화를 걸다(=ring up, dial, give a ring[buzz]), 소집하다, 상기시키다, 컴퓨터 화면에 자료를 불러오다 (d) draw up 세우다(=halt, pull up, bring to a standstill), 정렬시키다(=put into position, arrange, line up, stand in a row, array, put[set]-in order), 작성하다(=write out, make out, complete)
   정답 (b) wrap

3. ✍(해석) A: 제인이 예일 대학교 장학금을 탈 수 있을 것이라고 생각해?
   B: 그녀는 가망이 없어.
   stand a chance 가망이 있다 stand a good[fair] of …의 가망이 충분히 있다 give one a chance …에게 시간[기회]을 주다, 조금 기다려 주다 (d) dismiss 해고하다
   정답 (b) stand

4. ✍(해석) A: 소리를 낮추어 주시겠어요? 쉬려고 해요.
   B: 미안합니다. 그렇게 크게 말하고 있는 줄 몰랐어요.
   (d) hold down 억제하다, 제지하다, 만족스럽게 일하다(=keep in obedience; keep control of; continue authority or rule over; work satisfactorily at) (a) shut down 폐쇄하다(=close down; stop all working; stop work

entirely; stop operations in) (b) turn down 줄이다, 약하게 하다, 거절하다 (=lower, lessen; refuse, reject, decline, disallow, dismiss) (c) put down 기록하다(=write[take/set] down, record, register), 진압하다(=suppress, check, subdue), 내려놓다(=lay down), …의 탓으로 돌리다(to)(=ascribe, attribute, impute, refer)

정답 (d) hold

5. ✎(해석) A: 김씨가 성폭행 죄로 체포당했다는 이야기를 들었니?
    B: 물론이지. 나는 그 일의 자초지종을 알고 있어.
빈칸에는 내용상 '자초지종'의 뜻을 가진 'ins and outs'가 와야 한다.
(d) ins and outs 여당과 야당, 여러 가지 부분, 자초지종(=the different parts; the details and complexities) (a) part and parcel 중요 부분(=an essential part) (b) odds and ends 자질구레한 것, 잡동사니(=small articles, bits and pieces) (c) give and take 타협(=compromise), 양보(=mutual concession), 주고받음

정답 (d) ins and outs

6. ✎(해석) A: 내가 너의 문제를 해결할 수 있어.
    B: 네가 참견할 일이 아니야. 내 일에 간섭하지 마라.
빈칸에는 내용상 '간섭하다'의 뜻이 와야 한다.
(d) poke[put/thrust/stick] one's nose into 간섭하다, 말참견하다 (=interrupt). (a) pull one's nose 놀리다(=ridicule) (c) hold one's nose 코를 쥐어 막다. jam 틀어박다, 고장 나다. It's none of your business 참견하지 마라(=Mind your own business=It is no concern of yours)

정답 (d) poke

7. ✎(해석) A: 캐시가 가짜 시계를 자랑하고 있어.
    B: 그래. 하지만 진짜처럼 보였어.
빈칸에는 내용상 '가짜의'의 뜻이 와야 한다.
(c) counterfeit 위조의, 가짜의(=false, sham, forged, bogus, spurious, fake, phony) (a) authentic 진정한, 믿을 만한(=genuine, real, true, trustworthy; credible, reliable) (d) realistic 현실적인, 사실주의의, 실존적인

정답 (c) counterfeit

9. ✍(해석) A: 내 차가 거의 기름이 떨어져 가요.
B: 여기서 유턴 합시다. 한 블록 전에 주유소를 찾았거든요.
(b) spot 발견하다(=place, locate), 더럽히다(=stain, blemish) (c) check 방해하다(=hinder), 억제하다(=restrain, hold back, curb, block), 막다(=prevent), 대조하다

정답 (b) spotted

10. ✍(해석) A: 이 소포를 영국에 보내고 싶은데요.
B: 항공우편으로 아니면 선박우편으로 하시겠어요?
(c) surface mail 차량[선박]우편 registered mail 등기우편 priority mail 빠른 우편 snail mail 전통적 우편 express mail 특급우편

정답 (c) surface

실력문제 4회

1. ✍(해석) A: 나는 뢴트겐이 아주 우연히 '엑스레이'라는 위대한 발견을 했다는 것을 들었어.
B: 너는 매우 박식하구나.
(b) stumble on[across] 우연히 발견하다(=discover by accident, find unexpectedly), 우연히 마주치다(=come across, chance on, fall in with, hit on, encounter)

정답 (b) stumbled

2. ✍(해석) A: 극장 건너편에 일식집이 새로 개업했어.
B: 일식이 끌려. 그 식당에 가자.
(d) go for -에 끌리다, 좋아하다(=be attracted by, want, like), 얻고자 노력하다(=try to get), 공격하다(=attack)

정답 (d) for

3. ✍(해석) A: 차가 시동이 걸리지 않아서 가게에서 집까지 걸어가야만

했어요.

B: 정말 지겨운 일이었군요.

(a) a pain in the neck[ass] 불쾌감, 안달, 불쾌하게[안달, 지겹게] 하는 사람[것] It's a pain in the neck(=It's something one doesn't like but must be endured away =It's a pain=It's a drag). (b) the apple of one's[the] eye 눈동자, 매우 소중한 것

정답 (a) pain

4. ✎(해석) A: 마이클은 어떻게 지내?

B: 잘 지내. 요즈음 그는 정말로 컴퓨터 게임에 푹 빠져 있어.

(c) be hooked on 열중해 있다(=be devoted to, be fascinated by), (마약에) 중독되어 있다(=be obsessed with, be addicted to) (a) book 장부에 기입하다(=list), 예약하다(=reserve, engage ahead of time)

정답 (c) hooked

5. ✎(해석) A: 내일 시험 준비했니?

B: 아니. 걱정으로 마음이 두근거려.

(c) have butterflies in one's stomach (걱정으로) 마음이 두근거리다[조마 조마하다](=feel very nervous before doing something) (a) nerve 신경(=sinew), 용기(=courage) (d) bug 곤충, 비밀도청장치, 병원균(=germ, virus)

정답 (c) butterflies

6. ✎(해석) A: 나는 영국이 인도네시아를 쉽게 이길 것을 알았어.

B: 그래. 그 게임의 결과는 미리 결정된 것 같아.

(c) cut and dried 미리 결정된(=arranged beforehand), 활기 없는(=listless, dull), 진부한, 틀에 박힌 (a) be out of contact with -와 접촉하고 있지 않다 (b) fall behind 뒤지다, 늦어지다, 추월 당하다(=drop to the rear of) (d) take up 차지하다(=occupy, cover), 집어 올리다(=raise, lift, pick up),태우다, 싣다 (=load), 시작하다(=begin), 맡다(=assume), 공부하다(=study)

정답 (c) cut and dried

7. ✍(해석) A: 너무 더워.
   B: 그래. 차가운 물이 정말 좋아.
   (d) hit the spot 말할 나위 없다, 만족스럽다(=refresh fully or satisfy; bring back one's spirits or strength) (a) hit the road 여행을 떠나다 출발하다(=become a wanderer[tramp/hobo]; leave) (b) hit the hay[sack] 자다(=go to bed, turn in) (c) hit the ceiling[roof] 몹시 성나다(=become violently angry; go into a rage)
   정답 (d) spot

8. ✍(해석) A: 스미스씨, 내일 저녁 우리 집에 오셔서 저녁 식사를 하실 수 있나요?
   B: 가고 싶기는 한데요, 선약이 있어서 미안합니다. 다른 날에 가도 될까요?
   (b) rain check 언제나 유효한 초청장(=standing invitation), 우천교환권, 후일의 약속 (a) break 갈라진 틈 단절, 잠깐의 휴식 Let's take a coffee break.(커피 마시면서 잠깐 쉽시다) (c) session 개회, 회기, 수업 in session (개회[개정, 회의]중)
   정답 (b) rain check

9. ✍(해석) A: 아드님의 파티 때문에 손해가 엄청나요.
   B: 걱정 마세요. 모든 비용을 지불하겠어요.
   (b) cover expenses 비용을 보상하다(=protect financially), 계산하다
   (a) bill 계산서(=account), 목록(=list), 지폐, 법안(=draft), 계산서를 보내다
   정답 (b) cover

10. ✍(해석) A: 당신은 약속을 했나요?
    B: 나는 약속이 필요한지 몰랐어요. 예약 없이 만날 수 없나요?
    (a) take walk-ins 예약 없이 만나다. (c) makeover 개조(=change, renovation) (d) impromptu 즉석에서(=without preparation; offhand)
    정답 (a) walk-ins

어휘 · Part II

실력문제 1회

1. 빈칸에는 문맥상 '성형수술'의 뜻을 가진 'plastic surgery'가 와야 한다.

(b) plastic 조형의, 성형의, 유연한 plastic surgery 성형수술(=plastic operation) (a) aesthetic 미의, 심미적인, 미학의 (c) artistic 예술적인, 예술[미술]의

✐(해석) 많은 영화배우들이 젊게 보이기 위해 성형수술을 하고 있다.
정답 (b) plastic

2. 빈칸에는 문맥상 '욕하다'의 뜻을 가진 'swear'가 와야 한다.

(d) swear 욕하다(=use profane language, curse, blaspheme), 맹세하다(=vow, pledge), 단언하다 (b) exclaim 외치다, 소리지르다(=cry out, shout, say vehemently)

✐(해석) 아이들 앞에서 욕하지 마세요. 나는 그들이 그런 말을 배우는 것을 원치 않아요. **정답 (d)**

3. 빈칸에는 문맥상 '가정하다'의 뜻을 가진 'postulate'가 와야 한다.

(a) postulate (자명한 일로) 가정하다(=assume to be true, real; take for granted), 요구하다, 성직에 임명하다 (b) proscribe 추방하다, 금지하다(=outlaw; banish, exile; denounce or forbid the use of) (c) preempt 선취하다(=seize before anyone else can), (프로를)바꾸다(=replace) (d) recapitulate 요약하다(=summarize), 반복하다(=repeat briefly)

✐(해석) 지그문트 프로이드는 우리 모두가 생존본능 뿐만 아니라 죽음 본능도 가지고 있다고 가정했다. **정답 (a)**

4. 빈칸에는 문맥상 '땀을 흘리다'의 뜻을 가진 'perspired'가 와야 한다.

(b) respire 호흡하다(=breathe), 휴식하다 (c) expire 만기가 되다, 끝나다, 죽다(=exhale; come to an end; die) (d) inspire 격려하다, 불어넣다, 영감을 주다(=stimulate, impel, spur; inhale; motivate)

✐(해석) 그는 지나친 운동 후에 땀을 많이 흘려 셔츠가 젖었다. 정답 (a)

5. 빈칸에는 '발효시킨'의 뜻을 가진 'fermented'가 와야 한다.

(a) ferment 발효시키다, 자극하다, 불러일으키다(=cause fermentation in; excite, agitate; stir up) (b) famish 굶주리게 하다(=starve) famished to death 배고파 죽다 (c) feeble 연약한, 희미한, 무력한(=weak, fragile, frail, brittle, delicate; faint; ineffective) (d) grumpy 성미 까다로운, 심술 난 (=grouchy; peevish)

✐(해석) 김치는 매우 매운 한국의 전통적인 발효시킨 배추이다. **정답 (c)**

6. 문맥상 '세밀히 조사하다'의 뜻을 가진 'comb through'가 와야 한다.

(b) go through 통과되다(=pass through, get through, be carried), 관통하다(=penetrate, pierce), 겪다(=undergo, suffer, experience), 견뎌 내다(=bear, endure, stand), 조사하다(=look into, investigate, examine) (c) get through …을 통과하다, 합격하다, 연락이 되다(to), 끝마치다(with) (d) put through …의 전화를 연결하다(to), (괴로움을)당하게 되다

✐(해석) 그 형사는 용의자에 관한 더 많은 정보를 얻기 위해 오래된 잡지들을 세밀히 조사했다. **정답 (a)**

7. 빈칸에는 문맥상 '누군지 생각나다'의 뜻을 가진 'ring'의 과거형 'rang'이 와야 한다.

(b) ring[hit] a bell 생각나게 하다(=make you remember something; sound familiar) It doesn't ring a bell. 전혀 기억이 안 나요. (a) peal (소리가) 울리다, (명성을) 떨치다, (소문을) 퍼뜨리다 (c) chime (종을) 울리다, (종소리가 시각을) 알리다, 일치하다(=agree) (d) toll 울리다, (종, 시계가) 치다, 사용세, 사상자수

✐(해석) 앤이 아버지에게 새로운 선생님의 이름을 말했을 때, 생각이 나서 아버지가 "제임스 카슨"이라고 말했다. **정답 (b)**

8. 빈칸에는 문맥상 '고갈'의 뜻을 가진 'depletion'이 와야 한다.

(a) depletion 고갈, 소모(=exhaustion, consumption, deficiency) (b) depiction 묘사, 서술 (c) deposition 파면, 퇴적, 공탁 (d) depreciation 가치하락, 감가상각, 경시

✐(해석) 그 논문의 주장에 따르면 동물 자원이 고갈되었기 때문에 그 종

족의 일인당 단백질 배급량이 실제적으로 감소되었다는 것이다. **정답 (a)**

9. 빈칸에는 문맥상 '꼼꼼하게'의 뜻을 가진 'scrupulously, meticulously' 등의 단어가 와야 한다. (a) reluctantly 마지못해(=unwillingly) (c) abjectly 천하게, 비열하게 abject 비천한, 비열한(=servile, degraded, contemptible; miserable, wretched)
✎(해석) 감염을 피하기 위해서 외과 의사들은 수술하기 전에 그들의 손을 꼼꼼하게 닦는다. **정답 (b)**

10. 빈칸에는 문맥상 '호소하다'의 뜻을 가진 단어가 와야 한다.
(a) appeal 애원하다, 호소하다, 항소하다, 흥미를 끌다(= be attractive or interesting) (b) attest 증명하다, 증언하다(=prove, testify, bear witness, certify, swear, vouch) (c) attribute-의 탓으로 돌리다(=ascribe, impute, assign) (d) addict 중독 시키다, 빠지게 하다(=devote)
✎(해석) 현대의 많은 광고들은 잠재적인 고객들의 감정에 호소하도록 만들어진다. **정답 (a)**

실력문제 2회

1. 빈칸에는 문맥상 '만장일치의'에 해당하는 'unanimous'가 들어가야 한다.
(a) unanimous 만장일치의(=without dissent, with one voice, of one accord) (b) associated 연합한, 조합의 (c) connected 일관된, 관계가 있는 (d) similar 비슷한
✎(해석) 월요일 회의에서 고용위원회의 회원들은 해리슨을 인사부장으로 승진시키는 것에 대하여 만장일치의 지지를 보였다. **정답 (a)**

2. 빈칸에는 문맥상 '생산성'의 뜻을 가진 'productivity'가 들어가야 한다.
✎(해석) 직원들의 생산성이 상당히 증가했기 때문에, 회사의 총수익은 엄청나게 늘어나고, 모든 직원들은 봉급 인상을 받을 것이다. substantial 상당한 tremendously 엄청나게(=enormously) (a) pursuance 실행 (b) provocation 분개, 도발, 자극 (d) prosecution

기소. **정답 (c)**

3. 빈칸에는 문맥상 '꽉 찬, 만원의'의 뜻을 가진 'packed'가 들어가야 한다.
(d) be packed with …으로 꽉 차다(=be filled with, be stuffed with, be crowded with). (a) heavy 무거운, 대량의, 힘겨운, 맹렬한, 침울한 (b) be covered with …으로 덮여 있다(=be topped with) (c) busy 바쁜, 통화중인, 번화한 be busy+(in)+V-ing …하기에 바쁘다 squeeze 헤치고 나아가다, 밀고 들어가다, 압착하다, 꽉 쥐다, 밀어 넣다
✍(해석) 버스가 너무 만원이어서 우리는 밀고 들어가서 탈 수 없었다.
정답 (d)

4. 빈칸에는 문맥상 '상을 받다'는 뜻을 가진 어구가 들어가야 한다.
(d) walk away[off] with 상을 휩쓸어가다, …에 낙승하다, …을 무심코 갖고 가다(=take, get, or win easily; take and go away with; take away)
✍(해석) 우리 팀이 너무 잘 해서 세 개의 큰상을 받았다. **정답 (d)**

5. 빈칸에는 문맥상 '어디에나 존재하는'의 뜻을 가진 ubiquitous가 와야 한다. (a) assiduous 부지런한(=diligent, sedulous, industrious) (b) superficial 피상적인(=shallow, dilettante, skin-deep, surface) (d) gregarious 군거성의 (=living in herds), 사교적인(=sociable)
✍(해석) 어디에나 존재하는 세계적 디지털 통신망의 선두주자인 인터넷은 원격통신과 방송적인 측면들을 결합하고 있다. **정답 (a)**

6. 'take a long rest'(오래 쉬다)로 보아 빈칸에는 '힘드는, 어려운'의 뜻을 가진 laborious가 와야 한다. (a) languid 나른한, 기운이 없는, 흥미 없는 (=weak, feeble, weary; listless, apathetic, indifferent; slow, dull) (b) fastidious 까다로운(=finicky, meticulous, squeamish) (d) insolent 거만한 (=arrogant, haughty, proud, pompous, puffed, toplofty, supercilious)
✍(해석) 그 산에 올라가는 것이 너무 힘들어서 내려오기 전에 오래 쉬어야만 했다. **정답 (c)**

7. 빈칸에는 문맥상 '묻혀 있다'의 뜻을 가진 단어가 와야 한다.
(d) inter 묻다, 매장하다(=bury; put into the earth or in a grave) (a)

excavate 파다, 발굴하다(=dig out, shovel, empty, hollow out) (b) torch 불을 지르다(=set fire to) (c) defile 더럽히다, 모독하다(=make filthy, dirty, foul, tarnish; profane, sully, drag in the dust, give a bad name)

✍(해석) 많은 미국의 영웅들이 알링톤 국립묘지에 묻혀 있다. **정답 (d)**

8. 빈칸에는 문맥상 '강좌'의 뜻을 가진 단어가 와야 한다.

(c) session 개회, 회기, 수업 summer session 하기강좌 emergency session 긴급 회기 (a) secession 탈퇴, 분리(=withdrawal, seceding, retraction) (b) section 부분, 구역, 계층, 절단, 단면 (d) succession 연속, 계승

✍(해석) 대부분의 대학생은 학위를 얻는데 4년이 걸리지만, 어떤 학생은 하기 강좌에 출석하여 더 빨리 학위를 얻는다. **정답 (c)**

9. 빈칸에는 문맥상 '억누르다'의 뜻을 가진 단어가 와야 한다.

(c) repress 억누르다, 억압하다, 진압하다(=hold back, restrain, check; put down, subdue) (a) reprove 꾸짖다, 나무라다, 비난하다(=blame, reprehend, rebuke, censure, chide) (d) reprieve 형 집행을 유예하다, 잠시 경감하다 (=give temporary relief to)

✍(해석) 어떤 심리학자들은 감정을 너무 억누르면 건강에 좋지 않다고 주장한다. **정답 (c)**

10. 빈칸에는 'desert'(사막)와 어울리는 단어가 와야 한다.

(a) parched 바짝 마른, 목마른(=very dry, thirsty) (b) arable 경작할 수 있는, 경작에 알맞은(=suitable for plowing) (c) fertile 비옥한, 다산의, 풍부한(=prolific, productive, fruitful, rich) (d) aqueous 물의, 물 같은, 수성의(=watery) '…하는데 어려움을 겪다'의 표현: have difficulty[trouble/bother/a hard time] (in)+V-ing, have struggle (in)+V-ing, be hard put to it to+동사

✍(해석) 개척자들은 바짝 마른 사막에서 작물을 재배하는데 어려움을 겪었다. **정답 (a)**

실력문제 3회

1. 빈칸에는 문맥상 '짐을 싸다'의 뜻을 가진 'pack'이 와야 한다.

(a) pack 짐을 꾸리다, …에 가득 채우다, 찜질하다 (b) rack 고문하다, 괴롭히다(=torture; torment, bug, plague, harass) (c) sack 해고하다, 약탈하다(=fire, dismiss, lay off; plunder, ravage, pillage, despoil) (d) lack …이 없다, 결핍하다, 모자라다(=be deficient in or entirely without) ['…이 부족하다'의 표현]: lack in, be in want[need] of, be[come/fall/run/drop] of, want, be devoid[destitute] of

✎(해석) 그들은 머지 않아 짐을 싸서 다른 도시로 이사 가게 되어 있다. **정답 (a)**

2. 빈칸에는 문맥상 '입장'의 뜻을 가진 'shoes'가 와야 한다.

(d) put oneself in[into] one's shoes[place] 남의 입장이 되어 보다 (=understand one's feeling imaginatively; try to know one's feelings and reasons with understanding; enter into one's trouble) ['내가 만약 당신의 입장이라면'의 표현]: If I were in your shoes[place/position]

✎(해석) 당신이 고객의 입장이 된다면 그 물건이 안 팔리는 이유를 알 수 있다. **정답 (d)**

3. 빈칸에는 "…이 없다면, …을 제외한다면"의 뜻을 가진 전치사 barring 이 들어가야 한다.

(a) bar 잠그다, 막다, 금하다(=obstruct, close, block, forbid, restrict) fluctuation 변동 profitable 수익성 있는(=lucrative, moneymaking)

✎(해석) 극도의 시장 변동이 없다면, 이번 투자 계획이 안전하면서도 수익성 있는 퇴직금을 마련하도록 도울 것을 확신할 수 있다. 정답 (c)

4. levy 부과하다, 징집하다, 시작하다(=impose; enlist; wage [war])

levy는 전치사 'on'을 동반한다. levy taxes on a person (…에게 세금을 부과하다), levy war on[against] (…에 대해 전쟁을 개시하다). in accordance with …에 따라서, …와 일치하여(=according to, in conformity to[with], agreeably [comfortably] to, in obedience to).

✎(해석) 최근 통과된 법률에 따라서 1월 1일 현재로 본 주의 모든 호텔 객실에 대해 5% 의 판매세가 부과될 것이다. **정답 (b)**

5. 빈칸에는 문맥상 '자발적으로'의 뜻을 가진 'voluntarily'가 들어가야 한다.
voluntary recall 자발적 리콜. (a) volubly 유창하게, 수다스럽게(=fluently; garrulously) (b) visually 시각적으로 (d) voraciously 게걸스럽게(=greedily, gluttonously)
✍(해석) 오늘 아침 현지 신문의 보도에 따르면 지인 스태포드는 오염에 대한 우려 때문에 많은 선적 제품을 자발적으로 리콜 했다는 것이다.
정답 (c)

6. (a) still, (c) hardly는 동사 뒤에 위치하므로 답에서 제외된다. 'Given her impulsive nature'(그녀의 충동적인 기질을 고려하면)와 어울리는 것은 (d) spontaneously이다. (d) spontaneously 자발적으로, 자연스럽게(=voluntarily; naturally) (b) simultaneously 동시에(=at the same time, concurrently, synchronously) given …을 고려하면(=taking into account, considering, under certain circumstances) come up with 생각해내다, …을 따라잡다, 제 안하다(=think of, produce; catch up with, overtake, reach, catch[get] up to, overhaul, run down, gain on; propose, suggest)['…하는 경향이 있다'의 표현]: tend to, be inclined[liable/prone/likely/disposed] to, be apt to, have a tendency to
✍(해석) 제인은 그녀의 충동적인 성질을 고려하면, 아이디어를 자연스럽게 생각해내는 경향이 있다. **정답 (d)**

7. 빈칸에는 문맥상 '위협하다'의 뜻을 가진 'cow'가 와야 한다. (b) favor 호의를 보이다, 편들다(=side), 찬성하다, 베풀다 (d) screen 가리다, 보호하다(=conceal; protect)
✍(해석) 아트로 토스카니는 한 때 "하늘에 있는 스타를 제외한 어떠한 스타도 그에게는 없다"는 풍자적인 말을 해서 한 유명한 오페라 가수를 위협했다. **정답 (c)**

8. acknowledge receipt of(…을 받았다고 통보하다). 영어 표현에서 collocation(연어)이 중요하므로 나올 때마다 기억해 두는 것이 좋다.
✍(해석) 동봉된 양식에 서명해서 이 문서를 받았다는 통보를 해 주십시오.

정답 (b)

9. 'broad A into B'(A를 B까지 확대하다)구문을 묻는 문제이다.
(a) multiply 증가시키다 (b) dictate 받아쓰게 하다, 지도하다 (c) impress 인상을 주다
✍(해석) 제인의 제안들은 동기를 부여하여 우리의 연구를 전에 간과했었던 부분까지 확대하도록 했다. **정답 (d)**

10. 빈칸에는 '요청하다'의 뜻을 가진 put in for(=request)가 와야 한다.
(b) put up with 참다(=endure, stand, bear, tolerate, persevere) (c) put back in 이전하다(=transfer) (d) put over to 의사를 전하다(=communicate)
✍(해석) 그 프로젝트가 끝난 후 그녀는 본사로 전근할 것을 요청했다. **정답 (a)**

실력문제 4회

1. 빈칸에는 문맥상 '예금'의 뜻을 가진 deposit가 와야 한다.
(a) withdrawal 인출 (b) contribution 기여, 기부금 (c) accumulation 축적(=pileup, amassment, hoard, storing up)
✍(해석) 이 은행에서 당신의 신용 기록을 개선하기 위해서는 당신의 보통 예금 계좌에 많은 돈을 입금해야 할 것이다. **정답 (d)**

2. 빈칸에는 문맥상 '아주 간단한'의 뜻을 가진 단어가 와야 한다. (c) foolproof 바보라도 할 수 있는, 아주 간단한(=so simple, well-designed) (a) shatterproof 산산이 부서지지 않는(=that will resist shattering) (b) airproof 공기가 통하지 않는 내기성의 (d) childproof 어린 아이에게 안전한, 어린아이는 다룰 수 없는 [참고] -proof (1) impervious to [waterproof: 방수의] (2) protected from [rustproof: 녹슬지 않는] (3) resistant to [fireproof: 방화의, 내화성의]
✍(해석) 이메일은 정보를 아주 빠른 속도로 한 장소에서 다른 장소로 전달하는 아주 간단한 방법이다. **정답 (c)**

3. 빈칸에는 문맥상 '병석에서 일어나다'의 뜻을 가진 어구가 와야 한다.

(a) be free and easy 마음이 편하다, 자유스럽다(=be unceremonious) (b) be neck and neck 비슷비슷하다(=be side by side; be abreast; be tied) (c) be up and out 병석에서 일어나다(=be out of bed and active) (d) be on pins and needles 매우 불안해하다(=be worried, be nervous)

✍(해석) 나는 그녀가 사고 직후에 아주 빨리 좋아진 것에 놀랐다.

정답 (c)

4. 빈칸에는 문맥상 '서로 얽혀 있는'의 뜻을 가진 단어가 와야 한다.

(a) unalterable 바꿀 수 없는, 불변의 (b) enigmatic 수수께끼의 (c) intertwine 서로 얽히게 하다 (d) regulate 규정하다, 조절하다, 조정하다 (=control, direct, adjust)

✍(해석) 손과 눈과 두뇌의 기능은 너무나 서로 얽혀 있기 때문에, 아동기에 손을 사용하는 것은 아동의 전반적인 인지 발달을 향상시키는데 도움이 된다. **정답 (c)**

5. 빈칸에는 문맥상 '강우, 강수량'의 뜻을 가진 '(d) precipitation'이 와야 한다.

(a) prediction 예언 (b) preservation 보존 (c) trepidation 공포

✍(해석) 대기권에 해로운 물질의 강우가 보호적 오존층의 고갈을 유발하고 있다. **정답 (d)**

6. 빈칸에는 문맥상 '준수하다'의 뜻을 가진 '(c) comply'가 와야 한다. ['규정을 준수하다'의 표현]: comply with the regulation[codes]

(a) go along 해나가다, 찬성하다, 협력하다(=continue; go for fun; agree; cooperate) (b) obey 복종하다, 따르다 (d) seek 찾다, 추구하다, 노력하다 (=search for; try, attempt)

✍(해석) 현지 교통 규정을 준수하지 않으면 벌금을 부과하거나 한 달까지 투옥될 수 있다. **정답 (c)**

7. 빈칸에는 문맥상 '군침이 도는'의 뜻을 가진 '(a) mouth-watering'이 와야 한다. (b) mind-boggling 경탄스러운, 믿기 어려울 만큼 놀라운 (c) eye-opening 괄목할만한, 놀랄만한 (d) breath-taking 아슬아슬한, 깜짝 놀라게 하는

✎(해석) 내가 커피를 기다리는 동안, 수석 웨이터가 큰 바구니에 군침이 도는 복숭아를 가득 담고 나에게로 가까이 왔다. **정답 (a)**

8. 빈칸에는 문맥상 '전부를 얻거나 전부를 잃는'의 뜻을 가진 (d) an all-or-nothing 이 와야한다. (a) ongoing 전진하는, 진행중의 (b) wining-and-dining 뇌물성 접대 (c) mud-slinging 추한 싸움 (d) all-or-nothing 전부를 얻거나 전부를 잃는

✎(해석) 내가 이미 말한바와 같이 협상은 전부를 얻거나 전부를 잃는 과정이 아니다. 즉, 협상에는 수준과 정도가 있고, 사실 하나의 연속체이다. **정답 (d)**

9. 빈칸에는 문맥상 '보답이 된다'의 뜻을 가진 (c) pay off 가 와야한다. (a) luck out 운이 좋다, 재수 있다 (b) make do ~으로 때우다(견디다) (d) hit the jackpot 상금을 타다, 대성공하다

✎(해석) 세상은 빨리 돈버는 곳이 아니다. 근면과 정직이라는 전통적 가치는 결국 여전히 보답이 된다. **정답 (c)**

10. narrow down the list 리스트의 목록을 몇 명으로 압축하다 (b) cut down 줄이다(=lessen; reduce; limit) (c) cut out 베어내다, 제거하다(=stop; quit)

✎(해석) 이 사건에 대한 새로운 증거에 비추어 우리는 이제 혐의자의 목록을 줄일 수 있다. **정답 (a)**

3. 독해 - Part 1

실력문제 1회

1. 많은 사람들은 병원이라고 다 똑같지는 않다는 사실을 알고 있다. 하지만 대부분 그 차이란 것이 규모와 전반적인 질의 차이라고 생각한다. 사실, 관상동맥 수술에 탁월한 능력을 자랑하는 병원은 암 치료의 경우 최선의 선택이 아닐 수도 있다. 대부분 종합병원들은 모든 분야의 치료를 똑같이 잘 해낼 수 있는 의료진과 장비를 갖추고 있지 못하다. 인생의 다른 부분에서도 그러하듯, 연습을 해야 완벽하게 되는 것이다. 의료처치와 시술의 기술 역시 그러한 시술들을 자주 시행하는 전문가에 의해 발전하는 법이다.

covonary 왕관의, 관상동맥의, 심장의. bypass 보조관, 우회로, 바이패스. cancer treatment 암 치료.

(해설) 빈칸이 있는 문장에 힌트가 있다. **정답 (c)**

2. 온라인상에서 사람들은 개인 정보에 관한 한 너무 순진하고 쉽사리 남을 믿어버린다. 그러나 사람들은 생각보다 온라인에서 더 많이 위험에 노출되어 있다. 대부분의 사람들은 일상생활에서 우연히 만난 사람에게는 절대로 공개 하지 않을 정보를 알려주곤 한다. 당신이라면 식료품가게 계산대 앞에서 줄을 서 있다가 옆에 서 있는 사람에게 주소와 전화번호를 알려주겠는가? 물론 그럴 리가 없다. 그러나 흔히 부지불식중에 채팅에서 그런짓을 저지르는 것은 이와 다를 바가 없다.

vulnerable 상처를 입기 쉬운, 비난[공격] 받기 쉬운, 약한.

(해설) 첫째 문장을 잘 읽고, However에 주의하면 답을 고를 수 있다.

정답 (b)

3. 물질은 눈에 보이지 않는 미세한 입자들로 이루어져 있다. 그 입자들의 조합의 움직임은 물질의 상태를 구별 짓는다. 고체 상태의 물질은 일정한 형태를 갖는다. 액체 상태의 물질은 일정한 형태는 없지만 일정한 부피는 있다. 기체 상태의 물질은 일정한 형태도, 일정한 부피도 없다. 물질은 온도를 변화시킴으로써 한 상태에서 다른 상태로 변환될 수 있다. 예컨대 액체 용액을 빙점까지 냉각시키면 고체 상태가 되고, 가열하면 수증기가 된다.

🔖 (해설) 빈칸 뒤에 오는 문장에 힌트가 있다. **정답 (c)**

4. 여성 근로자들은 참된 희생을 감내하고 있으며 출산 때는 큰 위험을 무릅쓴다. 노동조합 대표부가 없는 직장의 82%에서 임신한 여성 근로자들은 관행상 해고당한다. 나머지 여성들은 출산 후 복직했을 때 신규 채용으로 재조정되어 고참권을 상실한다. 새내기 엄마가 된 많은 여성들은 적당한 놀이방을 찾지 못해, 집에서 가깝고 근무시간이 짧은 변변찮은 직업을 택할 수밖에 없다.

new hire 신규 채용. marginal 가장자리의 한계의, 최저한의.

🔖 (해설) 주제문인 첫째 문장에 힌트가 나와 있다. '희생', '위험'이란 단어에 키가 있다. **정답 (b)**

5. 이혼은 결코 가벼운 문제가 아니다. 특히 아이들이 연루되어 있다면 더 더욱 그러하다. 부모의 이혼을 겪는 아이들에게는 종종, 부모의 불화에도 불구하고 두 사람이 모두 자신을 여전히 사랑한다는 확신을 주는 것이 필요하다. 아이들은 부모가 항상 함께 살 것이라고 추측하는 경우가 자주 있다. 그런 지속성의 의식이 흔들린다면, 그들은 앞으로 자신들에게 어떤 일이 일어날지, 누가 자신을 돌보아 주게 될 것인지 불안해하게 된다. 아이들에게 자신들의 건강, 교육, 집에 관련된 여러 문제들이 진심에서 아이들의 최선을 생각해 결정될 것이라는 사실을 알릴 필요가 있다. 자녀를 위해 당신이 할 수 있는 가장 중요한 일은, 이혼이란 서로의 문제로 헤어지는 두 부모의 문제이지 부모와 자식간의 문제가 아니라는 사실을 반복해서 이야기해 주는 것이다.

shelter 피난 장소, 차폐물 보호, 피난, 집.

🔖 (해설) 빈칸 바로 다음 문장에 힌트가 나와 있다. '아이들 문제'가 언급되고 있다. **정답 (c)**

6. 심한 외상 후 스트레스 질환을 겪는 베트남 참전 군인을 치료하는 정신과 의사로서 나는 어떻게 치유되지 않은 전투 외상이 민주적인 참여에 요구되는 기본적인 사회적, 인지적 능력을 무력화시키는지를 봐왔다. 민주적 절차에 그들이 참여할 수 없다는 것은 슬픈 일이지만, 외상 후 스트레스 질환을 갖고 있는 베트남 참전 군인들은 현재 미국 인구의 천 분의 일 정도

에 불과하므로, 이것이 민주적 절차 자체를 위협하지는 못한다. 그러나 고대 아테네의 경우에서 보듯이, 모든 시민이 군인이나 전직 군인이고 전쟁이 끊이지 않는 곳에서의 민주주의에서는 무슨 일이 생길까?

　post-traumatic stress disorder 외상 후 스트레스 질환. trauma 외상, 마음의 상처. leave out 빠뜨리다, 무시하다. maim 병신을 만들다, 망쳐 놓다.

　🕯 (해설) 빈칸이 있는 문장 특히 but이하에 힌트가 나와 있다.　정답 (a)

　7. 난 지금 등에 메는 배낭을 가지고 다니는데, 진작 이걸 사지 않았다는 것을 믿을 수 없다. 전에 다니던 직장에서 플래너 하나를 얻어 지갑, 수첩, 주소록, 메모 용지첩으로 활용하고 있다. 다 좋긴 한데 좀 무겁다. 해가 바뀌어도 그것을 계속 쓸지는 모르겠다. 난 항상 책, 회사 신분증, 사무실 열쇠, 작은 화장품 통, 휴대폰도 가지고 다닌다. 뭘 사러갈 때 아주 편리한데, 배낭 안에 구입한 것들을 모두 집어넣을 수 있어 손에 물건을 들지 않아도 된다! 그래서 내 손은 자유롭다.

　hang on 꼭 붙잡다, 놓지 않다, 잠시 기다리다, 전화를 끊지 않고 두다. handy 알맞은, 편리한, 가까이 있는. errand 심부름, 용건.

　🕯 (해설) 빈칸 바로 앞 문장에 힌트가 나와 있다.　**정답 (b)**

　8. 지구를 보호하는 오존층은 2000년이나 2001년이면 역사상 가장 엷게 될 것이라고 세계 기상 기구가 월요일 밝혔다. 오존층이 엷어지는 것을 막기 위한 국제적인 조치를 통해 다음 세기 중반까지 오존층이 두터워지리라는 예보가 있다고 할지라도, 오존층은 현재 가장 침해받기 쉬운 단계에 와 있으며 상황이 나아지기는커녕 더욱 나빠질 것이라고 세계 기상 기구는 말했다. 오존층은 태양의 해로운 자외선을 흡수하는 약한 가스 보호 방패인데, 인공 화학물질로 인해 점점 많은 구멍이 뚫리고 있다. 이 구멍들은 피부암을 일으키는 요인으로 문제가 된다.

　hit its all-time thinnest 가장 엷게 되다. meteorological 기상학. ultraviolet ray 자외선. sophisticated 순지하지 않은, 세련된.

　🕯 (해설) 주제문인 첫째 문장과 빈칸이 있는 문장에 힌트가 나와 있다.
　정답 (d)

9. 19세기 후반에 기업 옹호자들은 사회적 다원주의를 열광적으로 수용했는데, 그것은 찰스 다윈의 [종의 기원] 이론을 [자유 방임주의]의 원리에 대강 적용시킨 것이다. 인간 사회는 자연적으로 진화해 왔으며, 기존 제도들에 가해지는 어떠한 간섭도 발전을 저지하고 약자를 도울 뿐이라고 사회적 다원주의자들은 생각했다. 적자 생존 원리에 따라 움직이는 자유 사회에서는 권력이 가장 능력 있는 자들에게로 자연스럽게 흘러갈 것이다. 따라서 재산의 소유와 획득은 신성한 권리였으며, 부는 누려 마땅한 권력과 책임을 나타내는 징표였다.

(해설) 빈칸이 있는 문장에 힌트가 나와 있다. **정답 (b)**

10. 언어를 평가하는 것은 전통적으로 언어에 관한 지식을 평가하는 형태를 띠었는데, 일반적으로 어휘나 문법에 관한 지식을 평가하는 것이었다. 그러나 언어를 사용할 수 있으려면 언어에 관한 지식보다 더 중요한 것이 있다. Dull Hymes는 의사소통 능력이라는 개념을 제안했다. 그는 의사소통 능력에 정확한 문장을 형성하는 능력뿐 아니라 이 문장들을 적절한 때에 사용할 수 있는 능력을 포함시켰다. Hymes가 1970년대 초에 그러한 생각을 처음 제안한 이래로, 그것은 상당히 확장되었고 다양한 형태의 능력이 제안되었다. 하지만 의사소통 능력에 대한 기본적인 생각은 여전히 실제 상황에서, 언어 수용적인 면과 생산적인 면에서 언어를 적절하게 사용할 수 있는 능력이라는 것이다.

(해설) 빈칸이 있는 문장에 힌트가 나와 있다. **정답 (b)**

실력문제 2회

1. 원유의 공급 과잉과 경기 후퇴에 대한 두려움으로 인해 국제 시장가격이 2년 만에 최저가로 되었다. OPEC 관리자측은 11월 10일 회의에서 1일 생산량을 백만 배럴씩 줄임으로써 가격을 인상시키는 안에 대한 투표를 할 것이라고 전했다. 그러나 주요 산유국이면서 OPEC에 가입하지 않은 멕시코, 러시아, 노르웨이가 석유 수출량 감소를 반대하고 있기 때문에 가격 급감을 막으려는 OPEC의 능력에는 한계가 있을 것이다.

shore up 가격을 인상하다. cut down cost 가격을 내리다.

🖐 (해설) 빈칸이 있는 문장 특히 by이하에 힌트가 나와 있다. **정답 (c)**

2. 여러 가지 요인들이 법체계가 범인을 다루는 방식에 영향을 미친다. 한 예로 범죄자의 성별이 처벌의 경중에 영향을 미친다. 여성이 남성보다 사형을 받을 가능성이 적다. 또한 법정은 아버지보다는 어머니를 감옥에 보내기를 더 꺼려한다. 범죄자를 다룸에 있어서 또 한 가지 요소는 범죄자의 인종이다. 백인이 아닌 자들은 집행 유예나 보호 관찰 선고를 덜 받는다. 끝으로, 범죄자의 연령이 판결에서 고려된다. 나이 어린 범죄자들은 특별취급을 받는다. 그리고 연장자들은 보다 관대한 형을 선고받는다.

be likely to+동사: -하는 경향이 있다, -하기 쉽다(=be apt to, be liable to, be inclined to, be disposed to) death penalty 사형 선고 parole 집행 유예, 가석방 probation 보호 관찰 lenient 관대한(=generous, magnanimous, broad-minded) reluctant 꺼려하는(=unwilling) loathsome 싫은, 기분 나쁜 (=hateful, obnoxious, abhorrent, odious, abominable, repulsive, offensive, despicable, disgusting)

🖐 (해설) 빈칸이 있는 문장과 바로 앞 문장에 힌트가 나와 있다. **정답 (b)**

3. 어디서나 볼 수 있는 카나페, 찍어먹는 소스, 감자칩, 넘쳐나는 요리들, 화려한 후식으로, 끊임없이 계속되는 휴일 파티 후에 이제는 보다 건강한 식습관으로 돌아가야 할 때입니다. 탐식가가 아닌 사람들도 이 간단하고 가벼운 식사를 즐기게 될 것입니다. 운 좋게도 몸에 좋다고 해서 맛이 없을 필요는 없습니다. 우리가 이번 달에 특별히 다루는 주요 요리는 최고의 지방질에 훌륭한 맛을 제공하며 상상만큼이나 몸에 좋고 맛이 있습니다. 그리고 이 모든 조리법은 즉시 준비할 수 있기 때문에, 주중의 가장 바쁜 스케줄에도 적합할 것입니다.

entree 앙트레, 주요 요리, 입장 spectacular 화려한 recipe 조리법 gratify 만족시키다, 기쁘게 하다 palate 구개, 미각 picky 성미 까다로운, 법석대는

🖐 (해설) 빈칸이 있는 문장에 힌트가 나와 있다. **정답 (c)**

4. 예술이 생계를 이어가기에 급급하던 국민 사이에 아직은 하찮은 활동

으로 간주 되었던 1950년대와 1960년대에 한국은행은 작품을 구입함으로써 엄선한 예술가들을 지원하기로 결정했다. 이것은 금융기관으로서는 흔치 않은 조치였고, 예술계로부터 큰 호응을 받았다. 시간이 흘러 경제가 나아지면서 한국은행의 소장품도 늘어나게 되었고, 이제는 약 1,800점의 예술작품을 자랑하게 되었다. 이 작품들 중 70여 점이 다음 달 덕수궁 국립현대미술관 별관에서 전시될 것이다.

frivolous 경박한, 사소한(=trifling, trivial) make(both) ends meet 수지 균형을 맞추다.

▣ (해설) 빈칸이 있는 문장에 힌트가 나와 있다. **정답 (c)**

5. 한 관료가 그 수치들은 음주운전과의 전쟁에서 "상당한 진전"을 보여주었다고 말했다. 정부 기관은 음주운전 사망의 극적인 감소에 기여한 여러 가지 요소들을 열거하였다. 이러한 요소들에는 법적 음주 가능 나이의 확대, 개선된 법의 시행, 그리고 음주운전과 관련된 문제에 대한 제고된 대중적인 인식이 포함 되어 있었다.

list 열거하다. associate A with B(=A is associated with B) A와 B를 관련시키다.

▣ (해설) 빈칸이 있는 문장에 힌트가 나와 있다. **정답 (a)**

6. 종종 침 시술소에서 암 환자를 볼 수 있다. 그들 중 몇몇은 침술이나 한약 처방으로 병세가 호전되기도 한다. 그러나 침술에 의존하는 환자들은 대부분 암 말기 단계이며 자포자기 상태에서 침술을 찾는다. 대다수는 50세 이상이며 병세는 심각하다. 부분적으로 이런 이유로 암환자들은 치료로부터 단순히 증상만 덜어주는 효과밖에 보지 못한다. 어떤 경우에 있어서는 중요하다고도 할 수 있으나, 이 증상 치료는 암의 진전을 막거나 돌이키기에는 충분하지 않다. 그러나 암 초기 단계에서는 놀라운 침술의 효과를 볼 수 있다.

acupuncture 침술. herbal treatment 한약 처방. resort to …에 의존하다.

▣ (해설) 빈칸 앞의 문장에 힌트가 나와 있다. **정답 (b)**

7. 최근의 한 과학적, 경제적, 정치적 연구에 따르면 식량의 수요와 공급

곡선이 길어도 60년이 지나면 만날 것이라고 한다. 그 때까지는 인구과잉, 증가하는 오염, 식량공급의 감소가 인간의 생명의 종식을 위협할 수 있다.
　astounding treaten 위협하다.
　🖐 (해설) 빈칸이 있는 문장에 힌트가 나와 있다.　정답 (d)

8. 모든 고난의 느낌은 그 고난에서 벗어나고자 하는 욕망과 분리할 수 없는 것이다. 즐거움에 대한 모든 생각은 즐기고자 하는 욕망과 분리해서 생각 할 수 없다. 모든 욕망은 결핍을 품고 있고, 결핍은 모두 고통스럽다. 따라서 우리의 비참함은 우리의 욕망과 능력의 불균형에서 생기는 것이다. 의식 있는 존재가 지닌 능력이 그가 갖고 있는 욕망과 같다면 그는 완벽하게 행복한 사람일 것이다.
　wretchedness 비참함. disproportion 불균형.
　🖐 (해설) 빈칸 앞의 문장과 빈칸이 있는 문장에 힌트가 나와 있다.　**정답 (c)**

9. 유추는 새로운 발견을 비추어 주는 단서들을 제공함으로써 현대과학에 기여한다. 하지만 신중히 적용되지 않으면 위험하다. 한때는 유추가 사실에 대한 명확한 예를 제공한다고 생각되었다. 이러한 생각 때문에 많은 오류와 그릇된 이론이 양산되었다. 아무리 명확하고 훌륭해 보여도 유추는 증거가 되지 못한다.
　🖐 (해설) 첫째 문장의 but이하와 마지막 문장에 힌트가 나와 있다.　**정답 (b)**

10. 윌리암스 씨 귀하,
　귀하의 모든 노력과 훌륭한 고객 서비스에 대해 감사를 드립니다. 저희는 최근까지 꿈만 같았던 주택 담보 대출 승인을 이제 막 받았습니다. 신용 문제를 다룰 때 겁날 필요가 없다는 것을 잘 알게 되었고, 또한 시간을 내어 저희에게 신용 세계의 예상치 못한 위험 요인들을 가르쳐 주셔서 감사 드립니다. 이젠 막연히 좋은 조건을 바라기보다는 배운 내용에 근거하여 선택할 수 있습니다. 저희는 귀하의 업무에 대해 문의해 오는 모든 사람에게 귀하를 꼭 추천할 것입니다.
　mortgage 저당, 담보대출. pitfall 함정
　🖐 (해설) 빈칸 앞의 문장과 빈칸에 힌트가 나와 있다.　**정답 (a)**

실력문제 3회

1. 정신분석 치료 자체의 목적은 이드의 유동성, 초자아의 인내, 그리고 자아의 통합 능력을 동시에 증가시키는 것으로 정의되어 왔다. 이중 마지막 요인에 대해 덧붙일 말은 자아의 분석에는, 개인의 자아 정체성을 어린 시절을 지배한 역사적 변화와 관련하여 분석하는 것이 포함되어야 한다는 것이다. 개인은 현재의 자신을 만들었던 역사적 필연성을 받아들일 수 있을 때 자신의 신경증을 정복하기 시작하기 때문이다. 개인은, 자유의지로 자신의 자아 정체성과 자신을 동일시할 때, 그리고 주어진 것을 해야만 하는 것에 맞추는 법을 배우게 될 때 자유롭다고 느낀다. 그때에야 비로소 개인은 자신만의 개인적 역사와 특정 시기의 인간역사가 서로 부합한다는 사실에서 자아의 능력을 도출할 수 있게 된다.

neurosis 신경증. milieu 주위, 환경

(해설) 첫째 문장과 빈칸 앞의 문장, 빈칸이 있는 문장에 힌트가 나와 있다. **정답 (b)**

2. 놀랄 정도로 많은 사람들이 영어가 주요 영어사용국에서 전통 언어를 위협하고 있다고 믿고 있다. 이러한 믿음은 우리가 힌다-우르두어, 아랍어, 스페인어 같은 언어의 엄청난 성장을 고려해 볼 때, 그리고 영어를 모국어로 하는 세계 인구의 비율이 몇 십 년 동안 줄고 있고, 안정을 되찾을 때까지 수십 년은 더 감소할 것이 확실해 보인다는 점을 고려해 볼 때, 우스울 정도로 엉터리이다.

enormous 엄청난(=prodigious). level out 한결같이 되다, 안정 상태로 되다(=level off). obsessive 강박관념의, 비정상일 정도의.

정답 (b)

3. 미국에서 비만은 큰 재난이다. 비만은 예방 가능한 죽음의 주원인으로서 담배를 밀어젖히고 정상의 자리를 차지할지도 모른다. 이를 방지하기 위해서는 학교들과 패스트푸드를 겨냥한 반 비만운동이 있어야만 한다. 특히, 학교는 보다 건강에 좋은 음식을 제공해야 하고, 전 학년에 체육 수업을 의무화해야 한다. 덧붙여 도시에는 산책로가 더 많아져야 하고, 회사 사장들은 직원들에게 근무시간에 산책로를 이용할 기회를 주어야 한다.

fatness 비만(=obesity)

🔖 (해설) 첫째 문장과 빈칸이 있는 문장에 힌트가 나와 있다. **정답 (b)**

4. 아마도 가장 흥미로운 사실은 애완동물을 기르는 것이 수많은 보통 사람들에게 어떤 영향을 끼치는가에 관한 최근의 연구에서 나타났다. 애완동물로서 개와 고양이를 기를 때 사람들은 그전보다 감기나 두통, 위통 등 건강상의 문제에 덜 시달렸다. 일부 의사들은 이런 현상에 대한 이유가 애완동물을 통한 스트레스의 감소가 뇌 속에서 방출된 화학원소들의 반응을 통해 신체의 면역 체계를 강화시킨 때문이라 믿고 있다.

immune system 면역체계

🔖 (해설) 빈칸이 있는 문장과 다음 문장에 힌트가 나와 있다. **정답 (d)**

5. 제왕절개에 의한 분만이 지난 10년 동안 너무나 많이 증가되어서 전국적인 의학 논쟁을 불러일으켜 왔다. 수요자집단 에서는 많은 제왕절개가 불필요하며 산부인과 의사의 치료 계획의 편의를 위해 행해지고 있다고 주장한다. 의사들은 제왕절개를 많이 하는 것은 위험도가 높은 임신의 경우에 산모나 태아의 사망률을 줄이는데 도움을 준다고 주장하고 있다.

paternal 아버지의, 온정주의의. adolescent 청년기의, 미숙한. Caesarean section[operation] 제왕 절개 수술. obstetrician 산부인과 의사.

🔖 (해설) 빈칸이 있는 문장에 힌트가 나와 있다. **정답 (b)**

6. 인간은 관용과 탐욕을 교묘하게 조합함으로써, 수용소의 약자를 돕기도 하고 전쟁에서 강한 자를 죽이기도 한다. 기지와 무능을 교묘하게 조합함으로써 인간은 가능한 한 필요이상으로 생필품을 대량생산하지만, 결국 효율적인 배분을 하지 못했기 때문에 수백만의 인간을 배고프고 헐벗게 하고 있다.

🔖 (해설) 빈칸 뒤에 힌트가 나와 있다. **정답 (c)**

7. 독자로든 저자로든 전기에 몰두해 본 적이 있는 사람은, 위대한 인물과 작별하고 다시 스스로를 직면하게 될 때, 왠지 오싹한 느낌을 갖게 된다는 사실을 알고 있다. 그러나 전기에는 언제나 위대한 인물의 불멸성과 우

리 자신의 불멸성을 확인시켜 주는, 영원히 기억될 만한 인용구가 있다. 예를 들어, 제퍼슨의 수사적 표현을 우리 시대의 심리학적 통찰에 적용해 보면, 제퍼슨은 다음과 같이 그의 생각을 밝히고 있다. "내가 살아온 시절들, 그리고 내가 등장하는 풍경에서 지성은 언제나 행동에 신경쓸 것을 요구받았기에 행동의 법칙을 자세히 연구할 여가는 가질 수 없었다."

🔔 (해설) 빈칸 앞에는 사실이고 빈칸 뒤에는 예를 들고 있다. **정답 (c)**

8. 특허제도는 발명가보다는 훌륭한 특허변호사를 살 수 있고 독점 보호를 위해 소송할 돈이 있는 대기업에 가장 잘 적용된다. 특허를 따내는 사람은 좋은 아이디어를 가진 사람이 아니라, 영리하고 재빠르고 돈 많은 사람이다. 특허과정이 순차적인 과정이 아니라, 인맥이 좋고 보다 공격적인 사람이 이기는 고속 경주라는 사실은 그 행위를 더욱 부정한 거래로 만든다.

patent system 특허제도. litigation 소송(=lawsuit). rig 장비, 장치

🔔 (해설) 빈칸 앞뒤의 문장에 힌트가 나와 있다. **정답 (b)**

9. 야만인이란 조야하고, 문명화되지 못했으며, 문화가 결핍된 사람이다. 고대 그리스인들은 그들 자신을 고대 세계의 어떤 다른 민족보다 훨씬 더 문명화되고 진보된 것으로 생각했다. 그리스인들에게 있어서 야만인이란 그리스 민족이 아닌 사람들이었다.

crude 가공하지 않은, 천연 그대로의. **정답 (b)**

10. 휴가 장소를 선택할 때, 우리 중 많은 사람들이 조용한 장소를 찾는다. 그러나 당신은 소리 없는 세계를 상상할 수 있겠는가? 유명한 탐험가는 완전한 고독과 함께 그리고 모든 인간의 소리로부터 멀어진 남극에서 몇 주를 보냈다. 후에 그 경험을 기록할 때, 탐험가들은 친구의 목소리나 다른 친숙한 소리만큼 그리웠던 것은 없었다고 말했다. 그러한 경험은 사람들로 하여금 귀머거리의 세계를 약간 간파할 수 있게 한다.

🔔 (해설) 빈칸 앞 문장에 힌트가 나와 있다. **정답 (c)**

실력문제 4회

1. 구조주의 이론가들은 현대 교수법에 지대한 영향을 끼쳐왔다. 그들은 학습자에게 적절한 방식으로 가르침과 배워야 될 지식을 체계화하면서, 배움에 대한 각 학생의 관점에 입각한 학습법을 연구한다. 즉, 각 학습자는 자기가 원하는 방법으로 학습에 접근한다. 구조주의 이론에서 지식은 배우는 사람의 편의를 도모하기 위해 만들어진다는 의미를 내포한다. 이와 대조적으로 구태의연한 교육 방식은 보편적인 진리가 존재하며, 그것을 이해하고 깨치는 것은 전적으로 학습자의 몫이라는 것을 함축한다.

(해설) 빈칸 앞 문장과 In contrast에 힌트가 나와 있다. **정답 (d)**

2. 두 사람 또는 그 이상의 사람들이 각자가 사는 동안 부동산을 사용하기 위해서 동등한 권한을 가지고 한뙈기의 부동산을 소유한다. 이런 종류의 소유권은 공동차지라고 불린다. 소유자들 중 한 사람이 죽으면 고인에게 상속인이 있다 해도, 그 부동산은 살아남은 소유자들에게 속한다. 공동차지의 마지막 생존자가 유일한 소유인이 되어야 한다. joint tenancy 공동차지

(해설) 빈칸 앞 문장에 힌트가 나와 있다. **정답 (d)**

3. 영국 교회, 즉 성공회는 때때로 그것이 공식적인 국가 교회로서의 의회에 의해 설립되었기 때문에 국교회로 불린다. 국왕은 영국 교회의 회원이 되어야 하지만 그 나라의 모든 다른 사람들은 자신들의 종교를 자유롭게 선택 할 수 있다. 영국에는 이슬람 사원, 불교 사원, 유대교 회당, 로마 카톨릭 교회, 많은 개신교 종파 교회들이 있다. 영국은 매우 광범위한 종교적 자유를 가지고 있다.

the Establishment 국교회. mosque 이슬람 사원. synagogue 회당. denomination 종파.

(해설) 둘째 문장에 힌트가 나와 있다. **정답 (d)**

4. 대중에게 보여지는 과학적 천재의 얼굴은 늙고 고령화되는 경향이 있다. 우리는 앨버트 아인슈타인의 산발한 머리, 찰스 다윈의 위엄 있는 턱수염, 아이작 뉴턴의 주름진 얼굴을 떠올린다. 매년 노벨상을 받는 대머리의

권위자들은 말할 것도 없이, 하지만 사실상 우리의 상상력을 발화시키고 우리의 삶을 바꾸는 획기적인 발견이나 발명은 보통 그들이 아직 30대나 40대일 때 이루어진다. 여기에는 아인슈타인, 다윈, 뉴턴이 포함된다. 이것은 전혀 놀라운 일이 아니다. 젊은 과학자들은 그 시대의 지적인 정론에 그들의 선배보다 덜 투자했기 때문이다. 그들은 본능적으로 권위에 의문을 제기한다. 그들은 새로운 생각이 미친 것이라는 말을 들을 때 그것을 믿지 않는다. 그래서 그들은 불가능한 것을 자유롭게 행한다.

　disheveled 산발한. not to mention …은 말할 것도 없이. luminary 권위자. breakthrough 획기적·발견.

　ⓐ (해설) 빈칸 다음 문장에 힌트가 나와 있다. **정답 (b)**

5. 우리는 모두 삶 속에서 일정량의 스트레스를 필요로 하지만, 그것이 일상생활을 제한할 때 그것은 문제가 되고 우리의 건강에 영향을 줄 수 있다. 우리는 모두 서로 다른 개인들이며, 한 사람에게 긍정적인 스트레스는 다른 사람에게 부정적일 수 있다. 따라서 우리가 자신의 능력을 인식하고 생활 속에서 스트레스를 주는 상황에 대처하는 방법을 찾는 것이 중요하다.

　positive 적극적인, 긍정적인. nonetheless 그럼에도 불구하고.

　ⓐ (해설) 빈칸 앞에는 사실이고 빈칸 뒤에는 적용이므로, 빈칸에는 therefore가 와야 한다. **정답 (a)**

6. 우리가 아는 바로 현대과학의 시작은 대개 프랜시스 베이컨에게서 찾는다. 경험과학의 원리와 실험이 가설 입증에서 하는 역할을 천명한 공로를 대개 17세기 초 수십 년간 저술 활동을 한 베이컨에게 돌린다. 그러나 정말 묘한 것은 뉴턴 이래 과학자들에게 내내 끼친 그의 엄청난 영향력에도 불구하고, 베이컨 자신은 한번도 시험관을 만져보지 않았다는 사실이다. 그는 단지 안락의자에 앉아서 과학자들이 앞으로 어떻게 해야 할 것인지를 준비하여 알려 주었다.

　chart 도표로 만들다, 계획하다 be credited with ~에게 공로를 돌리다 spell out 천명하다 set the scene 준비하다 bottom line 핵심, 결론, 경비 crucial 결정적인, 중대한

　ⓐ (해설) 첫째 문장과 빈칸이 있는 문장 특히 주절에 힌트가 나와 있다.

빈칸에는 주어로서 명사구가 와야 하므로 (c)는 답에서 제외된다. **정답 (b)**

7. 학교는 학부모들을 격려하여 자녀들을 능력 이상으로 몰아세우지 말라고 한다. 그러나 유교사회에서 교육은 더 높은 사회적 신분으로 나아가는 전통적인 통로이다. 결과적으로 학부모는 자녀들을 교습시키는 데 엄청난 돈을 들인다. 그러나 일단 들어가고 나면 압력은 사라진다. 업무 부하가 대체로 가볍다. 그러나 대기업에 취직을 하고 싶어 한다면 열심히 노력을 해야만 할 것이다. 대학졸업생 실업률이 요즘 20퍼센트에 달하고 있기 때문이다.

🔥 (해설) 빈칸 앞의 문장과 바로 뒤의 문장에 힌트가 나와 있다. **정답 (c)**

8. 비록 일본이 거의 가축을 기르지 않는다 할지라도, 생선이 풍부하기 때문에 일본인들은 적절한 단백질 섭취를 한다. 일본의 수산업자들은 사람들이 먹을 수 있는 양보다 더 많은 생선을 가공하기 때문에 생선의 상당 부분은 수출된다. substantial 상당한 **정답 (d)**

9. 모든 요리는 기본적으로 퓨전 요리라는 말이 있다. 역사상 음식은 여러 문화를 가로질러 전파되어 왔다. 가령 중국인들이 유럽에 국수를 전했고, 아프리카 출신 노예들은 미국 백인들에게 쌀 재배법과 요리법을 가르쳐 주었다. 몇몇 음식 전문가들은 고유 음식이라 할 만한 것은 존재하지 않는다고 주장 한다. cuisine 오리.

🔥 (해설) 빈칸 다음 문장에 힌트가 나와 있다. **정답 (a)**

10. 사막은 모든 종류의 생명과는 친하지 않은 것 같다. 물이나 식물이 거의 없으며, 강렬한 태양으로부터의 보호도 빈약하다. 그러나 사막에는 많은 종류의 곤충, 파충류, 조류, 포유류가 있다. 인간은 물에 너무 의존적이어서 우리에게 충분한 물이 공급되는 것처럼 보이는 것이 없이 어떤 동물의 생명이 존재할 수 있는 방법을 이해하는 것이 어렵다는 것을 알았다. 그것들은 알려질 수 없고, 단순하게 사막의 동물들에게 충분한 양이 우리들에게 는 불충분하다는 것이다.

🔥 (해설) 첫째 문장과 빈칸이 있는 문장에 힌트가 나와 있다. **정답 (d)**

독해 · Part II

실력문제 1회

1. 하나의 기억처럼 보이는 것도 사실은 복합적인 구성물이다. 망치를 생각해 보라. 당신의 두뇌는 재빨리 그 연장의 이름과 모양, 기능, 무게, 부딪힐 때의 소리를 두뇌의 각기 다른 부분에서 기억해 낸다. 기억력 감퇴는 뇌의 각기 다른 곳에 저장되어 있는 조각을 한데 모으지 못하는 것이다. 우리들 중 많은 사람들은 20대가 되면 이러한 조립 공정의 쇠약을 경험하기 시작한다. 그리고 50대가 되면 이 문제는 걱정할 수준이 된다.

heft 무게, 무게가 나가다(=weigh). symptom 증상. debilitate 약하게 하다. aggravate 악화시키다, 성나게 하다.

(해설) 셋째 문장에 힌트가 나와 있다. **정답 (c)**

2. 어떤 자격증을 취득해서 대학을 졸업하는 일은 매우 중요하지만, 인생에서 성공하기 위해서는 그것 말고도 많은 일을 각자가 해내야 한다. 정상에 오르려는 의지가 있다면 서류상의 자격은 그다지 중요하지 않다. 과거에 대학교 학위를 가진 대기업의 대표이사나 중역이 얼마나 있었는가? 그들 중 상당수는 아마도 가게 매장을 거쳐 정상까지 노력해서 올라간 사람들일 것이다. 요즘은 이름난 고등교육기관에서 학위를 따려고 애쓰는 사람이 점점 많아지기 때문에, 서류상의 자격증이 중요하게 보일지도 모른다. 그러나 내가 확고하게 믿는 것은, 한 장의 종이에 불과한 학위증서보다는 건실한 경험과 기술이 더 중요하다는 것이다.

diploma 졸업증서, 공문서. must 절대로 필요한 것.

(해설) 첫째 문장과 둘째 문장에 힌트가 나와 있다. **정답 (b)**

3. 경찰은 불법으로 자동 현금 인출기에서 돈을 인출하려 했던 용의자 2명을 쫓고 있다. 이번 주 일요일 밤 12시경에 20-25세로 보이는 두 남자가 오션가의 유니언 은행에 들어와서 로비에 있는 자동 현금 인출기에 접근하려 했다. 용의자들은 몇 차례 시도에도 현금박스로의 접근이 불가능하자 포기하고 달아났다. 경찰은 용의자 제보에 최고 1,000달러의 현상금을 걸었다.

ATM 자동 현금인출기(=automated-teller machine). withdrawal 인출 foyer 로비(=lobby), 휴게실.

🔎 (해설) 셋째 문장에 힌트가 나와 있다. **정답 (d)**

4. 10년과 1년 기한 변동 금리 주택담보 대출에 대한 평균 이자율이 전국적으로 이번 주에 조금 내려갔다. 반면 15년 기한 주택담보 대출 금리는 현 상태를 유지했다. 10년 기한 주택담보 대출의 고정 금리는 7.17%에서 7.16%로 하락했다. 15년 기한 대출금리는 6.48%로 변동이 없었다.

mortgage 저당, 주택담보대출. dip 가라앉다. 내려가다. **정답 (d)**

5. 교역산업부의 위렌 스프링 연구소의 연구진들에 따르면 혼합된 쓰레기를 재활용하는 실질적인 목표는 무게로 따져 15-25% 중간이라고 한다. 이 비율은 금속과 아마도 약간의 유리도 포함할 수 있는 것이다. 이스트 앵글리아 대학의 연구진들이 집계한 통계는 '모으기' 계획(현관의 층층대에 신문 모으기와 같은)과 '가져가기' 계획(병 저장소와 같은), 그리고 금속 추출 공장들을 조화시키면 매립지로 가져 갈 가정에서 나오는 쓰레기의 전체 무게를 거의 절반으로 줄일 수도 있다는 것을 보여 준다.

halve 이등분하다, 반감하다. landfill 매립지. **정답 (c)**

6. 심리학과 응용언어학 문헌에서 가장 널리 쓰이고 있는 용어는 '스키마'이며, 이 용어는 심리학자 바틀렛에 의해 1932년만큼 오래전에 인간의 기억력의 작동 원리에 대한 그의 고전적 연구에서 처음 쓰인 말이다. 틀 이론과 마찬가지로 스키마 이론은 우리가 머리에 지닌 지식이 여러 가지 상호 관련된 형태로 이루어졌다는 것이다. 이러한 형태는 경험 세계의 어떤 면에 대한 우리의 이전 경험 전부로 구성되며, 미래의 경험에 대해 우리가 예측을 할 수 있게 해준다. **정답 (c)**

7. 경제계에서 "확장국면"은 회복과 번영을 포함한다. 회복기에는 기존의 생산시설이 증대되고, 새로운 시설은 개발되고, 기존 시설물의 확대로 새로운 사업들이 생겨난다. 이러한 발달에 의해 야기된 낙관적인 분위기 때문에 노동과 원자재의 수요가 증가할 뿐만 아니라 기계의 자본 투자가 증가한다. 경제의 한 부분의 확장으로 인해 다른 분야들에 공명 효과를 일으

킨다. 예를 들면, 자동화 산업이 번성하면 철강, 유리, 고무의 생산도 번성한다. 결과적으로 보다 확대되는 번영의 순환이 이루어진다.
　phase out 제거하다, 점차로 정지하다.　**정답 (a)**

　8. 오염에 대한 철저한 해결책은 거의 불가능한 것이기 때문에 대중적 행동을 단호하게 해야만 한다. 한꺼번에 오염을 제거할 수 없지만 오염을 감소시킬 수 있다. 그러나 우리는 각자 역할을 맡아야 한다. 자동차 오염방지 장치가 작동하는지 점검하라. 전기사용을 줄이라. 에어컨은 정말로 필요한 것인가? 땅이나 물에 쓰레기나 다른 폐기물을 버리지 말라. 오염을 발생시키는 자들에게 단호한 조치를 취하도록 정부에 요구하라. 깨끗한 세상을 만들 수도 있고 아무 것도 안 할 수도 있다. 선택은 당신에게 달려 있다.
　part 역할(=role). dump garbage 쓰레기를 버리다. have no choice but to+동사. …하지 않을 수 없다.　**정답 (c)**

　9. 자본주의 체제는 사유재산 보유와 자신들의 물질적인 복지를 진전시키기 위한 수단으로 각자 선택하여 경제활동에 종사할 수 있는 개인의 자유로 특징지어진다. 개인의 이윤추구는 그러한 경제를 이끌어 나가는 원동력이며, 경쟁은 이를 조절하거나 제어하는 장치로서 작용한다. 자본주의적 생산은 정부 계획에 기초하여 편성되는 것이 아니라, 무엇을 생산하고, 어떻게 생산하며 또 어떻게 유통시킬 것인가를 정하는 무수한 개개인들의 결정들을 체계화하고 유효하게 만드는 수단으로서의 가격제도를 특징으로 한다.
　feature 얼굴의 생김새, 특징, …의 특징을 이루라. myriad 무수, 무수한. shortcoming 결점, 부족.　**정답 (c)**

　10. 마침내 예루살렘은 해방되었다. 십자군이 첫째로 고려한 것은 예루살렘을 통치하는 방법이었다. 대다수의 십자군은 자신들이 익숙한 통치 형태인 봉건 왕국을 건설하는 것이 최선이라고 결정했다. 봉건 왕국은 중앙집권적인 통치 체제를 갖추어 새로이 획득한 영토의 방어를 조정할 수 있었다. 이 생각은 성직자의 불만에 부딪혔는데 그들은 거룩한 도시(예루살렘)의 통치 방식에 유일하게 적합한 방식은 교회 통치이며, 그 지역의 세속적 통치자는 성직 통치자에 종속되어야 한다고 믿었다. 하지만 새롭게 획득

한 동쪽영토를 위협하는 긴급한 위기상황은 대부분의 군주에게 강력한 세속적 통치자의 중요성과 필요성을 확신시키는데 충분했다.

Crusader 십자군. feudal kingdom 봉건 왕국. ecclesiastical 교회의. imminent 긴급한. **정답 (d)**

실력문제 2회

1. 일어나는 일들을 지켜보면서 TV 시청자들은 새로운 방식으로 사건의 일부가 된다. 그러나 가장 사건의 일부가 되는 것은 일어나는 일이 아무 것도 없을 때이다. 사람들은 늘 무엇인가를 보고 싶어 하며, 맨 벽과 깜박이는 광고 방송 사이에서 우리의 눈은 광고방송을 택할 것이기 때문이다. 화로와 불이 한때 집의 중심이었던 것처럼, 이제는 텔레비전이 현대인의 존재의 중심이 되었다. 방의 모든 점들은 이 물건의 존재에 모아지며 우리의 조상들이 불길을 보며 몽롱해지곤 했던 것처럼 심지어는 딴 생각을 하고 있으면서도 우리 눈은 화면을 응시한다.

flicker 깜박이다. 흔들리다, 명멸. converge 한 점에 보이다. 집중하다. doze 졸다. narcotize 마취시키다. **정답 (b)**

2. 귀하를 플래티넘 카드 특별 회원으로 모시게 되어 기쁩니다. 당신을 위한 몇 가지 특별한 혜택에 대한 정보와 함께 새 카드를 보내 드립니다. 지금 즉시 카드 뒷면에 서명하시고 바로 활용하십시오. 가게, 식당, 호텔, 주유소, 그 밖의 많은 곳에서 사용가능 합니다. 닐 플래티넘 카드는 세계 천백만 군데 이상의 장소에서 환영을 받습니다. **정답 (b)**

3. 과학의 핵심은 기초연구분야에 있다. 원자구조의 이해, 지진의 원인, 아니면 두 사람 이상이 만날 때 일어나는 사회작용의 역학 관계에 대한 연구이던지, 기초연구는 스스로를 위해 지식을 추구한다. 응용연구는 특정한 실제적인 문제에 목표를 둔다. 결과를 볼 수 있고 그 혜택을 누릴 수도 있다. 결과는 즉시 실용성을 갖기 때문에 기초연구보다도 더욱 더 많이 응용연구에 시간을 투자하게 된다. (정부는 기초연구분야에 연구 기금의 7%만을 사용한다.) 주의해야할 것은 응용연구로 인하여 기초연구를 없애지 말

아야 한다는 것이다. 기초 연구는 정교하고 개선된 기술에 이르는 최종적인 열쇠이다.

　　earmark 배당하다, 충당하다, 표를 하다. **정답 (d)**

　4. 노화의 신비는 생명의 신비만큼 심오하다. 지난 세기 동안 선진국의 평균 수명은 두 배가 되었다. 그것은 영양, 위생, 그리고 의학의 개선 덕분이었다. 그러나 어떤 한 인간의 잠재 수명은 할라와카가 뱀을 만났던 이후로 크게 변하지 않았다. 50세가 되면 아무리 건강하다 할지라도, 기관의 기능과 감각의 예민함이 천천히 쇠퇴한다. 그리고 비록 일부 사람들이 한 반 세기를 튼튼한 건강을 누리며 산다고 할지라도, 120세 이상 살 수 있는 가능성은 실제로 없다. 그렇게 절묘하게 건강에 이로운 것들이 조화를 이루고서도 우리들은 왜 그렇게 예상할 수 있는 방법으로 무너지고 마는가? 우리는 개보다 오래 산다. 그러나 거북이보다는 오래 살지 못하는 이유가 무엇인가? 거북이들을 따라 잡을 수 있는 우리의 가능성은 무엇인가?

　　life expectancy 수명(=life span, expectation of life). sensory acuity 감각의 예민함. **정답 (d)**

　5. 15년 이상 동안 바이러스 학자들은 인간이 침팬지 아종으로부터 에이즈 바이러스를 얻었다고 믿어 왔다. 새로운 연구는 에이즈 병원균이 제일 처음 생겨난 장소를 대서양 연안의 가봉, 적도 기니, 카메룬 근처 지역으로 좁혔다. 이 연구는 에이즈 바이러스가 언제 어떻게 '종의 장벽'을 뛰어 넘었는지에 관한 신비를 밝히지는 못했다. 그러나 그 연구 덕택에 좀 더 실용적이고 임상적으로 관련된 문제들이 분명해 질 수 있을지도 모른다. 왜냐하면 침팬지 아종은 에이즈 조상 바이러스로부터 병에 걸리지 않는다는 것을 예비 증거가 암시적으로 보여주었기 때문이다. 그 이상의 연구가 이것이 사실임을 증명한다면, 유전자의 98%가 침팬지와 동일한 침팬지의 사촌인 인간에게는 에이즈 바이러스가 왜 치명적인지를 명백히 하는데 침팬지 아종이 도움이 될 것이다.

　　virologist 바이러스 학자. microbe 세균, 미생물. shed light on …을 비추다.
　　정답 (b)

　6. 몇 해 전 겨울 12명의 연구자들이 항히스타민제에 대한 통계수치를

따로 따로 발표했다. 각 수치는 상당한 정도의 감기 증상이 치료 후에 나아졌음을 보여 주었다. 최소한 광고계에서는 엄청난 파장이 뒤따랐고, 의약품 생산 붐이 일어났다. 이는 끊임없이 솟아오르는 희망뿐만 아니라 통계수치 저편의 오랫동안 알려져 온 사실을 바라보지 않으려는 기이한 거부에 기초하는 것이었다. 유머작가인 헨리 G. 펠슨 지적했듯이 적절한 치료를 받으면 감기는 7일이 지나면 낫지만 그대로 놔두면 1주일은 지속된다.

antihistamine pill 항히스타민제, ensue 결과로서 따르다. **정답 (c)**

7. 당신이 "종교 전쟁"이라는 논문에서 기술한 것처럼, 이스라엘에는 열정적으로 교리를 준수하는 일부 유대인과 비슷하게 열렬한 세속적인 일부 유대인 사이에 갈등의 여지가 확실하게 있을 수 있다 할지라도, 대부분의 유대교 이스라엘인들은 단일민족으로서 종교적 전통으로 묶인 한 가족으로 느끼고 행동한다. 구성원들이 종교규정을 다소라도 준수하기로 선택한다. 이스라엘 국민은 양극화되어 있지 않으며, 종교적 내란의 직전에 있지도 않다. **정답 (a)**

8. 항공기의 안전 운항을 보장하는 일은 핵심적인 3원칙에 달려 있다. 즉, 내공성 인증을 담당하는 국가 규제 당국과 정비와 감사 및 부품 교체에 대한 기술적 자문을 담당하는 항공기 제조업체, 그리고 제조업체의 지시대로 운항 하도록 되어 있는 항공기, 이 세 가지이다. N73711기의 경우 알로하 항공의 정비 과정은 심각한 결손을 보여 주었다. 항공기가 섬과 섬을 오가는 단거리 비행으로 과다 사용되었고, 염기 있는 대기의 부식에 노출되어 있었지만 이렇 다할 부식 제어 대책이 불충분했다. **정답 (b)**

9. 한국의 놀라운 회복은 작년 10.7 퍼센트의 경제성장률을 기록함으로써 동아시아는 물론 세계 시장을 선도하게 되었다. 이러한 급속의 반전은 1998년 나라 경제를 6.7퍼센트나 주저앉혔던 파란만장한 금융위기를 딛고 일어난 것이다. 극도의 어려움에도 불구하고 금융위기는 개방과 개혁을 통하여 한국을 세계화하는 기회로 만들어준 것처럼 보인다. 정부의 한 관리는 말한다. "우리는 최상의 상품과 용역을 세계 시장에 제공할 때만 살아남을 수 있다는 교훈을 배웠다."

rebound 회복, 반전(=turnaround) tumultuous 소란스러운, 파란만장한

plunge 던져 넣다, 가라앉히다 stringency 절박, 핍박, 박력 recession 후퇴, 경기후퇴, 불경기 **정답 (b)**

10. 많은 동물들이 서로 의사소통을 할 수 있다. 물론 그들 중 어느 것도 우리처럼 말할 수는 없다. 실제로 말을 사용할 줄 아는 동물은 없지만 그들은 의사소통 수단을 갖고 있다. 가령, 새를 예로 들어보자. 병아리를 가진 암탉이 경고음을 내면, 그 새끼 병아리들은 어미 닭이 그들을 불러 모을 다른 소리를 낼 때까지 움직이지 않고 쭈그리고 있다. 야생 조류는 밤에 이동할 때 울음소리를 낸다. 이런 울음소리는 새들이 무리에서 떨어져 나가지 않도록 한다. 만일 철새 중 한 마리가 길을 잃으면, 그것은 다른 새들의 울음소리를 듣고 무리로 돌아갈 수 있다. 우리 자신은 단지 말하지 말하는 것 이상의 상호 의사소통 수단을 갖고 있다. 동물들은 말할 수 없고, 단어나 문장을 사용할 수 없지만, 그들 중 어떤 것들은 우리가 놀라서 외치는 것 등에 해당하는 소리를 낸다.

crouch down 쭈그리다, 몸을 웅크리다. stray 길을 잃다, 헤매다. **정답 (d)**

실력문제 3회

1. 인간과 달리 로봇은 불평이나 결석도 없이 따분하고, 더럽고 또는 불쾌한 작업을 한다. 그들은 한 번 시작하면 아주 오랫동안 구멍을 뚫거나 철판 부품들을 만들어 내거나 한꺼번에 찢는다. 로봇은 또한 오랜 시간에 걸쳐서 인간 대신 아주 위험한 일을 수행한다. 그런 일들은 질병을 야기 시키거나, 연기나, 방사능으로 인해 잦은 사고를 일으킬 수 있는 것들이다. 게다가 조립 작업대에 있는 로봇들은 사람보다 비용이 덜 든다. 그들은 하루 24시간 일할 수 있다.

fume 연기, 가스, 흥분. radiation 방사(능), 복사. **정답 (b)**

2. 과학자들은 50년간 우주여행과 위성 발사에서 나온 쓰레기를 어떻게 처리할 것인가에 대해 난처해 한다. 작은 잔해의 궤도를 바꾸기 위해 레이저를 사용하는 것과 고속으로 움직이는 쓰레기 주위를 감싸 속도를 늦춰줄 커다란 거품공을 이용하는 것에 대해 연구가 이루어졌으나, 이러한 방법

은 아직 기술적으로 가능하지 않다. 그래서 과학자들은 쓰레기가 덜 생기는 우주선을 만드는 데 총력을 기울이고 있다. 하지만 이미 존재하는 쓰레기를 치울 수는 없다. 이 문제를 풀기 위해서는 아직도 많은 연구가 필요하다.
　stump 괴롭히다, 난처하게 하다, 유세하다.　debris 잔해, 파편. foam 거품.
　정답 (b)

　3. 형제자매가 없는 삶을 상상해 보라. 말다툼할 일도, 거실에서 레슬링 시합을 할 일도, 머리를 잡아당기는 일도 없을 것이다. 41퍼센트의 미국 가정은 아이가 한 명인 가족을 꾸려나가게 된다. 그러나, 그 나머지 가정과 점차 증가 추세에 있는 여러 명의 양자를 함께 키우는 가정에 있어 형제자매간의 관계는 중대 관심사이며, 그래야만 한다. 진실로, 긍정적인 형제자매 관계는 삶을 살아가는 힘의 원천일 수 있다.
　sibling 형제자매. bickering 말다툼.　**정답 (d)**

　4. 나는 콜롬비아 마약 조직과의 전쟁을 또 다시 시작해야 한다는 미국의 입장을 지지합니다. 콜롬비아 대통령 앙드레 파스트라나가 약자의 입장에서는 반군과 평화협상을 할 수 없다는 것을 이해하지 못하고 있는 것은 불행한 일입니다. 이 반군들은 법률과 명예에 복종하지 않고, 그 어떤 도덕적 원칙도 없으며, 마약 거래와 납치에서 부당 이득을 취하는 무자비한 사람들입니다. 대통령은 군대와 밀접한 관계를 유지해야만 합니다. 그를 도울 수 있는 유일한 힘은 반군들에게 그들의 행동이 위험하다는 것을 보여주는 것입니다.

조지 핀존
콜롬비아 보고타에서

　정답 (d)

　5. 사람의 전체 몸무게의 약 16%는 단백질이다. 근육조직 속의 단백질 미오글로빈은 산소를 저장하고, 고기가 붉은색을 띠게 한다. 음식물을 소화시키는 침, 위액, 장액 속에도 단백질이 있다. 뇌하수체는 성장을 조절하는 인간성장 호르몬이라 불리는 단백질을 분비한다. 췌장 속의 어떤 세포들은 혈액 속의 당분을 조절하는 단백질인 인슐린을 분비한다.
　saliva 침. gastric juice 위액. intestinal juice 장액. pituitary gland 뇌하

수체. secrete 분비하다. **정답 (b)**

6. 수신 : 전 직원
   발신 : 인사과
   　1999년 9월 1일자로 True Con社에서는 또 하나의 건강 보험 상품인 Blue Cross of Boston을 내놓습니다. 만일 여러분들이 신상품보험 보상범위에 대해서 더 알고 싶으면, 인사과로 연락하십시오. 상기시켜 드릴 것은, 신 기획상품이든 기존의 보험상품이든 1999년 12월 17일까지 모든 보험 신청서류를 제출해야 한다는 것을 잊지 마십시오. 이 날짜로 접수되지 않은 서류는 나중에 제기되는 어떤 청구에 대해서도 상환을 유예할 수 있습니다.
   　coverage 적용 범위, 보상 범위. turn in 제출하다. reimbursement 변제, 상환.
   정답 (d)

7. 자반은 시판되는 가장 효과적인 금연 제품 중 하나이다. 로젠지스는 자반보다 더 효과적이나 영국에서만 구할 수 있다. 붙이는 패치나 껌과는 달리 자반은 약국에서 바로 살 수 있는 니코틴 대체요법이 아니라, 실은 의사의 처방이 필요한 항우울성 치료제이다. 그것이 금연에 정확히 어떤 식으로 도움이 되는지는 확실하지 않다.
   　cessation 중지, 중단. over-the-counter 의사의 처방 없이 팔 수 있는. antidepressant 항울제. **정답 (b)**

8. 바르셀로나 — 아홉 명의 산악인들 일행이 에베레스트 산을 청소하기 위해 어제 네팔로 향했다. 이 세계 최고봉은 40여 년 전 처음 정복된 이래 많은 양의 쓰레기들이 산기슭에 버려져 왔다. 죽은 산악인들의 시신도 또한 그곳에 버려져 있다. 스페인 등정대는 20명의 셰르파들의 도움을 받아 10톤 가량의 쓰레기를 수거할 계획이다. 이 쓰레기는 1953년 뉴질랜드인 에드먼드 힐러리 경과 텐징에 의해 첫 등정이 이루어진 이래로 에베레스트 산을 오르는 수많은 산악인들에 의해 버려진 것이다. **정답 (c)**

9. 나이든 미국인에게 노인 격리는 양로원에서 가장 널리 행해지고 있다. 미국에는 현재 1,150만 명의 노인들이 별도리 없이 양로원에 살고 있다. 미국인 약 다섯 명 중 한 명 꼴로 생애의 어느 때인가는 결국 그런 집에서 살게 될 것이다. 이 노인들의 대다수는 몸이 쇠약해지거나 혼자 힘으로

사는데 필요한 자금이 모자라서 양로원으로 들어간다. 양로원에 들어간다는 것은 전체 시설의 일부가 된다는 것을 의미한다. 활동은 오로지 양로원에 의해 결정되며, 주거자들 개개인의 선호에 맞춰지는 일이 거의 없지만, 그들은 이를 받아들이지 않을 수가 없는 것이다. **정답 (a)**

10. 인간은 두 가지 기본 방식으로 사고할 수 있다. 집중적 사고는 일관성 있게 체계적으로 해답을 지향한다. 확장적 사고는 중심으로부터 여러 방향으로 동시에 흩어지며 특정 목적이 아닌 다양한 탐구 방법을 추구한다. 대체로 과학자들은 집중적 사고를 하지만, 확장적 사고야말로 과거와 단절하고 예기치 못한 결론을 유도해내는 사고방식이다. **정답 (d)**

실력문제 4회

1. 이번 주 전 미네소타 차량관리국에 배포된 새 지침서에 따라, 단기 비자 소지 외국인에게는 운전면허증이 발급되지 않을 것이다. 다른 주의 면허증을 가진 운전자들은 미네소타 운전 면허증을 따기 위해 적어도 하나 이상의 다른 신분증을 제시해야 할 것이다. 미국 내 1년 이하 체류 비자를 지닌 이민자들이 미네소타에서 운전하려면 본국의 운전면허증을 사용해야 할 것이다. 새로운 운전면허증 발급 법규는 신분증 위조 범죄를 집중단속하려는 정부 노력의 일환이다.

crack down on 단속하다. **정답 (d)**

2. 두툼하고 튼튼한 상자에 신문지를 각 측면마다 겹겹이 대어 상자 안에 제품이 꼭 맞게 들어가도록 주의해서 포장하십시오. 모든 부속품, 코드 등은 모두 흐트러지지 않도록 안전하게 포장해서 제품과 함께 두어야 합니다. 수송 도중 손상되지 않도록 주의해서 포장하십시오. 가장 인접한 서비스 센터의 이름과 주소, 귀하의 성함과 발송자 주소를 상자에 명확히 기재하십시오. 귀하의 성함, 제품을 구입한 날짜와 장소, 점검을 요하는 결함사항을 적은 편지를 꼭 동봉하도록 하십시오.

snug 아늑한, 아담한, 꼭 맞는. carton 판지상자, 마분지 상자. **정답 (c)**

3. 프랑스 과학자들은 금요일, 소화하기 쉬운 우유를 생산하는 동물들을

유전 공학으로 만들어 내는 방법을 발견했다고 발표했다. 그들은 생쥐에게만 실험을 실시했지만 동일한 유전자 변화가 소에서도 일어난다면, 낙농장은 소화하기 쉬운 우유를 대량으로 만들 수 있을 것이라고 말했다. 프랑스 의료 연구원의 버나드 조스트와 동료들의 말에 의하면, "전 세계 성인의 약 70퍼센트는 락토스 알레르기가 있다."고 한다. 이들은 락토스라는 젖당을 소화할 수 없어서, 설사와 메스꺼움, 복부 경련과 기타 불편한 증상을 보인다. 조스트 팀은 쥐의 유전자를 생쥐에 삽입하여, 생쥐가 젖을 분비하기 전에 우유를 쉽게 소화되기 쉬운 상태가 되게 했다. 락토스 알레르기가 있는 대부분의 사람들은 락타아제라 알려진 효소가 부족하다.

　churn out 대량 생산하다. diarrhea 설사. nausea 매스꺼움. abdominal cramp 복부경련. predigest 소화가 잘 되도록 요리하다. enzyme 효소. **정답 (c)**

　4. 좋은 탐정 소설은 모두 독자들로 하여금 빈틈없는 긴장감을 느끼게 한다. 사람들은 심지어 긴장감 그 자체를 위한 긴장감이 탐정 소설이 노리는 것이라고 말하기도 한다. 탐정 소설은 노골적이고 잔인하게 묘사될 수 있다. 피와 시체 위에서 만들어졌다 하더라도, 좋은 탐정 소설은 그러한 것이 주는 매력만으로 명성을 얻을 수 없다. 그것들은 순전히 수수께끼를 해결하고 범인을 찾아내는 지적인 훈련을 위한 구실에 불과하다. 이것은 사람을 끌어들여, 있음직한 올바른 단서를 찾기 위한 외견상으로는 정반대의 것, 즉 탐정과 독자간의 경쟁을 통해, 역설적으로 휴식을 제공하는 것이다. 성공적인 수사 자체는 이야기의 나머지 부분과 분리되어 묘사된다.
정답 (c)

　5. 정확하게 보자면, 과학은 인간의 점증하는 힘과 진보의 도구 이상의 것이다. 과학은 또한 모든 종의 진화 과정에서 개발된 도구 중 최고의 도구이며, 인간이 자신의 환경에 유연하게 적응하고 환경을 자신에게 맞게 조정하는 도구이기도 하다. 인간이 성공적으로 존속하려면 자연과 사회적·기술적 변화의 속도를 통제하는 한편 촉진하는데 있어서 과학이라는 도구를 보다 많이 이용해야 한다. 이런 의미에서 보면, 적어도 과학은 자연현상과 우리가 "자연 법칙"이라고 부르는 규칙간의 실제 관계를 이해하는 새로운 감각 기관의 역할을 훨씬 넘어선다. 과학은 또한 인간이 자연에 적응하는 수단이며, 이상적인 환경을 창조하기 위한 도구이다.

malleable 유순한, 유연한(=easily trained or adapted). **정답 (a)**

6. 크고 강한 것이 작고 약한 것보다 훨씬 덜 위험하다는 말은 사실인 것 같다. 자연은 (무엇이든) 작고 약한 것은 더 빠르게 재생산 되도록 만들어 놓는다. 하지만 물론 이것은 사실이 아니다. 죽는 속도보다 빠르게 재생산하지 못한 것들은 소멸하였다. 그러나 작은 실수들, 작은 고통들, 작은 근심거리들은 어떠한가? 우주적인 병폐는 커다란 근심이 아니라 사소한 노여움으로부터 비롯된다. 거대한 것은 사람을 죽일 수도 있지만, 만일 죽이지 못할 경우 사람이 그것들보다 강해지고 뛰어나게 된다. 사람을 파멸시키는 것은 성가신 잔소리, 잡다한 청구서들, (잘못 걸려온)전화, 무좀, 두드러기쑥, 감기, 권태 따위인 것이다. 이것들은 모두 부정적인 것들이며 사소한 좌절들이지만, 이보다 강한 것은 아무것도 없다.

ulcer 궤양, 병폐. nibble 갉아 먹다. nagging 성가신 잔소리. athlete's foot 무좀. ragweed 두드러기쑥, 금불초. **정답 (a)**

7. 문화는 경제와 마찬가지로 영역을 배열하는 방법이다. 문화는 경제와 일치할 수도 있지만 구별될 수도 있다. 문화적 지도와 경제적 지도는 예외없이 단순하게 중첩될 수 없고, 후자의 수명도 인상적이지만, 문화가 세계 경제보다는 훨씬 이전부터 시작되었다는 만으로도 이 사실은 논리적이다. 문화는 인간 역사에서 가장 오래된 특성이다. 경제는 서로 계승되고, 정치 제도들은 무너지지만 문명은 자신의 방식을 따라 지속된다. 로마는 5세기에 멸망했지만 로마 교회는 지금도 우리와 함께 있다. 18세기에 힌두교가 이슬람교에 대항했을 때, 이것은 영국이 정복할 수 있는 틈을 열어 주었지만, 힌두교와 이슬람교 사이의 분쟁은 아직도 계속되고 있다. 반면에 영국의 인도 지배는 30년 이전에 끝났다.

Raj 지배, 통치(=rule; government). life span 수명. crumble 부스러뜨리다, 무너지다, 망하다. insinuate 넌지시 비추다(=hint or suggest indirectly: imply). **정답 (a)**

8. 우리는 생활수준을 자동차, 생산추진력, 소득액으로 판단하는 것을 중지해야만 한다. 일이 고역이 되고 업무 시간이 지루해질 때, 젊은 남녀가 가정을 꾸려갈 여유가 없을 때, 어린이들이 벽돌로 인해 잔디와 하늘로부터 차단되어 있을 때는, 생활수준이 높은 것이 아니다. 우리는 우리의 교육

을 젊은이의 정신에 주입시키는 지식의 양보다는, 그것이 창조하는 삶의 지혜로 평가해야 한다. 지식의 축척은 그것이 사람들의 이익 때문에 가정보다는 사업을 우선순위에 둘 때, 그리고 여성들이 자녀들보다 직업을 먼저 생각하게 만들 때 부정적인 가치를 가진다. 또한 지식의 축척이 현대 무기들을 통제해야 하는 인간의 가치기준을 우리에게 가르쳐 주지 않은 채, 그 무기들을 방치하는 마술에 대해 가르칠 때 부정적인 가치를 가진다.
　　drudgery 고역. sod 잔디. instill 스며들게 하다, 주입시키다.　**정답 (c)**

9. 삶을 재미와 오락으로 바꾸려는 충동이 바로 스포츠의 원천이다. 놀이를 찾는 인간의 경향은 모든 사회, 모든 시대에서 스포츠와 게임으로 표현 되어 왔다. 예컨대 권투는 6,000년도 더 이전에 아프리카의 나일강 유역을 통해 퍼졌다. 이집트인의 예술은 무려 기원전 12세기 전의 펜싱을 묘사한다. 현대의 많은 구기 종목은 수세기 전 유럽의 수도원 회랑에서 최초로 경기했던 옛날식 핸드볼에서 그 유래를 찾아볼 수 있다.
　　wellspring 원천, 자원, 근원. penchant 경향, 취미, 기호. cloister 회랑, 수도원.　**정답 (b)**

10. 모든 유명한 담배 브랜드들에 똑같은 함량의 타르와 니코틴이 들어 있는 것은 아니다. 필터가 달린 담배는 다른 브랜드들보다 더 낮은 타르 함량을 갖고 있다. 그러나 흡연을 덜 위험하게 하는 방법들이 있다. 담배를 끝까지 다 피워서는 안 된다. 흡연자들은 1년마다 신체 검진을 받아야 한다. 담당 의사들은 그 검진에 폐기능 검사와 흉부 X-레이 혹은 타액 검사를 포함시킬 수 있다. 담배를 끊은 흡연자들은 기분이 더 좋아지고 호흡하기가 더 편해진다. 담배를 끊으면 호흡기 증상이 나아진다. 전에 담배를 끊은 자들의 사망률은 비흡연자의 사망률에 근접하고 있다.
　　sputum test 타액 검사 respiratory symptom 호흡기 증상　**정답 (d)**

독해 · Part III

실력문제 1회

1. 두 번째 단점은 혁신적인 노동력이 부족하다는 것이다. (a) 아시아가 '기업가적인' 문화를 가지고 있다고 자주 칭찬을 받는다고 할지라도, 이런 칭호는 두 가지 분명한 특성을 총괄하여 이르는 것이다. 다시 말하면, 그 특성은 이윤 추구욕과 영리하게 새로운 방법을 생각해내는 능력이다. (b) 가상대학이 옥스퍼드나 하버드를 대신하기엔 아직 이른 것처럼, 가상 실리콘 벨리도 아직은 팔로 알토의 적수가 되지는 못한다. (c) 그러나 그들은 종종 모방을 일삼는 기회주의자들이다. (d) 정말 창의적인 기업가는 아직 그 층이 엷고, 나타난다 해도 본국에 있기 보다는 모두들 미국으로 건너가기 바쁘다.
shortcoming 결점, 단점, 부족. supplant 대신 들어앉다, 대신하다. **정답 (b)**

2. 초자아에는 '선한' 행위와 '악한' 행위에 따른 보상과 처벌이라는 두 가지 측면이 있다. (a) 초자아의 긍정적인 측면은 고상한 도덕 원리들과 일치되는 이타적인 행동을 지지하는 데, 이러한 측면을 때로 이상적인 자아라고 한다. (b) 자아(에고)는 그 사람이 할 수 있는 것에만 관심이 있는 반면, 원아(이드)는 그 사람이 원하는 것과 관계가 있다. (c) 우리가 만약 좋은 옷을 입고서도 진흙탕에 빠진 돼지를 구했을 때 우리는 개인적으로 한껏 자긍심을 경험하게 된다. (d) 프로이드에 따르면 이것이 초자아가 자아에게 보상을 주는 것이다. **정답 (b)**

3. 거울은 디자인을 돋보이게 하는 위대한 도구이다. (a) 거울은 다루기가 쉽고 작은 공간을 크게 보이게 하는 굉장한 요술 능력을 가지고 있다. (b) 거울을 가진 사람은 부엌에서 일하면서도 바다의 전망과 나무들을 볼 수 있다. (c) 방에 거울을 마련하려는 사람은 거울을 방에 가져와 비추어 보아야 한다. (d) 또한, 방에 놓은 다른 물건들의 가격을 고려해 볼 때, 거울은 비교적 저렴하다. **정답 (c)**

4. 유전 공학에 의해 생산된 식품이 현재 시중에 다량 유통되고 있기 때문에 공상 과학 식품에 대한 두려움이 실제적이든 아니든, 최근 많은 관심

을 받고 있다. (a) 어떤 사람들은 이들 식품의 맛이 동일하지 않고 또 병을 유발 할 수 있다는 것에 대해 염려하고 있다. (b) 예를 들어 송어의 유전자는 현재 좀 더 오래 보존되는 토마토를 생산하는 데에 사용되고 있다. (c) 그러나 유전자를 접합하는 과정에서 송어 유전자가 충분히 순화되지 않았다면, 생선 알레르기가 있는 사람들이 이러한 토마토를 먹고 병에 걸릴 수 있다. (d) 송어 유전자로 인해서 사람들은 오래 보존되는 토마토를 그 색깔과 맛, 그리고 저장 기간 때문에 더 좋아하게 되었다.

sublimate 순화하다. gene-splicing process 유전자 접합 과정 **정답 (d)**

5. 에스키모인들은 매우 주의 깊게 자식들을 가르쳤다. (a) 결코 변함이 없는 이어온 말로써 옛날 얘기를 해 주었으며, 아이들은 그것들을 완전히 알 때까지 되풀이해서 다시 얘기해야 했다. (b) 그들은 자연과 영혼 세계에 대해 그들의 사상을 표현한 옛 에스키모 노래와 춤을 배웠다. (c) 나이 많은 에스 키모인들은 튼튼한 하얀 이를 갖고 있지만, 단 음식은 자식들의 이를 상하게 했다. (d) 그리고 무엇보다도 그들은 거친 땅에서 살아남기 위해 필요했던 기술, 즉 그 지역의 동물, 새, 물고기, 그리고 얼마 안 되는 식물과 나무의 모든 부분을 이용했던 기술을 배웠다. **정답 (c)**

실력문제 2회

1. 중국 시민은 만일 그들이 공식적으로 후원을 받는 교회 밖에서 종교 행사를 하면 괴롭힘을 당하거나 노동 수용소에서 오랫동안 구류를 당하게 된다고 미 국무부가 세계의 종교 탄압에 관한 새 보고서에서 밝혔다. (a) 그 보고서는 또한 티벳을 포함한 중국에서 불교 수도승과 비구니를 박해하고 있다는 믿을 만한 보고서를 내놓았다. (b) 중국은 종교적 자유에 대한 연례 시리즈 중의 첫 부분이 될 그 보고서에서 조사된 194개국 내지 영토 중의 하나이다. (c) 그 연구는 수요일에 의원들에게 공개되었고, 목요일에는 언론사에 제공될 것이다. (d) 자유시장 자본가 체제는 만일 그 경제에 참여하는 사람들이 그들의 최선을 다할 기회를 부여받지 못하면 효과를 충분히 발휘할 수가 없다.

detention 구류. **정답 (d)**

2. 에이즈라는 병이 출현한 이래로 사람들은 안전한 섹스를 하는 방법으로써, 그리고 에이즈와 다른 질병으로부터 자신을 보호하는 방법으로 콘돔을 사용할 것을 권장 받고 있다. (a) 콘돔은 약방에서 살 수 있고, 또는 술집이나 선술집의 화장실에 있는 자판기에서도 살 수 있다. (b) 사람들은 가게에서 너무 당황하여 콘돔을 달라고 요구하지 못하는 남자들, 특히 점원이 여자일 경우에 대한 농담을 종종 한다. (c) 콘돔을 칭하는 알려진 이름에는 French letter, Rubber, 그리고 Durex가 있다. (d) 에이즈, 즉 후천성 면역 결핍증은 1981년 미국에서 처음 보고 되었으며, 그 후 전 세계적인 주요 전염병이 되었다.

epidemic 전염병. **정답 (d)**

3. 혈압을 조절하는 것은 거대한 도전처럼 보일 수 있다. 어디서부터 시작할 것인가? (a) 첫째, 고혈압은 성공적으로 치료될 수 있다는 것을 기억하라. (b) 당신은 자신에게 적합한 치료계획을 수립하기 위해 당신의 건강 관리자와 함께 그 일을 해야 한다. (c) 어떤 치료 계획을 결정하느냐는 현재의 건강과 다른 약물에 중독되어 있는지 여부를 포함한 수많은 다양한 요인들을 평가하는 것을 의미한다. (d) 혈압이 높을수록 고혈압이 생명에 치명적이 될 가능성도 높다.

hypertension 고혈압. fatal 치명적인. **정답 (d)**

4. 흙 속의 염분은 농작물에 해를 줄 수도 있다. 어떤 염분 성분은 그 자체만으로도 일부 식물 종류에 유독성을 끼칠 수 있다. (a) 또한 식물 뿌리 주변의 흙 속에 있는 고농도 염분은 균형을 이루기 위해 물을 식물 밖으로 배출함으로써 삼투압을 감소시킬지도 모른다. (b) 고농도 염분은 강한 증발로 인해 흙 속에 염분을 축적시키는 건조한 땅에서 종종 발견된다. (c) 어떤 경우에는 고농도 상태의 염분이 작물을 파괴시키기보다는 그저 작물의 수확량을 감소시키고 식물이 병에 걸리기 쉽게 할지도 모른다. (c) 또한 고농도 염분은 잎의 끝과 가장자리를 태우거나 탈색시키거나 잎을 떨어지게 할 수도 있다.

osmotic pressure 삼투압. salinity 염분, 염도. defoliation 낙엽. **정답 (b)**

5. 우울함을 느낀다는 것은 '병적인 우울증'을 앓는 것과는 다르다. (a) 병

적으로 심각한 수준의 우울증은 우울함(예를 들어 슬픔을 느낀다든지 좋아하던 것에 대한 흥미를 잃어버리는 것)의 증세가 너무 심하고 오래 지속돼서 일상생활을 할 수 없을 정도가 되는 것을 일컫는 말이다. (b) 병적 우울증을 앓고 있는 사람은 그 증세가 심하고 끝없이 지속되며, 좋은 일이 있거나 기쁜 소식을 접해도 증세가 사라지지 않는다. (c) 이런 증상을 느낄 때면 이미 축복 받은 일들을 세어 보아라. (d) 병적인 우울증은 전문가의 도움을 받아야 한다.
  clinical depression 병적인 우울증. **정답 (c)**

실력문제 3회

1. 마약 소비 양상이 변하고 있다. (a) 많은 나라에서 마약 중독자들의 평균 연령이 높아지고 있다. (b) 비 상습적 복용은 감소된 것 같고, 상습복용은 계속되고 있다. (c) 더욱 많은 미국의 십대들이 대마초를 피우고 있지만, 코카인이나 헤로인을 경험한 청소년들의 수는 별로 증가하지 않고 있다. (d) 미국의 헤로인 유행은 1973년경에 절정을 이루었고, 그 이후로 새로운 중독자의 수는 1960년대 중반의 수준으로 다시 줄었다. / 미국의 대대적인 환각제 유행 또한 오래 전에 지나갔고, 코카인 사용은 1970년대의 절정기로부터 한 걸음 물러났다. 대마초에서 코카인이나 헤로인 같은 더 심각한 마약들을 복용할 가능성은 10년 동안 꾸준히 줄고 있다.
  addict 중독자. cannabis 대마초. hideous 끔찍한, 무시무시한. crack (속어) 값싼 농축 코카인. retreat 물러서다, 후퇴하다. **정답 (a)**

2. 사람들은 종종 발전을 비웃는다. 아마도 이는 과학 기술이 흔히 예전의 문제를 풀려고 하면서 새로운 문제를 만들어 내기 때문이다. (a) 과학자의 연구실에서 유전적으로 만들어진 유전자가 일단 외부 환경으로 유포된다면 어떤 일이 발생할지 상상해 보라. (b) 대부분의 사람들은 유전적으로 만들어진 제품이 우리의 삶을 발전시킬 것인가에 대해 확신할 수 있으려면 더 많은 정보가 필요하다는 사실에 동의한다. (c) 이 같은 유전자를 도입한 결과는 매우 놀랍다. 어떤 이는 인간 괴물, 혹은 프랑켄슈타인의 창조에 대

해서 얘기한다. (d) 실제로 몇몇 사람에 의해서 "프랑켄푸드"라고 불리는 유전적으로 조작된 음식이 이미 존재하고 있다.

poke fun at 비웃다. engineer 솜씨 있게 처리하다, 공작하다. offshoot 분지, 분파, 결과. **정답 (b)**

3. 미국 식민개척시대의 최초 음악은 교회음악이었다. (a) 사실은 이 시대에 출판된 최초의 책도 찬송가였다. (b) 식민개척시대 식민 개척시대에 최초의 작곡가들은 영국인 촌(村)이든 독일인 촌이든 찬송가와 교회음악에 국한되었다. (c) 아마 세계 음악에 대한 미국의 가장 큰 기여는 대중음악 분야였으리라. (d) 많은 노래들이 물론 식민개척자들에 의해 유럽으로부터 전래되었고, 이런 노래들은 종종 악보로 기록되지도 않았지만, 특히 사람의 왕래가 잦지 않은 산골 같은 곳에서는 아직도 이런 노래들을 들을 수 있다.

psalm 찬송가, 성가, 시편. **정답 (c)**

4. 환경론자들은 생명공학이 자연을 변환시킬 수도 있다고 두려워한다. (a) 예를 들어 동물의 유전자 조작은 급속도로 확산되고 있다. (b) 이미 잉어와 같은 고기들은 빨리 자라도록 유전자 변경이 이루어졌다. (c) 정보화 시대는 또한 생물의 시대이기도 하다. (d) 이론적으로 볼 때, 과학자들은 연어에 그들의 이동 패턴을 바꿀 유전자를 넣어, 바다에서 연어를 잡기 수월하게 만들 수도 있다.

biotechnology 생명공학. genetic manipulation 유전자 조작. **정답 (c)**

5. 역사를 통해 보면 자민족 중심주의가 낳은 파괴적인 결과들의 예는 많이 발견된다. (a) 고대에 유럽의 로마인들과 아시아의 중국인들은 외국인들을 야만인으로 여겼다. (b) 중국의 마지막 왕조는 만주족에 의해 세워졌는데, 이들은 한족과 함께 어울려 살기를 원했다. (c) 현대에는 독일의 독재자인 아돌프 히틀러가 독일인들은 '열등한 민족들'을 말살시킬 의무를 지닌 우월한 민족에 속한다고 주장했다. (d) 이러한 자민족 중심주의적 생각에 의거하여 히틀러는 '열등한 민족'이라고 생각했던 유태인, 집시, 슬라브족, 그리고 그 밖의 다른 집단들을 박해하도록 명령하였다.

ethnocentrism 자민족중심주의. **정답 (b)**

실력문제 4회

1. 광고에 등장하는 여성의 이미지는 인공적인 것이고 또한 인공적으로만 만들어질 수 있다. (심지어 "자연스런 표정"에도 많은 준비와 비용이 요구된다.) (a) 미는 외부에서 오는 어떤 것이기 때문에 백만 불 이상의 돈이 매시간 화장품에 사용된다. (b) 이상과 불가능한 기준에 부합하기를 갈망한 나머지 많은 여성들은 얼굴과 신체를 가꾸고 변화를 주는 일이라면 어떤 고생도 마다하지 않는다. (c) 광고에서 분석과 변화가 가장 필요한 부분은 일하는 남자들에 대한 묘사이다. (d) 여성은 얼굴을 가면으로 그리고 끊임없이 변화와 향상, 그리고 위장이 필요한 대상으로서 신체를 바라보는 데 익숙해져 있다.

go to all lengths 철저하게 하다, 어떠한 짓도 서슴지 않다(=go to great lengths). **정답 (c)**

2. 연구에 따르면 너무 많은 동물성 지방은 건강에 나쁘다. (a) 예를 들면, 미국인들은 많은 육류를 먹기 때문에 암과 심장병의 발병율이 높다. (b) 대조적으로, 한국인들은 많은 양의 곡류와 아주 적은 양의 육류를 먹기 때문에 암과 심장병의 발병율이 매우 낮다. (c) 불행하게도, 햄버거, 콜라, 그리고 지방함유도가 높은 다른 식품들이 한국에서 인기를 끌게 되면서 심장병과 암의 발병비율도 높아지고 있다. (d) 사실, 심장병과 암은 미국에서는 첫 번째와 두 번째로 보편적인 사망의 원인들이어서 5명 중 2명의 사망자가 이에 해당된다. 결론적으로, 의사들은 곡류와 과일, 야채를 더 많이 먹고 육류는 더 적게 먹도록 충고한다.

grain 낟알, 곡물, 극히 조금, 조직, 성질. **정답 (d)**

3. 인간에게는 들리지 않는 초음파는 의학에서 여러 용도로 사용된다. (a) 그것은 소노그램을 만드는 데 사용되는데, 소노그램이란 신체 내부를 그림으로 나타낸 것이다. (b) 의사들은 임신부와 자궁 속에 있는 태아의 성장을 살피고 종양이나 신장 결석, 심장병 발견에 이 장치를 이용한다. (c) 기형이나 종양, 그 밖의 다른 문제를 발견하면 즉각적인 수술이 필요하다. (d) 초음파는 또한 신경계통 수술이나 신장 결석 분쇄와 같은 외과적 치료과정에도

사용된다.

    ultrasonic sound 초음파. uterus 자궁. tumor 종양. kidney stone 신장 결석.

정답 (c)

    4. 여러분이 초속 80피트로 고속도로를 질주하며 내려갈 때 네 조각의 작은 고무만이 도로와의 유일한 접촉을 제공한다. (a) 시력검사를 갓 통과했을지도 모를 누군가가 불과 몇 피트를 사이에 두고 쏜살같이 2톤 차량을 몰고 지나갈 것이다. (b) 이따금씩 우리는 이런 사실을 상기해야만 한다. 차로 여행한다는 것은 우리들 대부분과 같은 비 전투요원이 감당하기에는 너무나도 위험이 많은 일이라는 것을. (c) 여러분의 쇼핑 목록에 이와 같은 항목들을 추가시켜 보라. (d) 여러분과 여러분 가족의 운전 시 안전을 보장하기 위해 더욱 발전된 기술들이 매년 쏟아져 나오고 있고 최신의 정보를 얻을 절호의 기회는 바로 새 차를 구입하려 할 때이다.

    hurtle 돌진하다, 고속으로 움직이다. **정답 (c)**

    5. 언어는 개인의 자유 획득에 있어서 왜 그렇게 중요한가? 최초의 위대한 발견은 고독을 경험하는 것이다. 고독은 부분적으로 감각을 통해 극복된다. (a) 뭔가를 보고, 만지고, 마침내 그것을 움켜잡는 것은 우리의 자아를 확대하고 우리의 고립을 극복하는 가장 초기의 표현이다. (b) 그때 소리와 언어는 타인에게로 가는 다리이다. (c) 언어는 자아 확대의 가장 자연스럽고 세련된 형태이다. (d) 배우고 자아를 실천하는 과정의 핵심은 언어이다.

정답 (d)

IV. 최종점검 문제

◉ 1. 문법 · Part 1

1. <would love[like] to+동사원형(…하고 싶다)>를 알아야 한다. B는 I would love to buy it로 써야 한다. 아니면, to buy it를 줄여서 to를 쓸 수 있다. 이 때 to를 '대부정사'라고 한다.
   ✍(해석) A: 제 차를 사는데 관심이 있는지 궁금하군요.
   B: 사고 싶지만, 살 만한 여유가 없어요.
   정답 (c)

2. 가정법 과거완료 구문으로 <If 주어+had+과거분사--, 주어+조동사의 과거형+have+과거 분사-->의 형태를 취한다.
   ✍(해석) A: 세상에 결국 그는 사기꾼이었어. 그리고 아무도 그 사실을 몰랐군!
   B: 만약 그가 사기꾼인 줄 알았다면, 우리는 그를 믿지 않았을 텐데.
   정답 (d)

3. 빈칸 뒤에 '주어+동사'가 왔으므로 (c), (d)는 답에서 제외된다. 'How [What] about+V-ing' 의 구문으로 사용된다. 빈칸에는 문맥상 '왜'의 뜻을 가진 '(b) How come'이 와야 한다. (a) What if-?는 '-하면 어쩌지'의 뜻이다.
   [참고] '나타나다'의 표현: show up, turn up, appear, emerge, come into sight[view], come to light, become visible, show[present] oneself, make one's appearance
   ✍(해석) A: 딕의 송별회에 왜 안 왔니?
   B: 너는 몰랐니? 나는 그를 보고 싶지 않아.
   정답 (b)

4. <possibility+that절/of+V-ing>의 구문을 묻는 문제이다. 따라서 (a), (d)는 답에서 제외. that절이 오면 추측을 나타내는 가능성을 나타내므로 (c)도 답에서 제외된다.
   ✐(해석) A: 무슨 생각을 하고 있니?
         B: 학교 농구팀에 가입할 수 있는가를 생각하고 있어.
   정답 (b)

5. 빈칸 뒤에 cost(비용이 들다)로 보아 How much를 써야 한다. think는 간접의문문에서 의문사 다음에 온다. 이와 같은 동사에는 believe, imagine, suppose, guess 등이 있다.
   (예문) What do you think it is? [비교] Do you know what it is?
   ✐(해석) A: 쥬디, 나는 올해 여름 동해안으로 여행하고 싶어요. 당신은 어때요?
         B: 글쎄, 나는 정말로 해외여행을 생각하고 있어요. 비용이 얼마나 들까요?
   정답 (a)

6. 헤어지면서 하는 말이므로 완료부정사(to have+과거분사)를 써야 한다.
   ✐(해석) A: 시간이 제법 늦었네. 이제 가 봐야겠어. 아주 즐거운 저녁 고마웠어.
         B: 만나서 반가웠어. 잘 가!
   정답 (a)

7. <It sure was>(정말 그랬어)는 상대방의 말에 강하게 동의를 할 때 사용되는 표현으로 기억해 두는 것이 좋다. 여기서 sure는 부사이다.
   ✐(해석) A: 꽤 지겨운 일인 것 같아.
         B: 정말 그랬어. 그 감자 검사하는 일을 사임한 이래 감자칩을 단 한 개도 먹은 적이 없어.
   정답 (c)

8. [참고] '어떻게 바꿔 드릴까요?'의 표현: What is it (that) you wish to change?

✍(해석) A: 잔돈을 좀 바꿀 수 있나요?
　　　　B: 물론이죠. 어떻게 바꿔 드릴까요?
정답 (b)

9. 과거에 대한 가정이므로 빈칸에는 가정법 과거완료가 와야 한다. '조동사+부사+동사'의 어순이므로 (d)는 답에서 제외된다. thought의 목적어가 that 이하이므로 (a)도 답에서 제외된다. [참고] '해고되다'의 표현: get fired; get pink-slipped; lay off; dismiss; discharge
✍(해석) A: 딕이 해고된 것을 믿을 수가 없어.
　　　　B: 그래. 그가 해고당할 거라고 누가 지금까지 생각했겠어?
정답 (b)

10. 빈칸에는 의미상 '가장 최근의'의 뜻을 가진 (b) the latest가 와야 한다.
(a) the last 지난 번　(c) the late 고인　(d) later 나중에
✍(해석) A: 이 드레스들 중 한 벌을 입고 싶어요.
　　　　B: 탈의실로 안내해 드리지요. 그런데 이것은 가장 최근의 스타일입니다.
정답 (b)

11. [참고] '자유롭게 …하다'의 표현:
　　　　Don't hesitate to+동사; Be free to+동사
✍(해석) A: 당신은 내게 너무 친절하게 대해 주었어요.
　　　　B: 문제가 있으면 주저하지 말고 내게 알려 주세요.
정답 (d)

12. [참고] '…하는 편이 좋다'의 표현:
　　　　had better+동사원형; would rather+동사원형
✍(해석) A: 빌에게 내가 그의 책을 잃어버려서 정말로 미안하다고 말해 줄래?
　　　　B: 네가 직접 말하는 편이 좋지 않겠니?
정답 (a)

13. hardly, scarcely, barely 등은 '거의 -아니다[-하지 않다]'의 뜻을 가

진 반부정어로 not과 함께 쓸 수 없다.
✎(해석) A: 하워드, 낚시 여행은 어땠니?
　　　　B: 이번에는 한 마리도 잡지 못했어.
정답 (b)

14. run out of …을 다 써 버리다. 본문의 시제는 현재완료로 써야 한다.
✎(해석) A: 세상에! 연료가 다 떨어졌어!
　　　　B: 걱정하지 마. 긴급 카 서비스에 전화하면 돼
정답 (d)

15. 'by then'(그 때까지는)으로 보아 빈칸에는 미래완료가 와야 한다.
✎(해석) A: 오늘밤에 영화 보러 가려고 하니?
　　　　B: 그래, 그 때까지는 일을 끝낼 거야.
정답 (a)

16. <with+목적어+형용사[분사/부사/명사구]>의 형태로 부대상황을 나타낸다. 본문에서는 부사 on이 쓰였다. (예) Don't speak with your mouth full.
✎(해석) A: 그 음악이 켜져 있는 채로 영어 에세이를 쓸 수 없어요.
　　　　B: 음악을 꺼 드릴까요?
정답 (a)

17. 영어에서 문장과 문장을 연결하는 방법에는 세 가지가 있는데, 그것은 접속사, 관계사, 그리고 분사구문이다. 본문에서는 분사가 들어가야 한다. B를 제대로 쓰면 'As the job is done'이다. 이것을 분사구문으로 만들면 The job being done이 되는데, 여기서 being 은 생략할 수 있다.
✎(해석) A: 왜 그들이 모든 장비들을 치우지요?
　　　　B: 일이 끝나서 짐을 싸서 떠나는 것이에요.
정답 (b)

18. <I wish+가정법>이고, 직설법 과거(when I was)는 가정법 과거완료이므로 빈칸에는 'had+과거분사'가 와야 한다.

✍(해석) A: 플로리다에 갔다 왔어요?
　　　　B: 아니오, 하지만 미국에 있을 때 갔었더라면 합니다. 그 곳이 아름답다고 하더군요.
정답 (a)

19. 의문문이 평서문에 들어가면 <의문사+주어+동사>의 어순이 된다.
✍(해석) A: 내가 포기할 것이라고 생각하지 마. 내가 할 수 있다는 것 알아.
　　　　B: 그럴지 모르지. 하지만 문제는 얼마나 오래 걸리느냐 하는 것이야.
정답 (c)

20. 주절에 필요나 요구의 뜻을 나타내는 동사, 명사, 형용사가 오면 종속절인 that이하에 동사원형이 온다. 단 should를 넣을 수 있다. submit 제출하다(=hand in, send in, turn in)
✍(해석) A: 내가 지금 해야 할 것이 무엇입니까?
　　　　B: 회사의 규정은 당신이 사고에 대한 완전한 보고서를 제출할 것을 요구합니다.
정답 (c)

 문법 · Part II

21. 빈칸에는 명사절을 이끌면서 주어의 역할을 하는 What이 와야 한다.
✍(해석) 나를 가장 좌절시키는 것은 지원서가 순전히 내 성별에 근거해서 판정되었다는 사실이다. **정답** (c)

22. Parallelism(병렬법)문제로 빈칸에는 과거분사가 와야 한다.
✍(해석) 내 말들이 도둑맞은 후 그 책에 전시되어 이방인처럼 나를 쳐다보는 모습과 마주 쳤을 때, 나는 즐거웠고, 우쭐했고, 섬뜩했으며, 어느 순간에 한 마디로 고통스러웠다. **정답** (b)

23. 타동사인데 뒤에 목적어가 없으면 수동태를 써야 한다. 본문에서 타동사 'write'의 목적어가 없으므로, 빈칸에는 write의 수동태가 와야 한다.

✍(해석) 경찰서 같은 관공서 건물들에는 안내문들이 영어와 함께 스페인어로 쓰여져 있어 많은 경찰관들이 스페인어를 공부한다.
정답 (a)

24. 빈칸에는 의미상 '이유'를 나타내는 접속사(since)가 와야 한다.
✍(해석) 그러나 결국 우리는 간호사들이 의사 역할도 한다고 결론을 내렸는데, 그 이유는 그 곳에서 의사를 대표하는 사람은 단 한 사람도 발견할 수 없었기 때문이다. **정답 (a)**

25. <사역동사+목적어+동사원형>구문을 묻는 문제이다.
✍(해석) 도시로 몰려드는 외지인들의 무리로 인해 그 도시가 그렇게 빨리 커진 것이다. **정답 (a)**

26. <조동사+부사+동사>의 어순을 묻는 문제이다.
✍(해석) 금번 회계 연도 중의 손실을 만회하기 위해 회사는 과감하게 비용을 줄여야 할 것이다. **정답 (b)**

27. [참고] '-하자마자'의 표현:As soon as+주어+동사=Hardly[Scarcely]--when[before] =On+V-ing =No sooner--than=The moment[instant/minute]+주어+동사. 부정의 뜻을 나타내는 부사가 문두에 나오면 <조동사+주어+동사>의 어순이 된다.
 (예) Little did I dream that I met him there. 'had+과거분사'에서 had가 조동사, 과거분사가 본동사이다.
✍(해석) 게임이 시작하자마자 비가 오기 시작했다. **정답 (c)**

28. <현재완료(진행)+for+기간>을 묻는 문제이다.
✍(해석) 종합시험을 준비하는 박사과정 학생들이 지난 3개월 동안 도서관에서 매일밤 공부를 해 왔다. **정답 (d)**

29. 타동사 recycle(재활용하다)이 목적어가 없으므로 수동태가 되어야 한다. 또한 빈칸과 other items와의 관계가 수동관계이다.
✍(해석) 우리는 알루미늄 깡통, 병, 그리고 재활용될 다른 물건들을 모으고 있다. **정답 (c)**

30. 콤마 앞에 완전한 문장이 왔으므로, 빈칸에는 부사구, 부사절, 분사구 문, 동격, 관계사절 등이 올 수 있다. 'A를 B로 부르다': call A B. 본문에서는 동격이 들어간다.
✐(해석) 오늘날 레이저는 또한 초고속 인쇄와 홀로그램이라 불리는 3차원 이미지의 제작에 사용된다. **정답 (c)**

31. '주어+빈칸+동사'이므로 빈칸에는 주어를 수식하는 어구가 와야 한다. 따라서 (b), (d)는 답에서 제외된다. (c)는 which이하에 동사가 없으므로 답이 될 수 없다.
✐(해석) 팔레스타인에서 마카비가 일으킨 반란은 작은 유대 국가의 회복을 의미했다. **정답 (a)**

32. <the reason is that+주어+동사>구문(이유는 that이하 때문이다)을 묻는 문제이다.
✐(해석) 대중의 압력은 가로등을 더 켜라는 것인데, 그 이유는 물론 밝은 거리가 더 안전하게 느껴지기 때문이다. **정답 (b)**

33. '[Most/Half/Majority/Burden/Rest/분수/Part]+of+A+동사'에서 A의 수에 따라 동사가 결정된다. [모하마부래분파]로 기억하자. 본문에서는 단수이므로 (b), (d)는 답에서 제외. 타동사 flood가 뒤에 목적어가 없으므로 수동태가 되어야 한다. flood 범람시키다, 넘치게 하다, 물에 잠기게 하다 monsoon 계절풍, 호우
✐(해석) 방글라데시의 삼분의 일 이상이 호우로 인해 물에 잠기게 되었다. **정답 (c)**

34. 본문의 주어가 materials이므로 빈칸에는 materials를 수식하는 형용사구가 와야 한다.
✐(해석) 금강사, 규사, 석영과 같이 자연적으로 발생하는 연마제들은 고무와 플라스틱을 마무리하는데 사용된다. **정답 (c)**

35. 한정사(the, most, some, any)는 겹쳐 쓸 수 없으므로 (b), (d)는 답에서 제외. (a) almost 거의 (c) mostly 대개(=for the most part), 주로

(=chiefly)

✎(해석) 컴퓨터 기술은 거의 어느 직업에나 필요하다. 반면에, 많은 사람들이 두려움 때문에 이 기술을 배우기를 거부한다. **정답 (a)**

36. <have no choice but to+동사>구문을 묻는 문제이다.
   [참고] '-하지 않을 수 없다'의 표현: cannot but+동사=cannot help[avoid]+V-ing=cannot help[choose] but to+동사=have no alternative[choice/option/other way]but to+동사 =cannot keep[abstain/refrain/forbear/desist] from+동사-ing=there is nothing for it but to+동사=cannot do otherwise than+동사=cannot do nothing but to+동사=be bound[forced/compelled/obliged/impelled/constrained] to+동사 'request that+주어+(should)+동사원형'에도 주의할 것.
   ✎(해석) 마침내 의사는 그 아이를 양육 시설에 보내지 않을 수 없다고 결정했다. **정답 (b)**

37. beyond:-의 범위를 넘어서, (예) beyond control 통제할 수 없는, beyond one's belief 믿을 수 없는
   ✎(해석) 통제할 수 없는 상황 때문에 생긴 피해에 대해서는 회사에서 책임을 안 진다. **정답 (d)**

38. 빈칸에는 increasing의 목적어가 와야 하므로 (d)는 답에서 제외. (c)에서는 that이 불필요함. 또한 of이하가 amount를 수식하므로 한정의 the가 붙어야 한다.
   ✎(해석) 더러운 눈은 반사를 둔화시켜 눈이 흡수하는 빛과 열의 양을 증가 시킨다. **정답 (b)**

39. <지각동사+목적어+동사원형/동사-ing>구문을 묻는 문제이므로 (a), (c)는 답에서 제외. rail against 욕하다, 꾸짖다, 불평하다(=speak bitterly; complain violently)
   ✎(해석) 나는 일부 유럽계 미국인들이 다른 모든 사람들과의 평화적인 경쟁관계를 파멸시킨다는 이유로 착취적인 일본 상인들을 욕하는 것을 들었다. **정답 (d)**

40. 빈칸에는 원인을 나타내는 접속사가 와야 한다. (c) given that=since

✍(해석) 내가 그 나라말을 모르기 때문에 거기에서의 경험이 유용할 수 없었다. **정답 (c)**

🌐 문법 · Part III

41. <주어+동사+간접목적어+직접목적어'>=<주어+동사+직접목적어+전치사+간접목적어> 4형식을 3형식으로 전환하는 것인데, 동사에 따라 전치사가 다르다. '주다', '보내다'의 뜻을 가진 동사(give, send)는 to를, '마련', '주선'의 뜻을 가진 동사(make, get, bring)는 for를 쓴다. under the weather 몸이 편치 않은(=ill)

✍(해석)(a) A: 창백해 보여. 무슨 문제가 있니?
　　　　(b) B: 글쎄, 몸이 좀 편치 않아.
　　　　(c) A: 또 감기니? 약 좀 사다줄까?
　　　　(d) B: 아니, 이번에는 배가 아파.

정답 (c) get some medicine to you→ get some medicine for you

42. 'when'은 특정 시점을 나타내므로 현재완료와 같이 쓸 수 없다.

✍(해석)(a) A: 아니, 이게 누구야! 존 맞지!
　　　　(b) B: 맞아, 오랜만이구나.
　　　　(c) A: 우리가 서로 마지막으로 본 것이 언제였지?
　　　　(d) B: 아마 5년 전인가?

정답 (c) we have seen each other→ we saw each other.

43. I doubt if[whether] …인지 아닌지 의심하다.

✍(해석)(a) A: 쥬디가 너한테 빌린 돈 갚았니?
　　　　(b) B: 적은 월급으로 갚을지 모르겠다.
　　　　(c) A: 쥬디의 월급이 올랐다고 생각했는데.
　　　　(d) B: 인상을 요구했는데 못 받았대.

정답 (b) I doubt as she ever will→ I doubt if she ever will.

44. (d)는 의미상 '나를 초대해 주어 고맙다'라는 어구가 와야 한다.

✎(해석) (a) A: 지난 토요일에 파티를 열었어.
  (b) B: 파티를 또 할거니?
  (c) A: 물론이지, 너도 올 거니?
  (d) B: 그래, 그러고 싶어. 초대해 주어 고마워.
  정답 (d) Thanks for being invited→ Thanks for inviting me.

45. '일주일 후에'라는 표현은 'a week later'라고 쓴다.
✎(해석) (a) A: 콜린스 박사님 좀 부탁합니다.
  (b) B: 미안합니다. 지방에 출장 갔어요.
  (c) A: 그는 언제 돌아옵니까? 나는 그와 의논하고 싶은 것이 있어요.
  (d) B: 일주일 후에 전화하세요.
  정답 (d) a week late→ a week later.

문법 · Part Ⅳ

46. depend on 뒤에 목적어가 나오므로 현재분사가 되어야 한다. dental plaque 치석 floss 플로스(이빨사이에 낀 것을 제거하는 명주실), 치실질하다
✎(해석) (a) 치석은 치아에 계속해서 형성된다. (b) 하루에 적어도 두 번 양치질을 하고 치실질을 하면 치석 축적을 최소화할 수 있다. (c) 집에서 하는 치아 관리 뿐 아니라 적어도 6개월에 한 번은 전문 스케일링을 받을 것을 강력히 추천한다. (d) 치석 축적의 양과 현재 잇몸의 상태에 따라 서너 달에 한 번씩 스케일링이 필요할 수도 있다.
  정답 (d) depended on→ depending on.

47. <전치사+명사>의 어순이므로 (a)가 틀렸다.
✎(해석) (a) 모든 아이의 내면에는 숨겨진 힘, 미지의 능력, 발견되길 기다리는 영웅이 자리 잡고 있다. (b) 과외 프로그램을 통해 아이들은 모든 종류의 활동에 참가한다. (c) 이런 활동은 아이들이 스스로 생각했던 것보다 더 잘할 수 있으며, 더 많은 것을 성취할 수

있다는 잠재력을 깨우쳐주는 데 도움이 된다. (d) 해당 거주 지역의 과외 프로그램에 대해 알고 싶으시면 문의를 주세요.

정답 (a) Every child inside→ Inside every child.

48. be used to+V-ing(…하는데 습관이 되어 있다) be used to+동사(…하는데 사용되다). bullfight 투우. charge 공격하다, 돌진하다. color-blind 색맹의

✍(해석) (a) 투우에서는 황소의 관심을 끌기 위해 붉은 색깔의 천조각이 사용된다. (b) 황소가 공격할 때, 투우사는 한편으로 비켜서서 황소 몸에 칼을 꽂아 황소를 죽인다. (c) 많은 사람들이 붉은 색깔의 물건이 황소를 성나게 만든다고 생각한다. (d) 그러나 황소는 사실 색맹이다.

정답 (a) attracting→ attract.

49. 주절의 주어 they와의 관계가 능동이므로 현재분사를 써야 한다.

✍(해석) (a) 불과 15년 전의 세계와 오늘의 세계는 매우 다름에도, 정치학은 여기에 적응하는데 늦다. (b) 대부분의 경우에 민족 국가는 정책 결정을 하는 주체가 아니다. (c) 하지만 정치학자들은 민족 국가 개념을 버리는데 여전히 주저한다. (d) 모든 증거들에 도전하거나 증거들을 무시한 채 그들은 여전히 민족 국가들이 정치 권력의 단위라고 믿고 있다.

정답 (d) Challenged, or rather ignored→ Challenging, or rather ignoring.

50. (d)는 주절이 없어서 틀렸다. foolproof 아주 간단한, 안전한.

✍(해석) (a) 유전 공학 실험은 여러 분야에서 새로운 경지를 개척해 왔다. (b) 여러 질병의 치료법을 개발하고 곤충의 수를 조절하고 식량 생산을 증진시켰다. (c) 하지만 대부분의 실험들이 안전한 것은 아니다. (d) 왜냐하면 이것들이 어떤 부정적인 결과를 야기할지 아무도 확실하게 알 수 없기 때문이다.

정답 (d) Because no one knows for sure→ That's because no one knows for sure.

2. 어휘 · Part I

1. I couldn't help it. 어쩔 수가 없었어. 여기서 'help'는 '피하다'(=avoid, escape, shun, eschew)의 뜻인 것에 주의할 것.
   [참고] go off (1) 출발하다(=leave, depart), 도망치다(=flee), 죽다(=die) (2) 발사[폭발] 되다(=explode, blow up, discharge, blast, set off, detonate) (3) 실신[기절]하다(=faint, lose consciousness, swoon) (4) 울리다
   ✎(해석) A : 또 지각했군요.
            B : 어쩔 수가 없었어요. 자명종이 울리지 않았거든요.
   정답 (a)

2. boss a person around(about) 사람을 부려먹다
   ✎(해석) A : 왜 그를 미워하죠?
            B : 그가 그런 식으로 우리를 부려먹는 것에 싫증이 나요. 도대체 자기가 뭔데?
   정답 (a)

3. keep an eye on 감시하다(=watch) 이 표현은 대개 주인이 부재중에 주인의 소유물을 보아 달라고 할 때 쓰여진다.
   ✎(해석) A : 내가 없는 사이에 우리 집을 봐 주시겠어요?
            B : 그럼요. 기꺼이 봐 드리지요.
   정답 (c)

4. kick the habit 버릇을 버리다. second-hand smoke 간접 흡연
   A : 제가 담배를 피면 꺼리시겠습니까?
   B : 사실은 그렇습니다. 그리고 이곳은 금연구역이기도 하고요.
   정답 (b)

5. a close call 구사일생, 간발의 차이의 모면(=a narrow escape) upset 속이 상한(=unhappy), angry나 mad, pissed off보다는 정도가 약한 말
   ✎(해석) A : 무슨 일 있니? 아주 속상해 보여.

B : 차에 치일 뻔했어. 하마터면 큰 일 날 뻔했지.
정답 (b)

6. [참고] '본론으로 들어갑시다'의 표현: Let's get down to business. Let's get to the point. (d) compact 계약, 맹약(=agreement), 치밀한 (=close), 밀집한 (=dense)
✍(해석) A: 본론으로 들어갑시다. 무엇을 원하지요?
　　　　B: 휴가를 원합니다.
정답 (b)

7. 빈칸에는 문맥상 '불충분한, 빈약한'의 뜻을 가진 '(b) skimpy'가 와야 한다. (b) skimpy 빈약한(=barely enough, scanty), 인색한 (a) haggard 여윈, 수척한(=gaunt), 야생의(=wild) (c) stinking 악취를 풍기는(=bad-smelling)
✍(해석) A: 추운 날씨에 얇은 옷을 입고 무얼 하고 있니?
　　　　B: 추울지 몰랐어.
정답 (b)

8. get at 파악하다, 이해하다, 도달하다, 착수하다
✍(해석) A: 어떤 일에 착수하고 있어요?
　　　　B: 자세히 설명하겠어요.
정답 (d)

9. 빈칸에는 문맥상 '무기력한'의 뜻을 가진 '(c) enervated'가 와야 한다. sultry 무더운(=very hot, sweltering) (c) enervated 활력을 잃은, 무기력한 enervate 기운을 빼앗다, 약화시키다(=weaken, devitalize, unnerve, emasculate, unman, debilitate, enfeeble, effeminate) (a) elated 의기양양한, 우쭐대는(=high-spirited; pompous) (b) energized 격려 받은 (d) enchanted 요술에 걸린, 매혹된(=fascinated, captivated, attracted)
✍(해석) A: 이 무더위 때문에 맥이 다 빠졌어.
　　　　B: 살 뺀다는 명목으로 매일 아침을 거르기 때문은 아니고?
정답 (c)

10. 빈칸에는 'on leave'(휴가 중)와 어울리는 단어가 와야 한다.
    be away on leave 휴가를 떠나다
    ✍(해석) A: 사장님 들어왔니?
          B: 아니, 그는 지금 휴가를 떠나신 것 같은데.
    정답 (c)

11. 문맥상 빈칸이하에 '고소하다'는 뜻이 와야 한다.
    (c) press 주장하다, 간청하다(=urge; entreat) press charges 고소하다, 고발하다 (a) petition 청원하다, 신청하다, 진정하다(=ask for) (b) pledge 맹세하다, 서약하다, 보증하다(=swear, vow, vouch) (d) plead 변호하다, 변명하다, 주장하다(=argue; answer to a charge)
    ✍(해석) A: 그가 데모해서 체포되었다고 들었어.
          B: 그는 지금 곤경에 처해 있어. 경찰이 고소할 것이라고 했어.
    정답 (c)

12. 빈칸에는 문맥상 '연쇄충돌'의 뜻을 가진 '(a) pileup'이 와야 한다.
    (a) pileup 연쇄충돌(=a collision involving several vehicles)
    (b) takeover 인계, 탈취, 경영권 취득 the military takeover 군사 혁명
    (c) blowup 폭발, 확대, 발끈 화냄 blow up 폭발하다, 화내다(=explode; get angry)
    (d) makeover 완전한 변형, 개조, 수선
    ✍(해석) A: 오늘 신문에 따르면 많은 차들이 서로 충돌했다고 해요.
          B: 예. 짙은 안개 속에서 연쇄 충돌이 일어나 도심지에 차가 밀렸어요.
    정답 (a)

13. 빈칸에는 문맥상 '연줄을 이용하다'의 뜻을 가진 단어가 와야 한다.
    (d) pull strings (인형극에서) 줄을 조정하다, 배후에서 조정하다, 연줄을 이용하다 (=secretly use influence and power; make use of friends to gain one's wishes)
    (a) cord 끈, 새끼, (복수) 굴레, 구속 the silver cord 탯줄(생명)
    (b) lever 지레, 수단(=a bar used as a pry; a means to an end

(c) connection 관계, 연락, 연결, 연줄 of good connection 좋은 연고를 가진 form a connection 관계가 생기다, 인척간이 되다, 정을 통하다
✍(해석) A: 어떻게 제가 주지사를 만날 수 있나요?
　　　　B: 그를 만나기 원하면 루트가 연줄이 될 수 있어요.
정답 (d)

14. 빈칸에는 문맥상 '승진'의 뜻을 가진 '(a) raise'가 와야 한다.
    rise와 비교해서 기억해 둘 것. deserve a raise 승진할 만하다.
    (b) lift 올림, 차 태워줌, 승강기, 올리다, 향상시키다
    (d) arousal 각성, 자극(=awakening; stimulus)
✍(해석) A: 소식 들었어. 낙심하지 마. 나는 네가 승진할 만 하다고 생각해.
　　　　B: 고마워. 사장도 그렇게 생각하기를 희망해.
정답 (a)

15. 빈칸에는 문맥상 '조사하다'의 뜻을 가진 어구가 와야 한다.
    (c) look over 일일이 조사하다, -을 대충 훑어보다(=inspect, scan, pass an eye over) (a) look up 방문하다, 찾아보다, 호전되다(=visit; consult, hunt up; improve) (b) look down 내려다보다, 하락하다
✍(해석) A: 오랫동안 너를 기다려왔어.
　　　　B: 늦어서 미안해. 열쇠를 잃어 버려서 그것을 찾기 위해 아파트를 모두 뒤졌어.
정답 (c)

16. 빈칸에는 문맥상 '자금을 쓸 수 있다'는 뜻을 가진 어구가 와야 한다.
    (d) come in handy[useful] 여러모로 편리하다, 곧 쓸 수 있다(=prove useful) get money for 융자하다, 자금을 조달하다(=finance) loan 대부, 대부금
✍(해석) A: 그 프로젝트에 어떻게 자금을 조달했나요?
　　　　B: 필요할 때 마침 대부를 받았어요.
정답 (d)

17. 빈칸에는 문맥상 '진심의'의 뜻을 가진 '(d) genuine'가 와야 한다.

(d) genuine 진짜의, 진심의, 참된(=sincere, real, authentic, true)
(a) suspicious 의심 많은, 의심스러운(=doubtful, dubious)
(b) malicious 악의 있는(=spiteful, ill-disposed, malevolent, hateful)
(c) irrelevant 부적절한(=not pertinent, not to the point)

✍(해석) A: 그는 자신의 제안에 대해 매우 진지한 것처럼 보였어요.
　　　　 B: 그래요. 확신컨대 그는 우리를 도와주려는 진정한 의도를 가졌어요.

정답 (d)

18. 빈칸에는 문맥상 '정당한'의 뜻을 가진 '(c) fair'가 와야 한다.
get a fair shake 정당한 대접을 받다 (a) prejudiced 편견이 있는

✍(해석) A: 그가 왜 직장을 그만 두었지?
　　　　 B: 아마 그는 회사로부터 정당한 대우를 못 받은 것 같아.

정답 (c)

19. 빈칸에는 문맥상 '합격하다'의 뜻을 가진 단어가 와야 한다.
pass muster 합격하다, 검열에 통과하다 make it 성공하다 (=succeed), 제대로 수행하다 (c) trial 시도, 시련, 재판 (d) ordeal 시련, 괴로운 체험

✍(해석) A: 어떻게 된 거야? 나는 네가 합격할 줄 알았는데.
　　　　 B: 나는 최선을 다 했지만 합격하지 못했어.

정답 (a)

20. 빈칸에는 문맥상 '피하다'는 의미를 가진 어구가 와야 한다.
give room 물러서다 take-- out on …에게 분풀이하다

✍(해석) A: 이유는 모르겠지만 오늘 아침에 사장의 기분이 정말 우울한 것 같아.
　　　　 B: 그래. 오늘은 그를 피하는 것이 좋겠어. 우리에게 분풀이할지도 몰라.

정답 (c)

21. 빈칸에는 문맥상 '붙들어 두다'의 뜻을 가진 (c) stay back이 와야 한다.
(b) watch out 조심하다

✍(해석) A: 이사회 임원들이 내일 아침에 계획안을 보기를 원해요.

B: 그 계획안을 완성할 때까지 밤늦게 팀 사람들을 붙들어두겠어요.
정답 (c)

22. 'a complementary ticket'(보완적인 표)으로 보아 빈칸에는 '보상하다'의 뜻을 가진 (c) compensate가 와야 한다.
✍(해석) A: 내가 나중에 비행기를 탈 수 있지만 다소 불편할 것 같네요.
　　　　　B: 보상하는 뜻에서 미국 어디나 갈 수 있는 비행기표를 더 드리지요.
정답 (c)

23. 빈칸에는 문맥상 '취급하다'의 뜻을 가진 단어가 와야 한다.
　(d) carry 팔다, 취급하다 (a) load 짐을 싣다, 탄알을 재다(=charge) (b) lift 올리다(=raise, hoist, elevate),향상시키다(=enhance),제거하다(=remove) (c) contact 접촉하다(=get in touch with)
✍(해석) A: 여기서 아스피린을 좀 살수 있는지 궁금해요.
　　　　　B: 미안합니다만, 저희는 의약품을 취급하지 않아요. 옆에 있는 약국으로 가세요.
정답 (d)

24. be held up in traffic 교통이 막히다(=be tied up in traffic, be caught in a traffic jam, be bumper to bumper)
✍(해석)A: 네가 약속을 잊었다고 생각했어.
　　　　　B: 늦어서 정말 미안해. 현대 백화점에서부터 길이 막혔어
정답 (b)

25. 빈칸에는 문맥상 '엄청난'의 뜻을 가진 단어가 와야 한다.
　(a) exorbitant 엄청난, 과대한(=excessive, immoderate, extravagant, unreasonable) (b) exclusive 배타적인, 전적인 (c) exquisite 절묘한, 정교한(=delicate), 예민한(=acute) (d) extraneous 외래의, 관계없는(=unrelated)
✍(해석)A: 대만의 지진이 엄청난 피해를 가져왔다고 들었어요.
　　　　　B: 예. 그것은 매우 불행한 일이지요.
정답 (a)

26. 빈칸에는 'mileage points'와 어울리는 동사인 'accrue'가 와야 한다. (c) accrue (자연증가로) 생기다(=happen, result), 획득[축척]하다 (a) account 생각하다, 책임 지우다, 설명하다(for)(=consider; attribute; explain) (b) assail 공격하다, 엄습하다, 괴롭히다 (d) annex 부가하다, 훔치다, 횡령하다(=add, append; steal; appropriate)
   ✍(해석) 같은 항공사로 비행하면 마일리지 포인트가 생겨서, 그것들을 사용하여 향후 비행편의 등급이 상향 조절될 수 있다. **정답 (c)**

27. 문맥상 빈칸에는 '고인플레이션'의 뜻을 가진 'hyperinflation'이 와야 한다. slip out of control 통제를 벗어나다 bonanza 일확천금
   ✍(해석) 러시아 경제는 이미 통제를 벗어나고 있었다. 만일 정부가 새 돈을 찍으라는 사회적 압력에 굴복하면, 이는 신속히 고인플레 로 가게 되는 결과를 낳게 될 것이다. **정답 (d)**

28. 문맥상 빈칸에는 '악의 있는'의 뜻을 가진 'malevolent'가 와야 한다. sniff off 코방귀를 뀌다, 우습게 여기다 amicable 우호적인
   ✍(해석) 케이블 모뎀과 같은 언제라도 네트워크 상에 올라갈 수 있는 연 결 방식의 수가 증가하면서 악의적인 해커들은 디지털 마스터 자물쇠를 비웃으며 사람들의 생명을 노릴 수 있다. **정답 (d)**

29. 빈칸 앞뒤의 키워드를 찾으면 된다. 'not be available'과 'complications'의 관계가 인과 관계이므로, 빈칸에는 'due to'(…때문에)가 와야 한다. (d) except …을 제외하고
   [참고] '…에 관하여'의 표현: as to, as for, with regard[respect/reference] to, in reference to, as regards, regarding, concerning **정답 (b)**

30. 문맥상 빈칸에는 '악화시키다'의 뜻을 가진 'aggravate'가 와야 한다.
   ✍(해석) 몸의 긴장을 풀고 정신을 안정시킴으로써 명상은 긴장과 스트 레스의 해악을 경감시키고자 하는데, 이 해악은 수많은 의학적 조건들을 악화시키는 것으로 알려지고 있다. **정답 (a)**

31. 빈칸에는 문맥상 '살피다'의 뜻을 가진 어구가 와야 한다. (a) see to …에 유의하다, 살피다(=attend to, take care of) (d) glimpse 흘 끗

보다(=catch[get] a glimpse of)
✍(해석) 나는 우리 건물 관리인에게 천장의 새는 곳을 고쳐 달라고 요청했다. 그는 그것을 오늘 살펴보겠다고 말했다. **정답 (a)**

32. 빈칸에는 문맥상 '억제하다'의 뜻을 가진 'check'가 와야 한다.
(b) arrest 체포하다, 끌다(=apprehend; attract) (c) lose one's temper 화를 내다(=get angry)
✍(해석) 만약 네가 불같은 성질을 억제하지 못하면, 언젠가 어려움에 빠지게 될 것이다. **정답 (a)**

33. 'the unknown and the uncharted'로 보아 빈칸에는 'unfamiliar'가 와야 한다.
uncharted 미지의 sally 출격 (a) intricate 복잡한(=complex, complicated, entangled) (b) incessant 끊임없는(=endless, continual, unceasing) (c) unfeasible 실행할 수 없는
✍(해석) 본국이나 외국에서 낯선 환경에 처하여 돌아다니는 것은 종종 미지의 세계를 항해하는 것과 비슷하다. 하지만 이러한 새로운 세계에 대한 모험은 문화 학습에 대한 연습이라고 생각한다면 두려움이 덜 할 수 있다. **정답 (d)**

34. 'a history of suffering from heart attacks'로 보아 빈칸에는 'hereditary'(유전적인)가 와야 한다. (b) chronic 만성적인(=habitual) (c) innate 타고난 (d) acquired 습득된
✍(해석) 심장병은 유전적이므로 가족 중 심장 발작으로 고생한 사람이 있으면, 수시로 검사를 받는 것이 좋다. **정답 (a)**

35. 빈칸에는 문맥상 '일치'의 뜻을 가진 'consensus'가 와야 한다.
(b) consensus 일치(=concord, agreement) (c) distraction 산만, 오락 (d) agenda 안건
✍(해석) 일반적인 견해와는 달리 민주주의 사회는 서로 경쟁적인 이해 관계가 있는 곳이다. 그러므로 일치가 자동적으로 이루어질 수 없다. **정답 (b)**

36. 빈칸에는 'slow scientific progress'로 보아 '비용 절감'의 뜻을 가진 단어가 와야 한다. unravel 풀다, 해결하다(=make clear, solve) hamper 방해하다(=hinder, impede, encumber) (a) burdensome 부담스러운 (c) uninhibited 억제되지 않은, 무제한의 (d) tax-exempted 면세의, 비과세의 exempt 면제하다, 면제된, 면역의
✍(해석) 농장 일과 수질 오염 간의 연결고리를 푸는데 있어 과학의 진보 속도가 늦어서 비용 절감이라는 면에서 문제를 해결할 수 있는 개혁이 계속해서 방해를 받을 것이다. **정답 (b)**

37. 빈칸에는 문맥상 '연장된'의 뜻을 가진 단어가 와야 한다.
recession 후퇴, 불경기 (b) protract 오래 끌다, 연장하다 (c) rejuvenate 원기를 회복하다 (d) elaborate 공들인, 정교한 (해석) 실업은 국가의 재정 위기 이후 길게 이어지는 불경기 동안 가장 심각한 문제가 되었다.
정답 (b)

38. 빈칸에는 'role'(역할)과 어울리는 단어가 와야 한다.
   (a) carnivorous 육식성의 (b) ambivalent 상극인, 양면 가치의
   (c) conspicuous 두드러진, 저명한 (d) ambidextrous 양손잡이의, 두 마음을 품은
✍(해석) 많은 일본 여성들은, 시민으로서 자신들이 사회에서 하기로 기대되는 역할에 대해 모순된 태도를 지니고 있는 것 같다. **정답 (b)**

39. '꾸준히 향상되는 생활 수준 때문에'로 보아 빈칸에 들어갈 단어를 고르면 된다. (a) prominent 두드러진(=remarkable, outstanding) (b) tractable 다루기 쉬운, 순종하는(=manageable, docile, pliant, malleable) (c) lenient 관용의(=tolerant, indulgent, merciful) (d) impassive 무감각한, 냉정한(=apathetic)
✍(해석) 여행 관련 산업의 성장은 꾸준히 향상되고 있는 생활수준 때문에 다른 산업 분야들과 비교해서 최근 몇 년 동안 두드러졌다.
정답 (a)

40. 빈칸에는 '부모'와 어울리는 '승낙'의 뜻을 가진 'consent'가 와야 한

다. adolescent 청소년 (b) connection 관계, 연락, 연결 (c) confession 자백, 고백
✍(해석) 많은 국가들이 특정 연령 이하의 청소년들이 부모의 승낙 없이 결혼할 수 없음을 규정한 법을 가지고 있다. **정답 (d)**

41. 빈칸에는 의미상 '성가신 물건'의 뜻의 어구가 와야 한다. (d) white elephant 성가신 물건, 처치곤란한 일 (a) black 검은, 암담한, 화난, 흑자의 (b) yellow 노란, 질투 많은, 겁 많은 (c) gray 회색의, 음울한, 노년의, 원숙한
✍(해석) 그 사람이 저택을 샀을 때, 그는 그것이 성가신 물건이 될 것이라는 것을 전혀 알지 못했다. **정답 (d)**

42. 빈칸에는 문맥상 '대패로 깎아내다'의 뜻을 가진 어구가 와야 한다. (a) plane—off[away, down] …을 대패로 깎아내다 (b) carry off 유괴하다 (=kidnap, abduct) (c) ship off -을 배에 실어 보내다, 쫓아버리다
✍(해석) 그 노련한 목수는 대패로 능숙하게 문짝을 1인치 깎아냈다. **정답 (a)**

43. 빈칸에는 문맥상 '실질적인'의 뜻을 가진 'substantial'이 와야 한다. (b) substantial 실체의, 실질적인, 중요한, 상당한(=real, true; important; ample) (a) superficial 피상적인, 얕은(=shallow) (c) subsidiary 보조(금)의, 종속적인(=auxiliary) (d) superstitious 미신의, 미신적인
✍(해석) 학생이 자기 공부를 마치면 이상적으로는 자기 나라의 사회적 발전에 실질적인 공헌을 할 수 있어야 한다. **정답 (b)**

44. 빈칸에는 문맥상 '체면을 지키다'의 뜻을 가진 단어가 와야 한다. obsession 강박관념 (a) save (one's) face 체면을 지키다(=maintain face), 체면이 서다 (b) lose (one's) face 체면을 잃다 (c) keep face 태연하다 (d) make[pull] a face[faces] 얼굴을 찌푸리다
[참고] pull[put on, have, make, wear] a long face 침울한[심각한, 슬픈]얼굴을 하다
✍(해석) 아이들은 약해 보이는 것을 정말 싫어해서, 친구들 앞에서 체면

을 지켜야 한다는 강박관념을 가진다. **정답 (a)**

45. 빈칸에는 문맥상 '성과를 거두다'는 뜻을 가진 어구가 와야 한다.
in the last[final] analysis 결국(=after all, in the long run, in the end, at last, finally) (b) pay off 성과를 거두다(=succeed), 이익을 가져오다, 모두 갚다, 보복하다 (a) make do …으로 때우다[견디다](=manage with what is available) (c) luck out 운이 좋다 (d) hit the jackpot 상금을 타다, 대성공하다
✍(해석) 세상은 빨리 돈 버는 곳이 아니다. 근면과 성실이라는 전통적인 가치는 결국 아직도 성과를 거두는 것이다. **정답 (b)**

46. 빈칸에는 'public reaction'과 어울리는 'gauge'(측정하다)가 와야 한다.(a) gauge 측정하다, 평가하다(=measure; judge, estimate, evaluate, assess, appraise, rate) (b) grant 주다, 양도하다, 승낙하다, 인정하다 (=give, transfer, concede) (c) guarantee 보장하다, 책임지다(=vouch, warrant, pledge; promise, insure, ensure) (d) grip 단단히 쥐다, 마음을 사로잡다, 이해하다(=grasp, clutch, seize; comprehend)
✍(해석) 인터넷 덕택에, 지금은 정치 연설을 하고 있는 중에도 그에 대한 대중의 반응을 측정할 수 있다. **정답 (a)**

47. 빈칸에는 'rather than a redundant one'으로 보아 'redundant의 반대말인 'terse'이 와야 한다. redundant 과다한, 장황한(=superfluous, excessive; verbose, talkative, wordy, prolix)
(b) terse 간결한(=concise, succinct, curt, brief, pithy, laconic, compact)
(a) consistent 일관된, 모순이 없는, 언행이 일치된(=compatible, congruous, coherent) (c) logistical 병참의 (d) tacit 무언의, 암묵의(=unspoken, unexpressed, silent, mute; implied)
✍(해석) 이런 종류의 과학 논문은 장황한 문체보다는 간결한 문체를 요구한다. **정답 (b)**

48. <금지동사+A+V-ing>구문(A로 하여금 …못하게 하다)을 알면 쉽게 풀 수 있다.

(a) deter 막다, 단념시키다(=keep or discourage from doing something)
(c) deplore 비탄하다, 개탄하다(=regret deeply, lament, mourn, grieve)
(d) degrade 지위를 낮추다, 품위를 떨어뜨리다, 타락하다(=lower; debase; degenerate)
✍(해석) 건강에 해롭다는 인식과 부모에게 벌을 받게 될 지도 모른다는 생각조차도 중고등 학생들은 여전히 담배를 피우려고 하는 것 같다.
정답 (a)

49. 'Despite'로 보아 빈칸에는 'neatness and polish'(깔끔함과 세련)의 반대 말이 와야 한다. (a) unkempt 너저분한(=uncombed, disordered; slovenly, untidy) (b) tidy 단정한, 상당한(=neat, orderly, trim; sizable, considerable) (c) alluring 유혹하는, 매혹적인(=fascinating, enchanting, captivating, engaging, intriguing) (d) prepossessing 매력 있는, 호감을 주는, 편견을 갖게 하는
✍(해석) 그녀의 너저분한 외양에도 불구하고, 그녀는 사장에 의해 깔끔함과 세련을 요하는 직책에 선정되었다. **정답 (a)**

50. 빈칸에는 '점심을 사지 않을 것'으로 보아 '인색한'의 뜻을 가진 'stingy'가 와야 한다. (a) stingy 인색한, 부족한(=penurious, miserly, niggardly, parsimonious; scanty, meager) (b) lavish 아끼지 않는, 풍부한(=generous, prodigal, abundant, bountiful, profuse) (d) extravagant 지나친, 낭비하는(=excessive, immoderate; wasteful, profligate prodigal)
✍(해석) 그녀는 너무 인색해서 점심을 사지 않을 것이라고 생각한다. **정답 (a)**

3. 독해

Part I

1. 전통적인 퓨리턴의 관점에서 성공을 보면, 우리는 돈을 벌기 위해서 일하는 게 아니라 우리 자신이 더 좋은 사람으로 되기 위하여 열심히 일을 해야 했다. 성공이라는 것은 자기 성장을 위한 도덕적 목적에서 성공한다는 것을 의미했다. 따라서 사람들은 자신을 개발시키기 위해 노력해야만 했고, 만약 여러분이 그것을 충분히 성공적으로 다했다면 물질적인 성취는 그에 대한 보답으로서, 말하자면 부산물로서 따라 왔다. 신과 동시대의 사람들, 그리고 자기 자신에 대한 인간의 의무는 그 자체를 위해 열심히 일하는 것, 즉 자기 자신의 직업에 충실하는 것이었다.
by-product 부산물. **정답 (d)**

2. 빠른 경우 생후 10개월 때쯤 아이들이 처음 감정을 표현하는 말로 내뱉는 것은 한 번에 한 단어 정도이다. 평균적으로 18개월 때 약 50개의 단어가 축적되고 이때부터 어휘량은 급격하게 증가한다. 두 살에서 여섯 살까지 아이들은 하루에 약 여덟 개 정도의 새로운 단어를 배운다. 학교에 들어갈 때쯤이면 만 천여 단어에 달하는 놀라운 어휘를 보유하게 된다. 이러한 어휘 폭발은 실제 두뇌가 엄청나게 발달하는 것과 관련이 있다. 각각의 언어 습득 단계에서 두뇌는 서로 다른 부분들이 왕성히 활동한다.
at a fiery pace 급격하게. mind-boggling 놀라운. **정답 (c)**

3. 안전한 사용을 위해서는 반드시 일반 가정에서 사용하는 전선으로 땅에 잘 접지된 표준 콘센트에 플러그를 끼워야 합니다. 이 기구를 끼우는 연결 코드 역시 땅에 올바르게 접지되도록 해야 합니다. 잘못 접지된 연결 코드는 사고의 주요 원인입니다. 전기 기구가 만족스럽게 작동한다고 해서 콘센트가 땅에 접지되어 있고 설치가 완전히 안전하다는 뜻은 아닙니다. 콘센트가 잘 접지되어 있는지 의문스러운 경우에는 당신의 안전을 위해서 전문 전기 기사에게 문의하십시오. **정답 (c)**

4. 지적인 생물의 본능적인 토대는 호기심이다. 호기심은 동물에게서도

초보적인 형태로 발견된다. 정보를 얻기 위해서는 경계를 늦추지 않는 호기심이 필요하다. 하지만 그것은 일정한 종류여야만 한다. 즉 마을의 이웃 사람들이 어두워진 뒤에 커튼 사이로 내다보려고 애쓰게 하는 종류의 호기심에는 높은 가치가 전혀 없다. 남의 뒷말에 대해서 널리 사람들이 관심을 갖는 것은 뭔가를 아는 것을 좋아해서가 아니라, 적의에 의해서 생겨나는 것이다. 사람들은 누구나 다른 사람의 알려지지 않은 미덕에 대해서는 말하지 않는다. 사람들은 오직 타인들의 은밀한 결점에 대해서만 떠들어댄다.
정답 (c)

5. "사업상의 용도가 인터넷을 사용하는 비율의 80퍼센트를 차지하고, 개인적인 용도로 사용하는 경우는 단 20퍼센트가 될 것이다"라고 이곳에서 열린 경제 포럼에 참석한 유명한 공학자가 화요일에 예견했다. Dell Corporation을 운영하고 있는 마이클 델은 "인터넷의 미래"에 대한 회의에서 이렇게 내다보았다. 또 월요일에는 마이크로소프트사(社)의 빌 게이츠 회장이 가상 공간에서 이뤄지는 무역과 금융에 대한 기대 섞인 전망을 한 풀 꺾이게 했다. 그는 "사람들 모두가 가상 공간에서 물건을 사고, 은행 일을 보게 될까요? 그것은 현실적이지 않습니다. 이러한 일들이 일어나려면 시간이 걸려야 합니다"라고 말했다.
account for 설명하다, 차지하다. dampen 꺾이다. 정답 (a)

6. 거친 생태계와 강력한 금융계 사이에는 유사성이 거의 없어 보이지만, 한 가지 공통점이 있다. 바로 다량의 자료이다. 그 차이점이라면 생태학에서는 자료로부터 중요한 동향을 추출하는 방법의 개발이 자료 자체의 수집보다 뒤떨어져 있다는 것이다. 그 결과 여러 세대에 걸친 생태학자들이 자료 수집을 목적 그 자체로 여기는 경향이 있었고, 그 활용에 대한 개념은 거의 없이 다량의 자료를 수집했다.
lag behind 뒤떨어지다. in itself 그 자체로. 정답 (d)

7. 가구와 집기를 집안에 장만하고 배치하는 것은 책을 쓰는 것만큼 끊임없는 편집의 과정이다. 사람들의 취향과 수요는 변화하기 쉽다. 방은 저마다 다른 목적과 기능이 요구된다. 가구는 재배치되거나 버려진다. 새 가구가 들어와 낡은 가구를 대신한다. 정답 (c)

8. 요즘 사람들은 어려움에 대해 지나치게 지적인 분석을 행하는 경향이 있다. 그렇게 함으로써 그들은 종종 단순한 실제적인 문제들을 복잡한 이론적인 문제들로 바꿔 놓는다. 그 결과, 문제들은 완전히 그들의 통제에서 벗어나 사람들이 효과적인 행동을 취하지 못하게 한다. **정답 (d)**

9. 속이기 위한 도장은 군사시설을 위장하는데 사용되지만, 솜씨 좋은 도장만이 사물을 숨기지 않는다. 만약 어떤 도장된 사물이 그림자를 나타내고 있다면, 그것은 망원경이나 카메라 렌즈에 의해 발견될 수 있다. 결과적으로 군사시설의 위장이나 가장은 빛과 그림자와 형태에 의해서 섞여서 풍경을 이루어야 한다. 평평한 표면에서 설치된 총은 평평해 보여야만하고, 정글 전투 중 군인의 군복은 그늘지게 하여 군엽과 비슷하게 해야 한다.
paintwork 도장. camouflage 위장하다. foliage 군엽. **정답 (a)**

10. 이태리 요리는 최근에 일본에서 인기가 높아졌다. 그러나 잘 알려진 이름은 파스타나 피자뿐만이 아니다. 에스프레소 커피의 판매도 또한 급상승했는데, 이것은 정교한 가정용 에스프레소 커피 기계에 대한 수요가 증가하는 결과를 가져왔다. 점점 더 많은 식당과 커티숍들이 그들의 메뉴에 이 유럽 스타일의 음료를 포함시킴에 따라 이 기계의 인기는 커질 것으로 기대된다.
cuisine 요리 household name 잘 알려진 이름 skyrocket 급상승하다 sophisticated 정교한 show off 과시하다. **정답 (d)**

11. 역사 해석은 과거에 대한 우리의 이미지를 형성하고 미래의 행동에 영향을 미친다. 개인들은 어떤 제도의 역사적 목적이라고 믿는 것에 입각한 결정을 내리는 경우가 자주 있다. 어느 특정한 날에 발생한 다양한 사건들이 주어지면, 역사가는 어떤 사건과 사회적 활동들의 조합을 강조할 것인가 선택할 수 있다. 그래서, 다른 두 명의 역사가는 역사적인 사건들에 관해 다른 해석을 내리면서도 역사적인 사실을 정확히 기록할 수 있는 것이다.
정답 (b)

12. 오늘날 우리는 경쟁을 버리고 협동을 확보해야 한다. 이는 국제적인 사안들을 고려할 때 가장 중심적인 사실이 되어야만 한다. 그렇지 않으면

우리는 어떤 재난에 부닥치게 될 것이다. 과거의 사고방식을 세계대전을 막는데 성공하지 못했다. 미래적 사고방식이 전쟁을 막아 줄 것이다. **정답 (b)**

13. 원시인들은 환자의 몸속에 침입한 악령이 병을 일으키는 것이라고 생각했다. 그들은 병든 사람을 구할 수 있는 유일한 방법은 몸에서 악령을 쫓아내는 것이라 생각하고 몇 가지 방법을 사용하였다. 악령을 달래서 나가도록 하는 경우가 보통이었다. 만약 그 방법이 성공하지 못한다면, 강제적인 방법을 동원하게 된다. 어떤 경우에는 톰톰북을 두드리고, 다른 경우에는, 환자의 가슴을 때리기도 했다. 악령이 도망가기 전에 환자가 죽는 경우가 보통이었다.

coax 달래다, 구슬리다. magic 마법, 마술. hypnotism 최면(술). **정답 (c)**

14. 지능검사에 대한 가장 진지한 논쟁은, 유전과 환경 중 지능에 더 지대한 영향을 끼치는 것이 과연 무엇인가라는 풀리지 않은 문제와 관련이 있다. 환경이 더 큰 영향을 준다고 주장하는 사회과학자들은 지능검사가 인종적, 문화적으로 왜곡되어 있다는 이유로 이를 공격한다. 그러나 유전이야말로 결정적인 영향을 끼친다고 믿는 사회학자들은 지능검사 결과를 비교함으로써 다양한 인종과 민족 사이의 유전적 차이를 설명한다. 이러한 논쟁이 지속되는 가운데도 지능검사는 계속 사용되고 있다. 그러나 오늘날 지능검사가 한 아이의 지적 수행 능력과 잠재력을 판단하는 유일한 자료로 쓰이는 경우는 거의 없다. 동기부여와 문화적 요인 역시 아이의 발달에 중요한 역할을 한다는 것이 당연한 것으로 받아들여지기 때문이다.

heredity 유전. rage 격노하다, 날뛰다. 한창이 되다. motivation 동기부여.
정답 (b)

15. 어른과 아이 모두 에너지와 광물 그리고 다른 재활용할 천연자원이 고갈되어 간다는 말을 듣는다. 이것은 전혀 허튼 소리이다. 모든 사실과 수치가 보여주는 바에 따르면, 에너지와 광물 보존량이 양적으로 크게 증가하고 있어 가격이 내려가고 있다는 것이다. 두려움을 터뜨리는 사람들은 현재의 값으로 이용할 수 있는 보존 자원만을 계산하는 "알려진 자원"이라는 까다로운 어구를 사용한다. 예를 들어 현재는 추출하는데 드는 생산비가 안 드는 이판암이 나 더 깊은 유전의 기름은 가격이 어느 정도 수준으로 올라

가면 쉽게 이용할 수 있을 것이다.
　monger 퍼뜨리는 사람 tricky 까다로운 shale 이판암 should price levels increase to a certain level= if price levels should increase to a certain level. **정답 (b)**

　16. 1930년대 미국 국민들이 라디오 연속극을 듣기 시작한 이후로, 문화비평가들은 일일연속극의 내용과 형식, 인기도를 탐구해 왔다. 오늘날 매체비평가들은 다양한 접근을 택한다. 어떤 비평가들은 청중의 반응을 살펴보고, 성별, 인종, 국적에 따라 사람들이 같은 이야기를 다른 방식으로 해독한다는 결과를 알아냈다. 다른 비평가들은 연속극을 여성의 깊은 불평거리를 떠받쳐주는, 일종의 파괴적인 형태의 대중문화라고 간주한다. 또 다른 비평가들은 연속극을 하나의 텍스트로 보고 그것을 분석하고자 시도하는데, 이는 문학비평가가 문학작품을 해부하는 것과 흡사하다.
　soap(opera)연속극. decode 해독하다. subversive 파괴하는, 타도하는. grievance 불평거리. grievance machinery 고충처리 기관. dissect 해부하다. archeologist 고고학자. **정답 (a)**

　17. 고대 그리스인들은 빛이 치유할 수 있다는 것을 알았다. 그들은 치유과정을 돕기 위해 환자를 햇볕에 노출시켰다. 하지만 현대 기술은 빛의 가능성을 엄청나게 증진시켜, 레이저와 광활성 약품들을 선보였다. 치료용 빛은 세포 조직 깊숙이 파고들어 신체가 지난 자연적 회복 능력을 높여 준다. 연구자들이 보여 준 바에 따르면, 어떤 적외선 파장은 혈관을 자극하여 팽창시킴으로써 상처 부위의 혈액순환을 더 높여 준다고 한다. 이런 자극은 노폐물의 제거는 물론, 산소와 영양소의 운반을 촉진시켜, 손상된 조직이 더 빨리 회복할 수 있도록 해준다.
　boost 밀어올리다, 경기를 부양하다. wave length 파장, 사고방식. dilate 넓히다, 팽창시키다. **정답 (c)**

　18. 몇 전 전에 나는 친구들 몇 명과 함께 시골에서 주말을 보낸 적이

있다. 내 아내인 헬렌은 그 때 임신 7개월이었다. 나는 헬렌이 저녁 때 벽난로 앞에 혼자 앉아서 뱃속에 있는 아기에게 아름다운 자장가를 나지막하게 불러주는 것을 보곤 했다. 아들을 낳은 뒤에 헬렌은 나에게 그 자장가가 아들에게 마술 같은 효과를 낸다고 말했다. 아무리 자지러지게 울다가도 그 자장가를 불러주면, 아기는 울음을 그친다는 것이다. 정신과 의사로 태아기의 경험에 대해서 특별하게 관심을 갖고 있던 나는 흥미가 생겼고, 어머니의 행동이 뱃속에 있는 태아에게 영향을 줄 수 있는지에 대해서 알고 싶었다. 그래서 나는 태아의 정신을 이해하는 데 도움을 줄 정보를 얻기 위해서 과학문헌들을 찾아보기 시작했다.

lullaby 자장가. prenatal 태아기의. intrigue 호기심[흥미]를 돋우다, 음모를 꾸미다. **정답 (d)**

19. 14시간 동안 토론을 벌이고 나서, 오스트레일리아 북부 준주의 의회는 의학적으로 도와서 자발적으로 안락사하는 것을 허용하는 법률을 세계 최초로 통과시켰다. 15대 10으로 승인된 논쟁의 소지를 안고 있는 이 법률은 그 환자의 상태가 말기이고 또 사리를 분별할 수 있는 정신 상태라고 내과 의사와 정신과 의사가 결정한다면, 불치 환자가 자신의 생명을 종식시키는 것을 허용하고 있다.

euthanasia 안락사(=mercy killing). abortion 유산, 낙태, 실패. **정답 (d)**

20. 그 파괴행위는 철저히 계획된 것이었는가? 기계적 실수로 의한 인재는 아니었는가? 아니면 단순히 번개에 맞아서였나? 어떤 정신 이상자가 하늘에 대고 총을 쐈던 것이었나? 대서양 횡단 기구의 시작인 동시에 끝을 장식한 힌덴부르크 비극에 대해서는 많은 이야기와 추측들이 있다. 7백만 세제곱 피트가 넘는 수소를 채운 804피트 크기의 힌덴부르크는 한 시대의 최고 업적이었다. 그러나 1937년 5월 6일 힌덴부르크 폭발이 일어나면서 공기보다 가벼운 기구의 전망은 영원히 바뀌었다.

sabotage 파지[방해]행위. airship 비행선, 조종할 수 있는 기구(=dirigible). **정답 (a)**

21. 우울증과 불안을 경험해 본 사람은 누구나 이런 병들이 치료하기 어렵다는 것을 알 것이다. 이런 질병의 치료에서, 흔히 간과되어온 두 가지

영역은 호르몬에 의한 원인들과 생화학과 뇌의 연관관계이다. 또한 우울증과 불안은 중독의 원인이 되는데, 사람들은 기분이 좋아지기 위해 어떤 형태로든 스스로 약물투여를 시도하기 때문이다. 요즘은 환자들이 합성약품의 부작용을 기피하기 때문에, 자연적 치료법이 인기다. 비결은 각 환자의 건강을 극대화하기 위해 자연적 치료법과 합성약품 투약을 병행하는 것이다.

depression 우울증. medication 약물 치료[처리], 약물. side effect 부작용. key 해답, 비결. **정답 (a)**

22. 슈퍼마켓의 지배인들은 사람들을 자극해서 돈을 더 많이 쓰게 하는 모든 종류의 계략들을 확보하고 있다. 그들의 목표는 손님들이 상점 안을 더 천천히 돌아다니게 하는 것이다. 지배인들은 화려한 진열품들을 의외의 장소에 배치해서, 고객들의 주의를 끌게 한다. 그들은 또한 계산대 근처의 통로를 다른 곳보다 더 좁게 만든다. 그러면 커다란 수레를 끄는 손님은 옴짝달싹 못하게 되거나 천천히 갈 수밖에 없게 된다. 심지어 일부 슈퍼마켓에서는 바닥을 출구 쪽으로 가는 손님들에게는 약간 오르막이 되게 만들어 놓는다. 지배인들은 고객들이 천천히 지나가면, 더 많이 구매할 것을 바라기 때문이다.

corridor 복도, 회랑. get struck 옴싹 달싹 못하게 되다. **정답 (d)**

23. 아이들의 마음을 어른들의 마음보다 훨씬 빠른 속도로 성장하고, 발달하고, 학습하므로 특히 텔레비전의 영향을 받기 쉽다. 텔레비전은 아이들을 위해 교육수단으로도 활용할 수 있지만, 흔히 교육적 가치가 거의 없거나 전혀 없는 오락 만화들이 방영된다. 사회학자들, 교사들, 그리고 부모님들은 아이들이 선택하는 텔레비전 프로그램의 종류에 대해 우려하고 있다. 이 사람들은 어린 아이들에 대한 매체의 영향을 우려하고 있는 것이다. 이들은 표현상 매혹적인 식품들을 선전하는 광고방송들의 영향뿐만 아니라 텔레비전 방송의 폭력이 사회에 미치는 영향에 대해서도 우려하고 있다. 하지만, 가장 중요한 것은 이들이 텔레비전을 취학아동들의 산수와 읽기 점수를 낮추는 한 요소로 생각하고 있다는 것이다. 텔레비전을 시청하는데 너무나 많은 시간을 허비하기 때문에, 아이들은 책을 읽고 독립적으로 사고하는데 시간을 더 적게 쓰고 있다.

commercial 광고 방송. sugarcoated 표면상 매혹적인(=superficially

attractive). 정답 (b)

24. 아이들은 만화를 좋아한다. 그들은 몇 시간이고 만화를 보며 앉아 있을 수 있다. 그리고 오늘날에는 만화 전문 케이블 방송이 생겨나서 텔레비전에서는 한 프로가 끝나면 또 한 프로, 이렇게 하여 하루 24시간, 1주일 7일 내내 만화 프로를 보여 준다. 그러나 이 텔레비전 프로그램들의 많은 것들이 불온한 메시지를 전달한다. 즉 그것들은 세상은 하나의 커다란 전쟁터라는 것을 암시한다. 만화마다 사람과 짐승이 총을 쏘고 폭격하고 서로 폭파시켜 버리고 하는데도 어떤 심각하거나 치명적인 결과도 낳지 않는 것이다. 오늘날 우리 사회의 폭력 수준을 감안할 때 이것은 아이들에게 위험스런 메시지를 주고 있는 것이다.
disturbing 불안하게 하는, 불온한. 정답 (d)

25. 육체노동자와 사무원들은 모두 허리통증의 위험을 안고 있는데, 약간 신경에 거슬리는 정도의 통증에서 꼼짝도 하지 못할 정도의 극심한 통증까지 있다. 어떤 전문가들에 따르면 인간은 진화 과정에서의 약점 때문에 특히 쉽게 허리통증에 걸린다고 한다. 우리는 직립보행을 하는 방법을 찾아냈을지는 모르지만, 우리의 가냘픈 척추는 무거운 머리를 지탱할 만한 힘을 갖지 못했다. 무리하게 움직이면 부상을 입을 수 있지만, 그냥 앉아만 있는 것도 척추 아래쪽에는 부담을 줄 수 있다.
jockey 기수, 운전사, 조종자. spindly 호리호리한, 허약한. spine 척추.
정답 (d)

26. 컴퓨터와 꽤 쓸만한 소프트웨어만 있으면 실제로 누구든지 예술가가 될 수 있다. 사람들은 이미 실제 배우들을 컴퓨터 시뮬레이션으로 대체하고 있다. 예술가라고 왜 대체되지 않겠는가? 2100년쯤에는 아마 인간 예술가란 개념이 너무나 케케묵어서 22세기의 전문가들은 우리가 훌륭한 예술 작품을 만들기 위해 미약한 인간들에 의존할 만큼 서툴렀던가에 놀라워할지도 모른다. 실제로 다른 사람들과 다른 방식으로 사물을 볼 수 있는 한, 예술가는 항상 존재할 것이다. 그들은 자신들을 표현하기 위해 이전과는 다른 매체를 사용할 뿐이다.
passe 시대에 뒤떨어진, 케케묵은. gauche 어색한, 서투른(=awkward).
mortal 죽여야 할 운명의, 치명적인, 인간. 정답 (a)

27. 1978년 이전의 작품들은 28년간의 저작권 보호를 받았고, 첫 28년 보호 기간 동안 기한 연기 신청을 했을 경우 28년 더 보호받을 수 있었다. 1978년 현재로 아직 저작권법 하에 있는 작품들에 대한 기한연기 기간이 47년까지 연장되었고, 후에 20년이 더 추가되었다. 1998년부터는 저작권 보유자들이 더 이상 기한연기 신청을 할 필요가 없어졌다. 저작권 보호가 자동적으로 75년까지 연장되었고, 후에 95년까지 연장되었다. **정답 (a)**

28. 인간의 뇌는 부신에 신호를 보내어 에피네프린으로도 알려져 있는 아드레날린을 혈관 속에 더 많이 방출하도록 함으로써 갑작스런 공포에 반응한다. 이 물질은 종종 방위 호르몬이라고도 불리는데, 인체가 즉각적인 노력을 기울일 수 있도록 준비시켜 준다. 그것은 심장 박동을 더 빠르게 하고, 순환작용을 자극하고, 기관지를 이완시켜 더 많은 공기가 폐를 통해 보내질 수 있게 해준다. 이것은 갑작스런 위험에 대한 인체의 구명반응이기 때문에, 이 과정은 매우 빨리 발생할 수 있다.

adrenal gland 부신 fight or flight hormone 방위 호르몬 bronchial 기관지의
정답 (a)

29. 원원 정책은 보수적인 목표와 진보적인 목표를 동시에 달성할 수 있는 공공정책과 관련이 있다. 이에 대한 예는 경제, 사회, 환경, 법, 그리고 정치에 관한 정책과 같은 공공 정책의 모든 분야에서 찾아볼 수 있다. 원원 정책은 타협과 구분되어야 한다. 타협은 양측이 동의를 위해 각각의 목표 달성에서 부분적으로 후퇴하기 때문이다. 때때로 원원 정책은 극도의 낙관적인 정책으로 언급되기도 한다. 원원의 개념은 모든 주요한 쪽이 승리한다는 것을 의미하지만, 승리라는 개념은 모호할 수 있다. 양측이 한편으로는 승리하고 한편으로는 패배한다면 이는 간혹 원원식 해결이라고 불릴 수도 있으나, 이는 그야말로 미화된 이름의 전통적인 타협이다. **정답 (a)**

30. 한증막은 많은 질병을 치료하는데 이용되어 왔고, 땀을 내는 것이 바람직한 고열병의 경우에는 이러한 치료가 상당한 도움이 되는 것으로 드러났다. 한증막은 계속해서 불을 태우는 흙으로 덮인 오두막집이었다. 열이 높은 환자가 들어갔을 때, 단 하나만 있는 문이 단단히 닫혀진다. 그 사람은 그 오두막집에 남아서 가능한 한 오랫동안 숨막히는 열기를 견디어낸

다. 그 다음에 이 사람은 바깥으로 달려나와서 근처 호수나 시냇가로 뛰어 들어감으로써 그 치료를 끝낸다.

sweat house 한증막 treat 치료하다(=cure, heal) dirt-covered 흙으로 덮인 feverish 열이 많은 stifling 질식시키는 stifle 질식시키다(=suffocate, choke). **정답 (d)**

31. 우리가 걷는 땅, 우리가 숨쉬는 공기, 우리가 마시는 물이 우리가 만들어 내는 쓰레기에 의해 서서히 중독되어 가고 있다. 물질적인 상품들을 제조하고 소비하는 과정에서 우리 사회는 산더미 같은 쓰레기를 만들어 낸다. 가정에서 나오는 쓰레기들은 종종 그것의 해로운 결과를 고려하지 않고 버려진다. 그 결과 우리는 상상을 초월한 정도의 쓰레기 문제에 직면해 왔다. 우리는 우리가 만들어낸 쓰레기들을 쌓아 놓거나, 던져 버리거나, 에 파묻거나, 불에 태워버리는 식으로 처리한다. 그러나 쓰레기는 사라지지 않고 틀림없이 우리와 미래 세대에 되돌아와서 괴롭힐 것이며, 우리가 쓰레기를 제대로 처리하지 못했기 때문에 미래 세대의 문제는 더욱 심각해질 것이다.

poison 중독시키다 discard 버리다(=get rid of) dispose of -을 처분하다 (=settle; give away or sell; get rid of) dump 내버리다(=unload; throw away). **정답 (b)**

32. 우리 모두 자유가 중요하다고 생각하지만 궁지에 몰렸을 때 그것은 우리의 최대 관심사가 아니다. 위태로운 시기에 정부의 행위를 비판함으로써 자유를 외치는 사람들은 언제나 이 나라에서는 박해받는 소수가 될 것이다. 그들은 침묵해야 할 시기에 큰 소리를 내고, 단합해야 할 때 잘못을 지적하기 때문에 비웃음과 조롱을 받는다. 그러나 그들이 없었다면 우리나라는 오늘날의 자유국가가 되지 못했을 것이다. 오늘날의 시민 자유론자들은 여론에도 불구하고, 우리 모두를 위하여 자유를 옹호하는 사람들 속에 포함될 수 있다.

stand up for 옹호하다, 변호하다, 편들다. **정답 (d)**

33. 정부는 세 곳의 난민 보호시설 건립 발표 후 어제 이에 대하여 국민들에게 알리지 않고, 난민을 선거 이슈로 만들려 한다는 이유로 비난받았

다. 코소보 난민들을 수용했던 리머군 막사는 1,000명에 이르는 보호시설 희망자들을 수용할 시설로 건립될 것이다. 계약이 올해 말까지인 TPK 관리사가 새 시설들을 관리할 것이다. 출입국 관리 장관인 스미스 씨는 사람들을 보호 시설 밖으로 이주시키는 작업이 오래 지연되는 이유가 법정의 항소 금지 법안 통과를 노동부가 계속 거부하고 있으며, 정부가 정식 허가 없이 입국한 사람들을 국외로 추방하는 데 어려움을 겪고 있기 때문이라고 어제 말했다. "우리가 말하고자 하는 것은 강제 유치가 수용인원에 관계없이 엄격할 거라는 겁니다."라고 스미스씨는 말했다.

boat people 난민. house 수용하다. deport 추방하다. **정답 (c)**

34. 유로는 유럽이 무엇인지 확실히 정의하는 반면, 그것은 또한 무엇이 유럽이 아닌가를 강조할 것이다. 유로랜드는 단일 통화와 중앙 은행, 공동의 통화 정책을 가질 것이지만, 여전히 11개의 분리된 경제권에 의해 이끌어질 것이다. 중앙 은행을 가질 것이지만 11명의 재무 장관이 있을 것이다. 재정적 통합은 유로랜드 국가들을 경제적으로 단단하게 묶을 것이지만, 이 국가들을 감독하는 예산상의 혹은 정치적인 상부 구조를 만들지는 않을 것이다. 그리고 11개국은 유로의 창설에는 동의 할 수 있지만, 이라크나 혹은 좀 더 가까운 코소보 지역에서 어떤 정책을 추구할 것인지에 대해서는 거의 동의를 이루지 못해 왔다. 공동의 외교 정책은 여전히 요원한 꿈일 뿐이다.

underscore 강조하다. mesh 묶다. pursue 추구하다. **정답 (a)**

35. 1980년대 후반 이래로 정신 건강 전문가들은 가을과 겨울의 점점 짧아지는 낮 시간이 우울증을 초래할 수 있다는 사실을 알았다. 연구에 따르면 겨울철 우울증은 햇빛이 모자라서 일어나는 것이다. 반면, 여름철 우울증은 빛보다는 열과 더 밀접한 관계에 있는 것 같다. 더운 날씨가 주는 영향은 우울증과 비슷하다. 의욕을 잃고 하는 일 없이 시간을 보내는 경우가 많으며, 무엇이든 집중하기 어렵고 잠을 잘 자지 못할 수도 있다. 여름철 우울증은 신체가 더위에 나타내는 정상적인 생리 반응의 극단적인 표현일 수 있다.

the blues 우울증(=depression). physiological response 생리반응.

정답 (a)

36. 구름을 잡는다는 것은 무지개를 병에 담아보려는 시도만큼이나 어려운 일일지도 모른다. 그러나 칠레 북부의 가장 건조한 지역 중의 하나인 산악 마을, 칼레타 충궁고의 주민들은 구름을 잡을 방도를 알아냈다. 그들은 구름을 망으로 잡음으로써 그렇지 않고서는 비를 내리지 않는 하늘로부터 물은 짜낼 수 있게 되었다. 주변 계곡의 인근 지역들과는 달리 칼레타는 안데스 산맥에서 바다로 흘러가는 근처의 강들로부터 별 도움을 받지 못한다. 설상 가상으로 이 도시는 태평양 역선풍 고기압의 길목에 놓여있다.
wring water 물을 짜다. drought 가뭄. **정답 (c)**

37. 이 웹사이트는 넷스케이프 위주로 구축되었지만, 거의 모든 다른 브라우저들로도 탐색이 가능합니다. 주요 주제별 페이지들은 모두 맨 위에 안내 그래픽이 있습니다. 하지만, 만일 모든 주제들을 차례대로 모두 훑어보고 싶다면, 각 페이지 맨 밑에 있는 버튼들을 사용하셔서 사이트를 검색하십시오. 이 사이트 밖으로 탐색을 나갔더라도 늘 링크 버튼을 이용해 다시 쓰고 있던 주요 주제로 쉽게 되돌아 올 수 있습니다. 또 아주 멀리 있는 사이트까지 탐색을 나가야 한다면 새로운 창을 하나 더 열어서 사용하시면 인터넷에서 길을 잃을 염려가 없습니다. **정답 (b)**

Part III

38. 당신의 몸은 인생이 당신에게 준 선물이다. 이 감사함에 대한 보답은 당신이 할 수 있는 한 최대로 몸을 돌보는 것이다. (a) 독성 물질이나 비만으로 몸에 지장을 주지 말고, 몸이 최고의 수준에서 기능을 할 기회를 주어라. 즉 당신의 몸을 빛나게 하라. (b) 몸은 과잉 체중을 원치 않으며, 몸이 가질 수 있는 적절한 몸매를 원한다. (c) 당신이 해야 할 것은 몸의 자연스러운 과정을 촉진하는 것으로, 당신은 자랑스러워 할 몸의 기쁨을 경험하기 시작할 수 있을 것이다. (d) 당신이 아는 것처럼 항상 당신 안에 갇혀 있던 날씬한 몸매가 사라지는 것으로 즐겨라.
unimpeded 방해받지 않는 facilitate 쉽게 하다(=make easy), 촉진하다(=promote)

대부분 첫 문장이 주제문이다. 본문에서는 몸이 중요하다는 것을 설명하고 있다. **정답 (d)**

39. 천문학에서 16세기에 코페르니쿠스가 주장한 지동설은 시작에 불과했다. (a) 1632년에 갈릴레오는 지동설을 옹호하고 전통적인 천동설 지지자들을 조롱하는 책을 발행했다. (b) 그러나 교회는 갈릴레오를 종교재판에 회부했고, 그는 영구 가택 연금의 형을 받았다. (c) 공식적인 철회에도 불구하고, 갈릴레오는 "그래도 지구는 돈다."라는 최후의 한 마디를 했다고 전해진다. (d) 지동설은 특히 행성궤도의 관측이 코페르니쿠스의 믿음과 일치하지 않았을 때 많은 난점들이 제기되었다.

heliocentric 지동설의. geocentric 천동설의. Inquisition 종교재판소. recantation 취소, 철회. planetary orbit 행성궤도. **정답 (d)**

40. 근본적으로 좋은 결혼에서도, 우리는 얼마만큼의 외로움을 가지고 살아가야만 할지도 모른다. (a) 어떠한 두 사람도 완전하게 조화되지는 못한다. (b) 우리 자신의 어느 부분들은 우리가 영혼의 배우자가 되기를 희망했던 바로 그 사람에 의해 이해될 지도 모른다. (c) 내 남편은 그의 프로 축구에 대한 열광을 내가 공감할 수 있도록 하기 위해 할 수 있는 것이 아무 것도 없다. (d) 나는 그에게 예이츠의 시를 사랑하도록 하기 위해 할 수 있는 일이 아무 것도 없다.

match 필적하다(=equal), 조화하다(=suit, go with, harmonize) mania 열광, 열중 (=madness, frenzy, lunacy; obsession, craze)

완벽한 결혼 생활은 없다는 취지의 글이다. **정답 (b)**

제4부

빈출 어휘 정리

빈출 어휘 정리

001. abate 줄이다, 감소시키다(=subside, diminish; reduce)
002. abet 부추기다, 교사하다(=incite, encourage, instigate)
003. abhor 혐오하다(=shrink from, detest, loathe, abominate)
004. abject 비참한(=hopeless, miserable, wretched),
     비열한(=contemptible, despicable)
005. abolish 없애다, 폐지하다(=do away with, eliminate, remove,
     eradicate, wipe out)
006. abortive 유산의, 실패한(=unsuccessful)
007. absolve 용서하다, 사면하다(=forgive, pardon, exonerate,
     free from blame)
008. abstract 추상적인(=theoretical, unrealistic), 개요,
     발췌(=summary, epitome)
009. abuse 남용하다(=misuse), 학대하다(=mistreat)
010. access 접근(=approach), 이용할 권리, 격발, 발작(=outburst, fit)
011. acclaim 갈채[환호]하다(=applaud, hail, salute, give one a big hand)
012. accompany 동반하다, 동행하다(=go with)
013. account 설명하다(=explain), 고려하다(=consider), 거래,
     계좌(=bank account)
014. acerbic [맛이] 신, 신랄한(=bitter, sour, severe)
015. achieve 성취하다(=carry out, accomplish, execute, complete).
016. acute 격렬한(=severe, intense), 날카로운(=sharp, keen, shrewd,
     penetrating)
017. adapt 적응시키다(=adjust), 개조하다(=modify)
018. address 말을 걸다(=speak to), 연설하다(=deliver a speech),
     주소, 연설
019. adequate 적절한(=proper, suitable), 충분한(=enough, sufficient)
020. adherent 추종자. 지지자(=follower; supporter)
021. administer 관리하다, 운영하다(=manage, direct), (약을)바르다(=apply)
022. admonish 훈계하다(=urge, exhort), 경고하다(=warn)

023. adroit 교묘한(=skillful; dexterous), 영리한(=clever; shrewd)
024. adulterate 오염시키다(=contaminate, pollute), 더럽히다(=make inferior, impure)
025. advocate 지지하다(=support), 변호하다(=defend)
026. affinity 유사(=similarity), 친화력, 좋아함(=sympathy, attraction)
027. aggravate 악화시키다(=make worse), 괴롭히다(=annoy, exasperate)
028. aggressive 공격적인(=offensive, belligerent, bellicose), 적극적인(=active)
029. alleviate 완화하다, 경감하다(=ease, relieve, lessen, mitigate)
030. allocate 할당하다, 배분하다(=distribute, assign, allot)
031. ameliorate 개선하다(=make better, improve)
032. amiable 호감을 주는, 상냥한(=friendly, agreeable, amicable)
033. analogy 유사, 유추(=similarity)
034. animosity 적의, 원한, 악의(=resentment, hostility, ill will)
035. anticipate 고대하다(=look forward to, expect)
036. apparently 외관상(=seemingly), 분명히(=clearly, obviously, evidently)
037. appease 진정시키다, 달래다(=soothe, pacify, placate, alleviate)
038. appreciate 평가하다, 감상하다, 감사하다, 가격이 오르다 (=increase in value)
039. apprehend 체포하다(=arrest), 이해하다(=understand, make out)
040. arbitrary 임의의, 독단적인(=random, capricious)
041. arid 메마른(=dry), 무미건조한(=uninteresting, dull)
042. aroma 향기(=a pleasant odor, fragrance)
043. artificial 인공의(=man-made), 모조의(=simulated), 꾸며낸(=not natural)
044. assiduous 근면한, 부지런한(=hardworking, diligent, sedulous, industrious)
045. assuage 진정시키다, 누그러뜨리다(=soothe, pacify, ease, relieve)
046. astute 빈틈없는(=shrewd, keen), 교활한(=sly, cunning)
047. auspicious 길조의, 경사스런(=favorable, promising)

049. authorities 당국 the proper authorities=the authorities concerned 관계 당국
050. available 이용 가능한, 손에 넣을 수 있는(=usable, accessible)
051. ban 금지하다(=prohibit, inhibit, forbid)
052. banal 평범한, 진부한(=mediocre, common, unoriginal, ordinary)
053. bar 막대기, 장애(=hindrance), 창살, 술집, 법정(=law court), 제재
054. batter 난타하다, 강타하다(=beat, strike, pound)
055. belligerent 교전중인(=waging war), 호전적인(=combative, quarrelsome, bellicose)
056. beneficial 유익한, 이로운(=advantageous, helpful, salutary)
057. benevolent 인정이 많은, 자비로운(=generous, kind, charitable)
058. beset 둘러싸다, 포위하다(=surround, besiege, hem in), 괴롭히다(=harass)
059. bias 편견(=prejudice, preoccupation), 경향, 성질(=tendency, predisposition)
060. bitter 쓴, 쓰라린, 지독한(=sharp, disagreeable, harsh) bitterly 쓰게, 몹시, 심하게
061. bleak 황량한(=desolate, barren, unsheltered), 어두운(=discouraging)
062. border 가장자리(=edge, brim, brink), 경계(=boundary)
063. breakdown 고장, 붕괴, 쇠약 nervous breakdown 신경쇠약 (=crack-up)
064. breakthrough 큰 발전, 새 발견(=a very important advance or discovery), 돌파(구)
065. bulwark 성채, 보루(=rampart, citadel, fortification, safeguard)
066. capitulate 항복하다(=surrender, give up)
067. capricious 변덕스러운(=unpredictable, fickle, irregular), 충동적인(=impulsive)
068. casualty 불상사, 사고(=a fatal accident) casualties 사상자 수
069. catholic 보편적인(=universal, all-inclusive), 관대한(=broad)
070. celibacy 독신, 금욕(=abstinence from sex)
071. censure 비난하다, 나무라다(=condemn severely, chide, reprove, blame)
072. certificate 증명서, 면허장, 증권

073. chaos 혼돈, 무질서(=complete disorder, confusion)
074. checkup 건강진단(=a medical examination), 총 점검, 검사
075. cherish 소중히 하다(=hold dear), 품다(=cling to, hold to, nurture)
076. chronic 만성의 고질적인(=constant, recurring, habitual, inveterate)
077. circulation 순환, 유통, 발행 부수, 통화
078. circumspect 조심성 있는, 신중한(=cautious, prudent, vigilant, wary)
079. civil 시민의(=civilized), 예의 바른(=polite, courteous)
080. claim 요구하다(=require, demand), 주장하다(=assert)
081. clemency 관용(=mercy, mercifulness, forgiveness),
        온화(=mildness)
082. clue 실마리, 단서
083. clump 덩어리(=lump, mass), 수풀(=cluster)
084. clumsy 꼴사나운, 어색한(=awkward, cumbersome)
085. coarse 조잡한, 거친(=rough, crude), 천한(=vulgar)
086. coax 구슬려 --시키다(=cajole, wheedle, inveigle)
087. colleague 동료(=a fellow worker, associate)
088. collusion 공모, 결탁(=conspiracy, scheme, intrigue, cabal)
089. commission 위임(=delegation), 임무, 위원회
090. commitment 위탁, 약속, 책임, 헌신, 범행
091. commodity 상품, 물건(=goods, merchandise, article, wares)
092. compact 밀집한(=dense), 간결한(=concise, brief, succinct)
093. compendium 개략, 요약(=summary, abridgment)
094. compete 겨루다, 경쟁하다(=contend, rival, vie)
095. competent 유능한(=capable, fit), 충분한(=adequate, sufficient)
096. complex 복잡한(=complicated, intricate, entangled), 집합체, 고정 관념
097. comprehensive 포괄적인, 넓은(=wide, inclusive, extensive,
        sweeping), 이해가 빠른
098. comprise 포함하다(=contain), 구성되다(=consist of, be composed of)
099. conclude 끝내다(=finish), 결정하다(=determine, resolve),
        체결하다(=arrange, settle)
100. conclusive 결정적인, 단호한, 종국의(=decisive, final)
101. concurrent 동시에 일어나는(=happening at the same time),
        협력의(=parallel)

102. condense 압축하다, 농축하다(=distill, solidify), 요약하다(=digest, curtail)
103. conduct 안내하다(=guide), 지도하다(=direct), 행동하다(=behave)
104. confident 확신하는, 자신 만만한(=certain, sure of oneself)
105. confidential 심복의, 기밀의(=trustworthy, secret)
106. conflict 투쟁(=struggle, fight, war), 충돌, 대립(=opposition, difference), 갈등
107. confuse 혼동하다(=mix up), 어리둥절하게 하다(=bewilder, embarrass)
108. conjecture 추측하다(=guess, surmise, speculate)
109. consensus 일치, 여론(=unanimity or general agreement)
110. consequence 결과(=result, effect), 중요성(=importance)
111. considerable 중요한(=important), 많은, 다량의(=much, large)
112. constant 불변의, 충실한, 부단한(=faithful, regular; continual, persistent)
113. consult 상담하다, 의논하다(=advise, counsel; confer, discuss)
114. consume 다 써버리다, 소비하다, 낭비하다(=use up, exhaust, drain; waste)
115. contaminate 더럽히다, 오염시키다(=pollute, taint)
116. content 만족하는(=satisfied), 내용(=substance)
117. contribute 공헌하다, 기부하다(=subscribe, donate), 기고하다
118. controversial 논쟁의 여지가 있는(=subject to controversy, debatable)
119. convalesce 건강을 회복하다(=regain strength and health; get better)
120. conventional 전통적인, 협정상의, 형식적인(=common; customary; habitual)
121. convict 유죄를 입증[선고]하다(=condemn, find guilty, sentence)
122. copious 풍부한(=abundant, plentiful, ample, profuse)
123. countenance 용모(=face), 표정(=facial expression), 지지(=approval, support)
124. counterfeit 위조의(=forged), 허위의(=sham, pretended) 위조하다, 가장하다
125. covert 은밀한, 숨은(=secret, furtive, clandestine, stealthy, surreptitious)
126. curfew 만종, 통행금지, 소등 명령
127. currency 통화(=money), 유통(=circulation)
128. daunt 위압하다, 기세를 꺾다(=frighten, dishearten, intimidate)
129. deadline 사선, 마감 시간

130. deadlock 막다른 골목(=impasse, bottleneck, stalemate, standstill)
131. deadly 치명적인(=fatal, lethal, mortal)
132. debris 부스러기, 파편, 잔해(=rubble, wreckage)
133. defend 방어하다(=protect, guard), 변호하다(=plead)
134. deformity 기형(=disfigurement), 신체장애자, 추함(=ugliness, depravity)
135. degenerate 퇴보하다, 타락하다(=break down, deteriorate)
136. degrade 지위를 낮추다, 품위를 떨어뜨리다(=demote; lower, debase, dishonor)
137. delay 연기하다(=put off, postpone, defer, adjourn), 늦추다(=detain)
138. deluge 대홍수, 범람(=flood, inundation), 쇄도, 밀어닥치다
139. deposit 두다, 맡기다, 예금하다, 예금, 보증금(=pledge), 침전물(=sediment, dregs)
140. depress 내리 누르다(=press down), 기를 꺾다, 우울하게 하다 (=sadden, deject)
141. deride 조롱하다, 비웃다(=ridicule, laugh at, scorn, scoff, make fun of)
142. deserve …할 만하다, …할 가치가 있다(=be worthy of, merit)
143. detain 보류하다, 유치하다(=keep in custody, confine) detention 저지, 유치
144. deter 단념시키다, 막다(=discourage, restrain, hinder)
145. deteriorate 악화시키다(=worsen, degenerate)
146. detrimental 해로운(=harmful, injurious, deleterious, poisonous, pernicious)
147. dexterous 손재주가 있는(=skillful, adroit, deft), 영리한(=clever)
148. diagnosis 진단, 식별 diagnose 진단하다
149. dilute 희석하다(=thin down or weaken as by mixing with water)
150. directory 주소 성명록, 전화번호부
151. discard 버리다(=throw away, abandon, repudiate), 해고하다(=discharge)
152. discrepancy 불일치, 모순(=disagreement, discord, inconsistency)
153. disgust 혐오감, 넌더리(=aversion, nausea, loathing, abhorrence)
154. disparage 얕보다, 깔보다(=belittle), 비방하다(=discredit)
155. dispatch 특파하다, 급파하다(=expedite), 끝내다(=finish quickly, get through)

156. dispense 분배하다(=give out, deal out, distribute),
시행하다(=administer)
157. dispute 논쟁하다(=argue, debate), 싸우다(=quarrel),
의심하다(=doubt), 논쟁
158. disseminate 뿌리다(=scatter, disperse), 보급하다, 퍼뜨리다
(=spread, diffuse)
159. disturb 방해하다(=interrupt), 어지럽히다(=confuse)
160. divert 전환하다, 딴 데로 돌리다(=distract, digress, deviate,
diverge, swerve)
161. docile 유순한, 가르치기 쉬운(=submissive, obedient, tractable,
teachable)
162. domestic 가정의, 국내의(=native), 길들여진(=tame)
163. draft 기초하다(=outline, formulate), 선발하다,
징병하다(=conscript, enlist)
164. drastic 격렬한, 철저한, 과감한(=severe, harsh; rash, impulsive)
165. dreadful 무서운(=awesome, terrible), 몹시 불쾌한(=offensive), 엄청난
166. drive 충동, 욕구(=strong impulse or urge), 정력, 몰다,
질주하다, 공을 쳐 보내다
167. drought 가뭄(=long dry spell)
168. dubious 의심스러운, 애매한(=doubtful, uncertain, questionable)
166. dwell 거주하다(=reside, abide) dwell on
숙고하다(=speculate, ponder, brood over)
167. dwindle 점차 감소하다(=shrink, diminish, lessen, run low)
168. eccentric 별난, 괴벽스러운(=irregular, peculiar, odd)
169. ecology 생태학 ecosystem 생태계
170. emanate 발산하다, 퍼지다(=come forth, issue, emit, radiate)
171. embezzle 횡령하다(=steal, misappropriate, peculate, defalcate)
172. emerge 나타나다(=appear, show up, turn up)
173. empirical 경험의, 경험적인(=experiential)
174. emulate 겨루다(=rival, vie, compete, contend),
모방하다(=imitate, copy, mimic)
175. enchant 매혹시키다(=attract, charm, captivate, fascinate)
176. enforce 시행하다(=execute), 강요하다(=compel)

177. enhance 높이다(=elevate, raise, lift, heighten), 강화하다(=intensify)
178. enigmatic 수수께끼 같은, 불가사의의
179. enormous 거대한, 엄청난(=huge, vast, titanic, tremendous, colossal, immense)
180. ephemeral 하루살이 목숨의, 순식간의, 덧없는(=short-lived, transitory, fleeting)
181. erudite 박식한, 유식한(=scholarly, deeply learned)
182. evaluate 평가하다, 사정하다(=assess, estimate, appraise, value, rate)
183. evidence 증거(=proof), 징표, 흔적(=indication, trace)
184. exacerbate 분개시키다(=exasperate, irritate), 악화시키다(=aggravate)
185. exacting 엄한(=strict), 가혹한, 힘든(=arduous)
186. exclusive 배타적인(=selective), 유일한(=sole, unique)
187. exemplify 예증하다(=illustrate), …의 모범이 되다
188. exhausted 피곤한, 지친(=fatigued, worn out)
189. exhaustive 소모적인, 고갈시키는(=leaving nothing out)
190. exigency 위급, 긴급한 상태(=emergency, urgency)
191. exotic 이국적인, 색다른(=foreign, alien, outlandish, bizarre)
192. expedite 재촉하다, 촉진하다(=speed up, facilitate), 급파하다(=dispatch)
193. explicit 명백한, 뚜렷한(=definite), 노골적인, 솔직한(=outspoken)
194. explode 폭발하다(=blow up, go off, detonate)
195. exploit 이용하다(=utilize, capitalize on), 착취하다, 업적, 공적(=feat, merit)
196. extensive 광대한(=vast), 광범위한(=comprehensive, far-reaching)
197. extenuate 경감하다(=mitigate), 변명하다(=excuse)
198. extol 칭찬하다, 극찬하다(=praise highly, laud)
199. extraneous 불필요한(=unnecessary), 부적절한(=irrelevant), 외래의(=extra)
200. facile 손쉬운(=easy), 유창한(=fluent), 피상적인(=superficial)
201. fade 바래다, 사라지다(=disappear, die out), 시들다(=wither)
202. fastidious 까다로운, 괴팍스러운(=meticulous, demanding, finicky)
203. favorite 좋아하는, 마음에 드는(=highly regarded, preferred)

204. feasible 실행할 수 있는(=practicable), 가능한(=possible),
     그럴듯한(=likely)
205. fervor 열정, 열렬(=ardor, zeal, enthusiasm, passion)
206. fidelity 충실, 성실, 충성(=faithfulness, loyalty, allegiance)
207. figure 숫자, 형태, 인물, 그림, 계산하다(=calculate), 나타나다
208. file 제기하다: file a protest against -에 이의를 신청하다, 서류철, 열
209. financial 재정의, 금융의(=pecuniary, fiscal, monetary)
210. fire 불을 지르다(=ignite), 발사하다(=shoot), 해고하다(=discharge)
211. flagrant 악명 높은, 극악스런(=notorious, scandalous, infamous)
212. flourish 번영하다(=prosper, thrive, flower), 휘두르다(=brandish)
213. forbear 억제하다(=refrain, abstain), 참다
214. forerunner 선구자, 선조(=predecessor, ancestor), 전조(=herald)
215. forge 버리다, 위조하다(=counterfeit)
216. formidable 무서운(=appalling), 만만치 않은(=arduous)
217. forsake 버리다(=abandon, renounce, relinquish)
218. fortify 강화하다(=strengthen), 확증하다(=support, uphold, sustain)
219. fragile 부서지기 쉬운, 약한(=breakable, frail, delicate, weak)
220. frenzy 격분, 광포(=wild excitement; delirium), 격분하게 하다
221. frugal 검약한, 검소한(=economical, penny-pinching)
222. furtive 은밀한, 교활한(=stealthy; sly, secretive)
223. futile 쓸데없는, 효과 없는(=useless, hopeless)
224. garment 의복, 옷옷(=robe, dress, vestment)
225. garrulous 수다스러운, 장황한(=talkative, chatty, verbose,
     loquacious, long-winded)
226. genetic 유전학적인, 유전학의, 기원의 genetics 유전학
227. genuine 진짜의(=true, real, authentic, sincere)
228. gorgeous 호화스러운(=magnificent), 멋진(=beautiful, delightful)
229. gratify 만족시키다(=satisfy), 기쁘게 하다(=please)
230. gregarious 군거하는, 사교적인(=sociable)
231. grouch 불평하다(=grumble, complain), 불평꾼
232. guile 교활(=cunning, slyness, duplicity, artfulness)
233. hackneyed 낡아빠진, 진부한(=overused, trite, stale)
234. halt 멈추다, 정지하다(=stop, cease), 주저하다(=hesitate)

235. harass 괴롭히다(=worry, torment, torture, vex)
236. harsh 거친(=rough), 엄한, 가혹한(=stern, severe, cruel)
237. heyday 전성기(=golden age, prime)
238. hibernate 동면하다(=sleep all winter)
239. homogeneous 동질의, 같은 종류의(=uniform)
240. hypocritical 위선의, 위선적인 hypocrite 위선자
241. hypothetical 가설의, 가정적인(=assumed, supposed, uncertain, unproven)
242. identification 신분증
243. illicit 불법의(=illegal, illegitimate, unlawful), 불의의, 불륜의
244. imminent 절박한, 긴급한(=pending, impending, urgent, emergent)
245. impartial 공평한, 치우치지 않은(=fair, just, unbiased, unprejudiced, evenhanded)
246. impassive 무감각한, 의식 없는, 냉정한(=unfeeling; unconscious; calm)
247. impeach 탄핵하다, 비난하다(=discredit)
248. impeccable 결함 없는, 죄가 없는(=without defect or error; flawless)
249. impede 방해하다(=hinder, obstruct, block, bar)
250. impetuous 성급한, 격렬한, 맹렬한(=rash, impulsive; extremely impatient)
251. implement 실행하다(=carry out, execute), 도구(=tool, instrument)
252. impose 부과하다(=place), 강요하다(=force on others)
253. imposing 인상적인(=impressive), 당당한(=grand)
254. impoverish 가난하게 하다(=make poor), 약하게 하다
255. inborn 타고난, 선천적인(=innate, natural, native, inherent)
256. incarcerate 투옥하다(=imprison)
257. incense 몹시 화나게 하다(=enrage, infuriate, anger, ire)
258. incipient 처음의, 발단의(=beginning, emerging)
259. incoherent 일관성 없는(=inconsistent, disjointed)
260. indifferent 무관심한(=unconcerned, apathetic), 중요치 않은(=unimportant), 관계없는
261. indolent 게으른, 나태한(=idle, lazy, sluggish)
262. indomitable 불굴의(=invincible, unconquerable, unbeatable)

263. inept 부적당한(=unsuitable), 어리석은(=foolish), 서투른(=clumsy, awkward, gauche)
264. inexorable 무정한, 냉혹한, 용서 없는(=relentless, unrelenting, cruel, merciless)
265. infer 추론하다(=deduce), 나타내다, 암시하다(=imply)
266. influx 유입, 쇄도
267. ingenuous 솔직한, 꾸밈없는(=frank, open), 순진한(=simple, naive)
268. ingredient 성분(=component, element, constituent)
269. inhabit 거주하다(=abide, reside, dwell)
270. iniquity 부정, 죄악(=wickedness, sin, transgression; vice, immorality)
271. innocuous 해가 없는, 독이 없는(=harmless, inoffensive)
272. inordinate 지나친, 과도한(=excessive, unreasonable, immoderate), 무절제한
273. insatiable 만족할 줄 모르는, 탐욕스러운(=greedy, voracious, avaricious)
274. insidious 교활한, 방심할 수 없는(=treacherous, sly, sneaky)
275. insinuate 넌지시 비치다(=hint or suggest indirectly, imply), 교묘하게 불어넣다
276. insipid 김빠진, 무미건조한(=dull, bland, banal), 맛없는(=tasteless)
277. insolent 거만한, 오만한(=arrogant, insulting, disrespectful, impudent)
278. instigate 선동하다, 부추기다(=provoke, stir up, incite)
279. insulate 격리하다, 고립시키다(=set apart, isolate, detach)
280. intangible 손으로 만질 수 없는(=untouchable)
281. integrity 성실, 완전(=completeness, wholeness)
282. interrupt 가로막다, 중단시키다(=obstruct)
283. intervene 방해하다, 중재하다(=intercede, mediate)
284. intractable 다루기 힘든, 고집이 센(=obstinate, stubborn, obdurate, disobedient)
285. inundate 범람시키다, 침수시키다(=flood), 쇄도하다(=overwhelm)
286. invalid 병약한, 허약한(=weak and sickly), 무효의(=null, void), 병자
287. inventory 재고품, 재고 조사
288. invigorate 기운 나게 하다, 고무하다(=refresh, restore, animate)

289. invoice 송장
290. irascible 성급한, 화를 잘 내는(=easily provoked; irritable, hot-tempered)
291. issue 내다, 나오다, 유래하다, 발행, 유출, 결과, 논점
    issue an order 명령을 내리다
292. itinerary 여행일정(=detailed plan of a journey)
293. judicious 분별이 있는(=prudent, wary, cautious), 현명한(=wise)
294. knack 솜씨, 요령(=a clever expedient, adeptness, dexterity)
295. laborious 어려운(=difficult), 힘드는(=hard-working)
296. lament 슬퍼하다, 애도하다(=mourn, deplore, grieve, commiserate)
297. landmark 경계표, 획기적인 사건
298. languid 나른한, 기운 없는(=weak, listless, sluggish)
299. latent 숨어 있는, 잠재적인(=hidden; potential)
300. laud 칭찬하다, 찬양하다(=praise, applaud, extol; celebrate)
301. launch 진수시키다, 발사하다, 시작하다
302. layout 배치, 설계,
303. legitimate 합법적인(=legal, lawful), 이치에 맞는(=reasonable)
304. lenient 관용의, 인자한(=generous, magnanimous, merciful)
305. levity 경솔, 경거망동(=lightness, frivolity)
306. liabilities 부채, 채무(=debts)
307. limber 유연한(=flexible, supple, pliable, malleable)
308. litter 쓰레기(=rubbish, waste, trash, junk), 어지럽히다(=make untidy)
309. lucid 투명한, 알기 쉬운(=clear ; easy to understand), 제정신의(=sane)
310. lucrative 돈이 벌리는(=profitable, moneymaking, gainful)
311. lure 유혹하다, 꾀다(=attract, tempt, allure, entice, coax, decoy)
312. mandate 명령(=order, command), 통치, 위임, 영장
313. mandatory 강제의, 필수의(=compulsory, obligatory)
314. manifest 명백한, 분명한(=apparent, evident, obvious)
315. meager 메마른(=thin, lean), 빈약한(=poor), 불충분한(=inadequate)
316. meanwhile 한편, 그 동안에(=meantime)
317. meek 유순한(=mild), 순종적인(=submissive, tame)
318. mellow 달콤한, 부드러운(=soft, sweet)
319. meticulous 꼼꼼한, 너무 신중한(=very careful, scrupulous, finicky)

320. milieu 주위, 환경(=environment, surroundings)
321. modest 겸손한(=humble), 삼가는(=reserved)
322. mundane 세속의, 현세의(=worldly), 평범한(=commonplace, ordinary)
323. musty 진부한, 케케묵은(=stale, trite, antiquated)
324. mutation 변화(=change), 돌연변이
325. mutual 상호의(=reciprocal), 원조의
326. navigate 조종하다, 항해하다(=steer, direct)
327. neglect 무시하다, 소홀히 하다(=ignore, disregard)
328. notify 통지하다(=apprise, inform, give notice)
329. noxious 유해한, 해로운(=harmful, offensive, poisonous)
330. nuisance 남에게 폐를 끼치는 행위, 성가신 물건(사람)
331. object 목적, 목표(=purpose, aim, goal, target), 반대하다(=oppose, protest)
332. obese 비만의(=very fat, stout, plump)
333. oblivion 망각, 건망(=total forgetfulness)
    oblivious 잘 잊어버리는(=forgetful)
334. obscure 모호한(=vague), 흐린(=dim, hazy)
335. obsolete 구식의, 낡아빠진(=antiquated, out of date, old-fashioned)
336. obstacle 장애(=hindrance, impediment, barrier, obstruction)
337. optimistic 낙관적인
338. opulent 부유한(=rich), 풍부한(=luxurious, abundant)
339. ostensible 외면상의, 겉치레의(=apparent, seeming, professed)
340. outburst 폭발(=explosion, blowup), 분출(=sudden release)
341. outcast 버림받은(=driven out, rejected)
342. overlook 감시하다(=inspect), 간과하다, 무시하다(=ignore, neglect, disregard)
343. overt 드러난, 명백한(=not hidden, manifest)
344. overwhelm 압도하다(=crush, overpower) overwhelming 압도적인
345. pacify 달래다, 진정시키다(=placate, mitigate, assuage, allay)
346. pack 꾸러미(=bundle), 무리, 채워 넣다 pack up 포장하다, 짐을 꾸리다
347. palpable 만질 수 있는(=tangible), 분명한(=patent, obvious)

348. panacea 만병통치약(=cure-all)
349. paralyze 마비시키다, 무력하게 만들다(=cripple, disable)
350. parole 가석방, 집행유예
351. penitent 후회하는 참회하는, 죄를 뉘우치는(=sorry, repentant, contrite)
352. perform 공연하다(=enact), 수행하다(=execute, fulfil)
353. perish 멸망하다, 죽다(=expire, die), 사라지다
354. perjury 위증, 거짓 맹세(=lying under oath)
355. permeate 스며들다, 침투하다, 퍼지다(=seep through; penetrate, pervade)
356. persecute 박해하다(=oppress), 괴롭히다(=annoy, trouble)
357. pertaining to …에 속하는(=belonging), …에 관계된(=having reference)
358. petulant 화를 잘 내는, 까다로운(=cranky, rude, ill-tempered)
359. pious 경건한(=holy, religious, devout)
360. pinpoint …의 위치를 정확하게 나타내다, 꼭 집어 말하다
361. plague 전염병, 골칫거리(=nuisance), 괴롭히다(=torment, torture, vex)
362. plateau 고원(=an elevated tract of level land)
363. plentiful 풍부한, 많은(=abundant, copious)
364. potential 잠재하는(=possible, latent), 잠재력
365. pragmatic 실용적인, 실용주의의(=practical ; down to earth)
366. precipitous 가파른, 험한(=steep), 성급한(=rash, impetuous)
367. predecessor 전임자, 선임자, 조상(=ancestor, progenitor)
368. predict 예언하다, 예측하다(=foretell, prophesy, presage)
369. prestigious 이름이 난, 세상에 알려진
370. prevail 이기다(=be victorious), 우세하다, 보급되다, 설복하다(=persuade)
371. probation 검정(=testing), 견습 기간, 시련, 집행유예
372. probe 조사(=search, investigation), 조사하다, 연구하다(=examine, search for)
373. prodigal 풍부한, 낭비하는(=extravagant), 방탕한
374. procedure 진행, 절차
375. prodigious 비범한, 유별난, 거대한(=extraordinary; enormous, vast)
376. proficient 숙달된, 능숙한(=competent, capable, skillful)
377. prohibit 금지하다(=prevent, inhibit, ban, proscribe)

378. prolific 다산의, 비옥한(=productive, fruitful, fertile)
379. property 재산, 소유물(=possessions), 소유권,
　　　　특질(=characteristic, attribute)
380. propitious 순조로운, 상서로운(=favorable, auspicious), 좋은
381. proponent 옹호자, 지지자(=advocate, supporter)
382. proportion 비율(=ratio), 균형, 몫
383. prosecute 수행하다(=carry on, engage in), 기소하다,
　　　　고발하다(=sue, charge)
384. provisional 잠정적인, 일시적인, 임시의(=conditional;
　　　　temporary; tentative)
385. proximity (to) 근접, 인접(=nearness)
386. prudent 신중한(=discreet, cautious, wary),
　　　　검약하는(=thrifty), 빈틈없는(=shrewd)
387. qualify 제한하다(=modify, restrict), 자격을 주다, 권한을 부여하다
388. qualitative 질적인, 질에 관한
389. quarantine 격리(=isolation), 검역
390. radiation 방사, 발광
391. raid 침입하다(=invade), 불시 단속하다, 습격, 불시 단속
392. rail 욕하다, 조롱하다, 불평하다(=speak bitterly, inveigh, complain)
393. rain check 후일의 약속, 초대의 연기
394. rampant 만연하는(=widespread), 사나운(=violent)
395. rapacious 욕심 많은(=greedy), 강탈하는, 약탈하는(=plundering,
　　　　avaricious)
396. ratify 비준하다, 재가하다(=approve, confirm)
397. recede 물러나다(=retrogress), 감소하다(=diminish),
　　　　희미해지다(=wane)
398. reckless 무모한(=heedless, rash)
399. reckon 계산하다, 간주하다, 평가하다, 생각하다(=count;
　　　　regard; estimate; suppose)
400. recommend 추천하다, 권고하다(=advise, counsel)
401. recur 되돌아가다, 재발하다, 순환하다
402. redundant 여분의, 과다한(=excessive), 장황한(=wordy)
403. refer 언급하다, …에 돌리다, 관련되다(=mention; attribute to;

be relevant to)
404. refund 환불, 상환
405. refurbish 다시 닦다(=freshen or polish up again), 일신하다(=renovate)
406. register 기재하다, 기록하다(=write down), 등기부, 자동기록기
407. reimburse 상환하다(=repay), 변제하다(=indemnify)
408. relative 비교상의, 상대적인(=comparative), 적절한(=relevant), 친척
409. relax 늦추다(=loosen), 편하게 하다, 쉬게 하다(=rest)
410. release 풀어놓다, 석방하다(=set free, liberate), 방출하다
411. reluctant 마음 내키지 않는(=hesitant, unwilling)
412. remarkable 놀랄만한, 두드러진(=extraordinary, outstanding, conspicuous, salient)
413. renounce 포기하다, 단념하다(=give up; disown)
414. replenish 다시 채우다, 새로 보충하다(=fill again, resupply, restore)
415. represent 나타내다(=stand for, symbolize), 대표하다, 표현하다(=describe)
416. repress 억제하다, 억누르다(=hold back, restrain), 진압하다(=put down, subdue)
417. reproach 비난하다, 나무라다(=criticize, scold, blame, censure, reprimand, reprove)
418. rescue 구출하다, 구조하다(=free, save), 구출, 구원
419. residue 잔여, 나머지(=remainder), 찌꺼기
420. resolute 결심한, 단호한, 확고한(=determined; firm, steadfast; unwavering)
421. resolve 분해하다(=analyze), 결심하다(=determine), 결의하다, 해결하다(=solve)
422. respective 각각의(=individual) respectful 경의를 표하는, 공손한
423. respond 응답하다(=answer, reply), 반응하다(=react)
424. retard 지체시키다, 방해하다(=hinder, delay, hold back)
425. reticent 과묵한, 삼가는(=quiet; restrained; reserved, reluctant to speak)
426. revere 존경하다, 숭배하다(=respect highly; honor)
427. revitalization 소생, 경기 부양화, 경제력 활성화
428. rigorous 엄격한, 엄한(=strict; harsh; severe), 엄밀한, 정확한(=exact)

429. robust 강건한, 건전한(=strong and healthy; vigorous)
430. rudimentary 기본의, 초보의; 미숙한(=basic; crude; unformed or undeveloped)
431. ruminate 반추하다, 심사 숙고하다(=contemplate, ponder, mull over)
432. sagacious 현명한, 기민한, 총명한(=wise, discerning; shrewd; keen in judgement)
433. salient 두드러진, 현저한; 원기 왕성한(=sticking out, conspicuous; leaping)
434. salutary 건전한, 유익한(=healthful, remedial, curative)
435. sanction 인가, 재가(=authorization, support, approval), 제재
436. sanguine 다혈질의, 혈색이 좋은, 쾌활한(=cheerful; optimistic; hopeful)
437. saturate 흠뻑 적시다(=soak, drench), 가득 채우다(=fill)
438. scatter 흩뿌리다(=disperse, dissipate), 낭비하다(=waste, squander)
439. scrap 쓰레기로 버리다, 폐기하다(=discard, junk), 한 조각, 먹다 남은 것
440. scrupulous 빈틈없는, 세심한; 양심적인, 신중한(=strict; careful; conscientious)
441. sensitive 민감한, 느끼기 쉬운. sensual 관능적인, 음탕한
442. sentence 문장, 판결, 선고하다(=pronounce punishment upon)
443. serious 진지한(=earnest, grave, sober), 중대한(=dangerous)
444. settle 정착하다(=arrange), 해결하다(=solve), 결정하다(=decide)
445. servile 노예 근성의, 비굴한(=like a servant; submissive and subservient)
446. shatter 산산이 부수다(=break or burst into pieces), 손상시키다(=damage)
447. shift 변화, 교체(=transfer), 수단, 속임수(=trick)
448. shortcut 지름길(=a shorter route)
449. shrink 감소하다, 줄어들다(=contract; lessen), 움츠러지다 (=draw back, flinch)
450. singular 보통이 아닌, 뛰어난; 유일한(=superior; exceptional; strange unique)
451. slander 중상하다, 명예를 훼손하다(=defame; spread malicious rumor)

452. slovenly 단정치 못한(=untidy, unkempt, disorderly)
453. sluggish 느린, 불경기의, 부진한(=slow, stagnant, inactive; lazy, dull, indolent)
454. sober 술 취하지 않은(=not drunk), 냉정한(=serious, sedate)
455. solace 위안, 위로(=consolation), 위안하다, 위로하다(=comfort, console)
456. somber 어둠침침한(=dark and gloomy), 우울한(=dismal, sad)
457. somewhat 어느 정도(=to some extent), 다소(=a little)
458. sophisticated 약아빠진(=worldly-wise), 세련된(=highly complex or developed)
459. sordid 지저분한(=filthy, squalid), 누추한, 야비한(=mean, base, vile)
460. spawn 산란하다, 대량 생산하다(=bring forth; produce a large number)
461. specious 허울 좋은, 그럴듯한, 겉만 번드레한(=deceptively plausible or attractive)
462. speculate 사색하다(=ponder, contemplate), 투기하다(=gamble)
463. sporadic 때때로 일어나는, 드문드문한, 산발성의
464. spread 펴다(=stretch out, unfold), 퍼뜨리다, 확산시키다 (=distribute; extend)
465. squander 낭비하다(=waste, lavish, dissipate)
466. stability 안정, 확정(=steadiness; firmness) stabilize 안정시키다
467. stagnation 침체, 불경기(=motionlessness; inactivity)
468. stall 마구간, 구실, 지연시키다
469. static 정적인, 정지된(=stationary; not changing or moving)
470. staunch 견고한, 믿음직한(=steadfast, loyal; solid), 멈추게 하다, 지혈하다
471. sterile 불임의, 불모의(=barren)
472. sterling 파운드의, 진정한, 훌륭한(=excellent)
473. stick 찌르다, 내밀다, 붙이다 stick to 고수하다(=adhere to)
474. stifle 질식시키다(=smother, suffocate), 억누르다(=suppress, hold back)
475. stimulate 자극하다(=excite, rouse, stir, spur), 격려하다
476. stingy 인색한(=miserly), 부족한(=scanty)
477. stock 저장, 재고품, 가축, 주식, 줄기
478. strain 잡아당기다, 긴장시키다, 상하게 하다 strained 팽팽한, 긴장한, 억지의
479. strife 투쟁, 불화(=bitter conflict; discord; struggle, clash)

480. strike 치다, 찌르다, …에 충돌하다, 마음에 떠오르다, …에게 인상을 주다
481. stringent 엄중한, 절박한(=strict, severe; restrictive)
482. stumble 발부리가 걸리다, 비틀거리며 걷다
    stumble upon 우연히 만나다
483. stunning 아연하게 하는, 멋진(=attractive, excellent)
484. subjugate 정복하다, 가라앉히다(=subdue and dominate, enslave)
485. sublime 장엄한, 탁월한, 고상한(=majestic, awesome; extremely exalted; lofty)
486. submit 복종시키다, 제출하다(=hand in, send in, turn in)
487. subsequent 다음의, 그 후의(=coming after; following)
488. subsidiary 보조의(=auxiliary), 종속적인(=subordinate)
489. subtle 미묘한, 예민한, 교활한, 교묘한(=thin; ingenious; crafty)
490. subtract 빼다, 공제하다(=take away, deduct)
491. subversive 파괴적인, 전복하는(=overthrowing; undermining; insurgent)
492. succumb 굴복하다, 지다(=yield or submit),죽다(=die)
493. supercilious 거만한(=haughty; patronizing)
494. superficial 표면적인, 피상적인(=on the surface only; shallow; not thorough)
495. superfluous 남아도는, 불필요한(=extra; unnecessary; redundant)
496. superstition 미신
497. suspect 짐작하다, …이 아닌가 하고 생각하다, 의심을 두다, 용의자
498. suspend 매달다(=hang, dangle), 중지하다
499. symptom 징후, 징조(=sign, token)
500. synthesis 종합, 합성(=composite)
501. tablet 정제, 알약
502. tacit 무언의(=unspoken, silent), 암묵적인, 암시하는(=implied)
503. tangible 만질 수 있는(=touchable, palpable), 명백한, 확실한 (=definite, objective)
504. tantamount 동등한, 상당하는(=equivalent, as good as)
505. tariff 관세
506. tedious 따분한, 지루한(=boring, wearisome, long and dull, monotonous)

507. temerity 만용, 무모(=boldness; recklessness; audacity)
508. temperate 기온이 온화한, 온건한, 절제하는(=mild; moderate; restrained)
509. tenacious 고집 센(=persistent, obstinate, obdurate), 완고한(=stubborn)
510. tentative 잠정적인, 시험적인, 임시의(=experimental; temporary, provisional)
511. testimony 증언(=statement), 증거(=proof), 언명(=declaration), 고백
512. therapy 치료(=cure, healing) therapist 치료사
513. threaten 위협하다(=menace, intimidate, frighten, cow, bully, terrorize)
514. thrifty 검소한(=economical, frugal, saving, sparing)
515. topple 넘어뜨리다(=overturn), 쓰러지게 하다
516. tractable 다루기 쉬운(=docile), 가르치기 쉬운(=malleable)
517. transcend 초월하다, 능가하다, 우수하다(=go beyond or above; surpass)
518. transgress 범하다, 어기다(=violate)
519. transient 일시적인, 변하기 쉬운(=temporary)
520. treat 다루다(=deal with), 치료하다(=cure, heal), 지불하다 (=pay for food)
521. tremendous 무서운(=dreadful), 거대한, 굉장한(=wonderful, amazing)
522. trepidation 공포, 전율, 놀람(=fear; apprehension; nervous trembling)
523. turbulent 사나운, 떠들썩한(=violent, disorderly, uncontrolled)
524. ubiquitous 어디에나 있는, 편재하는(=present everywhere)
525. unanimous 만장일치의(=in complete agreement; without dissent)
526. uncouth 거친(=rough), 어색한(=awkward), 교양 없는(=uncultured)
527. undergo 겪다(=suffer), 경험하다(=experience)
528. ungrateful 배은망덕한(=unthankful)
529. unremitting 간단없는, 끈질긴(=unceasing; unabated; relentless)
530. unwitting 알지 못하는(=ignorant), 고의가 아닌(=unintentional)
531. uphold 받치다(=support), 찬성하다(=approve), 확인하다(=confirm)
532. utilities 공공 설비
533. utilize 이용하다(=make use of, avail oneself of, employ)

534. utter 전적인(=complete, total), 철저한(=absolute), 발언하다
535. vacillate 흔들리다, 동요하다(=waver), 망설이다
536. vanish 사라지다(=disappear), 희미해지다(=fade away)
537. vehement 열렬한, 열정적인(=intense; forceful; violent, impetuous)
538. venerate 존경하다, 공경하다(=revere, adore, respect, regard)
539. venue 재판지, 회합 장소, 개최지
540. verbose 말이 많은(=talkative, garrulous, loquacious), 장황한
541. vestige 자취, 흔적(=trace)
542. vex 초조하게 하다(=confuse), 괴롭히다(=annoy, pester)
543. vigilant 조심하는, 경계하고 있는(=watchful, alert)
544. vilify 헐뜯다, 중상하다(=defame), 타락시키다
545. virtually 사실상(=in fact)
546. vital 생명의, 극히 중대한(=essential, indispensable), 치명적인(=fatal)
547. vulnerable 상처받기 쉬운, 공격받기 쉬운(=susceptible)
548. wane 이지러지다(=fade, peter out), 약해지다(=abate)
549. withdraw 물러나다(=take back), 취소하다(=call back, retract)
550. zealous 열심인, 열광적인(=eager, fervent)

| 판권 |
| 소유 |

마스터 영어

2004. 8. 20 초판 인쇄
2004. 8. 25 초판 펴냄

지은이 조영태
발행인 김영무

발행처 도서출판 아가페문화사
156-094 서울 동작구 사당4동 254-9
등록 제3-133호(1987. 12. 11)

보급처 : 아가페문화사
156-094 서울동작구 사당4동 254-9
전화 02-3472-7252-3
팩스 02-523-7254
온라인 우체국 011791-02-004204(김영무)

값 16,000원

ISBN 89-8424-078-8 03230